Sometimes I happen to see myself in
the mirror when I'm not wearing glasses
and I jerk back. "Who's that?! Thief!"
After wearing glasses for twenty years,
you forget what you really look like!

–Yoshiyuki Nishi

Yoshiyuki Nishi was born in Tokyo. Two of
his favorite manga series are *Dragon Ball* and
the robot-cat comedy *Doraemon*. His latest
series, *Muhyo & Roji's Bureau of Supernatural
Investigati*on, debuted in Japan's *Akamaru
Jump* magazine in 2004 and went on to be
serialized in *Weekly Shonen Jump*.

MUHYO & ROJI'S
BUREAU OF SUPERNATURAL INVESTIGATION

VOL. 4
The SHONEN JUMP Manga Edition

STORY AND ART BY
YOSHIYUKI NISHI

Translation & Adaptation/Alexander O. Smith
Touch-up Art & Lettering/Brian Bilter
Design/Izumi Hirayama
Editor/Amy Yu

Editor in Chief, Books/Alvin Lu
Editor in Chief, Magazines/Marc Weidenbaum
VP of Publishing Licensing/Rika Inouye
VP of Sales/Gonzalo Ferreyra
Sr. VP of Marketing/Liza Coppola
Publisher/Hyoe Narita

Printed in the U.S.A.

Published by VIZ Media, LLC
P.O. Box 77010
San Francisco, CA 94107

SHONEN JUMP Manga Edition
10 9 8 7 6 5 4 3 2 1
First printing, April 2008

SHONEN JUMP MANGA EDITION

Vol. 4 Sad Times Ahead

Story & Art by Yoshiyuki Nishi

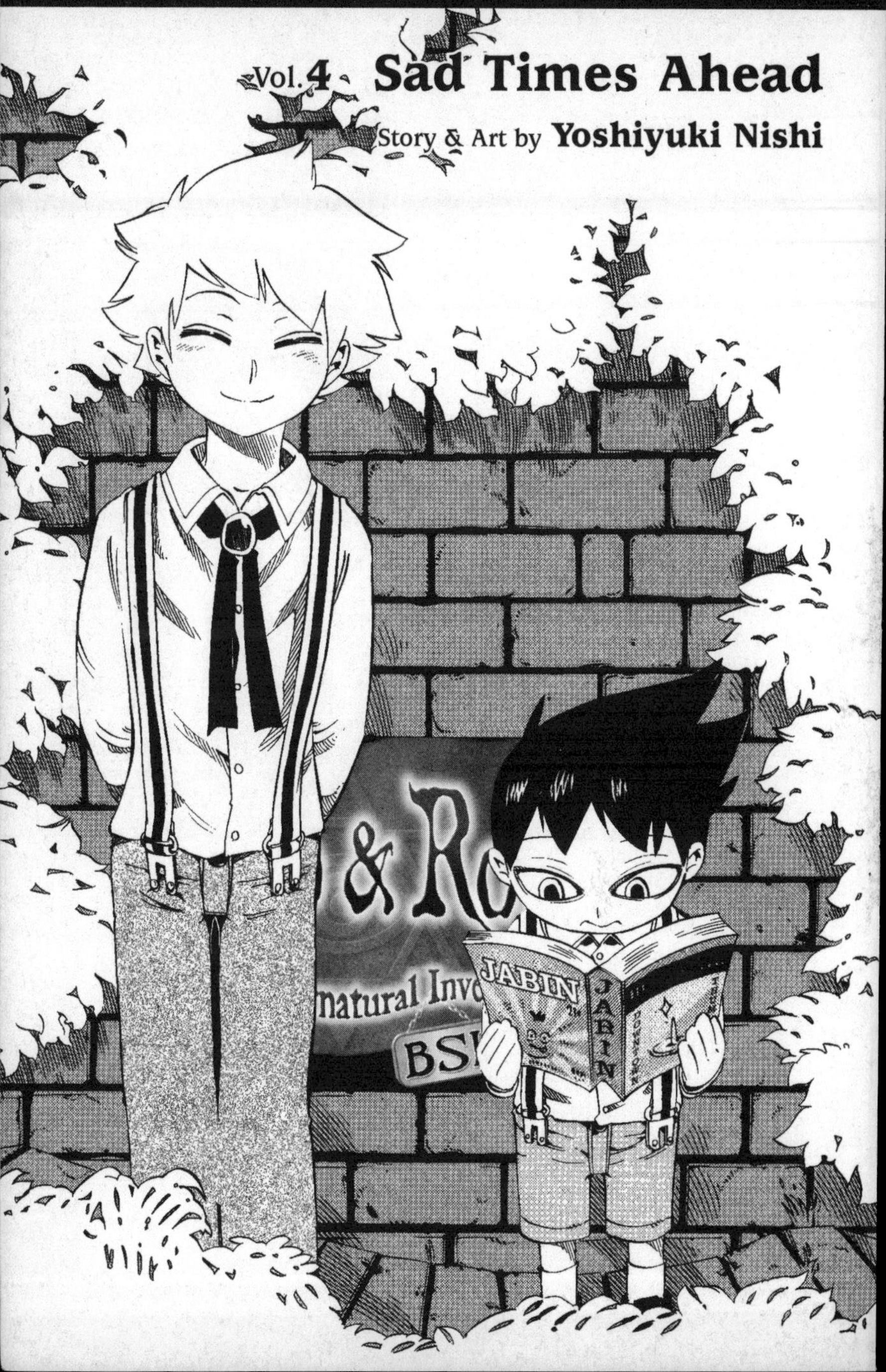
JABIN

Dramatis Personae

Toru Muhyo (Muhyo)

Genius elite practitioner of magic law, one of the youngest to achieve the highest rank of "Executor." Always calm and collected (though sometimes considered cold due to his tendency to make harsh comments), Muhyo possesses a strong sense of justice and has even been known to show kindness at times. Sleeps a lot to recover from the exhaustion caused by his practice. Likes: *Jabin* (a manga). Dislikes: interruptions while sleeping.

Jiro Kusano (Roji)

Assistant at Muhyo's office and a "Second Clerk," the lowest of the five ranks of practitioners of magic law. Roji cries easily, is meek and gentle, and has been known to freak out in the presence of spirits. Irritated at his own inability to help Muhyo, Roji has devoted himself to studying magic law. Likes: tea and cakes. Dislikes: scary ghosts and scary Muhyo.

Soratsugu Madoka (Enchu)

Muhyo's old classmate. Many thought he was destined to become an executor, but one event turned him traitor to the Magic Law Association.

Yoichi Himukai (Yoichi)

Judge and Muhyo's former classmate. Expert practitioner of all magic law except execution.

The Story

Magic law is a newly established practice for judging and punishing the increasing crimes committed by spirits; those who use it are called practitioners.

One day, Muhyo and Roji receive a visit from Biko, an artificer and one of Muhyo's old classmates. She asks them to come with her to Arcanum, a prison that holds dangerous spirits. One of Biko's seals, which was used to keep the prisoners in, has broken, with tragic consequences. What's more, the seal that broke was on the lowest level, where the most dangerous spirits are imprisoned. Muhyo, Roji, Biko, and Biko's teacher Rio head into the Arcanum to face the most feared of all the Arcanum inmates: Face-Ripper Sophie! Unfortunately, Muhyo wears himself out while fighting other ghosts on the way down. He's at the point of exhaustion, and they've only just reached the bottom level...

Yu Abiko (Biko)

Muhyo's classmate and an artificer. Makes seals, pens, magic law books, and other accoutrements of magic law.

Rio Kurotori (Rio)

Biko's teacher and a renowned artificer. While artificers can make the tools of the magic law trade, they cannot use them.

Muhyo & Roji's Bureau of Supernatural Investigation BSI

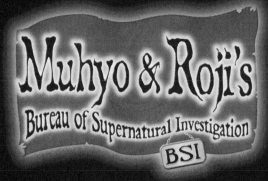

CONTENTS

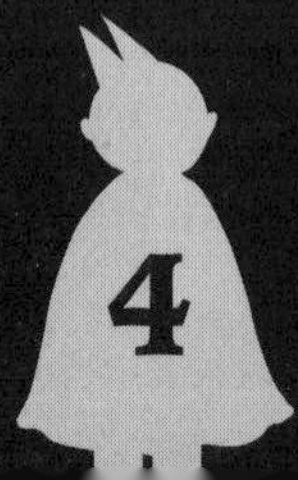

4

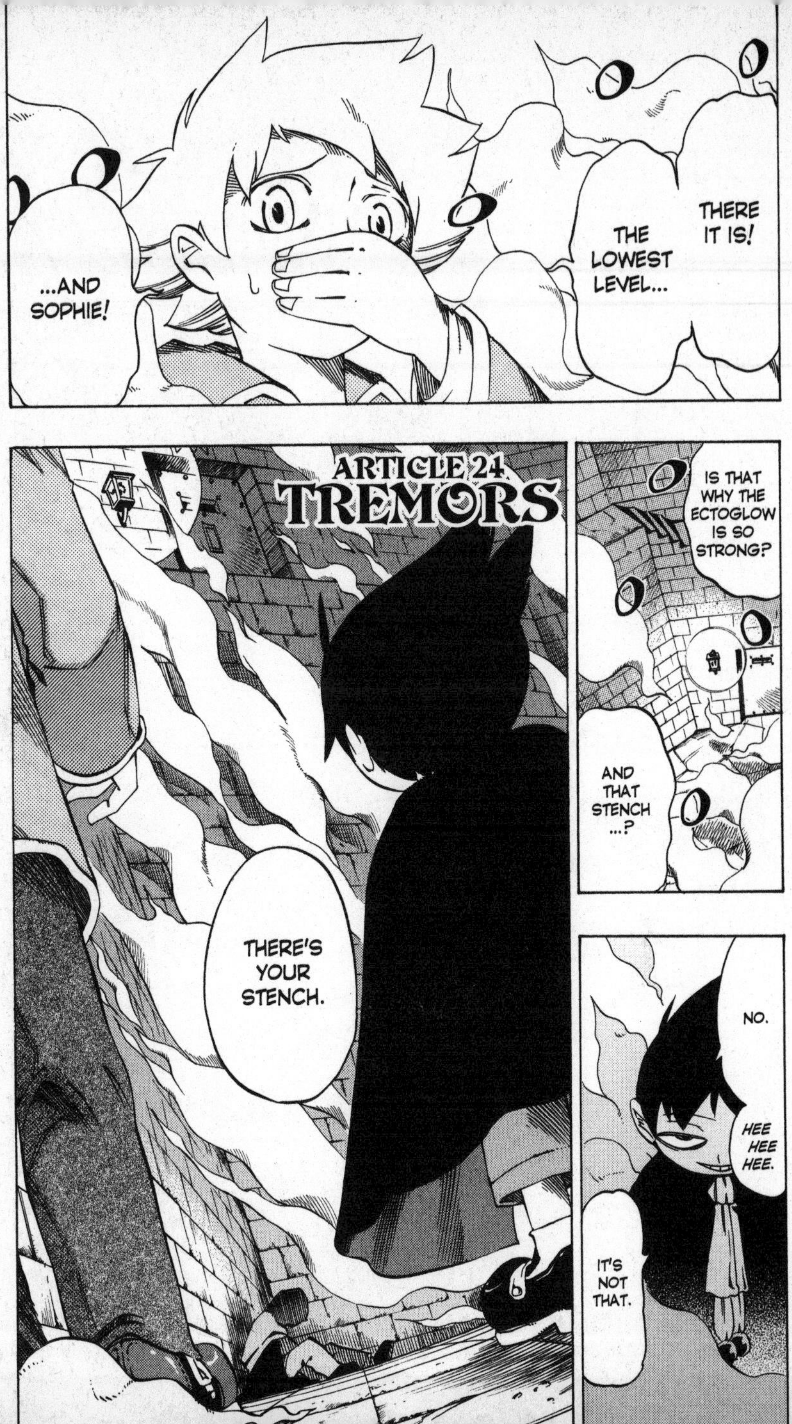
THERE IT IS!
THE LOWEST LEVEL...
...AND SOPHIE!
IS THAT WHY THE ECTOGLOW IS SO STRONG?
AND THAT STENCH ...?
NO.
HEE HEE HEE.
IT'S NOT THAT.
ARTICLE 24
TREMORS
THERE'S YOUR STENCH.

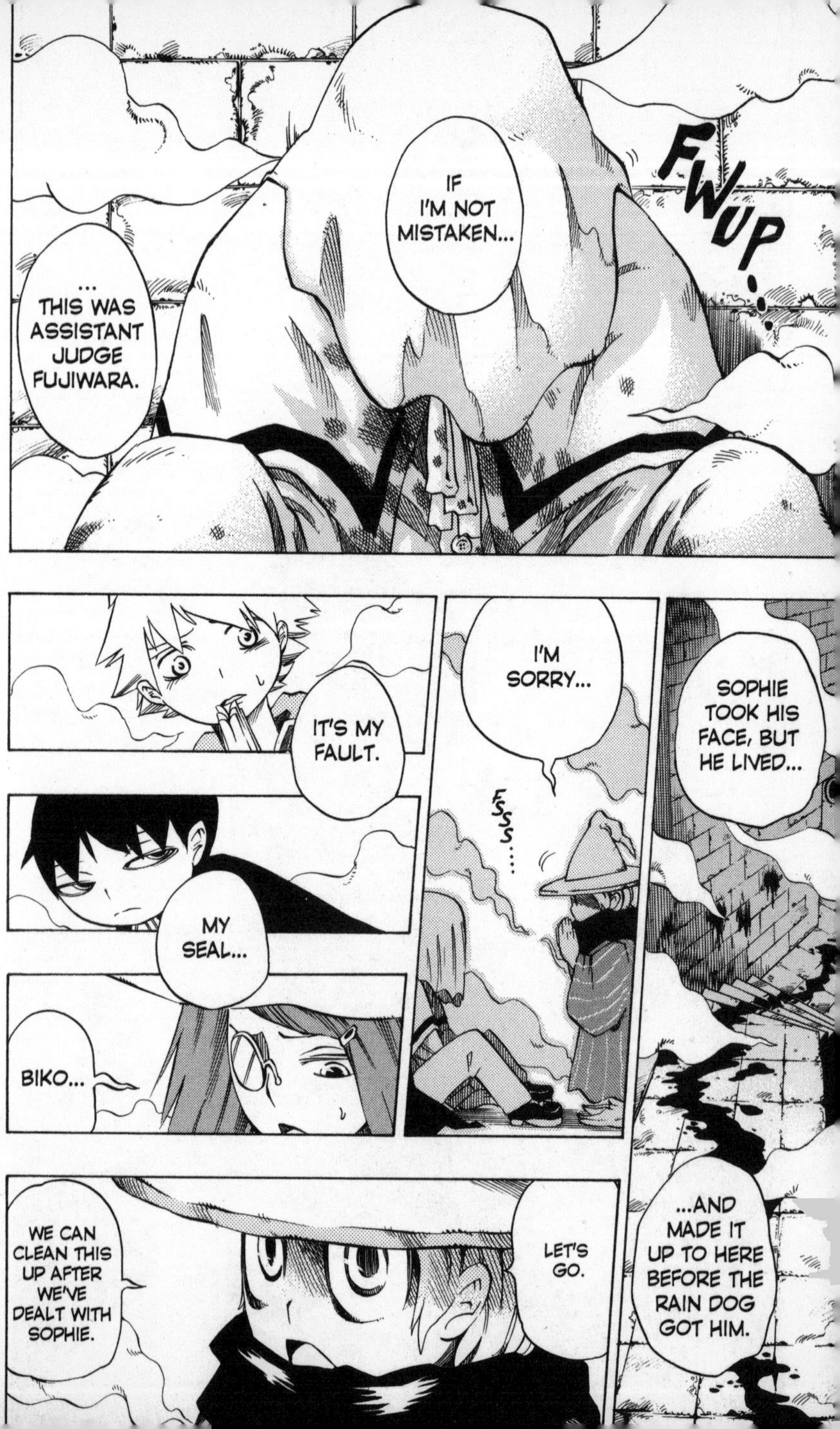
FWUP
IF I'M NOT MISTAKEN...
... THIS WAS ASSISTANT JUDGE FUJIWARA.
SOPHIE TOOK HIS FACE, BUT HE LIVED...
...AND MADE IT UP TO HERE BEFORE THE RAIN DOG GOT HIM.
I'M SORRY...
FSSS....
IT'S MY FAULT.
MY SEAL...
BIKO...
LET'S GO.
WE CAN CLEAN THIS UP AFTER WE'VE DEALT WITH SOPHIE.

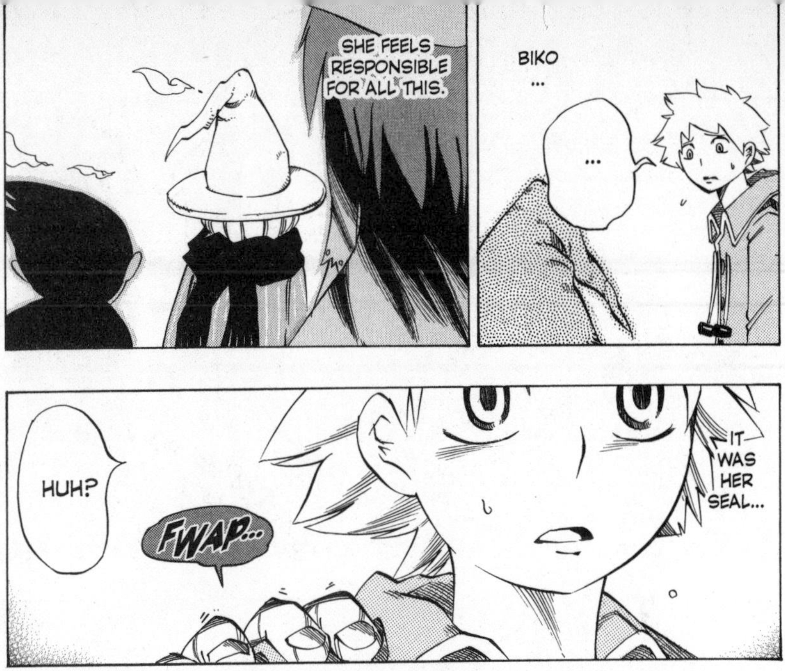
BIKO ...
...
SHE FEELS RESPONSIBLE FOR ALL THIS.
IT WAS HER SEAL...
HUH?
FWAP...

ARTICLE 24
TREMORS

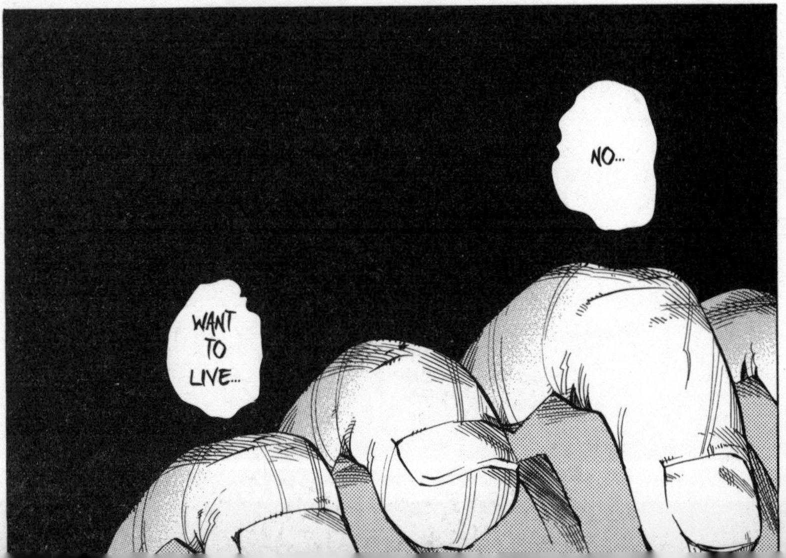
NO...
WANT TO LIVE...

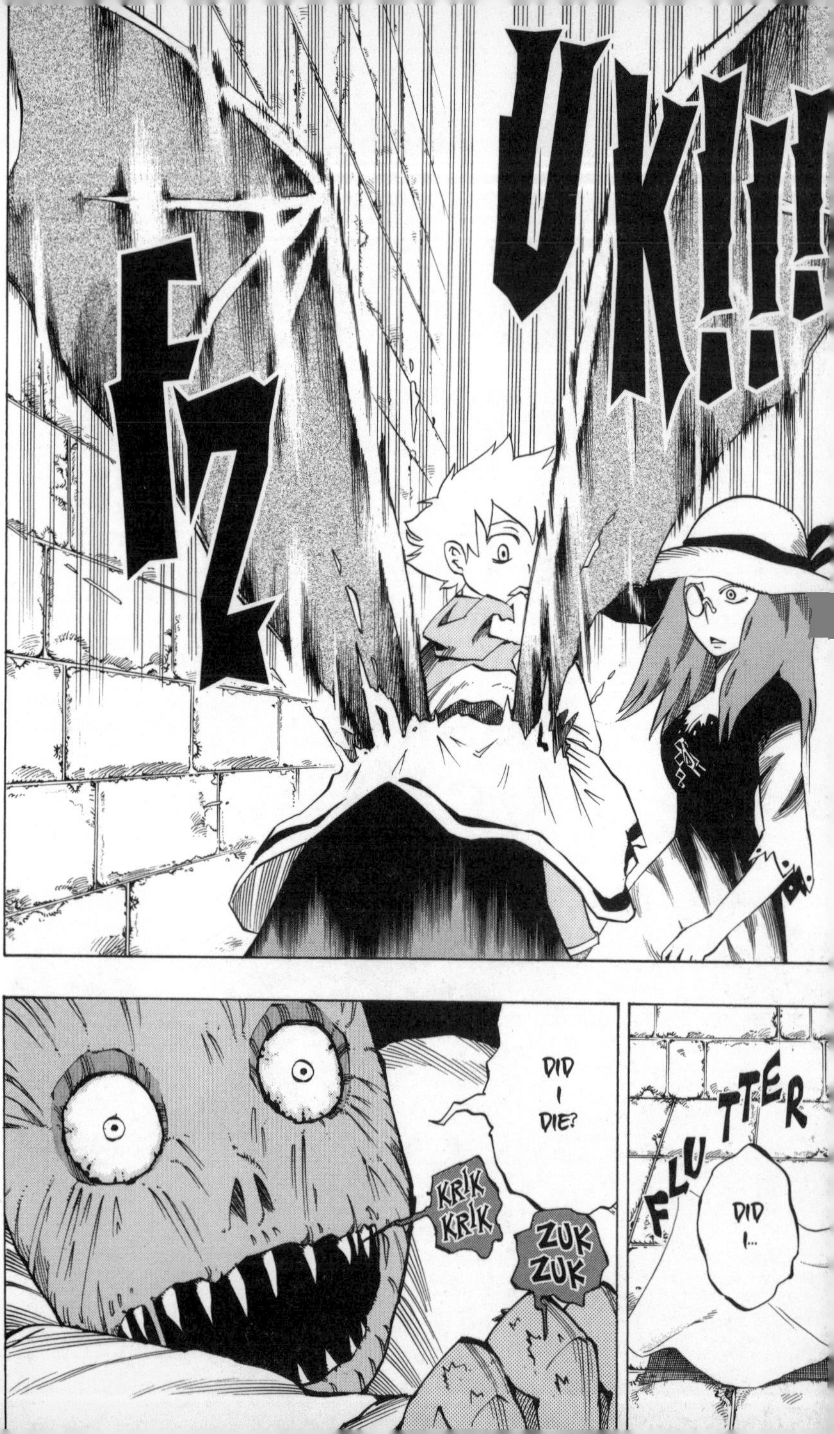
FZ
UK!!!
FLUTTER
DID I...
DID I DIE?
KRIK KRIK
ZUK ZUK

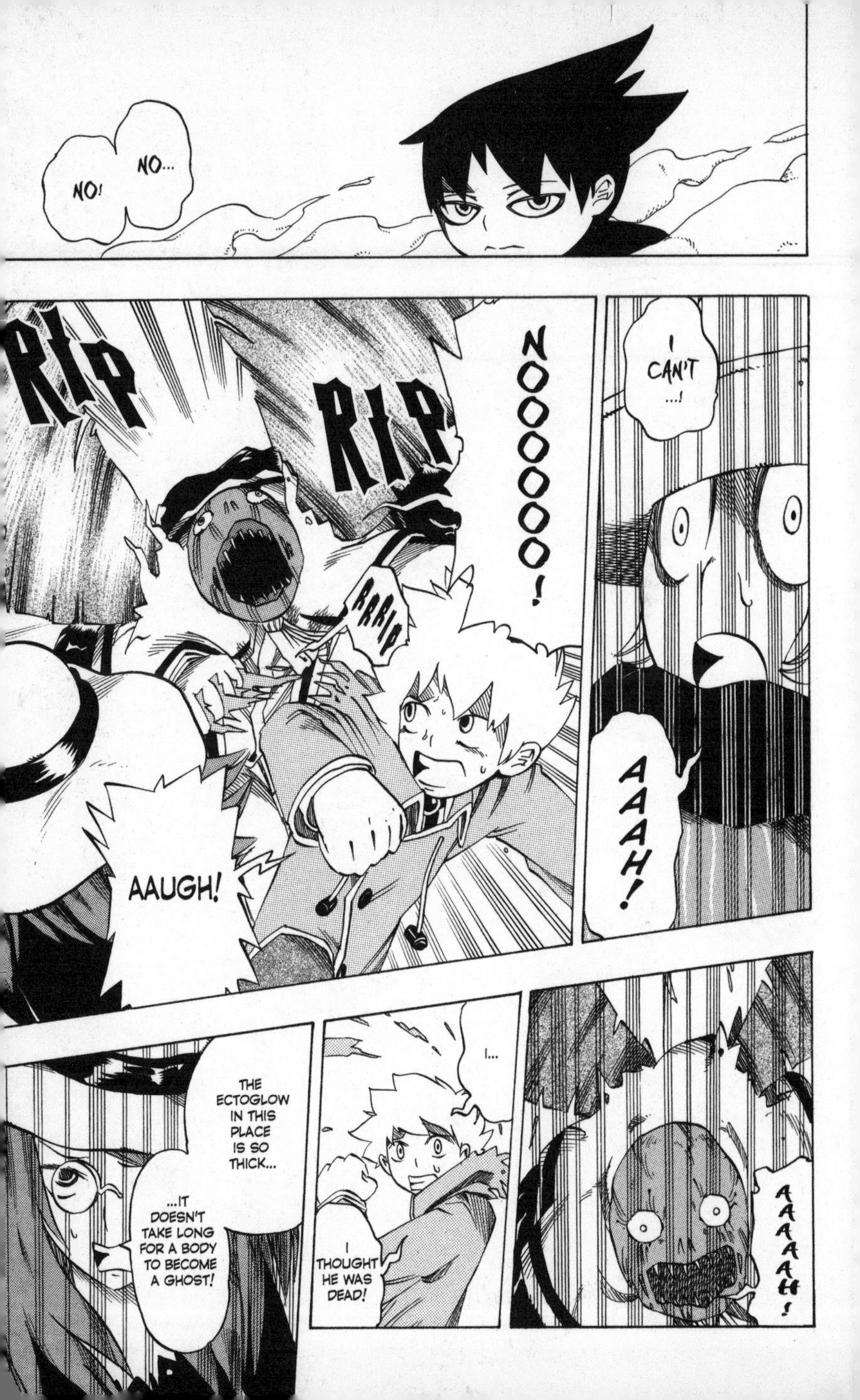
NO... NO!
I CAN'T ...!
AAAAH!
NOOOOOOOO!
RIP
RIP
RRRIP
AAUGH!
AAAAAAH!
I...
I THOUGHT HE WAS DEAD!
THE ECTOGLOW IN THIS PLACE IS SO THICK...
...IT DOESN'T TAKE LONG FOR A BODY TO BECOME A GHOST!

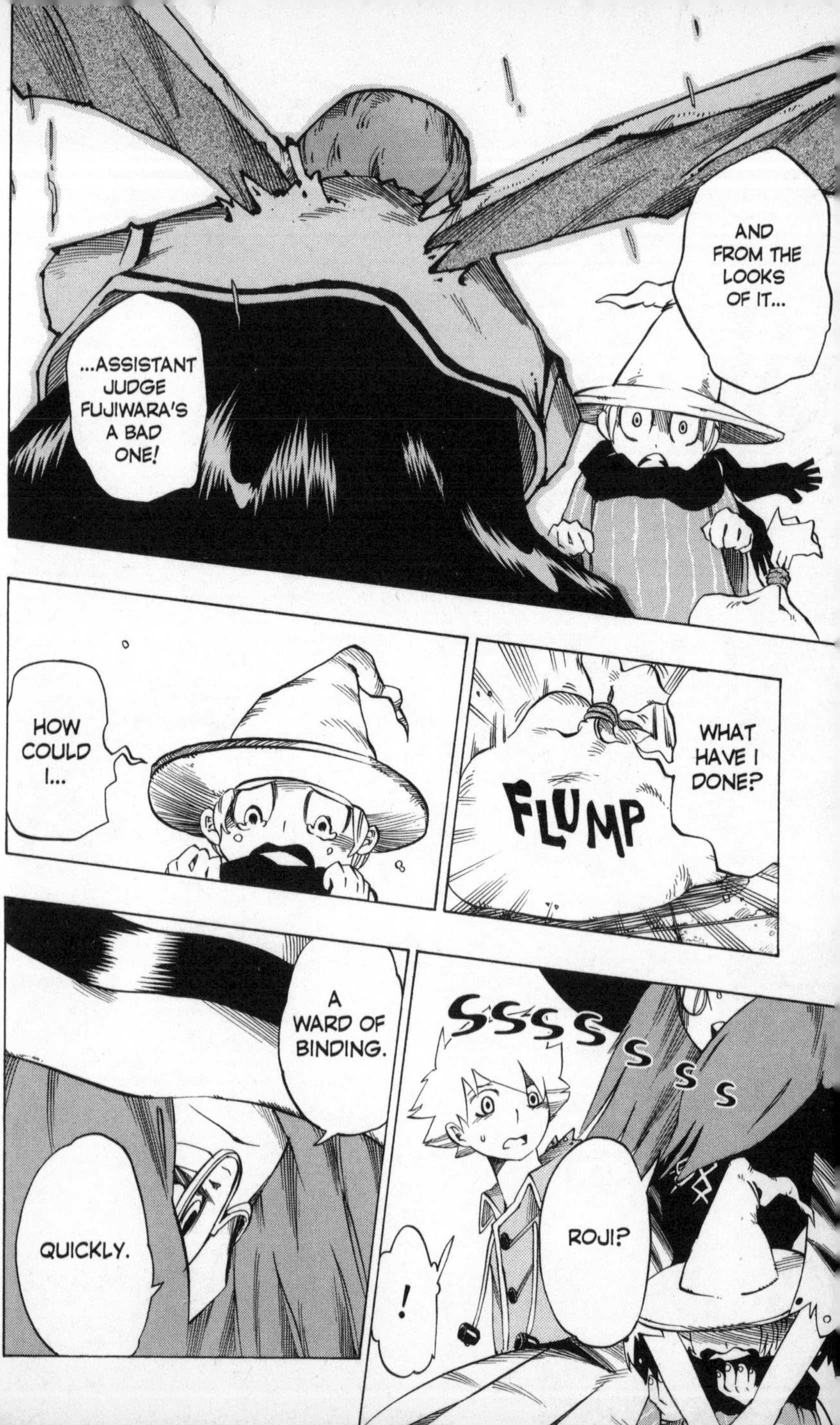
AND FROM THE LOOKS OF IT...
...ASSISTANT JUDGE FUJIWARA'S A BAD ONE!
WHAT HAVE I DONE?
FLUMP
HOW COULD I...
SSSSSSSSS
ROJI?
!
A WARD OF BINDING.
QUICKLY.

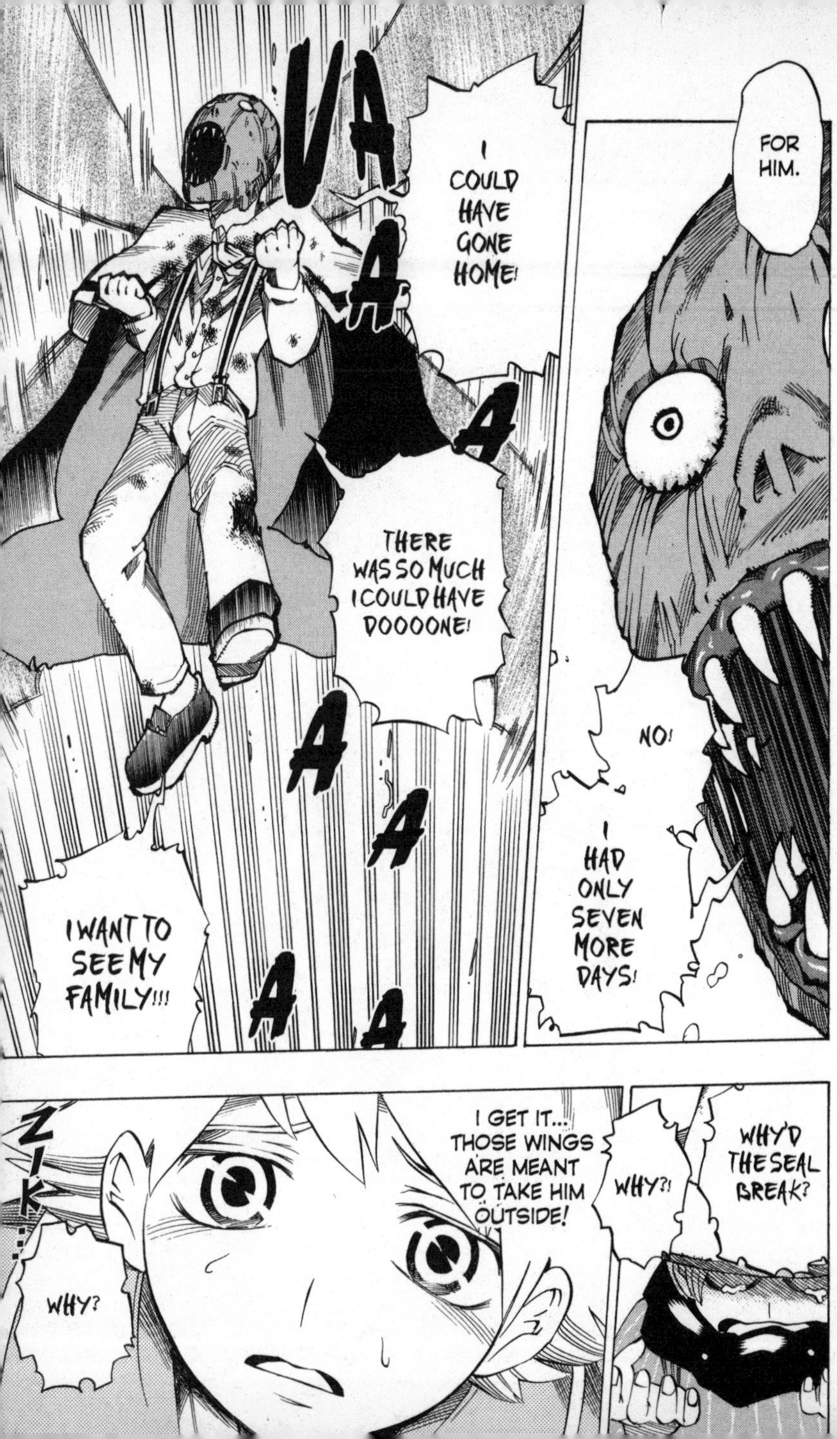
FOR HIM.
NO!
I HAD ONLY SEVEN MORE DAYS!
VAAAAAAA
I COULD HAVE GONE HOME!
THERE WAS SO MUCH I COULD HAVE DOOOONE!
I WANT TO SEE MY FAMILY!!!
WHY'D THE SEAL BREAK?
WHY?!
I GET IT... THOSE WINGS ARE MEANT TO TAKE HIM OUTSIDE!
ZIK...
WHY?

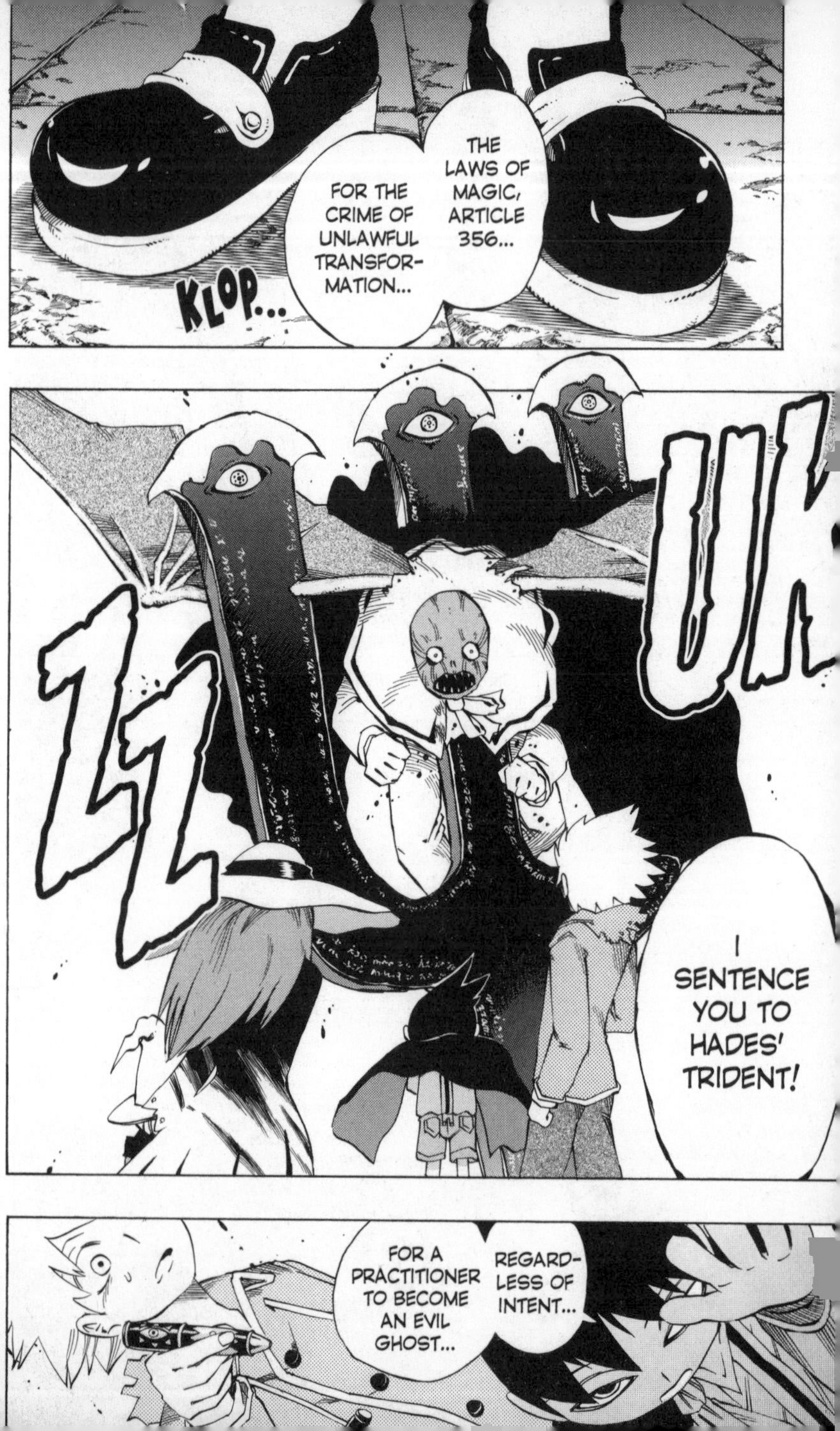
THE LAWS OF MAGIC, ARTICLE 356...
FOR THE CRIME OF UNLAWFUL TRANSFOR-MATION...
KLOP...
I SENTENCE YOU TO HADES' TRIDENT!
ZZ
UN
REGARD-LESS OF INTENT...
FOR A PRACTITIONER TO BECOME AN EVIL GHOST...

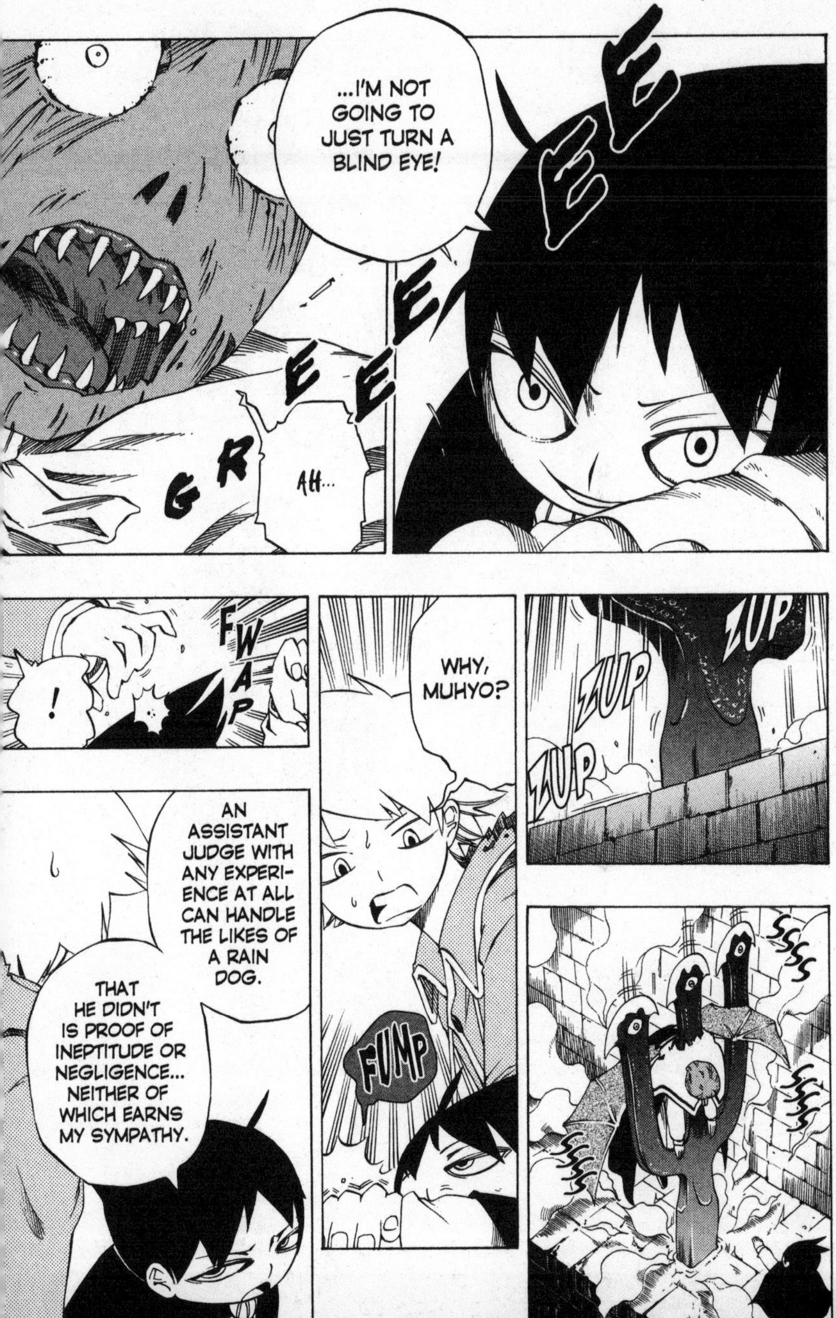
...I'M NOT GOING TO JUST TURN A BLIND EYE!
GREEEEEE
AH...
ZUP ZUP ZUP
SSSS SSSS SSSS
WHY, MUHYO?
FUMP
FWAP
!
AN ASSISTANT JUDGE WITH ANY EXPERIENCE AT ALL CAN HANDLE THE LIKES OF A RAIN DOG.
THAT HE DIDN'T IS PROOF OF INEPTITUDE OR NEGLIGENCE... NEITHER OF WHICH EARNS MY SYMPATHY.

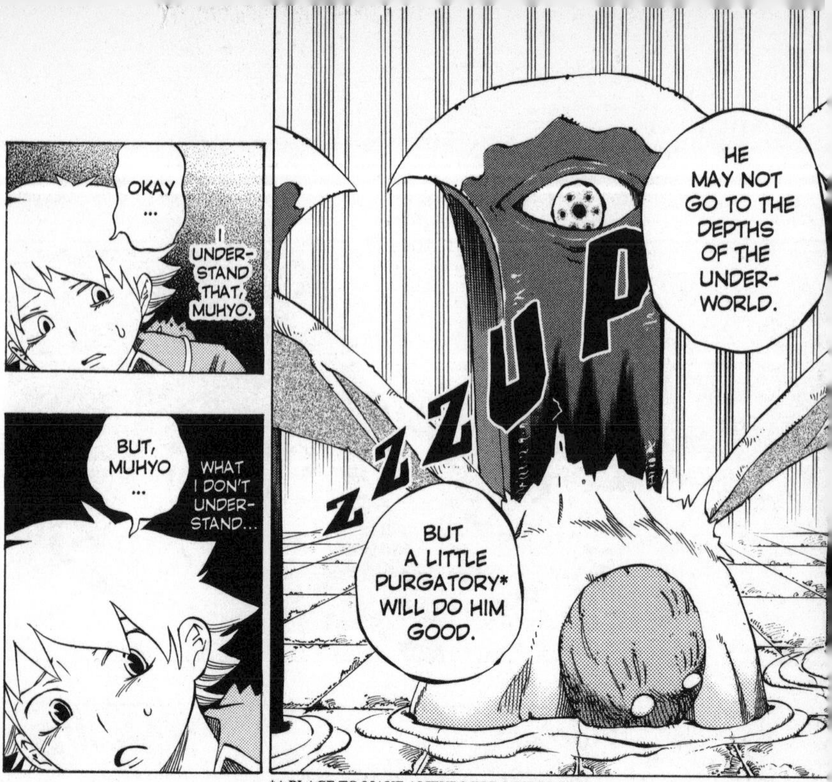
HE MAY NOT GO TO THE DEPTHS OF THE UNDER-WORLD.
ZZZUP
BUT A LITTLE PURGATORY* WILL DO HIM GOOD.
OKAY ...
I UNDER-STAND THAT, MUHYO.
BUT, MUHYO ...
WHAT I DON'T UNDER-STAND...

*A PLACE TO MAKE AMENDS FOR LESSER SINS, AFTER WHICH ONE MAY GO TO THE AFTERLIFE.

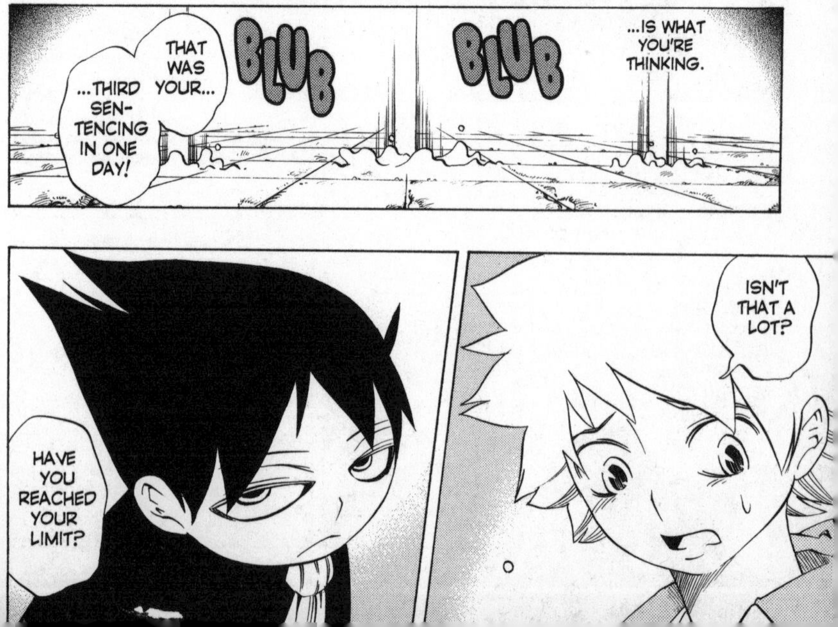
...IS WHAT YOU'RE THINKING.
BLUB
BLUB
THAT WAS YOUR...
...THIRD SEN-TENCING IN ONE DAY!
ISN'T THAT A LOT?
HAVE YOU REACHED YOUR LIMIT?

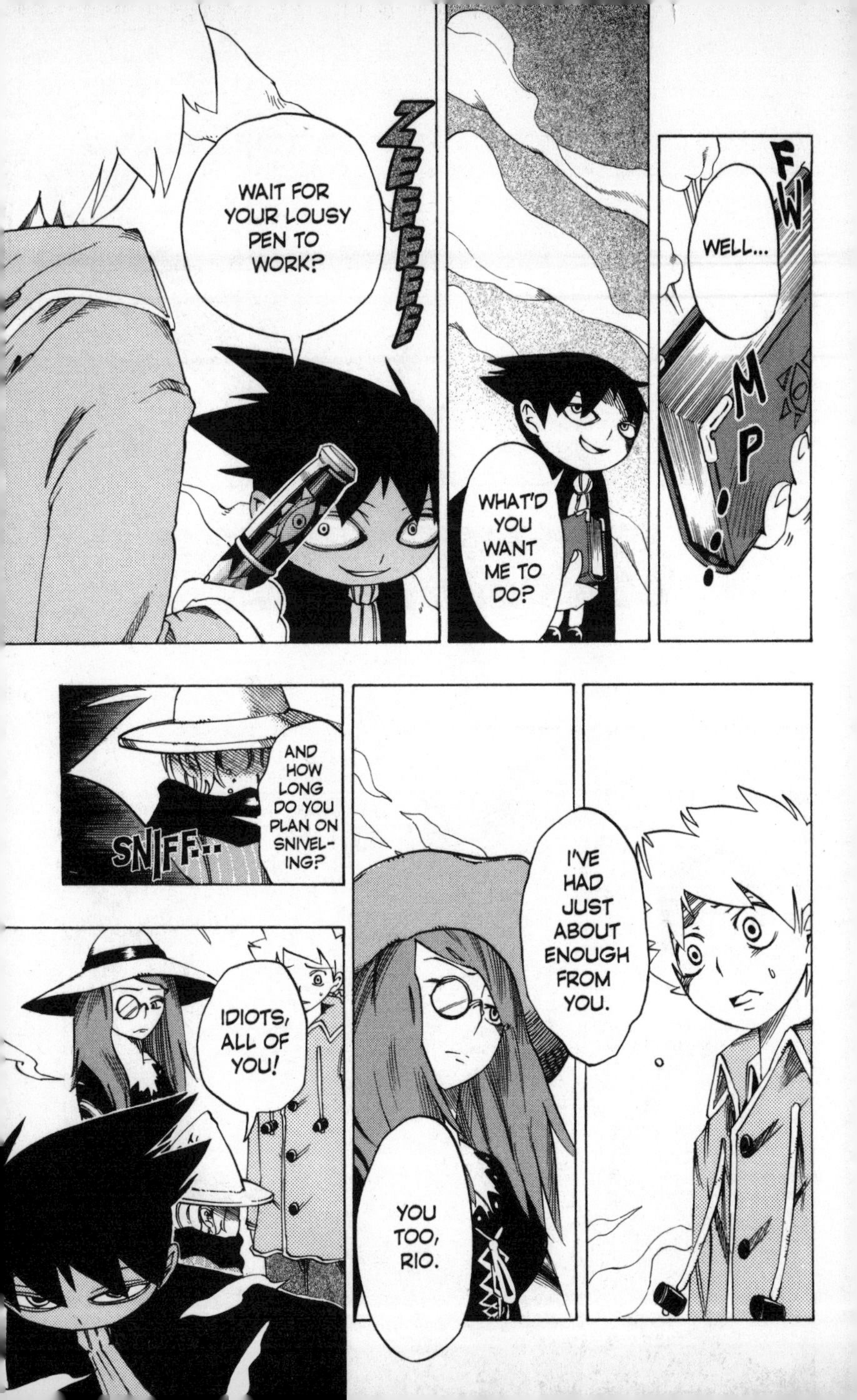
FWMP...!
WELL...
WHAT'D YOU WANT ME TO DO?
ZEEEEE
WAIT FOR YOUR LOUSY PEN TO WORK?
I'VE HAD JUST ABOUT ENOUGH FROM YOU.
YOU TOO, RIO.
AND HOW LONG DO YOU PLAN ON SNIVELING?
SNIFF...
IDIOTS, ALL OF YOU!

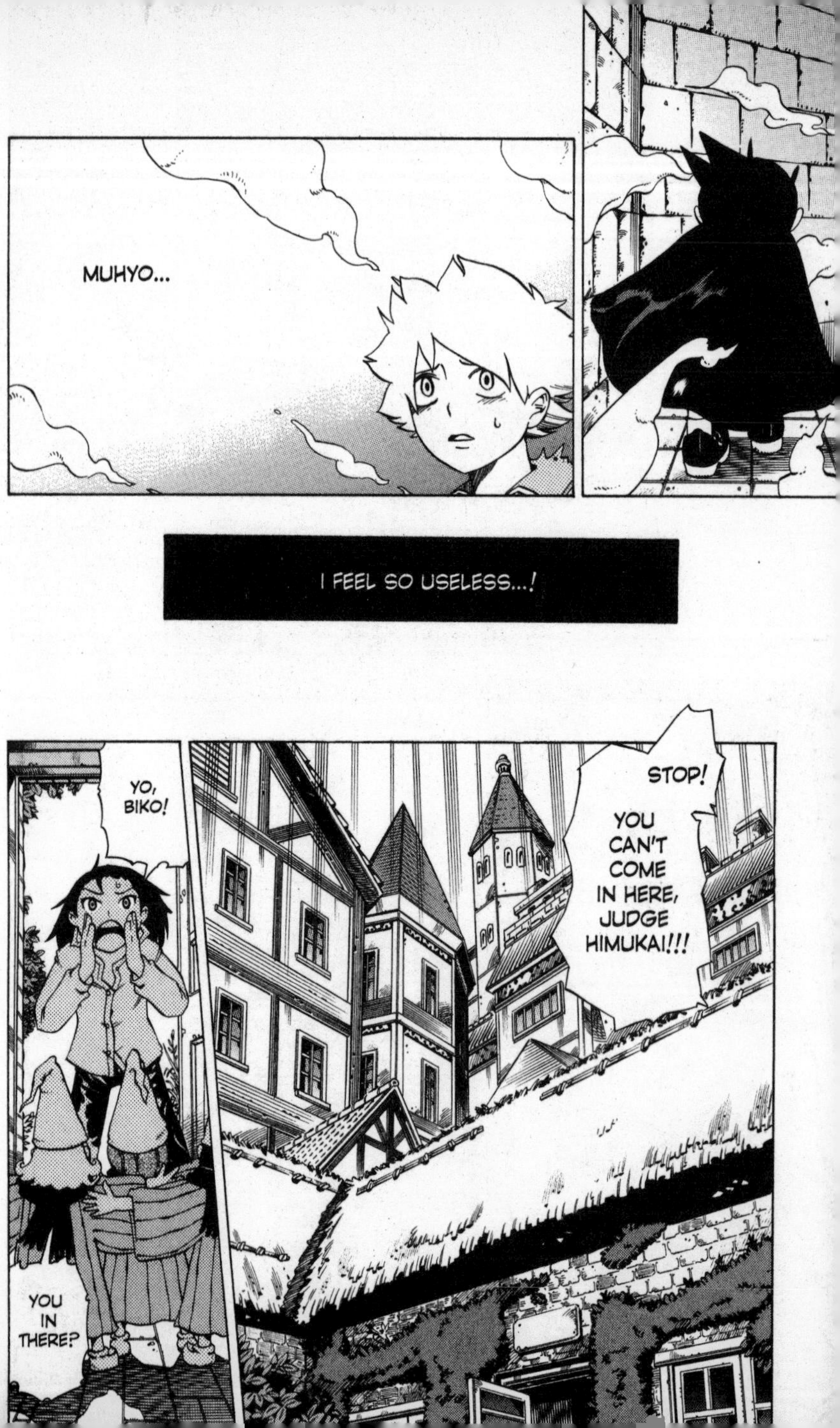
MUHYO...
I FEEL SO USELESS...!
STOP!
YOU CAN'T COME IN HERE, JUDGE HIMUKAI!!!
YO, BIKO!
YOU IN THERE?

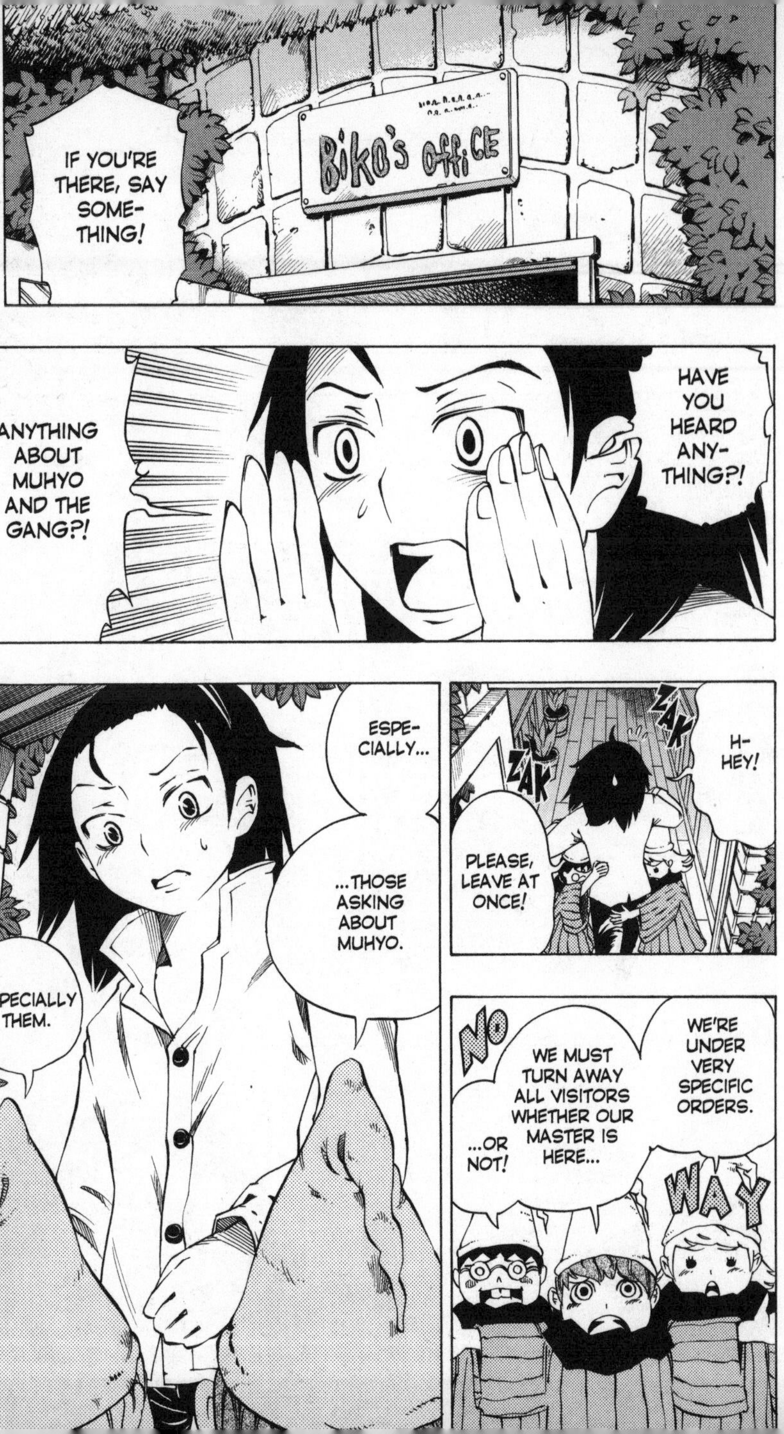
BIKO'S OFFICE
IF YOU'RE THERE, SAY SOMETHING!
HAVE YOU HEARD ANYTHING?!
ANYTHING ABOUT MUHYO AND THE GANG?!
ZAK
ZAK
H-HEY!
PLEASE, LEAVE AT ONCE!
WE'RE UNDER VERY SPECIFIC ORDERS.
WE MUST TURN AWAY ALL VISITORS WHETHER OUR MASTER IS HERE...
...OR NOT!
NO
WAY
ESPECIALLY...
...THOSE ASKING ABOUT MUHYO.
ESPECIALLY THEM.

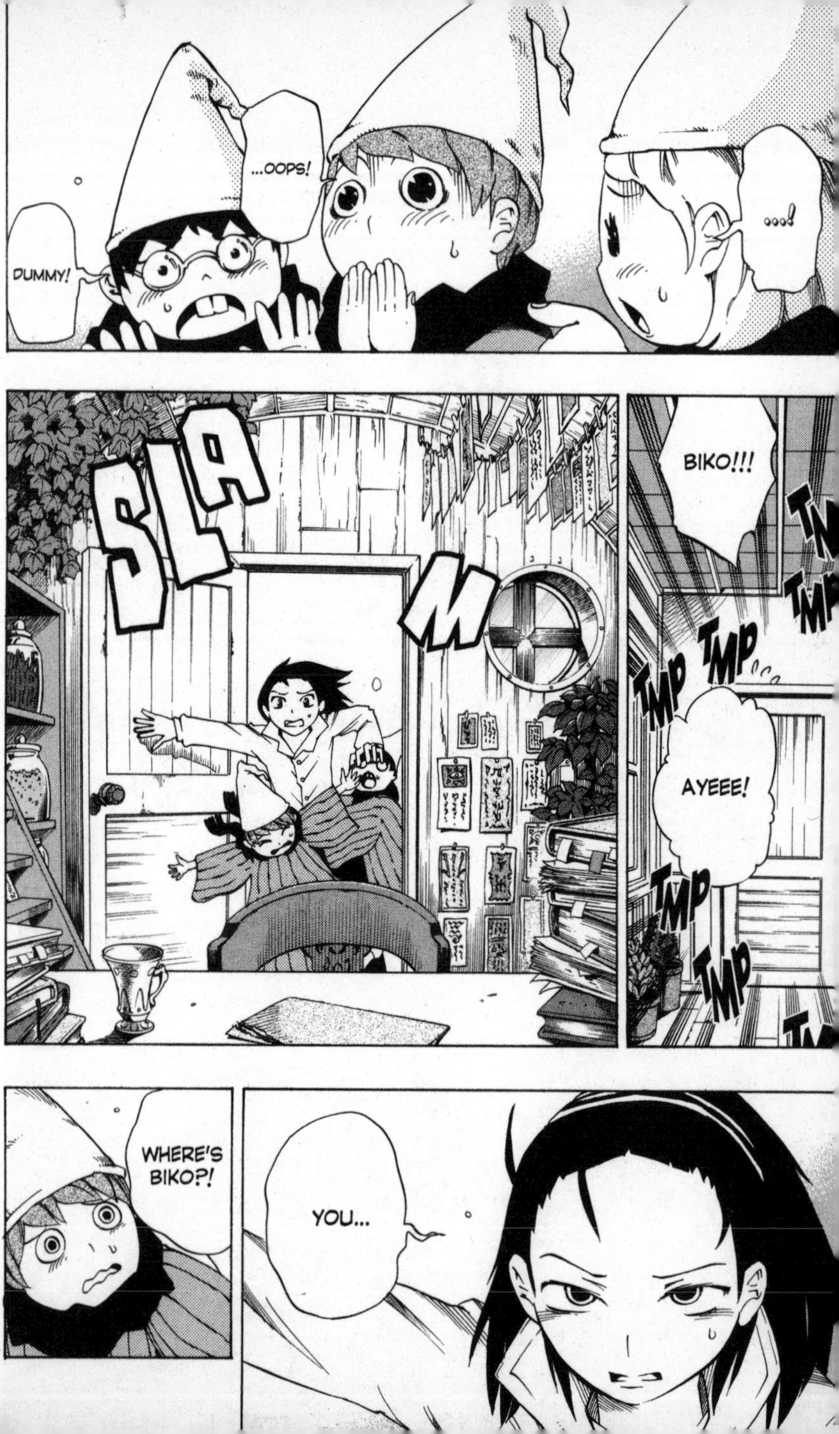
...!
...OOPS!
DUMMY!
BIKO!!!
TMP TMP
AYEEE!
TMP
TMP
SLAM
YOU...
WHERE'S BIKO?!

READ THIS WAY

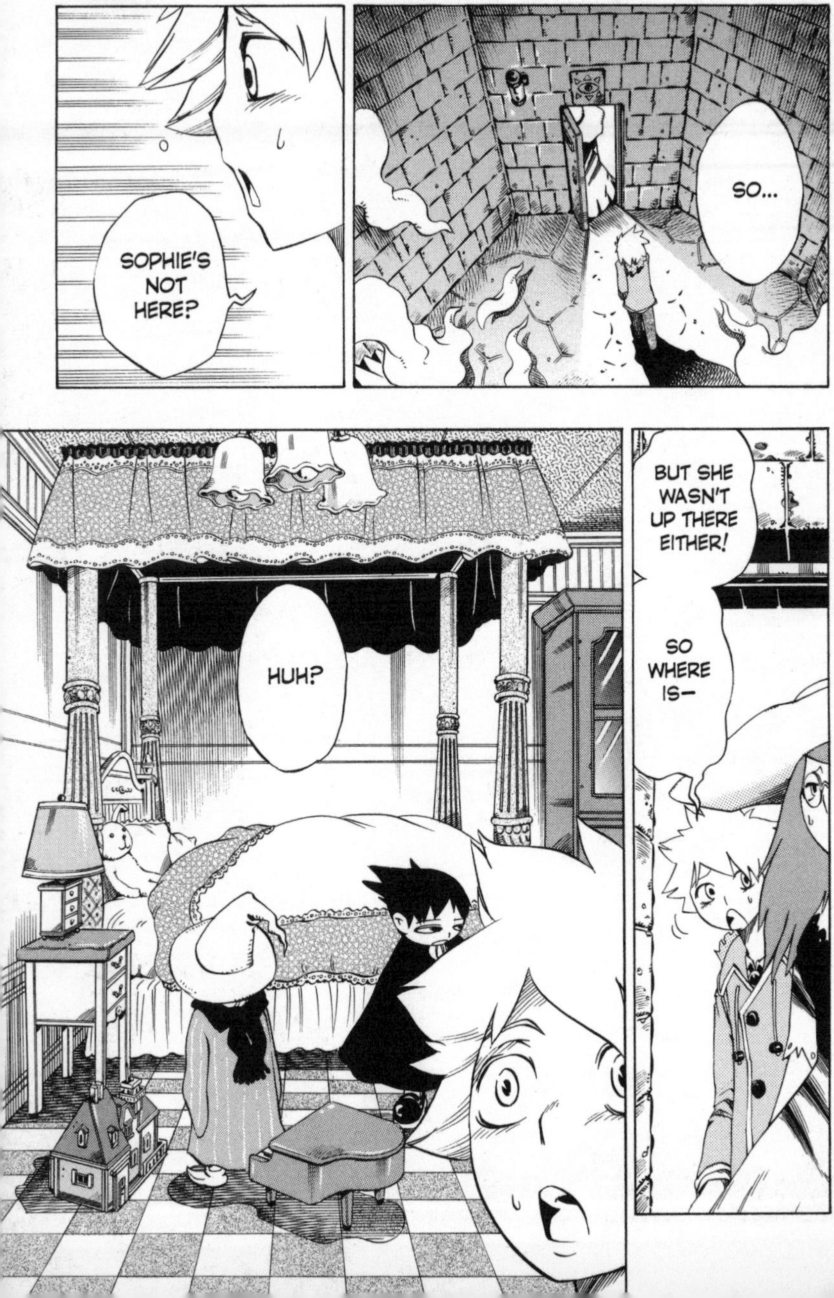
SO...
SOPHIE'S NOT HERE?
BUT SHE WASN'T UP THERE EITHER!
SO WHERE IS—
HUH?

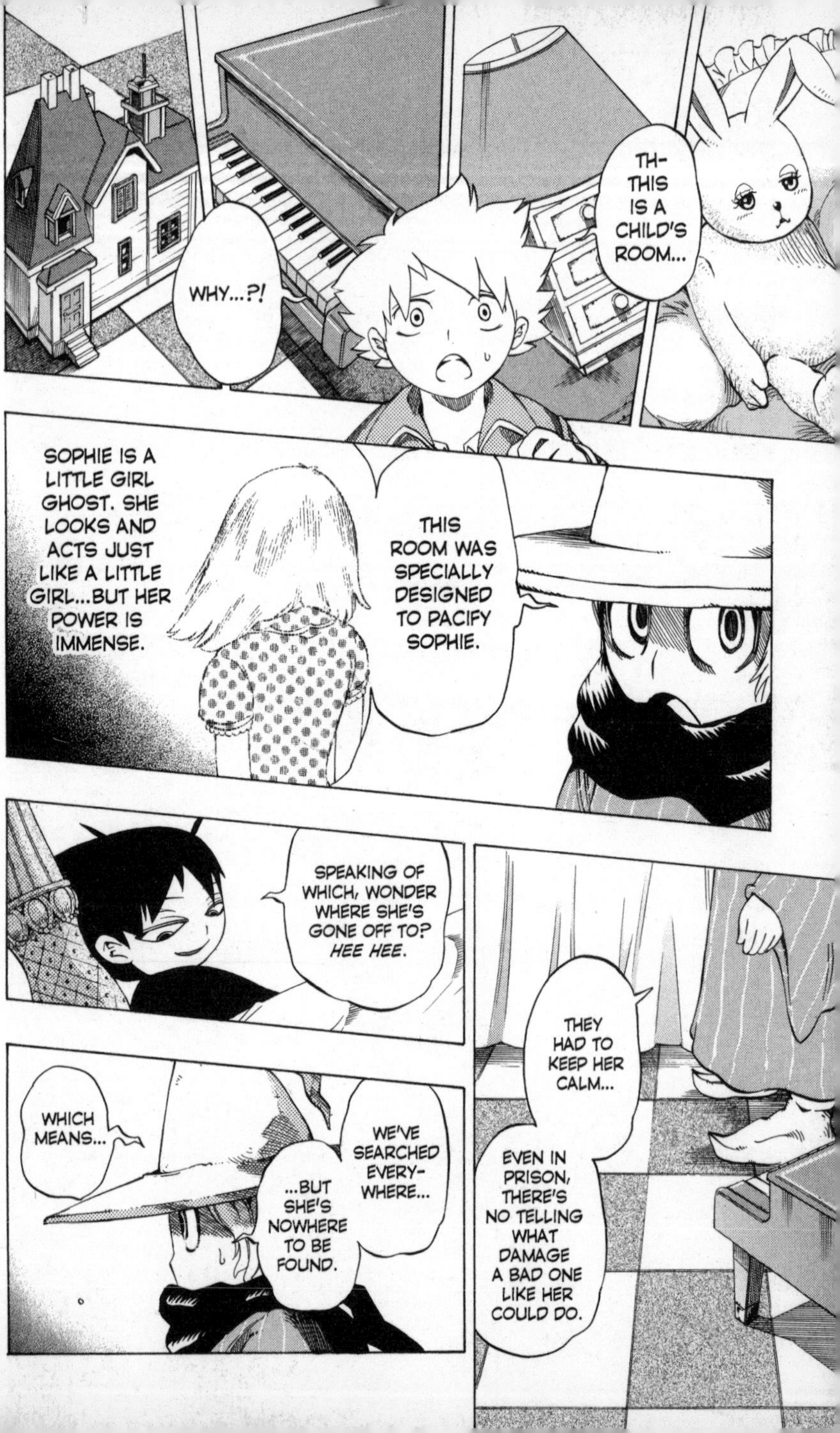
TH- THIS IS A CHILD'S ROOM...
WHY...?!
THIS ROOM WAS SPECIALLY DESIGNED TO PACIFY SOPHIE.
SOPHIE IS A LITTLE GIRL GHOST. SHE LOOKS AND ACTS JUST LIKE A LITTLE GIRL...BUT HER POWER IS IMMENSE.
THEY HAD TO KEEP HER CALM...
EVEN IN PRISON, THERE'S NO TELLING WHAT DAMAGE A BAD ONE LIKE HER COULD DO.
SPEAKING OF WHICH, WONDER WHERE SHE'S GONE OFF TO? *HEE HEE*.
WE'VE SEARCHED EVERY-WHERE...
...BUT SHE'S NOWHERE TO BE FOUND.
WHICH MEANS...

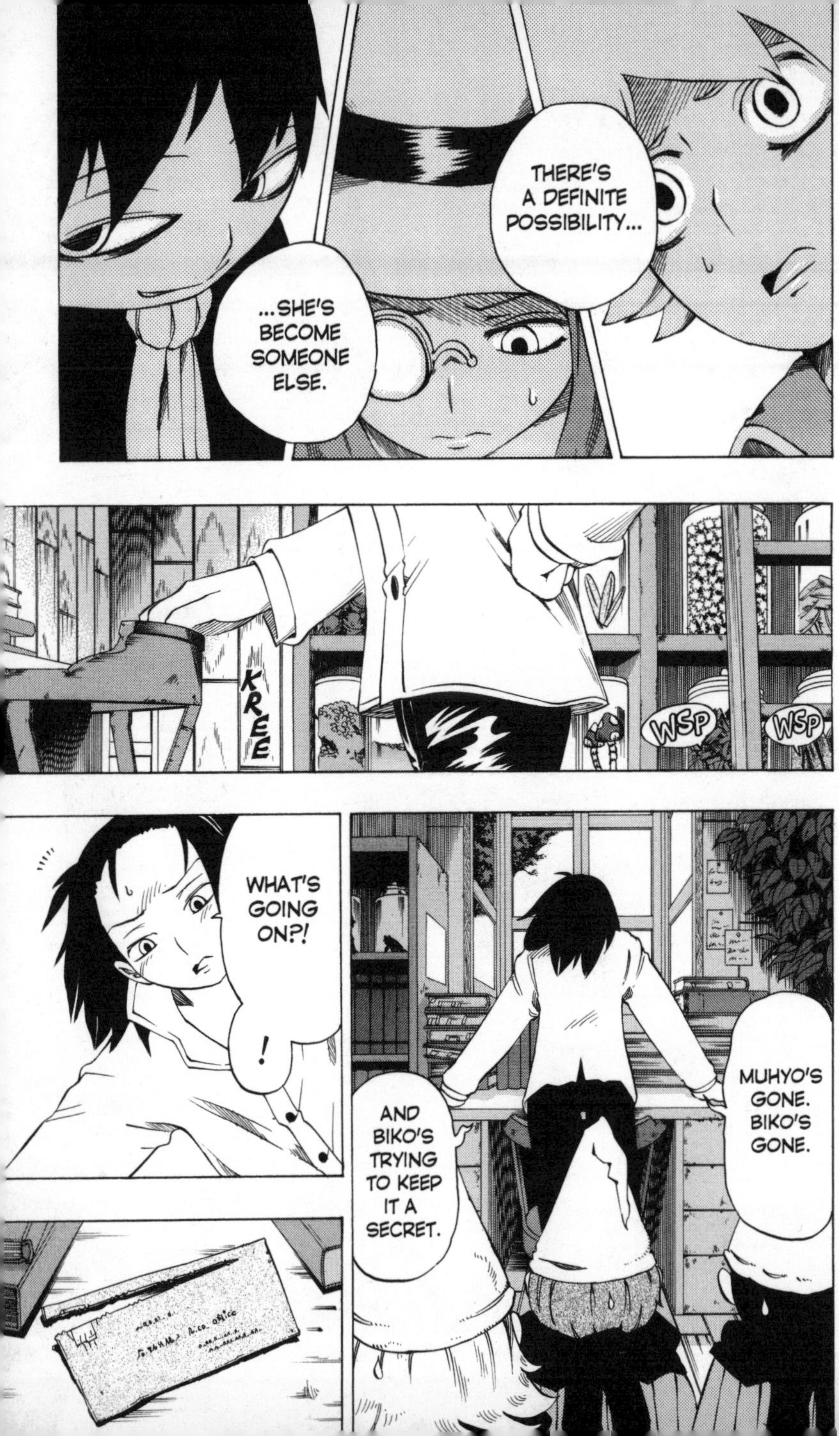
THERE'S A DEFINITE POSSIBILITY...
...SHE'S BECOME SOMEONE ELSE.
WSP
WSP
KREE
MUHYO'S GONE. BIKO'S GONE.
AND BIKO'S TRYING TO KEEP IT A SECRET.
WHAT'S GOING ON?!
!

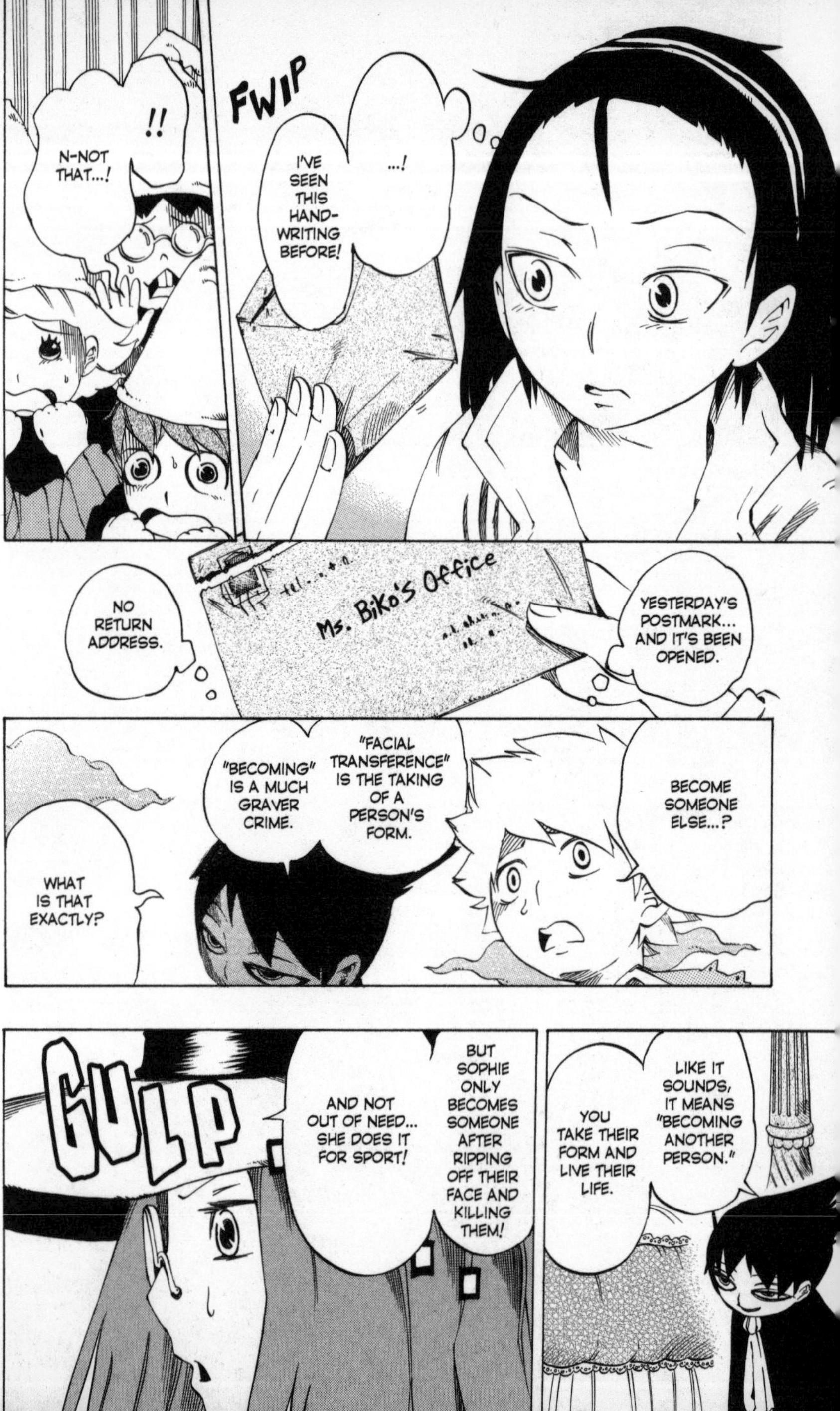
FWIP
...!
I'VE SEEN THIS HANDWRITING BEFORE!
!!
N-NOT THAT...!
Ms. Biko's Office
YESTERDAY'S POSTMARK... AND IT'S BEEN OPENED.
NO RETURN ADDRESS.
BECOME SOMEONE ELSE...?
"FACIAL TRANSFERENCE" IS THE TAKING OF A PERSON'S FORM.
"BECOMING" IS A MUCH GRAVER CRIME.
WHAT IS THAT EXACTLY?
LIKE IT SOUNDS, IT MEANS "BECOMING ANOTHER PERSON."
YOU TAKE THEIR FORM AND LIVE THEIR LIFE.
BUT SOPHIE ONLY BECOMES SOMEONE AFTER RIPPING OFF THEIR FACE AND KILLING THEM!
AND NOT OUT OF NEED... SHE DOES IT FOR SPORT!
GULP

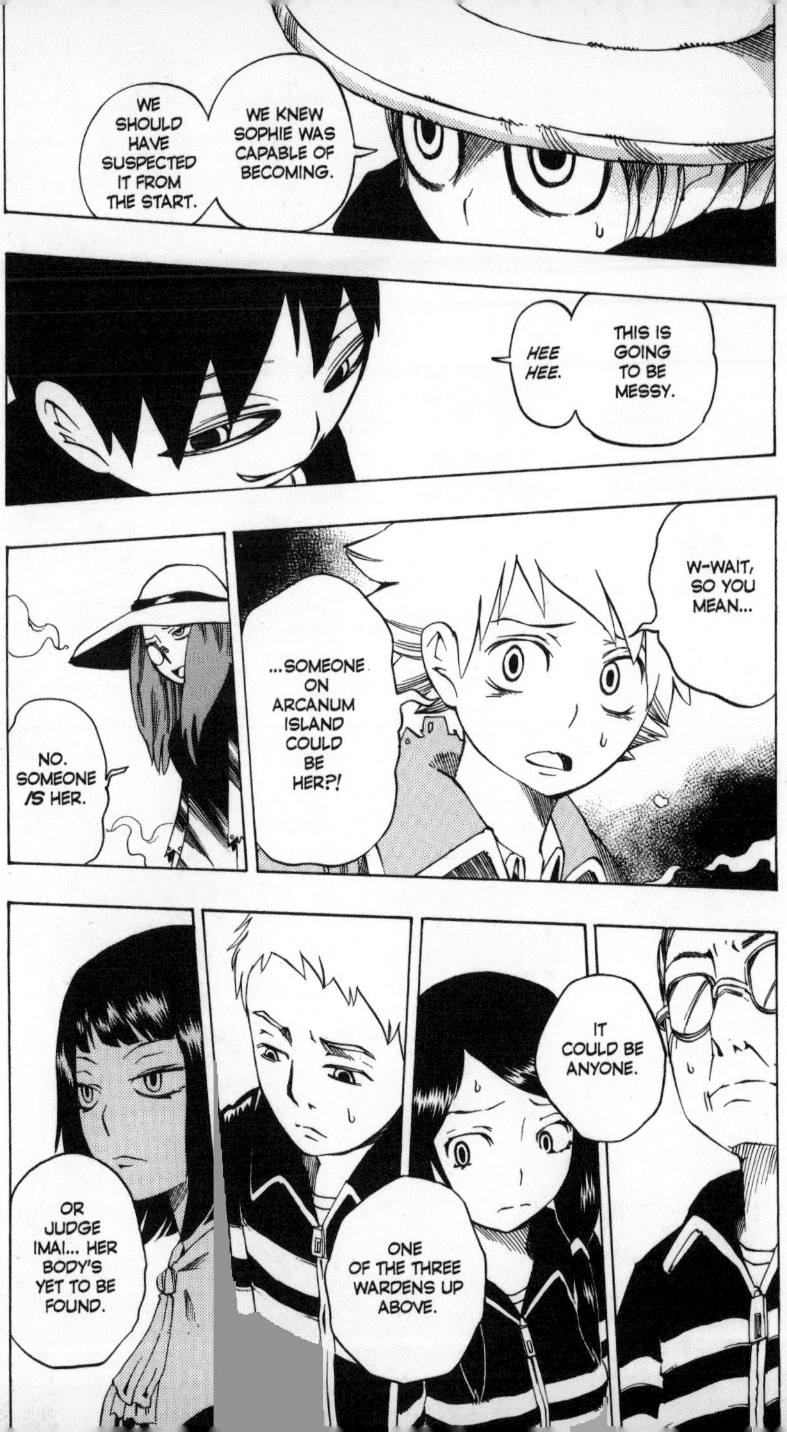
WE KNEW SOPHIE WAS CAPABLE OF BECOMING.
WE SHOULD HAVE SUSPECTED IT FROM THE START.
THIS IS GOING TO BE MESSY.
HEE HEE.
W-WAIT, SO YOU MEAN...
...SOMEONE ON ARCANUM ISLAND COULD BE HER?!
NO. SOMEONE *IS* HER.
IT COULD BE ANYONE.
ONE OF THE THREE WARDENS UP ABOVE.
OR JUDGE IMAI... HER BODY'S YET TO BE FOUND.

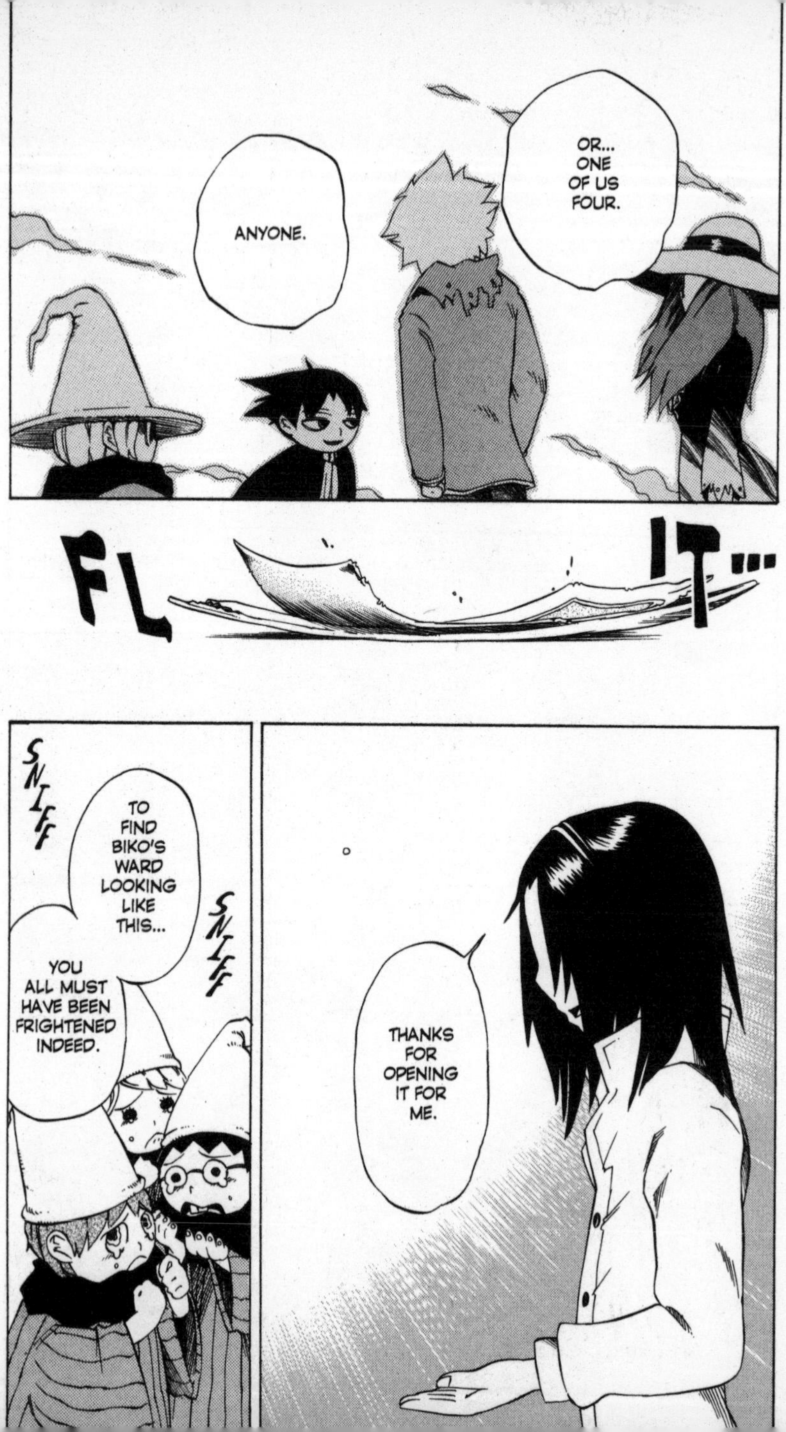
OR... ONE OF US FOUR.
ANYONE.
FL IT...
THANKS FOR OPENING IT FOR ME.
SNIFF
TO FIND BIKO'S WARD LOOKING LIKE THIS...
SNIFF
YOU ALL MUST HAVE BEEN FRIGHTENED INDEED.

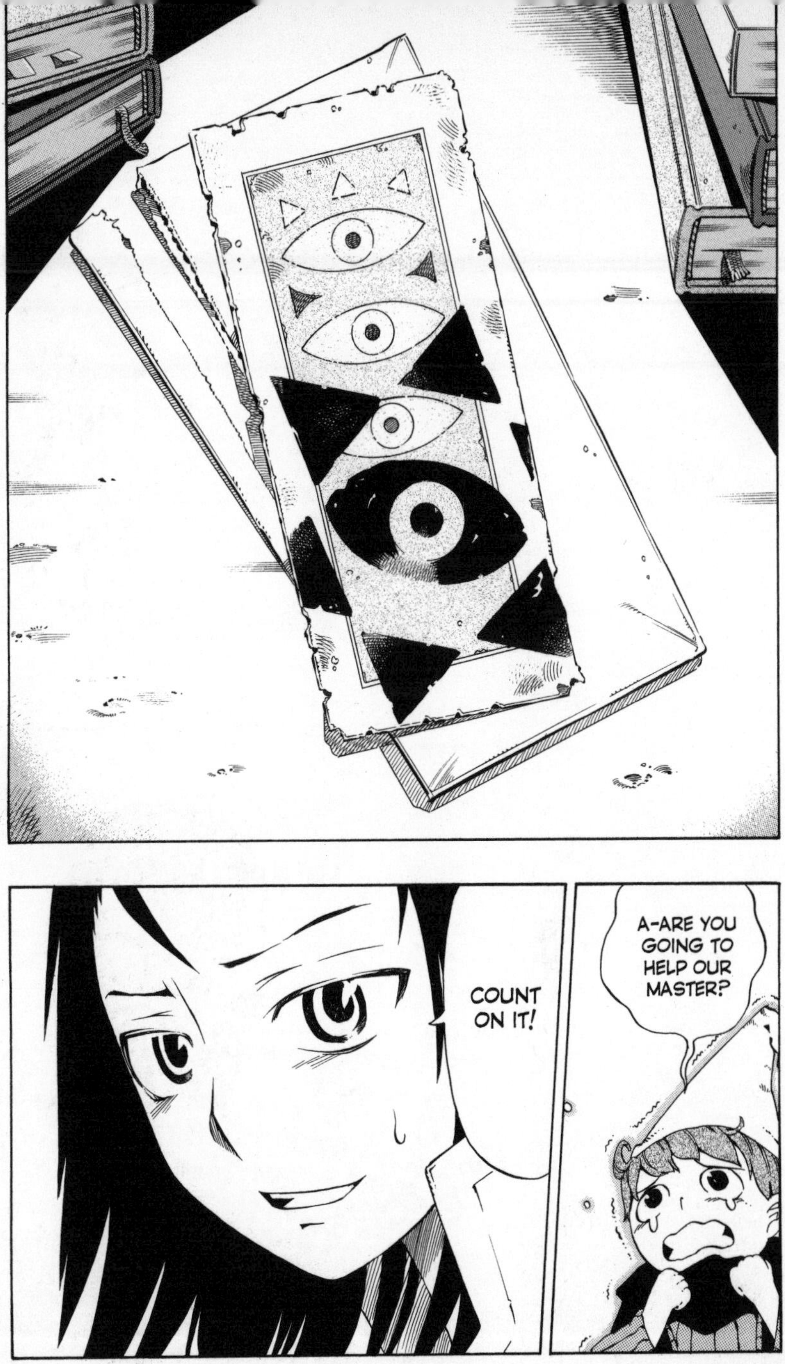
A-ARE YOU GOING TO HELP OUR MASTER?
COUNT ON IT!

A DAY IN BIKO'S OFFICE ①

JUDGE YOICHI WAS SO HANDSOME!

WHAA

HEY, GET TO WORK!

ARTICLE 25
RIO & ROJI

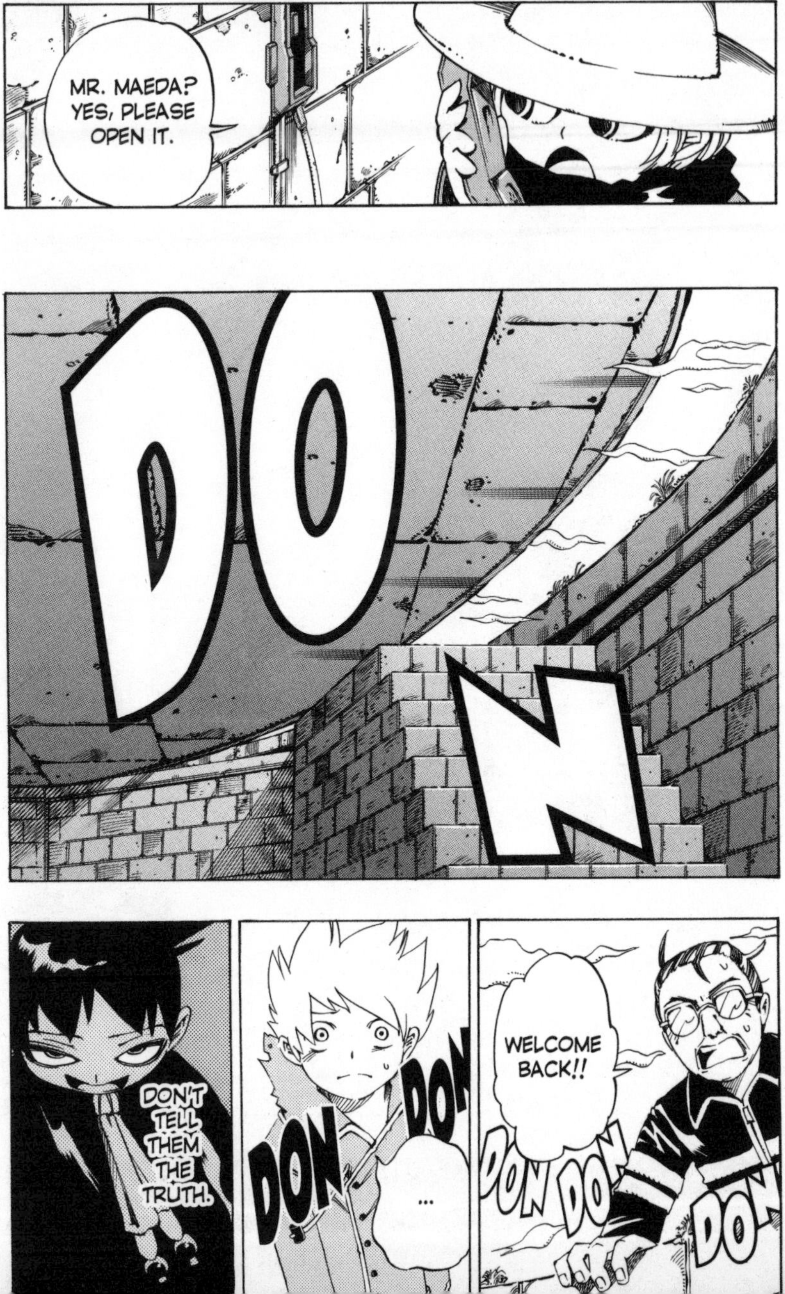

MR. MAEDA? YES, PLEASE OPEN IT.
DON
WELCOME BACK!!
DON
DON
DON
DON
DON
DON
...
DON'T TELL THEM THE TRUTH.

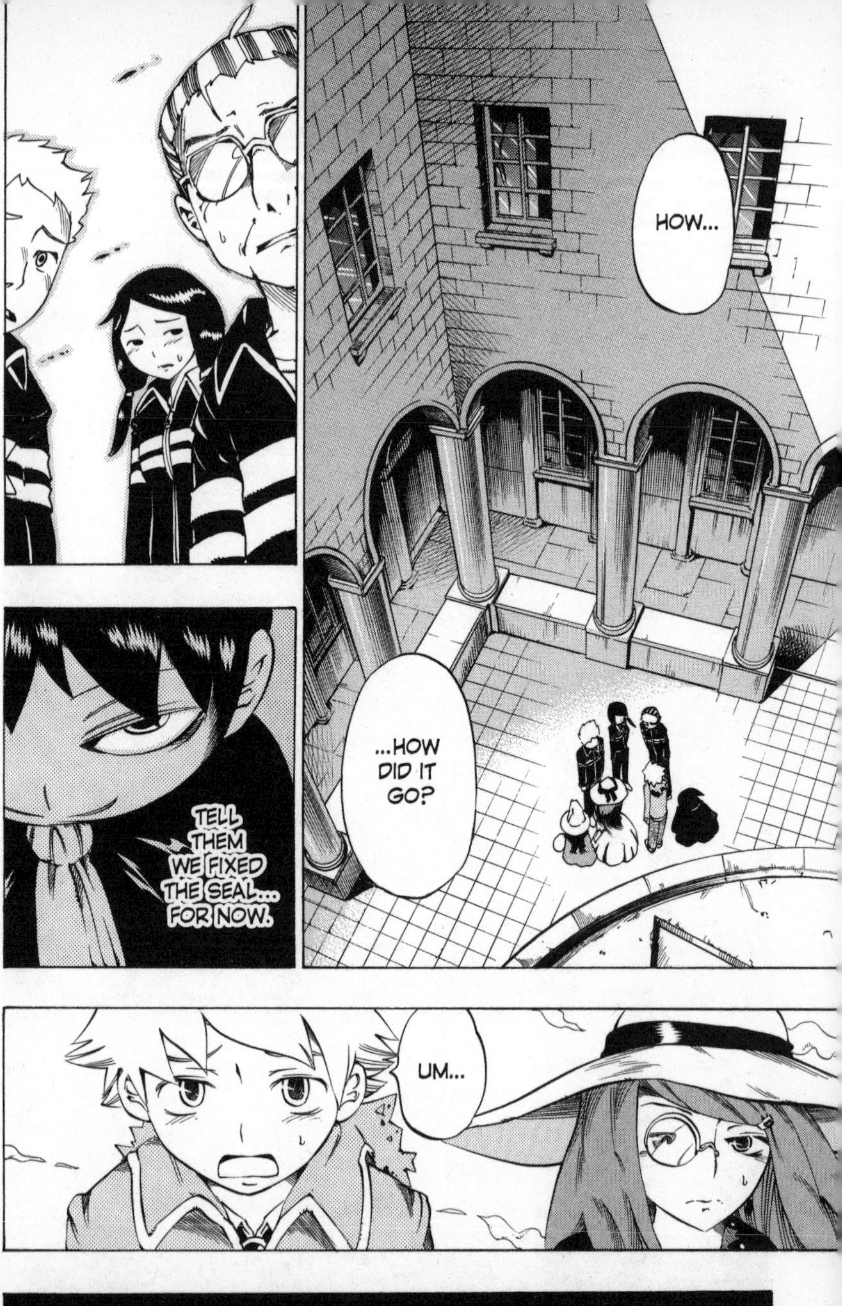
HOW...
...HOW DID IT GO?
TELL THEM WE FIXED THE SEAL... FOR NOW.
UM...
ONE OF US HERE IS SOPHIE!

ARTICLE 25
RIO & ROJI

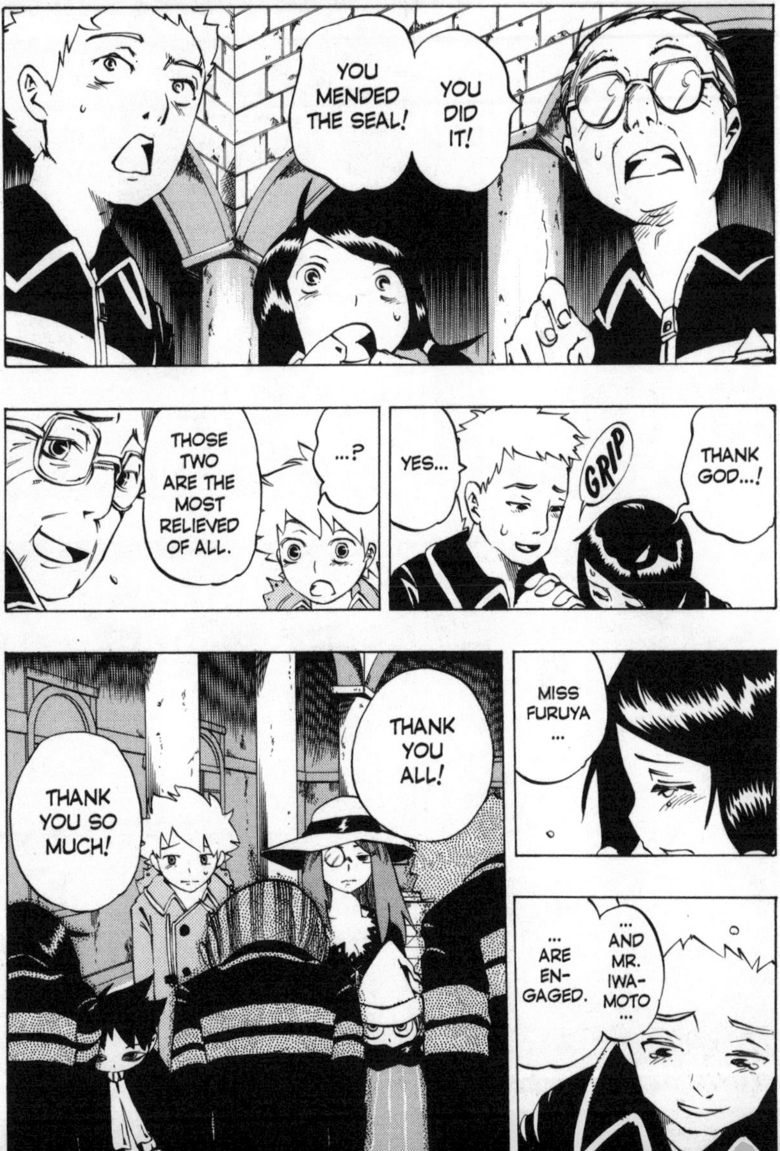
YOU DID IT!
YOU MENDED THE SEAL!
THANK GOD...!
GRIP
YES...
...?
THOSE TWO ARE THE MOST RELIEVED OF ALL.
MISS FURUYA ...
... AND MR. IWA-MOTO ...
... ARE EN-GAGED.
THANK YOU ALL!
THANK YOU SO MUCH!

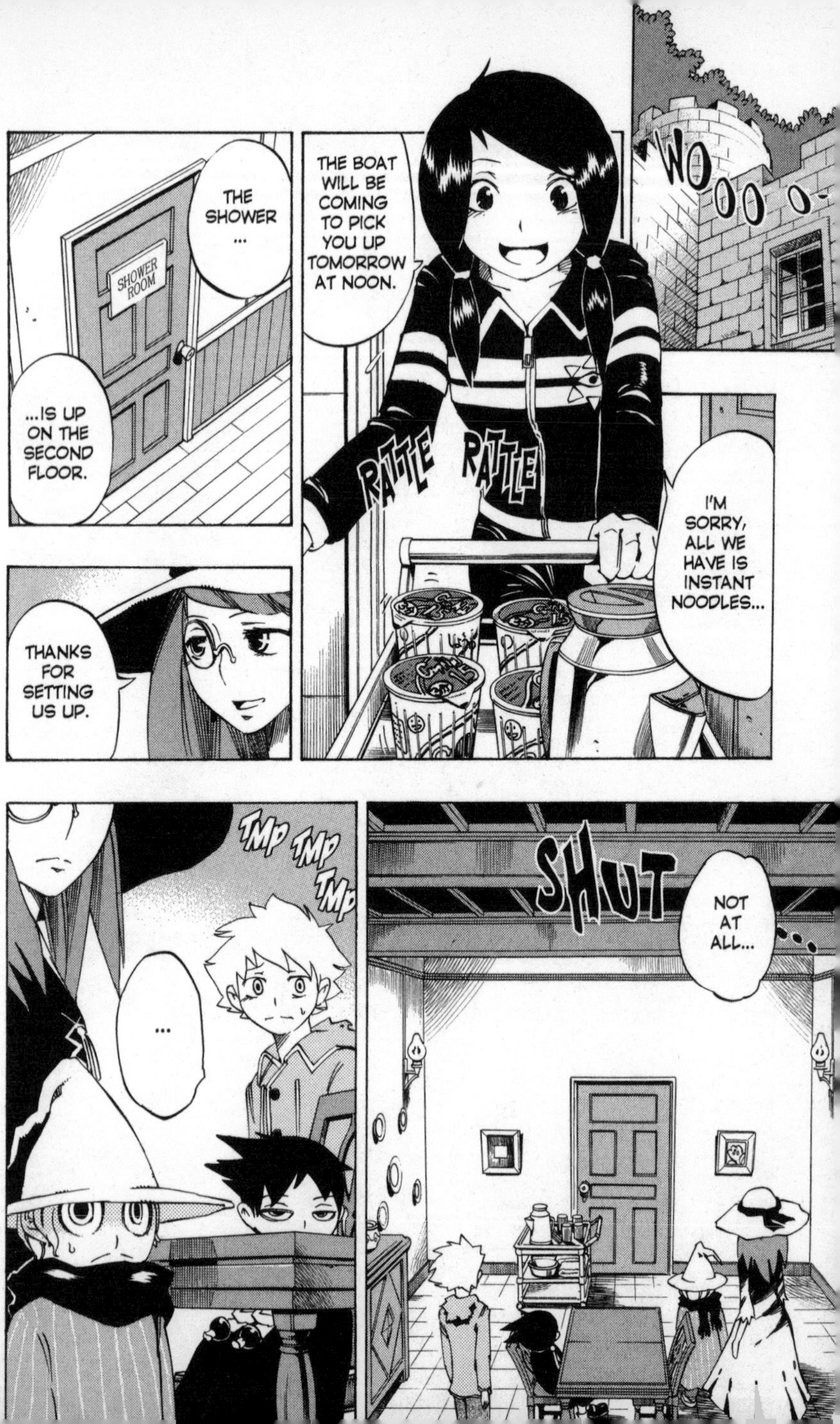
WOOOO...
THE BOAT WILL BE COMING TO PICK YOU UP TOMORROW AT NOON.
RATTLE RATTLE
I'M SORRY, ALL WE HAVE IS INSTANT NOODLES...
THE SHOWER ...
SHOWER ROOM
...IS UP ON THE SECOND FLOOR.
THANKS FOR SETTING US UP.
NOT AT ALL...
SHUT
TMP TMP TMP
...

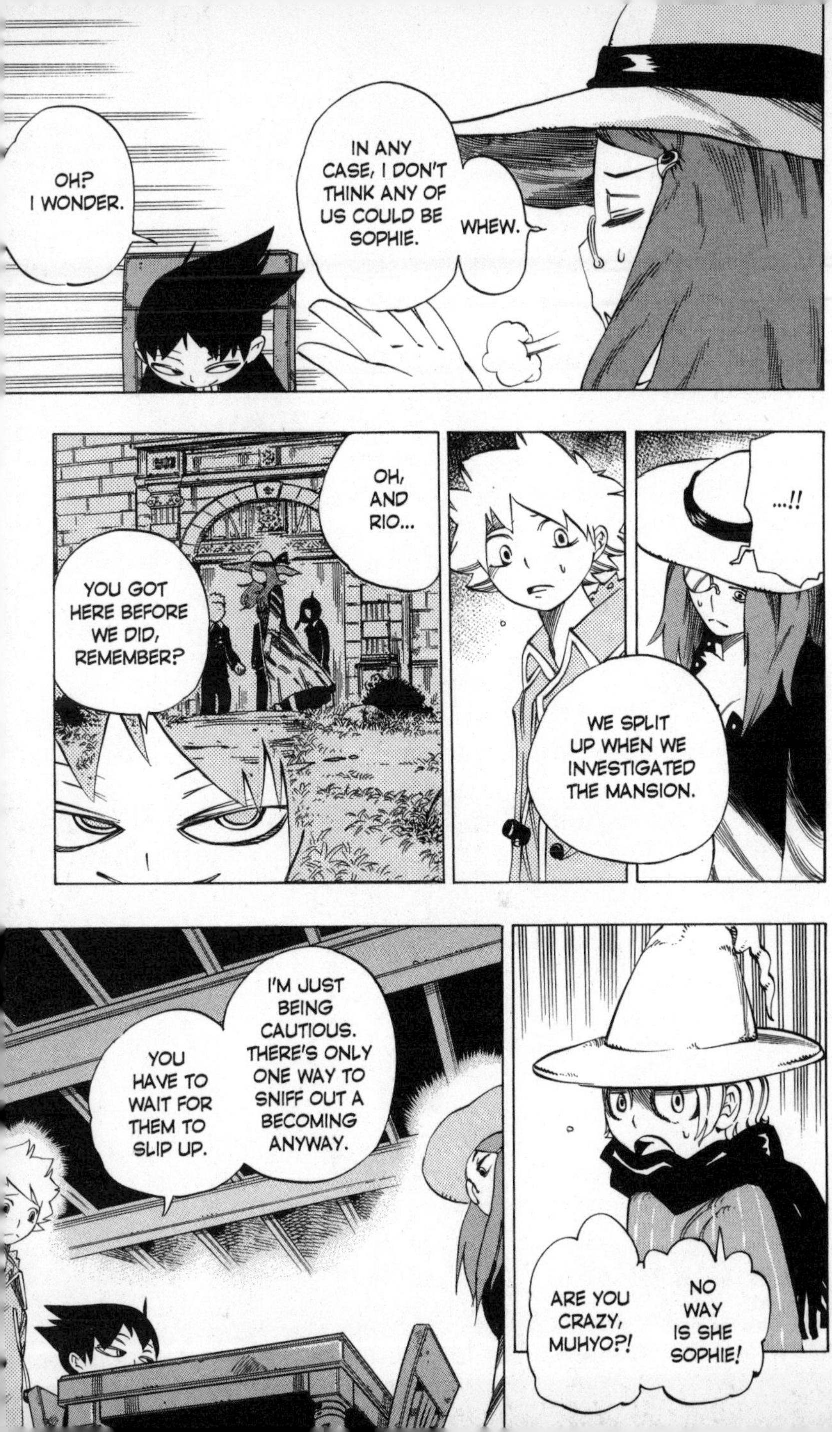
WHEW.
IN ANY CASE, I DON'T THINK ANY OF US COULD BE SOPHIE.
OH? I WONDER.
...!!
WE SPLIT UP WHEN WE INVESTIGATED THE MANSION.
OH, AND RIO...
YOU GOT HERE BEFORE WE DID, REMEMBER?
NO WAY IS SHE SOPHIE!
ARE YOU CRAZY, MUHYO?!
I'M JUST BEING CAUTIOUS. THERE'S ONLY ONE WAY TO SNIFF OUT A BECOMING ANYWAY.
YOU HAVE TO WAIT FOR THEM TO SLIP UP.

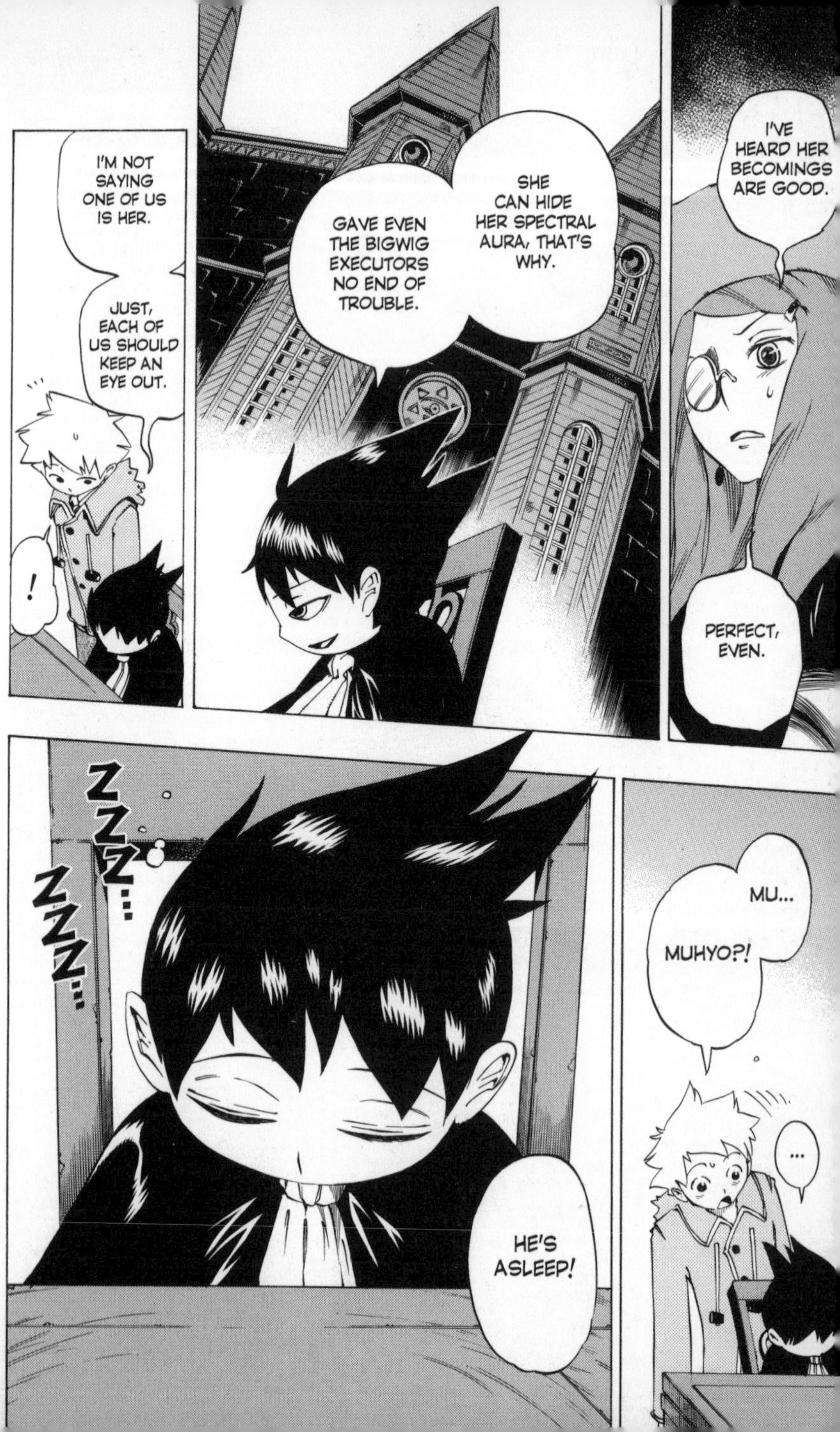
I'VE HEARD HER BECOMINGS ARE GOOD.
PERFECT, EVEN.
SHE CAN HIDE HER SPECTRAL AURA, THAT'S WHY.
GAVE EVEN THE BIGWIG EXECUTORS NO END OF TROUBLE.
I'M NOT SAYING ONE OF US IS HER.
JUST, EACH OF US SHOULD KEEP AN EYE OUT.
!
MU...
MUHYO?!
...
ZZZ...
ZZZ...
HE'S ASLEEP!

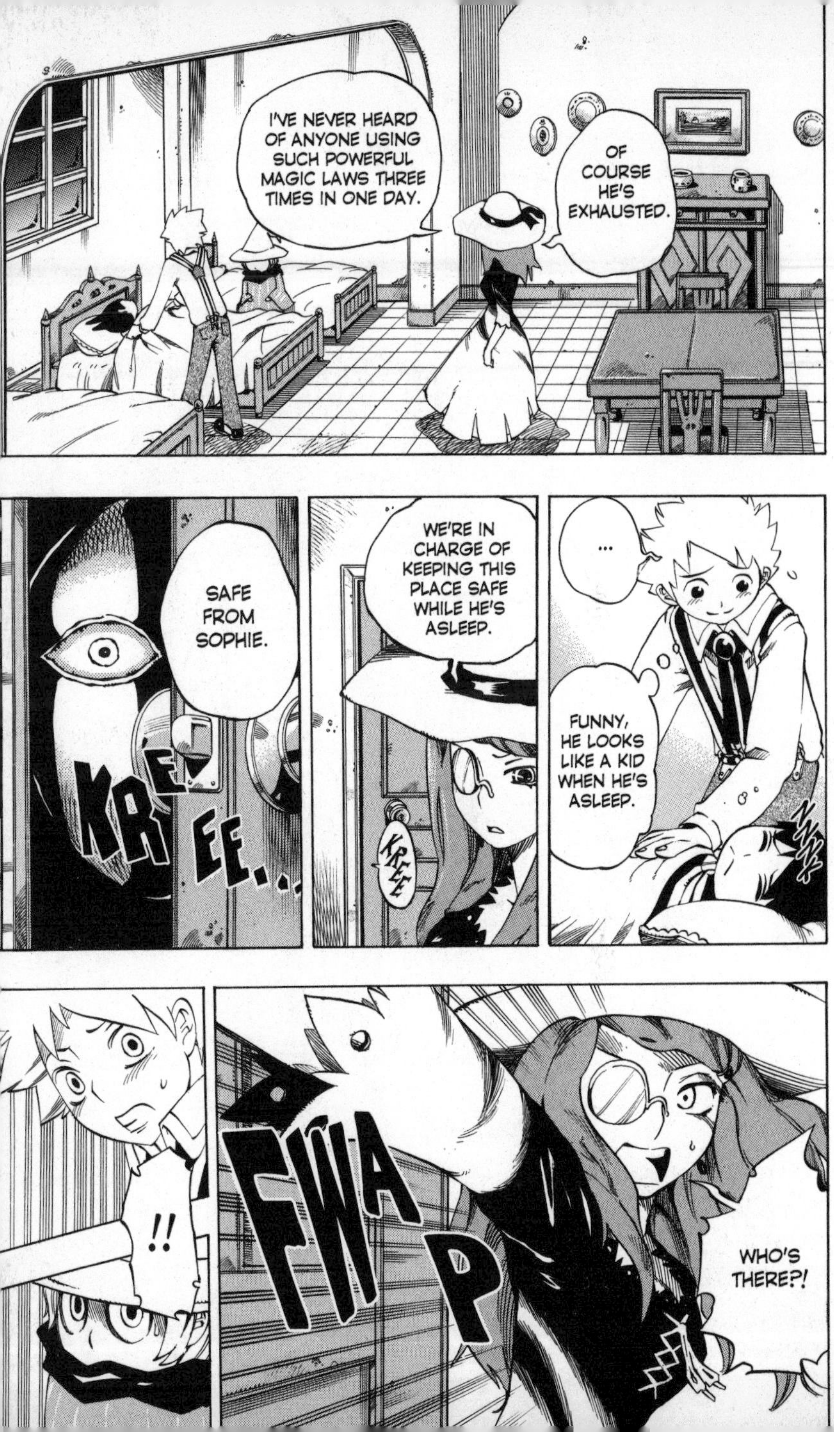
OF COURSE HE'S EXHAUSTED.
I'VE NEVER HEARD OF ANYONE USING SUCH POWERFUL MAGIC LAWS THREE TIMES IN ONE DAY.
...
FUNNY, HE LOOKS LIKE A KID WHEN HE'S ASLEEP.
NNNK
WE'RE IN CHARGE OF KEEPING THIS PLACE SAFE WHILE HE'S ASLEEP.
KREE
SAFE FROM SOPHIE.
KREEE...
WHO'S THERE?!
FWAP
!!

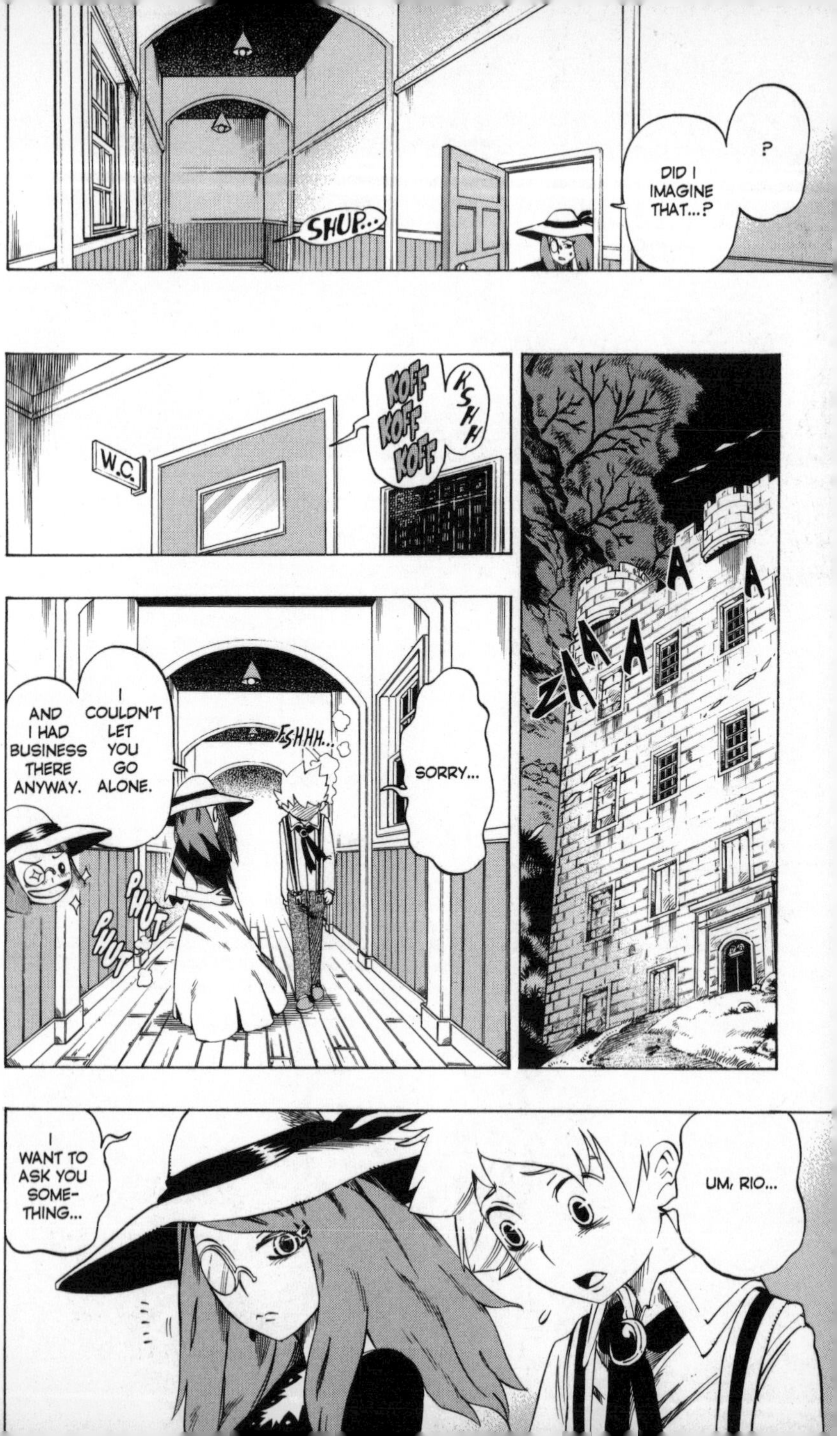

?
DID I IMAGINE THAT...?
SHUP...
ZAAAAAA
KSHH
KOFF KOFF KOFF
SORRY...
FSHHH...
I COULDN'T LET YOU GO ALONE.
AND I HAD BUSINESS THERE ANYWAY.
PHUT PHUT
UM, RIO...
I WANT TO ASK YOU SOME-THING...

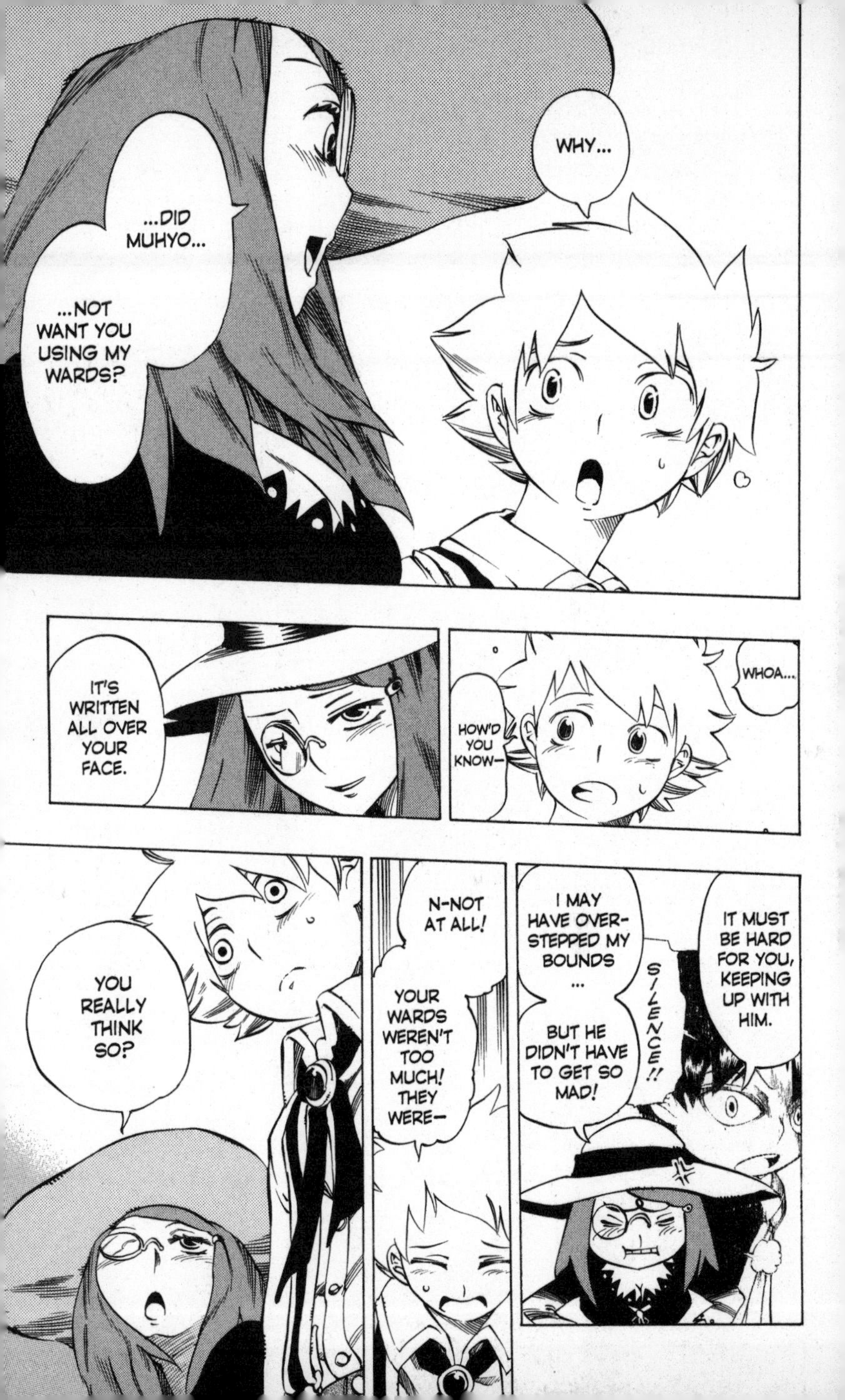
WHY...
...DID MUHYO...
...NOT WANT YOU USING MY WARDS?
WHOA...
HOW'D YOU KNOW—
IT'S WRITTEN ALL OVER YOUR FACE.
IT MUST BE HARD FOR YOU, KEEPING UP WITH HIM.
SILENCE!!
I MAY HAVE OVER-STEPPED MY BOUNDS ...
BUT HE DIDN'T HAVE TO GET SO MAD!
N-NOT AT ALL!
YOUR WARDS WEREN'T TOO MUCH! THEY WERE—
YOU REALLY THINK SO?

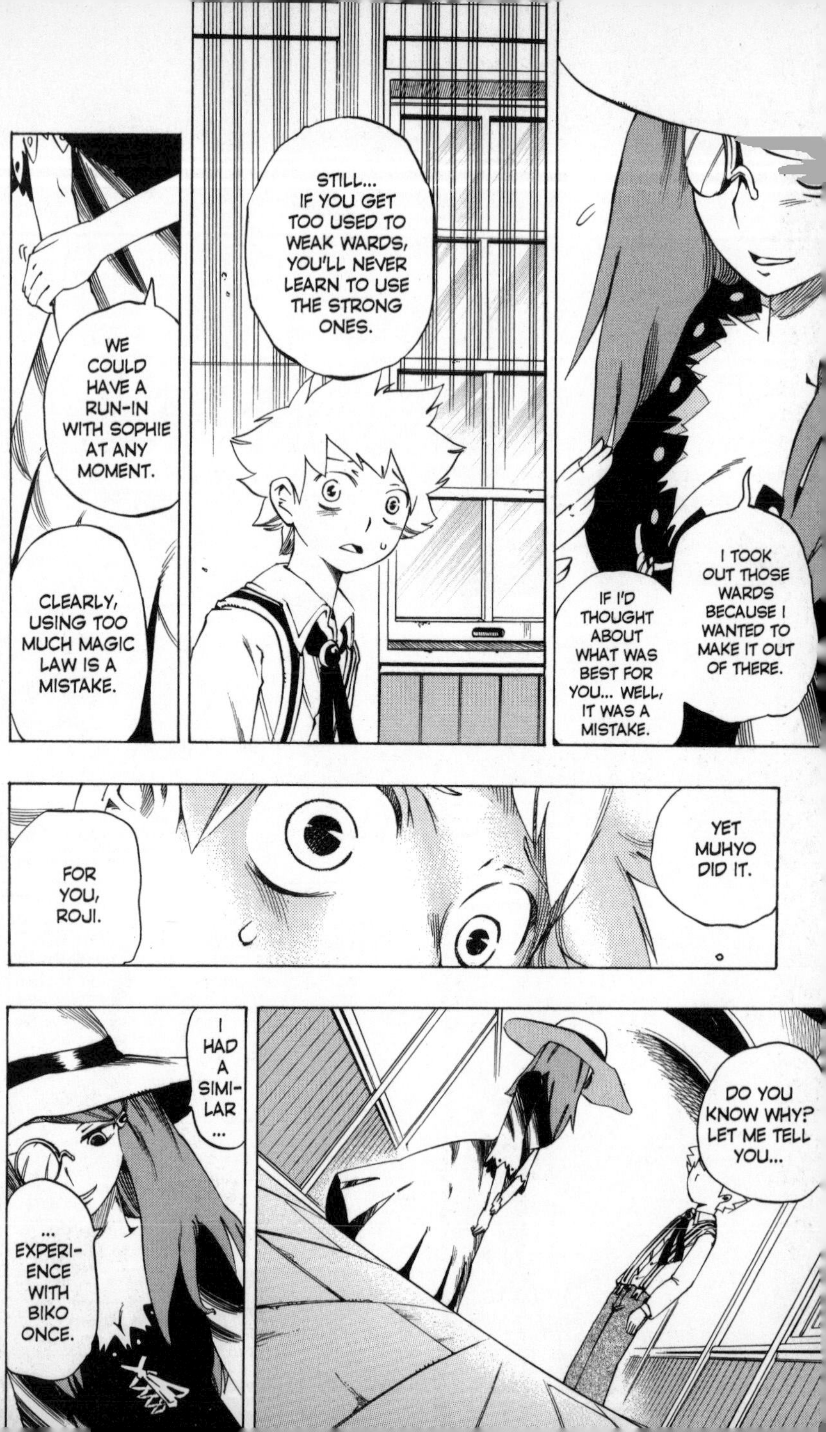
I TOOK OUT THOSE WARDS BECAUSE I WANTED TO MAKE IT OUT OF THERE.
IF I'D THOUGHT ABOUT WHAT WAS BEST FOR YOU... WELL, IT WAS A MISTAKE.
STILL... IF YOU GET TOO USED TO WEAK WARDS, YOU'LL NEVER LEARN TO USE THE STRONG ONES.
WE COULD HAVE A RUN-IN WITH SOPHIE AT ANY MOMENT.
CLEARLY, USING TOO MUCH MAGIC LAW IS A MISTAKE.
YET MUHYO DID IT.
FOR YOU, ROJI.
DO YOU KNOW WHY? LET ME TELL YOU...
I HAD A SIMILAR...
...EXPERIENCE WITH BIKO ONCE.

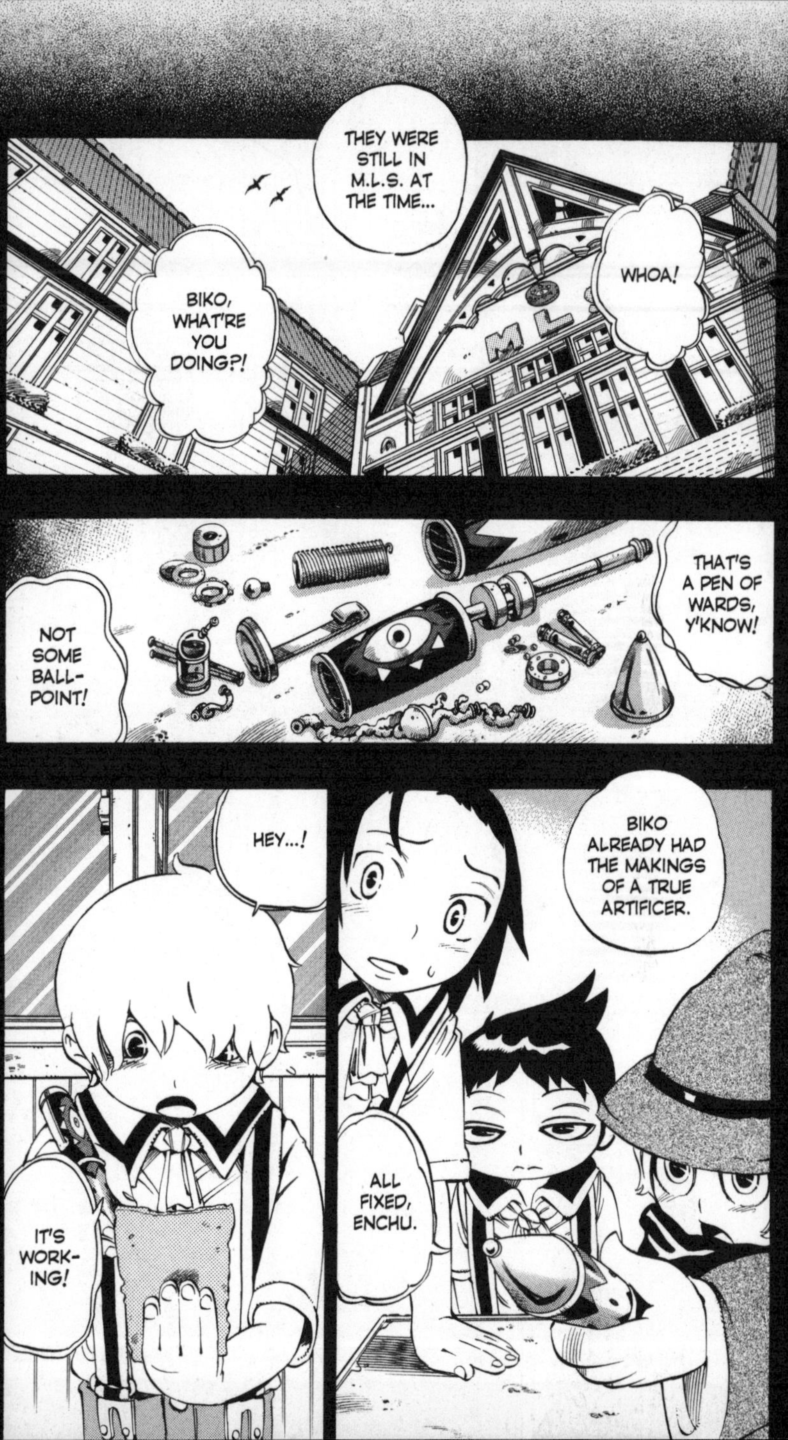
THEY WERE STILL IN M.L.S. AT THE TIME...
WHOA!
BIKO, WHAT'RE YOU DOING?!
M L
THAT'S A PEN OF WARDS, Y'KNOW!
NOT SOME BALL-POINT!
BIKO ALREADY HAD THE MAKINGS OF A TRUE ARTIFICER.
ALL FIXED, ENCHU.
HEY...!
IT'S WORK-ING!

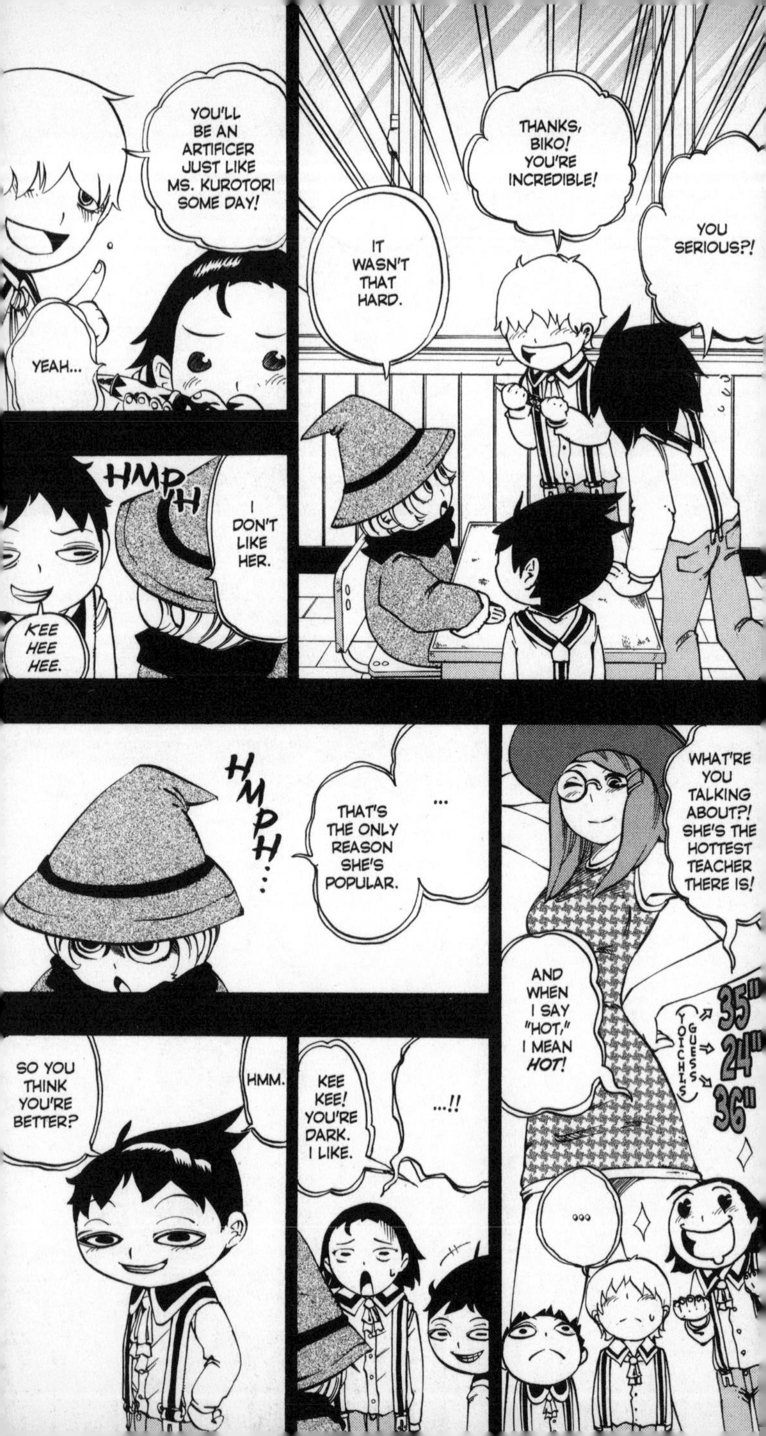
THANKS, BIKO! YOU'RE INCREDIBLE!
YOU SERIOUS?!
IT WASN'T THAT HARD.
YOU'LL BE AN ARTIFICER JUST LIKE MS. KUROTORI SOME DAY!
YEAH...
I DON'T LIKE HER.
HMPH
KEE HEE HEE.
WHAT'RE YOU TALKING ABOUT?! SHE'S THE HOTTEST TEACHER THERE IS!
AND WHEN I SAY "HOT," I MEAN HOT!
YOICHI'S GUESS
35"
24"
36"
ooo
...
THAT'S THE ONLY REASON SHE'S POPULAR.
HMPH...
...!!
KEE KEE! YOU'RE DARK. I LIKE.
HMM.
SO YOU THINK YOU'RE BETTER?

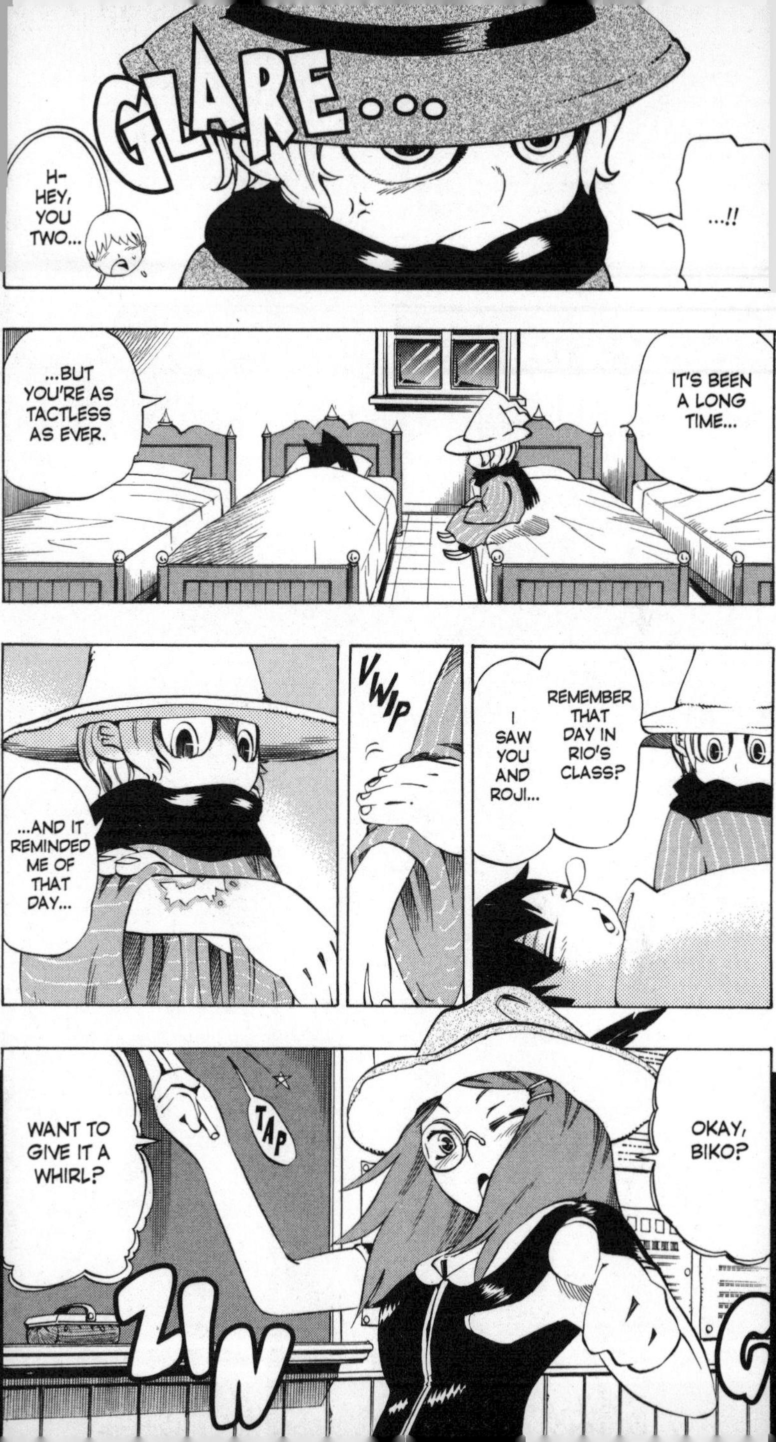
GLARE...
...!!
H-HEY, YOU TWO...
IT'S BEEN A LONG TIME...
...BUT YOU'RE AS TACTLESS AS EVER.
REMEMBER THAT DAY IN RIO'S CLASS?
I SAW YOU AND ROJI...
VWIP
...AND IT REMINDED ME OF THAT DAY...
OKAY, BIKO?
TAP
WANT TO GIVE IT A WHIRL?
ZING

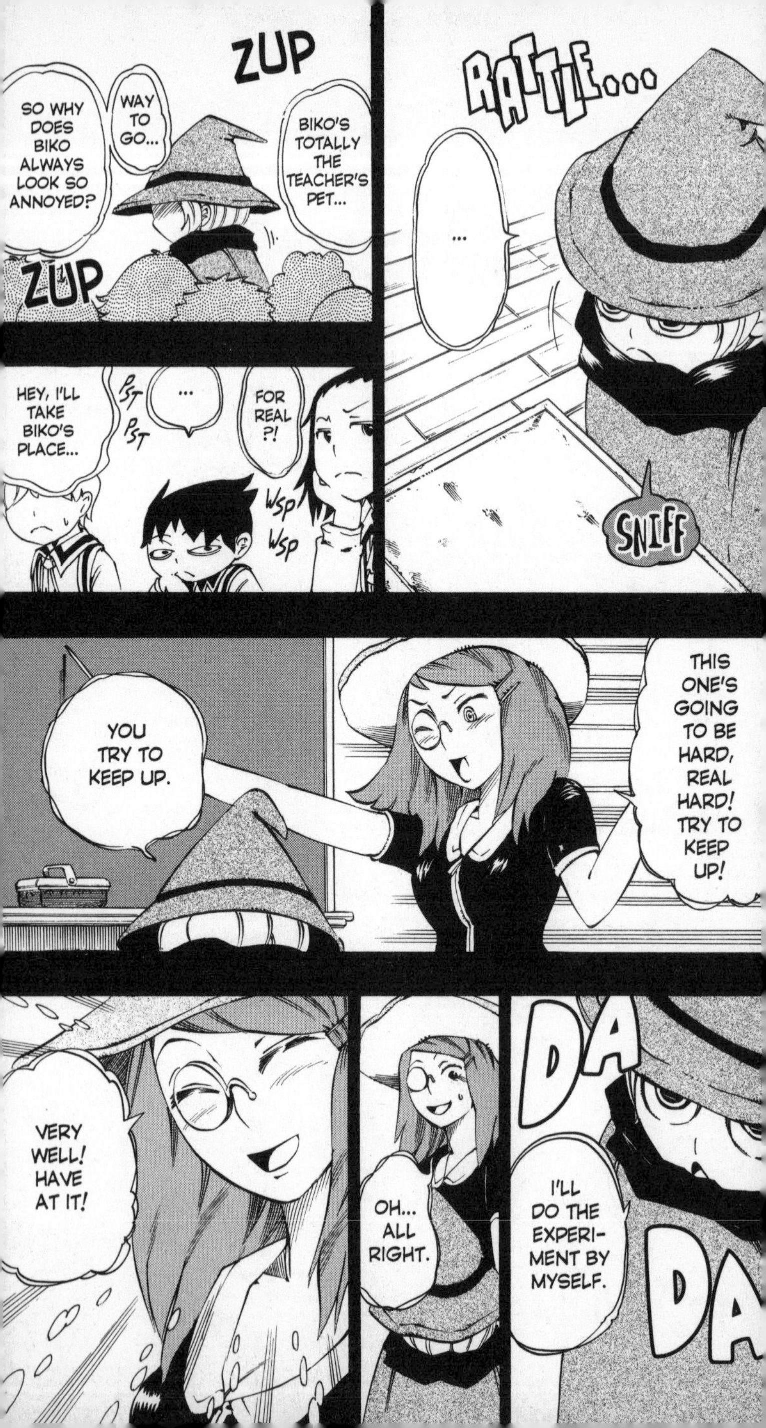
RATTLE...
...
SNIFF
ZUP
BIKO'S TOTALLY THE TEACHER'S PET...
WAY TO GO...
SO WHY DOES BIKO ALWAYS LOOK SO ANNOYED?
ZUP
FOR REAL?!
...
PST PST
HEY, I'LL TAKE BIKO'S PLACE...
WSP WSP
THIS ONE'S GOING TO BE HARD, REAL HARD! TRY TO KEEP UP!
YOU TRY TO KEEP UP.
DA
I'LL DO THE EXPERIMENT BY MYSELF.
DA
OH... ALL RIGHT.
VERY WELL! HAVE AT IT!

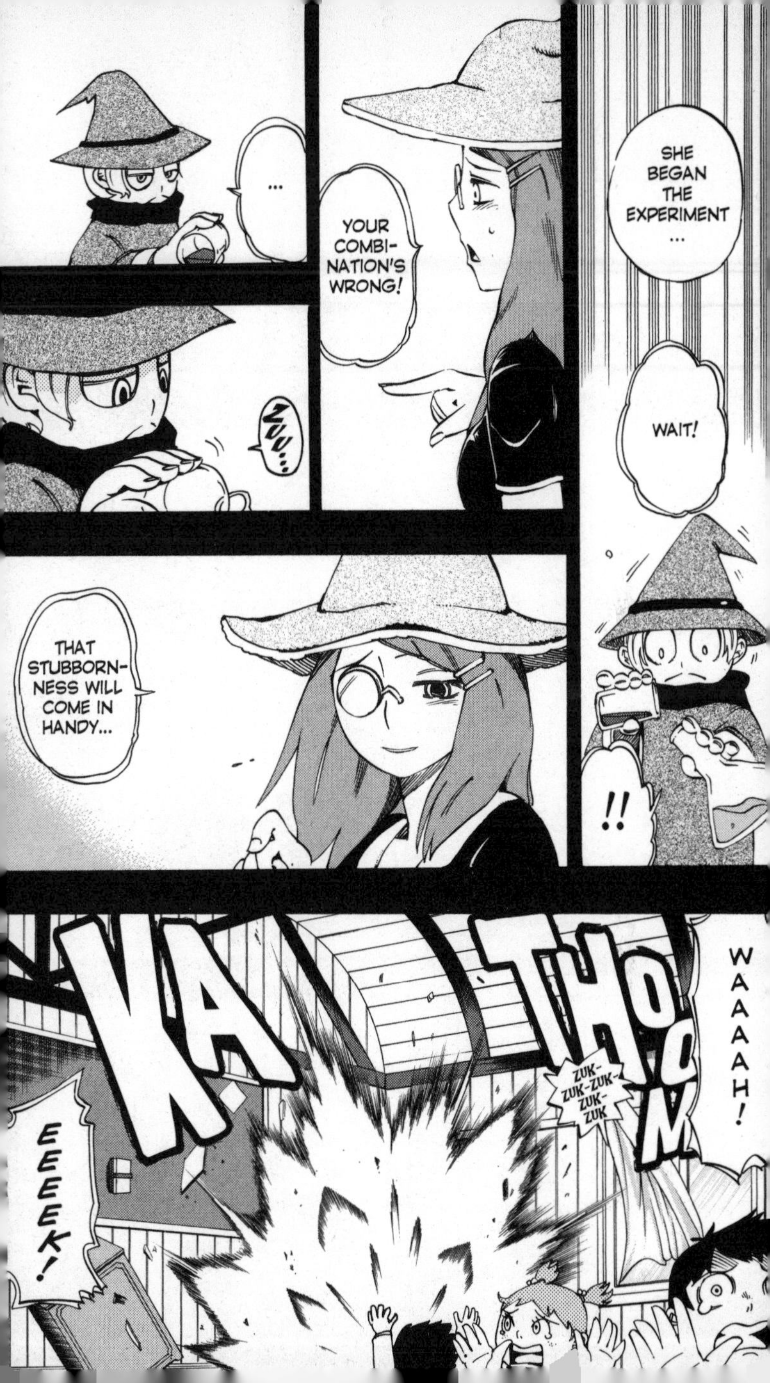
SHE BEGAN THE EXPERIMENT ...
WAIT!
YOUR COMBINATION'S WRONG!
...
ZUU...
!!
THAT STUBBORNNESS WILL COME IN HANDY...
WAAAAH!
ZUK-ZUK-ZUK-ZUK-ZUK
KA-THOOM
EEEEEK!

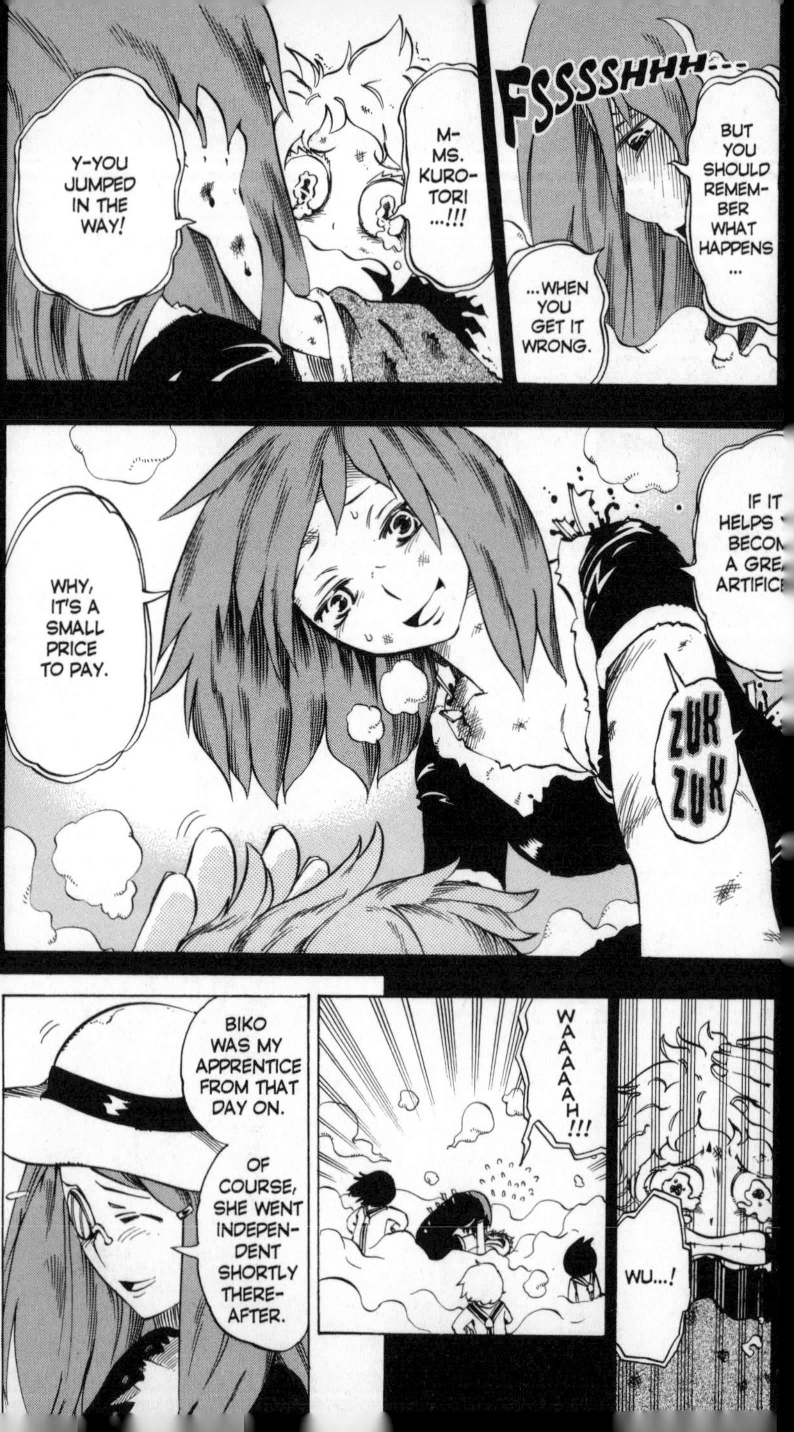
FSSSSHHH...
BUT YOU SHOULD REMEMBER WHAT HAPPENS...
...WHEN YOU GET IT WRONG.
M-MS. KUROTORI...!!!
Y-YOU JUMPED IN THE WAY!
IF IT HELPS
ZUK ZUK
WHY, IT'S A SMALL PRICE TO PAY.
WU...!
WAAAAAH!!!
BIKO WAS MY APPRENTICE FROM THAT DAY ON.
OF COURSE, SHE WENT INDEPENDENT SHORTLY THEREAFTER.

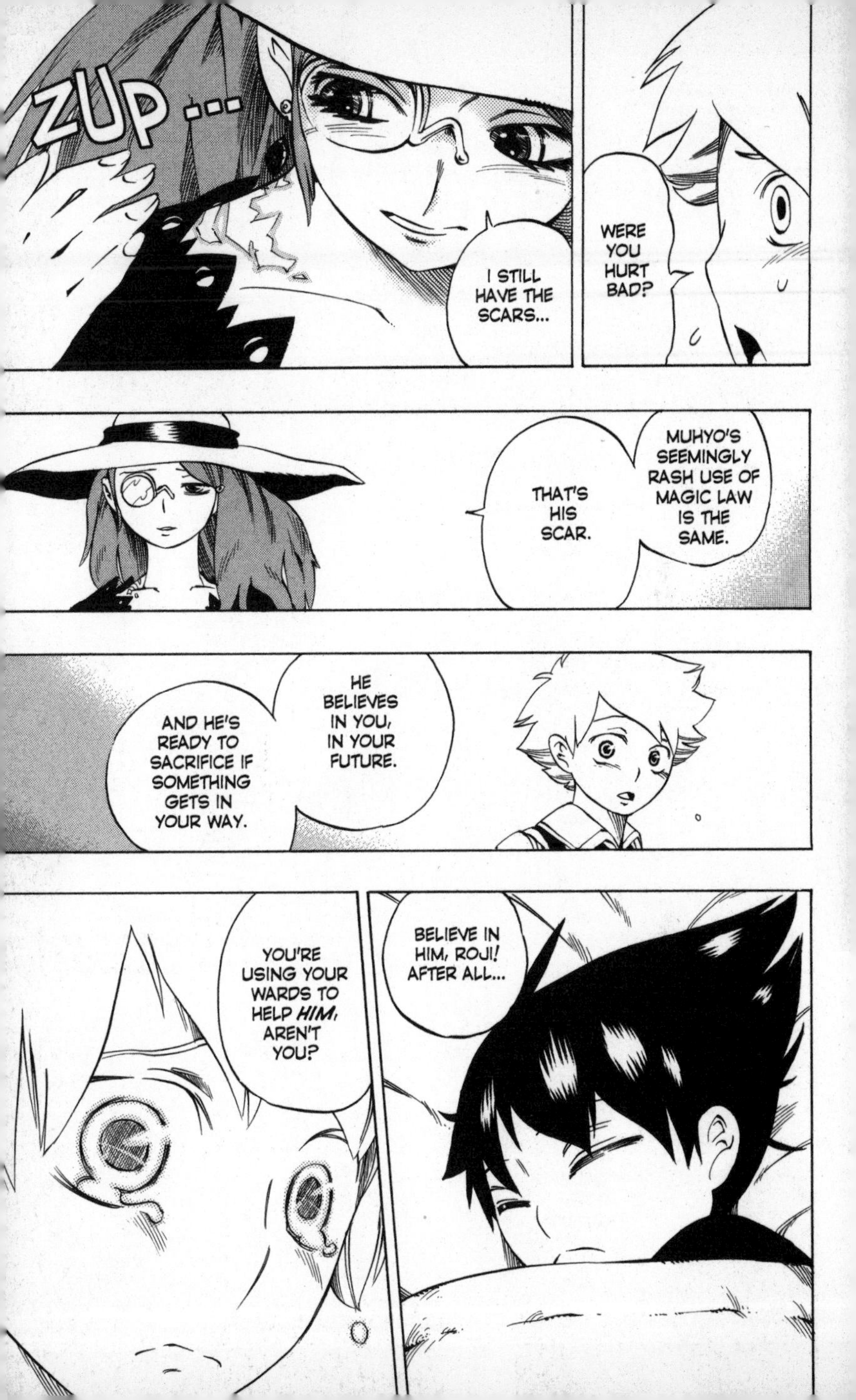
WERE YOU HURT BAD?
ZUP...
I STILL HAVE THE SCARS...
MUHYO'S SEEMINGLY RASH USE OF MAGIC LAW IS THE SAME.
THAT'S HIS SCAR.
HE BELIEVES IN YOU, IN YOUR FUTURE.
AND HE'S READY TO SACRIFICE IF SOMETHING GETS IN YOUR WAY.
BELIEVE IN HIM, ROJI! AFTER ALL...
YOU'RE USING YOUR WARDS TO HELP *HIM*, AREN'T YOU?

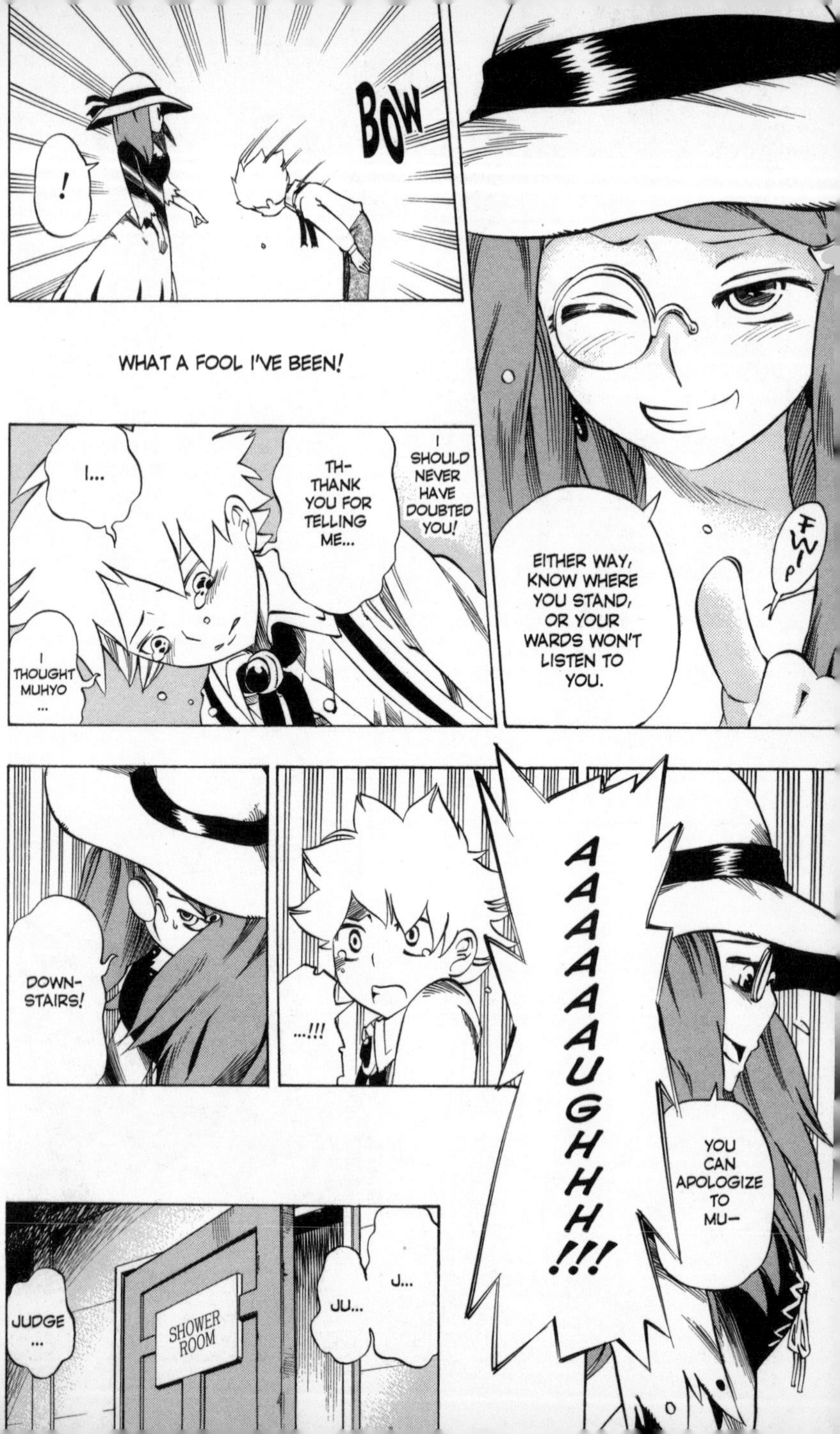
FWIP
EITHER WAY, KNOW WHERE YOU STAND, OR YOUR WARDS WON'T LISTEN TO YOU.
BOW
!
WHAT A FOOL I'VE BEEN!
I SHOULD NEVER HAVE DOUBTED YOU!
TH- THANK YOU FOR TELLING ME...
I...
I THOUGHT MUHYO ...
YOU CAN APOLOGIZE TO MU–
AAAAAAUGHHHH!!!
...!!!
DOWN-STAIRS!
J...
JU...
JUDGE ...
SHOWER ROOM

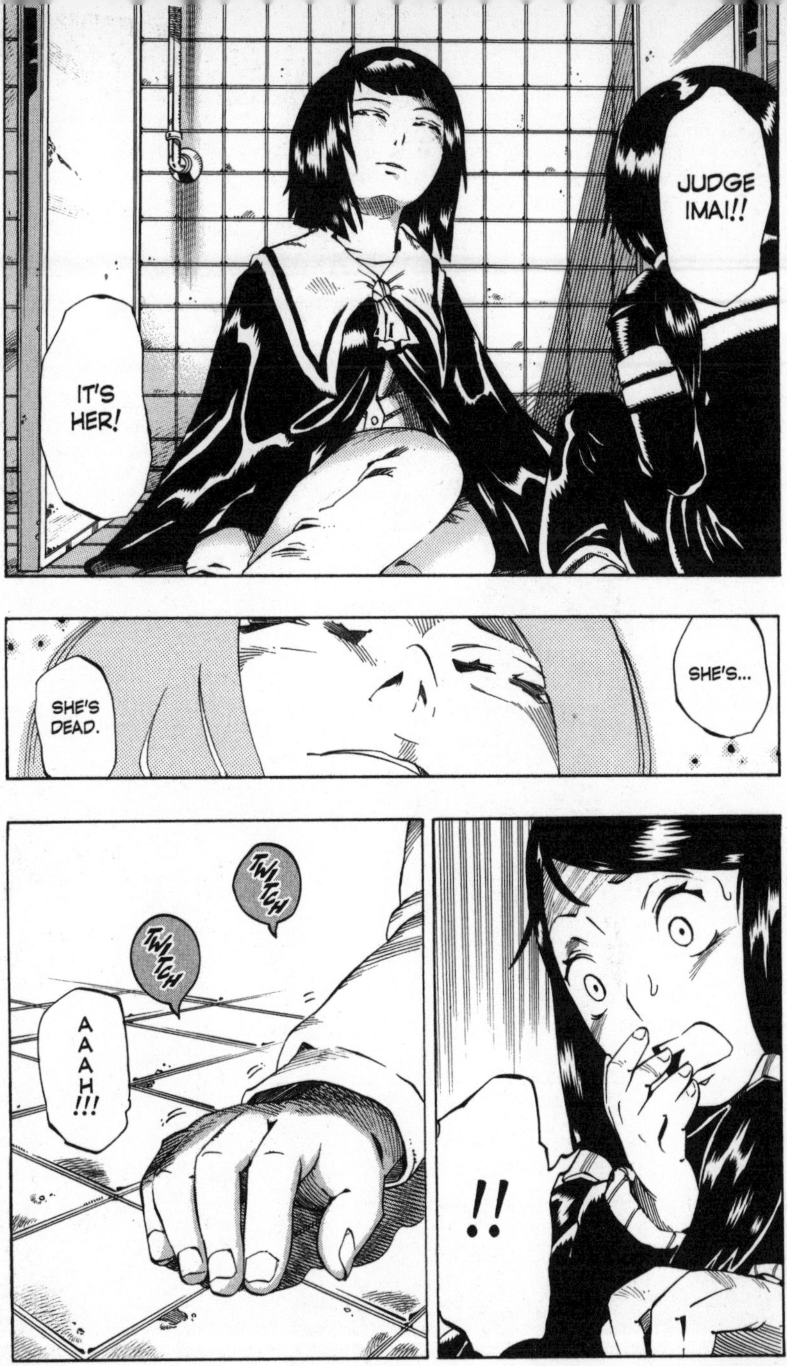
JUDGE IMAI!!
IT'S HER!
SHE'S...
SHE'S DEAD.
!!
TWITCH
TWITCH
AAAH!!!

RIO KUROTORI

BIRTHDAY: MAY 10

HEIGHT: 168 CM

LIKES: FRESHLY BAKED BREAD
(BAKED BY BIKO)
COFFEE
LONG BATHS

TALENTS: SHOPPING
(GOOD AT BARGAINING)
PUTTERING IN THE GARDEN
MAKING CHEESE GRATIN
(OVER 20 KINDS!)

NOT GOOD WITH: ALCOHOL (CAN DRINK
A LITTLE WINE BUT
BECOMES A THREAT
TO PUBLIC SAFETY WITH
OTHER BEVERAGES.)

ARTICLE 26
SOPHIE

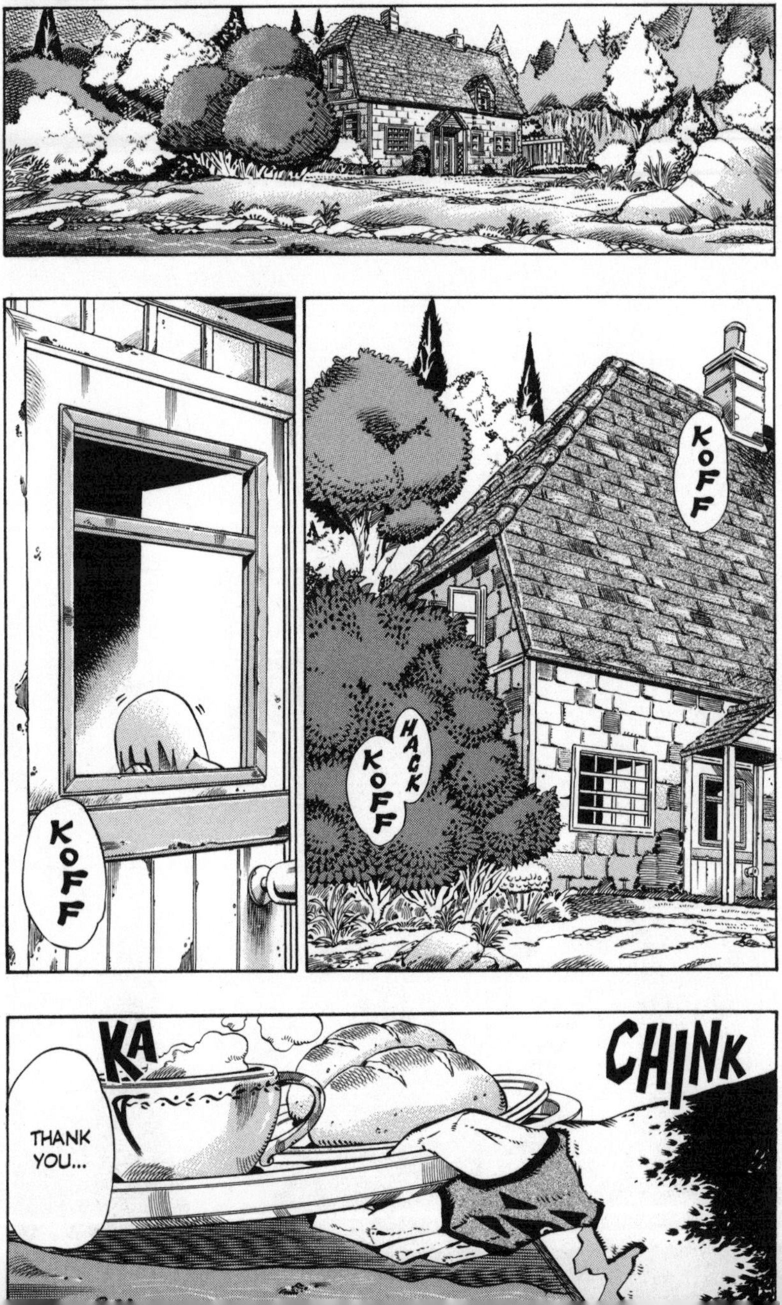
KOFF
HACK KOFF KOFF
KOFF
KA CHINK
THANK YOU...

...BUT I'M OKAY.

ARTICLE 26
SOPHIE

I FIND...

...I DON'T NEED TO EAT THESE DAYS.

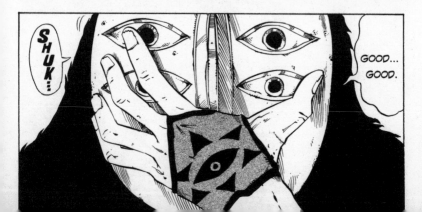

SHUK...

GOOD... GOOD.

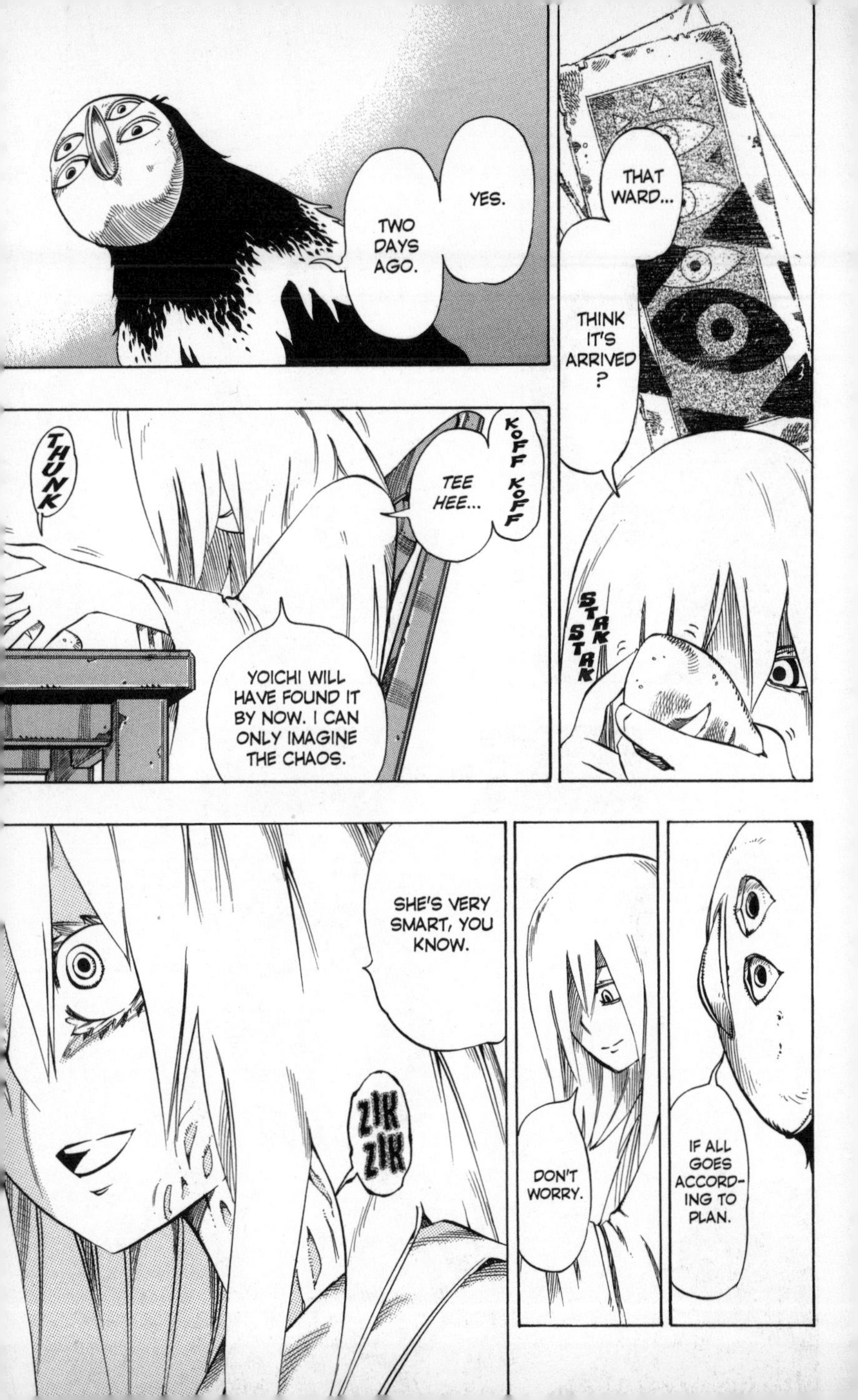

THAT WARD...
THINK IT'S ARRIVED?
STRK STRK
YES.
TWO DAYS AGO.
KOFF KOFF
TEE HEE...
YOICHI WILL HAVE FOUND IT BY NOW. I CAN ONLY IMAGINE THE CHAOS.
THUNK
IF ALL GOES ACCORD-ING TO PLAN.
DON'T WORRY.
SHE'S VERY SMART, YOU KNOW.
ZIK ZIK

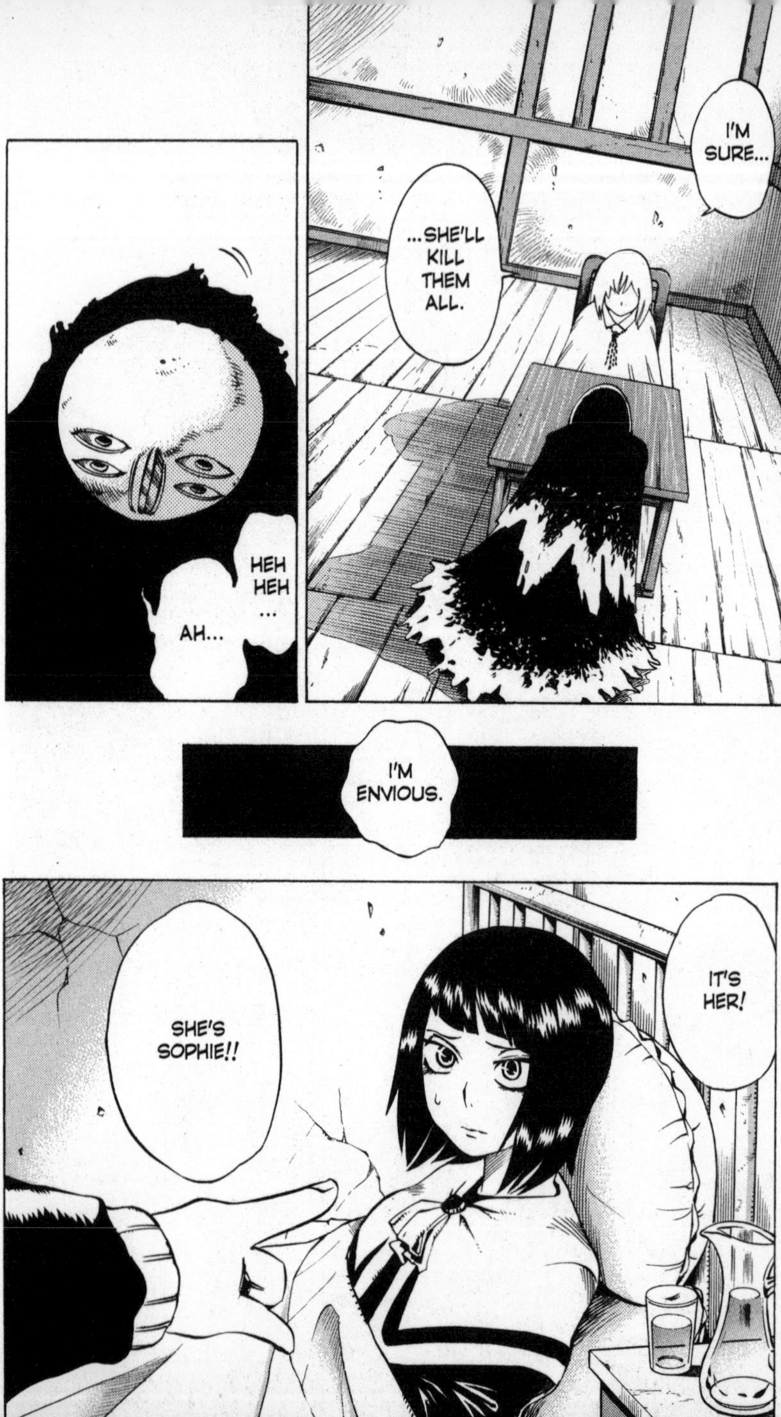
I'M SURE...
...SHE'LL KILL THEM ALL.
HEH HEH ...
AH...
I'M ENVIOUS.
IT'S HER!
SHE'S SOPHIE!!

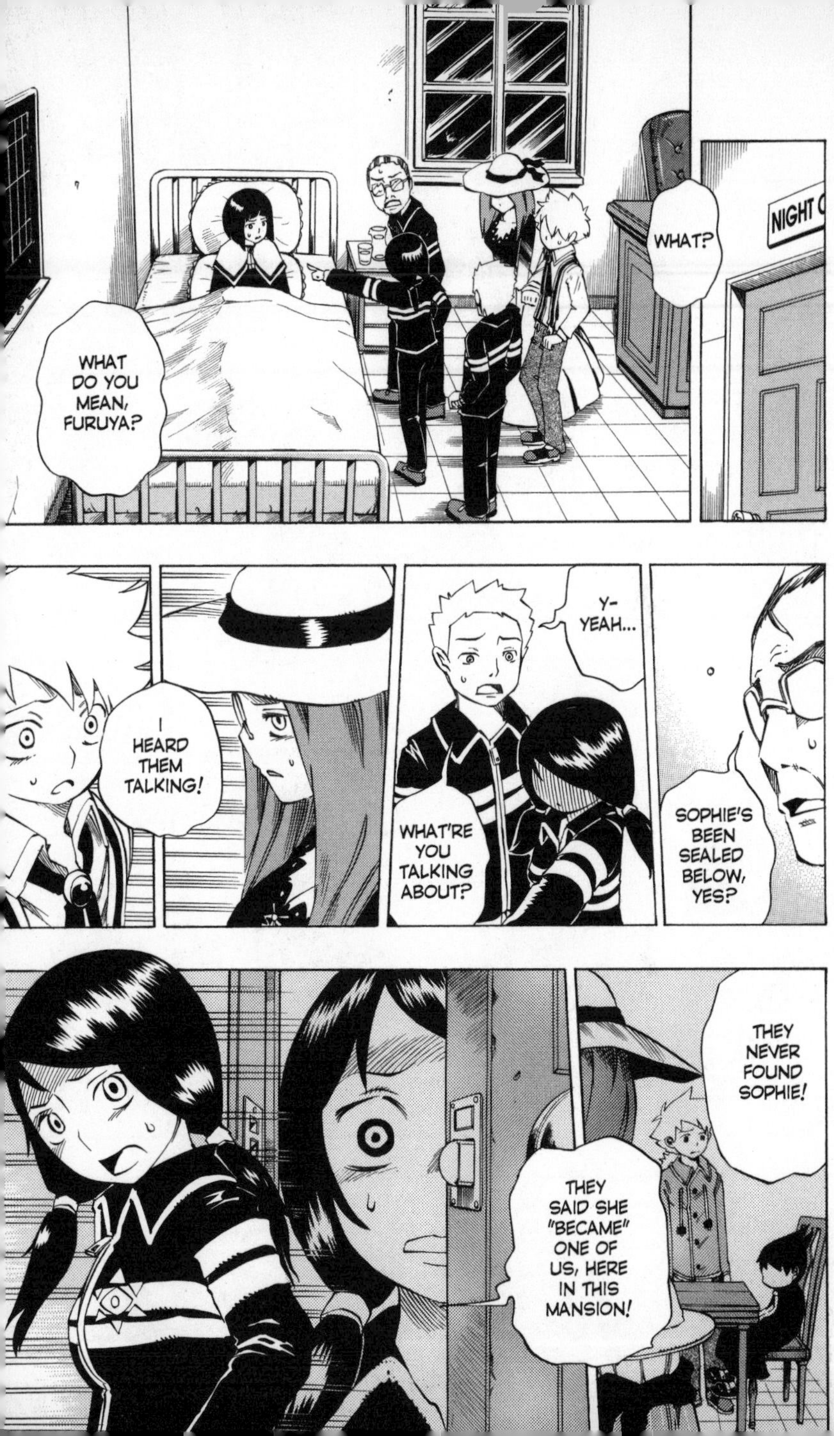
WHAT?
WHAT DO YOU MEAN, FURUYA?
SOPHIE'S BEEN SEALED BELOW, YES?
Y-YEAH...
WHAT'RE YOU TALKING ABOUT?
I HEARD THEM TALKING!
THEY NEVER FOUND SOPHIE!
THEY SAID SHE "BECAME" ONE OF US, HERE IN THIS MANSION!

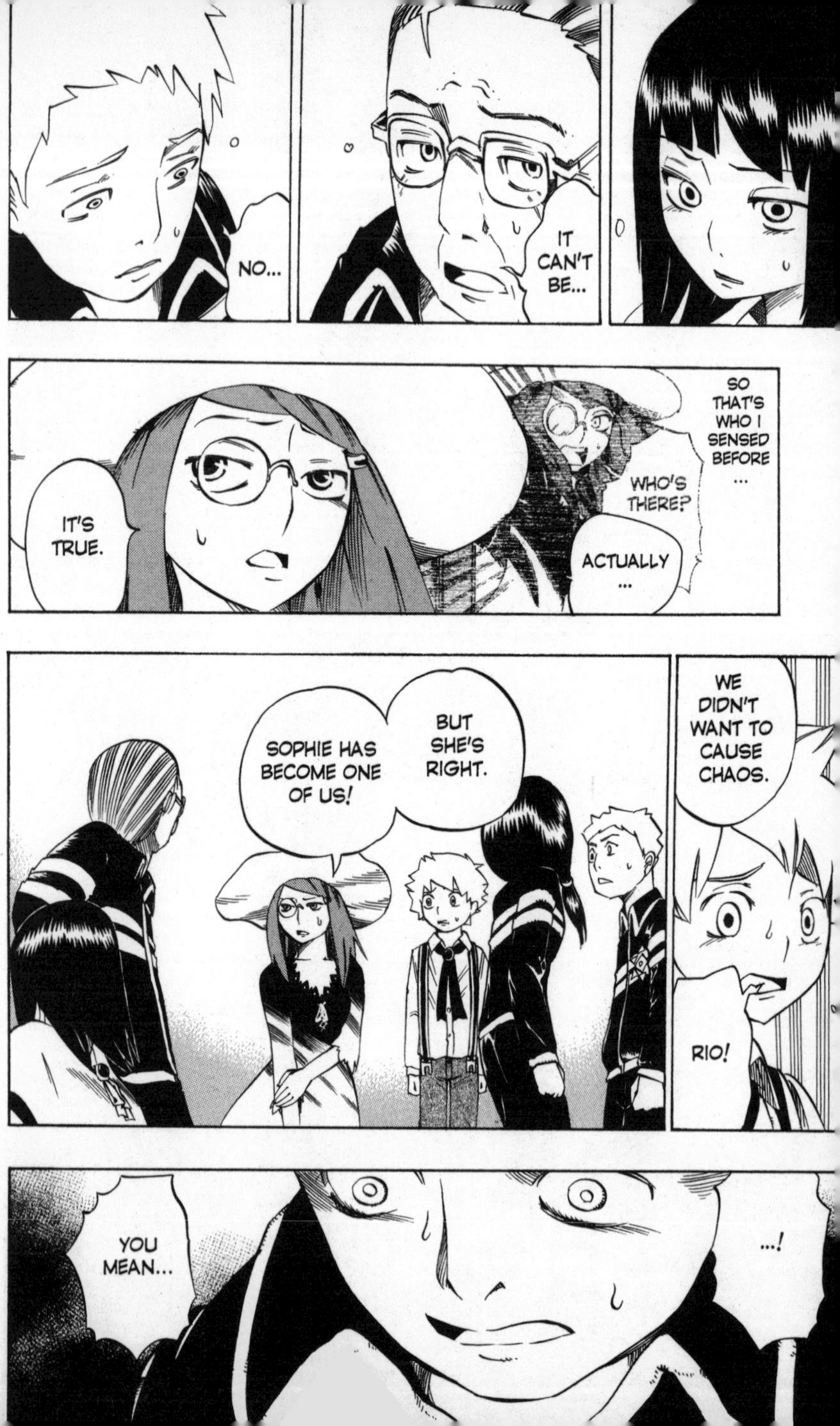
IT CAN'T BE...
NO...
SO THAT'S WHO I SENSED BEFORE ...
WHO'S THERE?
ACTUALLY ...
IT'S TRUE.
WE DIDN'T WANT TO CAUSE CHAOS.
RIO!
BUT SHE'S RIGHT.
SOPHIE HAS BECOME ONE OF US!
...!
YOU MEAN...

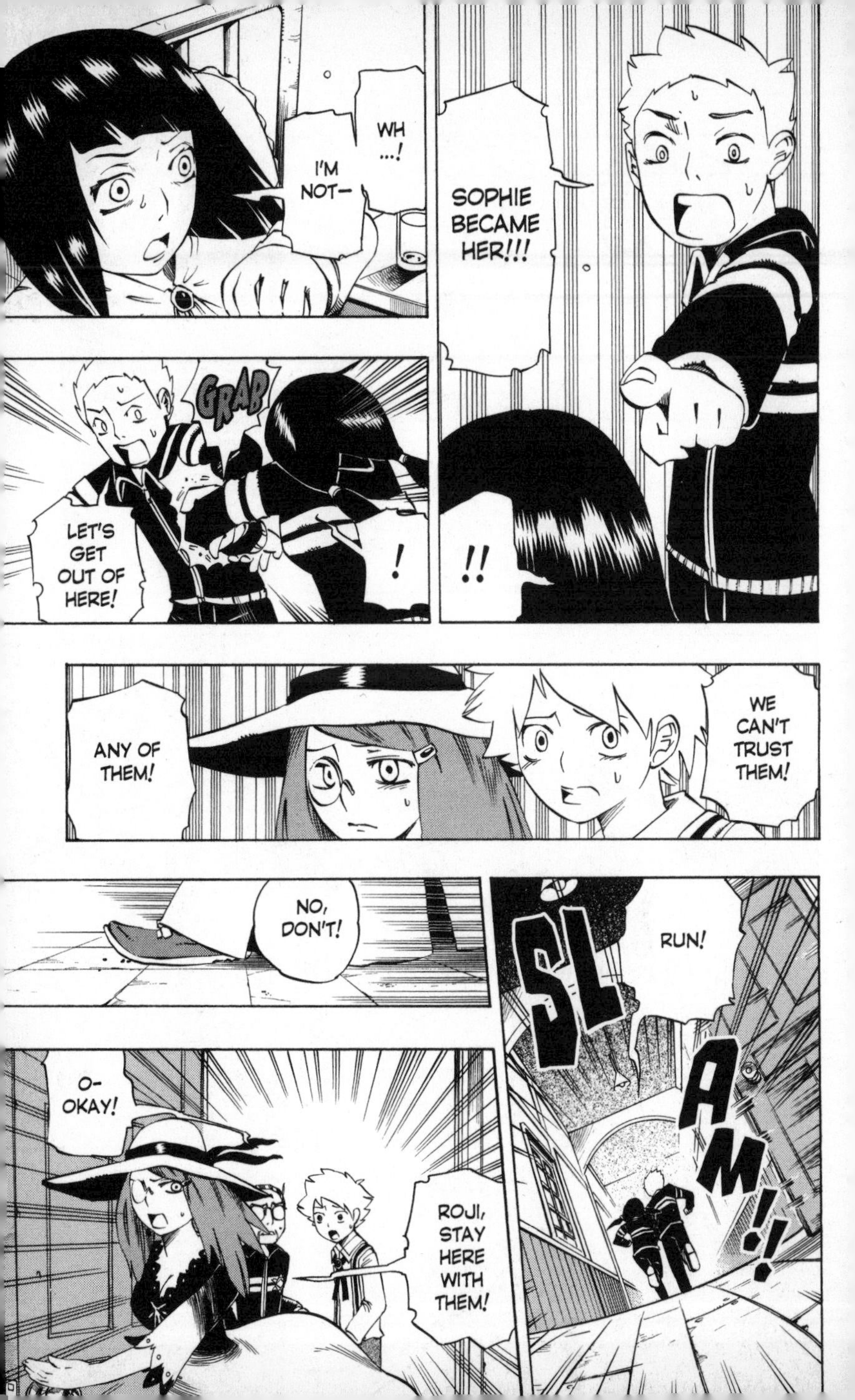
SOPHIE BECAME HER!!!
!!
WH ...!
I'M NOT—
GRAB
!
LET'S GET OUT OF HERE!
WE CAN'T TRUST THEM!
ANY OF THEM!
RUN!
SLAM!!
NO, DON'T!
ROJI, STAY HERE WITH THEM!
O-OKAY!

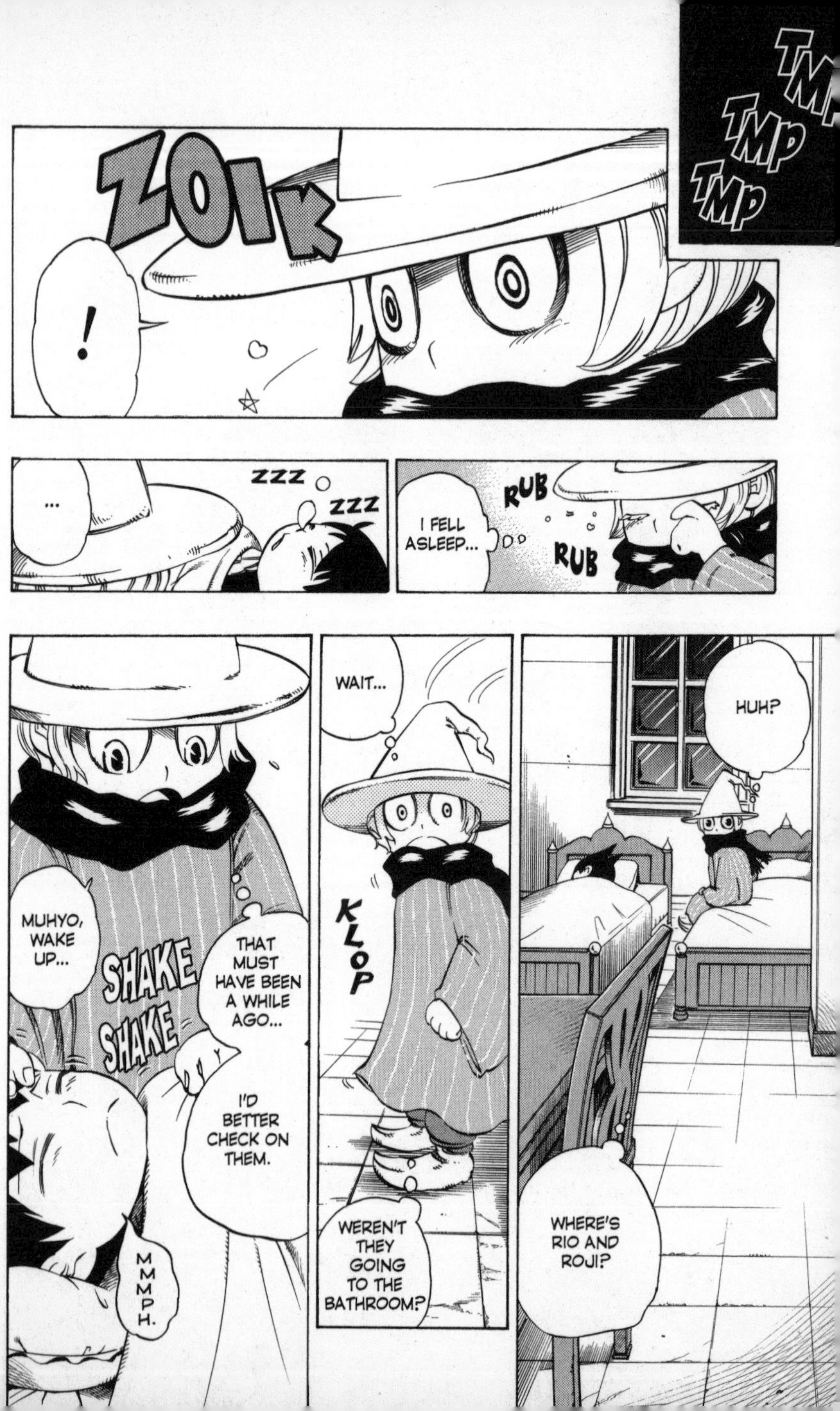
TMP
TMP
TMP
ZOIK
!
I FELL ASLEEP...
RUB
RUB
ZZZ
ZZZ
...
HUH?
WHERE'S RIO AND ROJI?
WAIT...
KLOP
WEREN'T THEY GOING TO THE BATHROOM?
THAT MUST HAVE BEEN A WHILE AGO...
I'D BETTER CHECK ON THEM.
MUHYO, WAKE UP...
SHAKE
SHAKE
MMMPH.

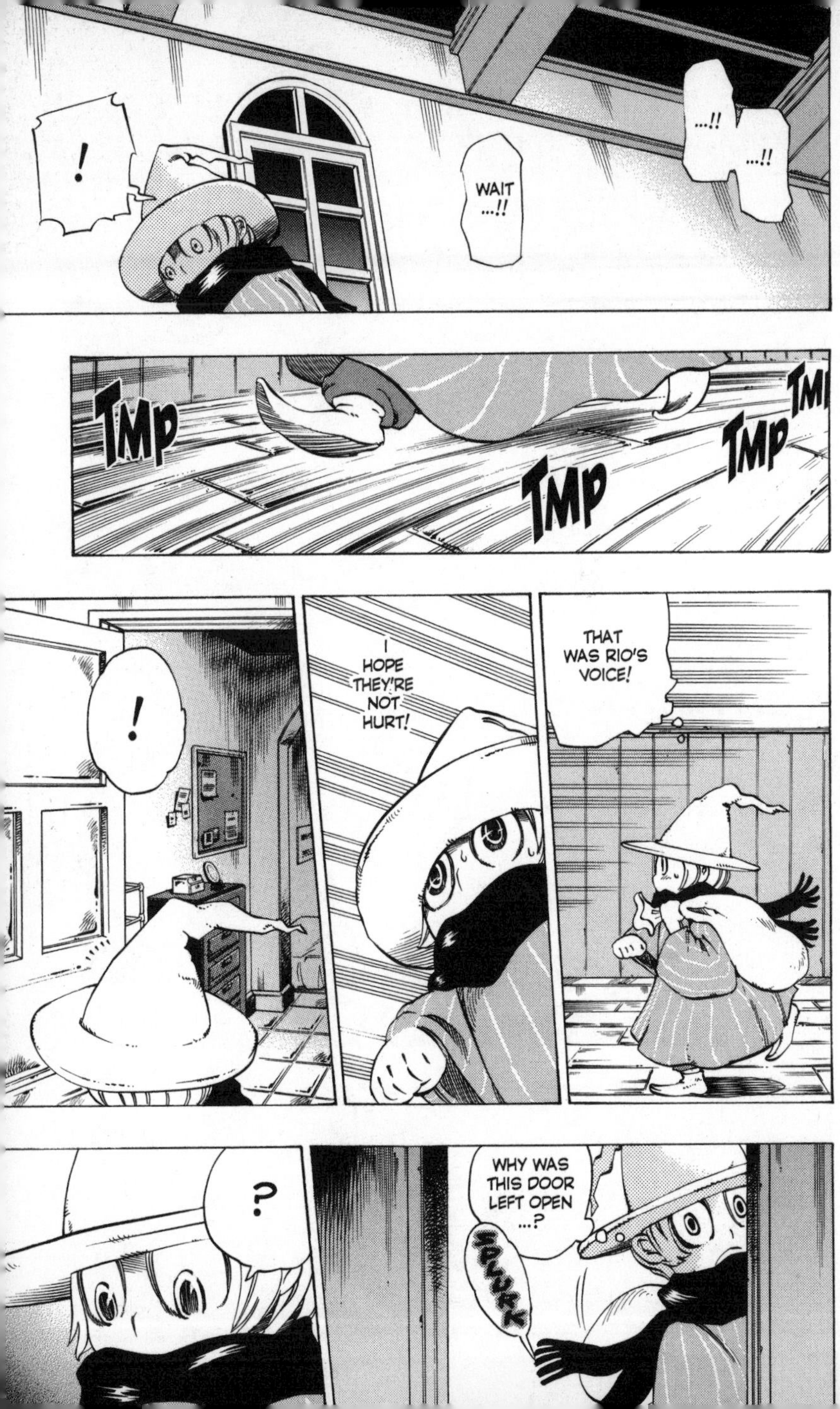
...!!
...!!
WAIT ...!!
!
TMP
TMP
TMP
THAT WAS RIO'S VOICE!
I HOPE THEY'RE NOT HURT!
!
WHY WAS THIS DOOR LEFT OPEN ...?
SPLURK
?

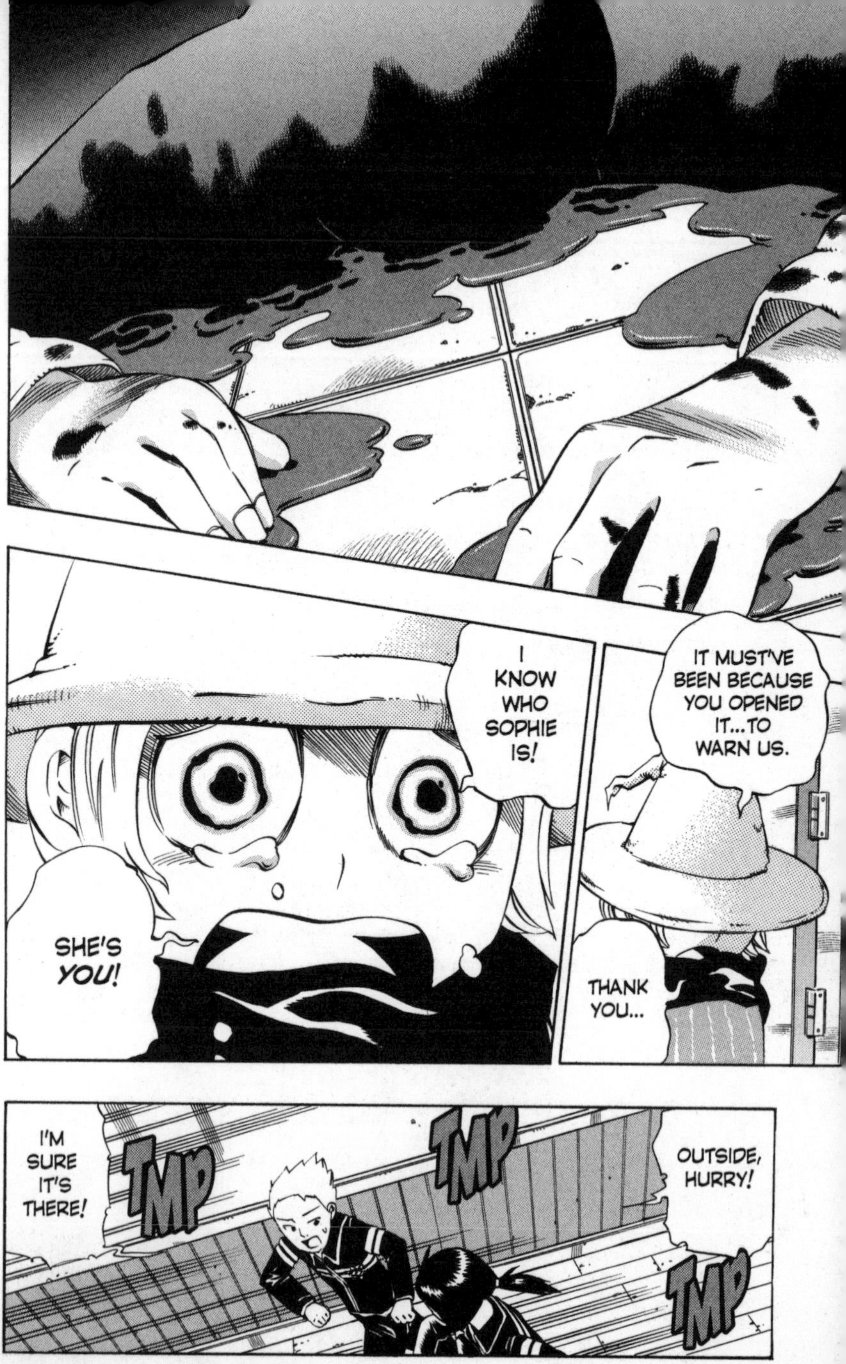
IT MUST'VE BEEN BECAUSE YOU OPENED IT...TO WARN US.
THANK YOU...
I KNOW WHO SOPHIE IS!
SHE'S *YOU!*
OUTSIDE, HURRY!
TMP
I'M SURE IT'S THERE!
TMP
TMP

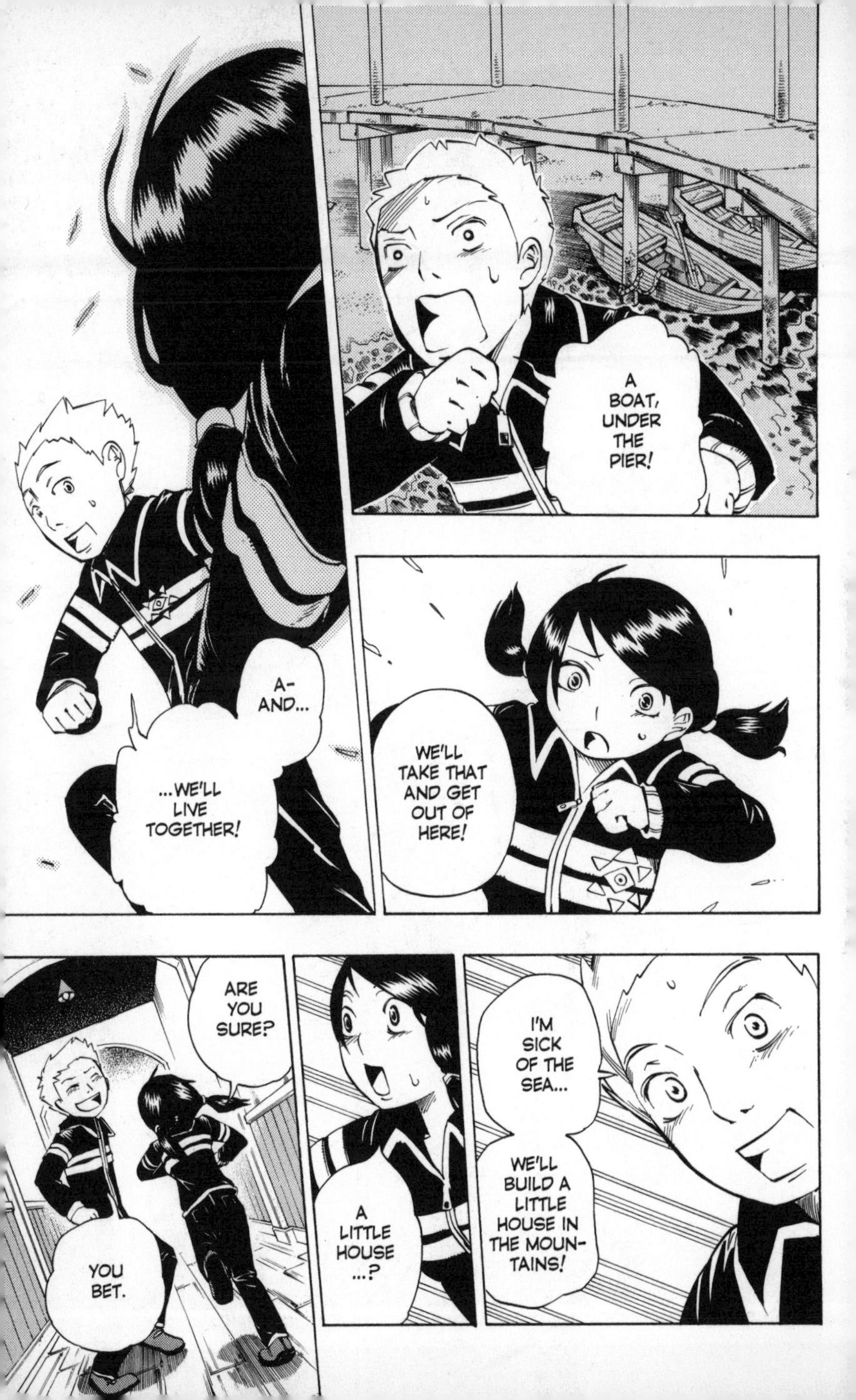
A BOAT, UNDER THE PIER!
WE'LL TAKE THAT AND GET OUT OF HERE!
A- AND...
...WE'LL LIVE TOGETHER!
I'M SICK OF THE SEA...
WE'LL BUILD A LITTLE HOUSE IN THE MOUN-TAINS!
A LITTLE HOUSE ...?
ARE YOU SURE?
YOU BET.

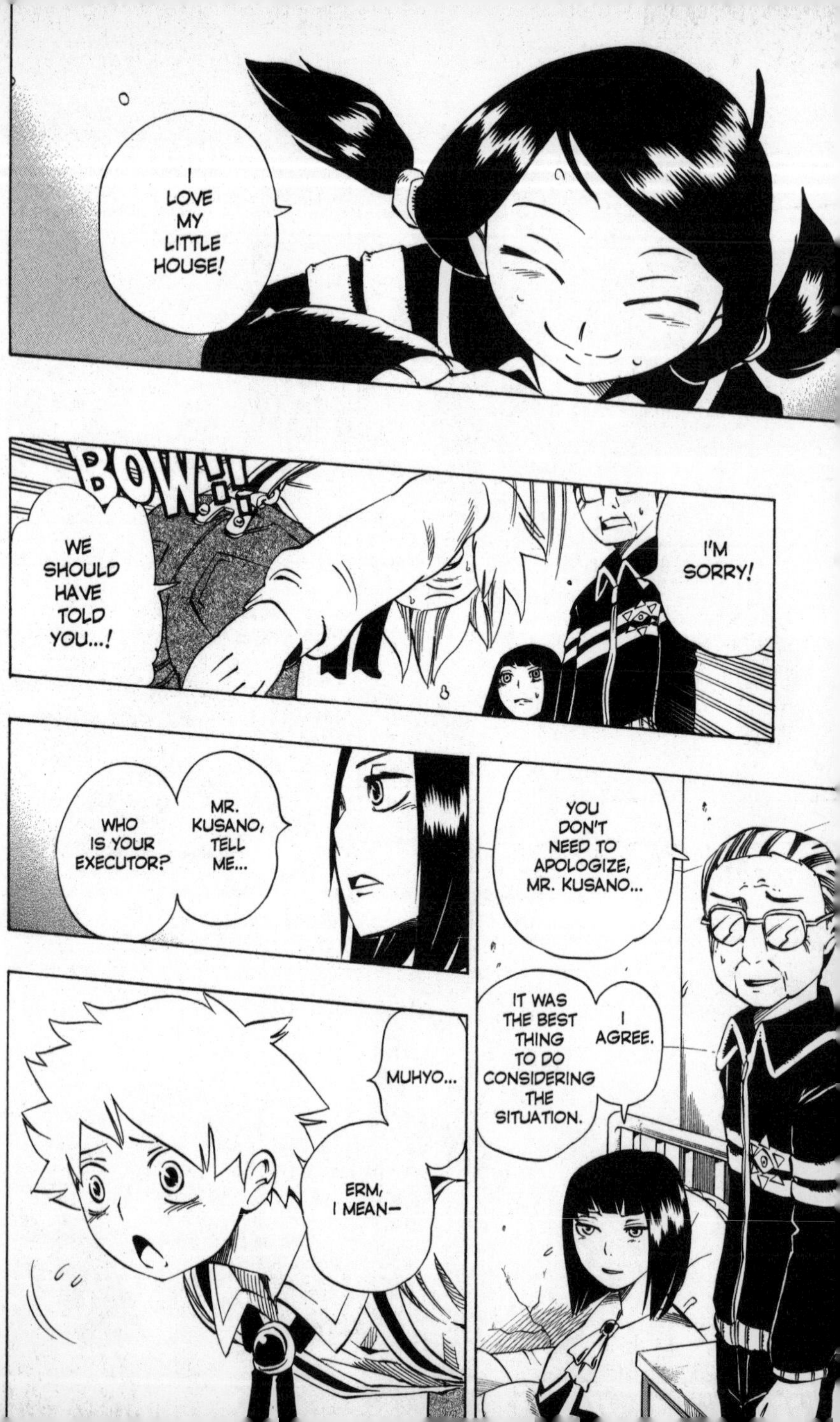
I LOVE MY LITTLE HOUSE!
BOW!!
I'M SORRY!
WE SHOULD HAVE TOLD YOU...!
YOU DON'T NEED TO APOLOGIZE, MR. KUSANO...
I AGREE.
IT WAS THE BEST THING TO DO CONSIDERING THE SITUATION.
MR. KUSANO, TELL ME...
WHO IS YOUR EXECUTOR?
MUHYO...
ERM, I MEAN—

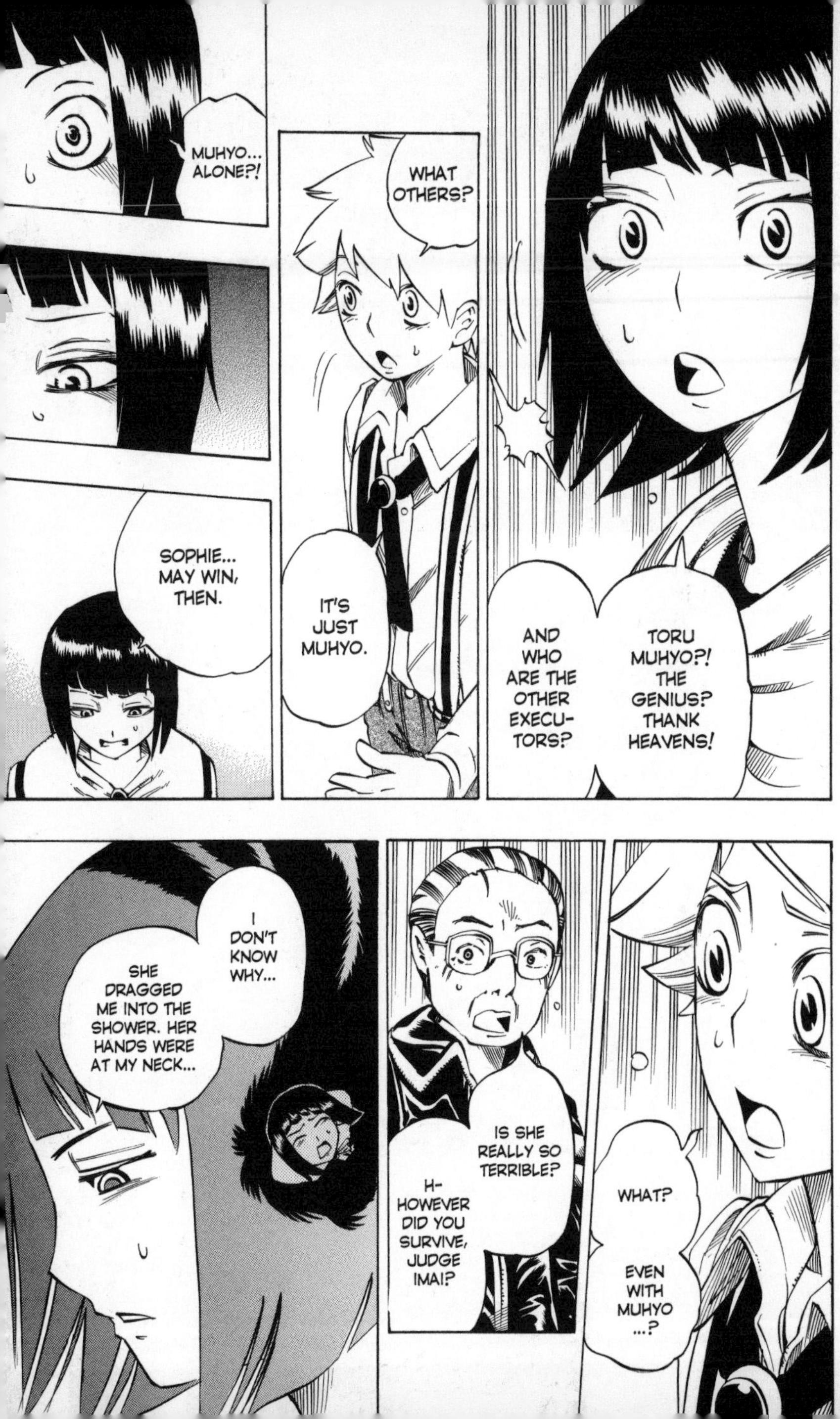
TORU MUHYO?! THE GENIUS? THANK HEAVENS!
AND WHO ARE THE OTHER EXECUTORS?
WHAT OTHERS?
IT'S JUST MUHYO.
MUHYO... ALONE?!
SOPHIE... MAY WIN, THEN.
WHAT?
EVEN WITH MUHYO...?
IS SHE REALLY SO TERRIBLE?
H-HOWEVER DID YOU SURVIVE, JUDGE IMAI?
I DON'T KNOW WHY...
SHE DRAGGED ME INTO THE SHOWER. HER HANDS WERE AT MY NECK...

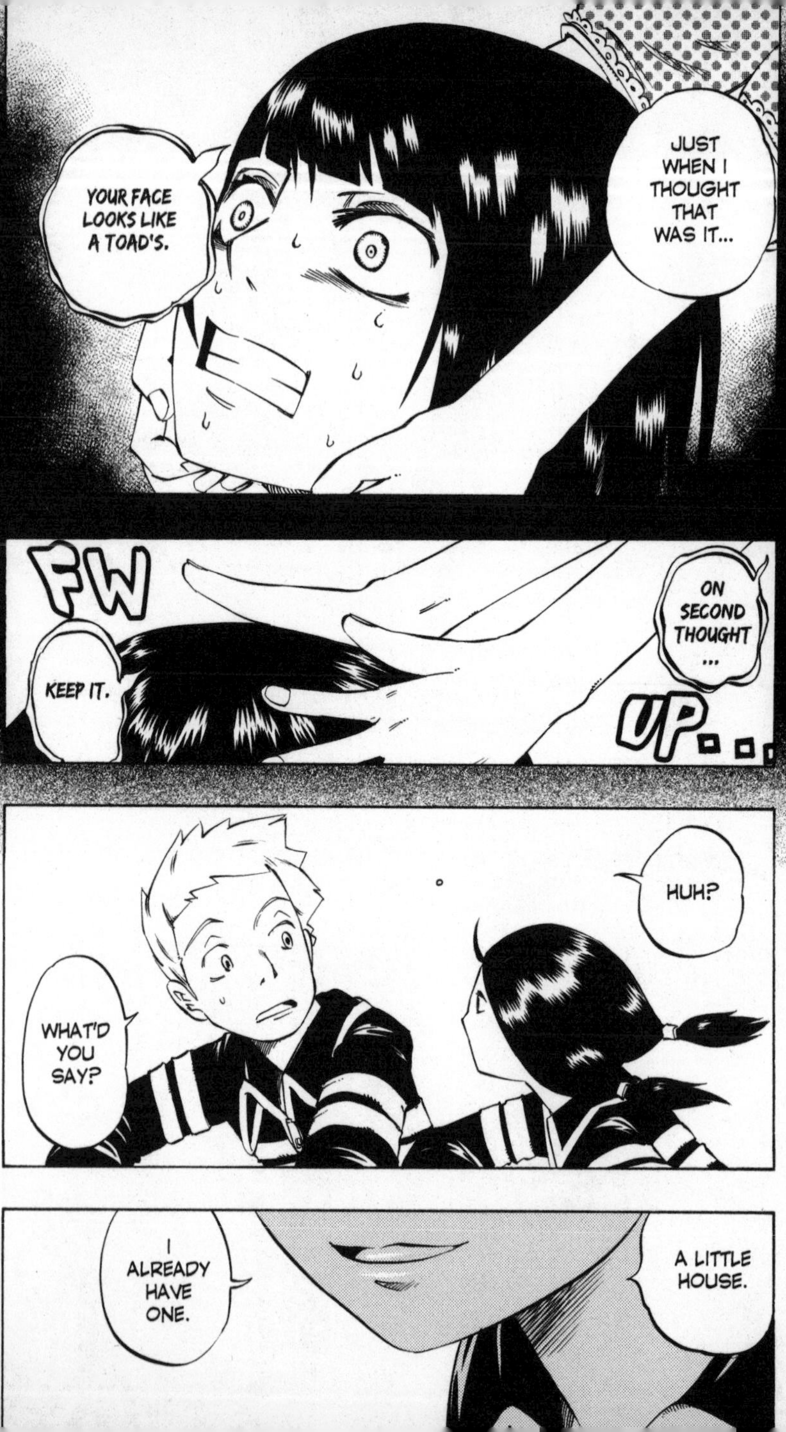
JUST WHEN I THOUGHT THAT WAS IT...
YOUR FACE LOOKS LIKE A TOAD'S.
ON SECOND THOUGHT ...
UP...
FW
KEEP IT.
HUH?
WHAT'D YOU SAY?
A LITTLE HOUSE.
I ALREADY HAVE ONE.

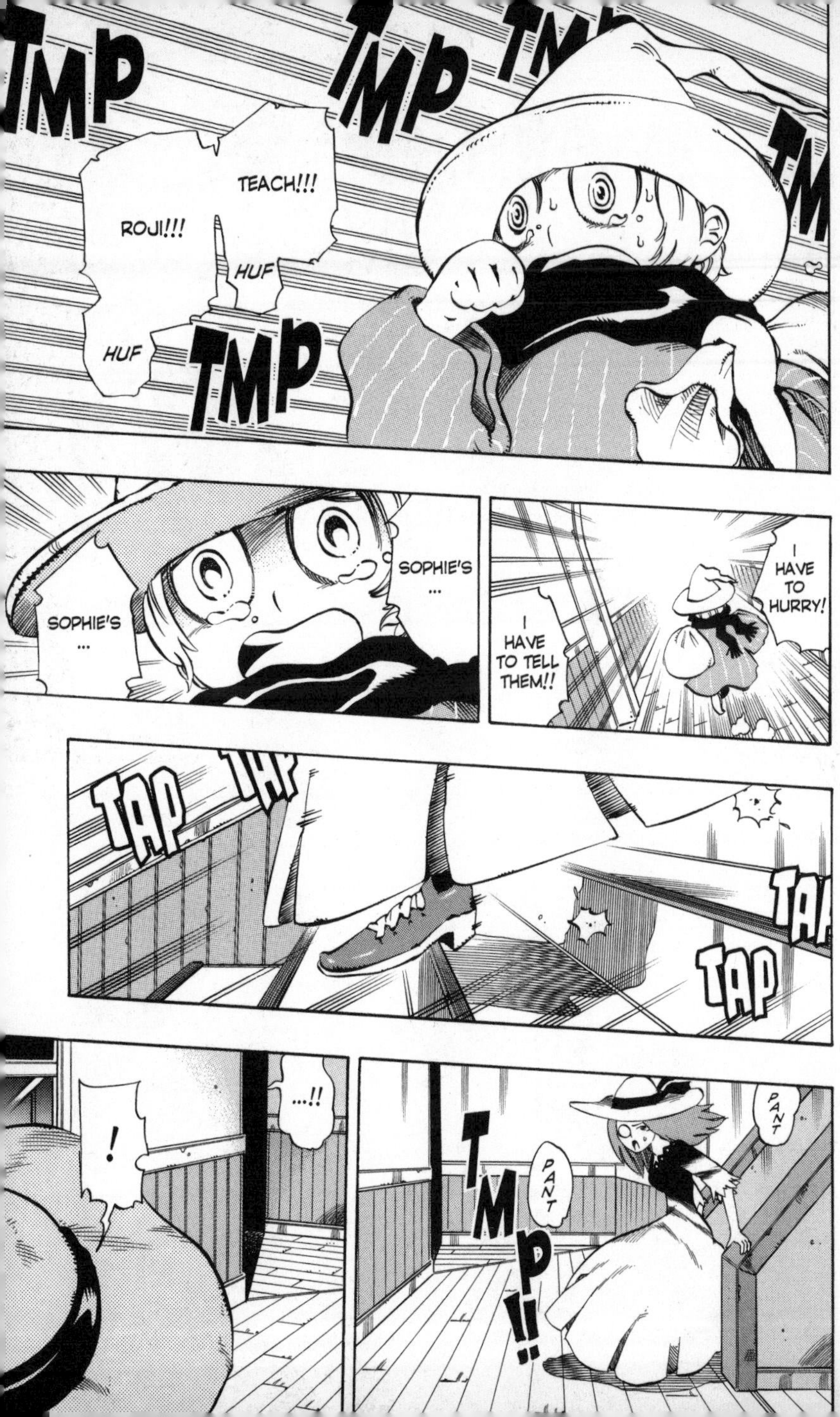
TMP
TMP
TMP
TMP
TEACH!!!
ROJI!!!
HUF
HUF
TMP
I HAVE TO HURRY!
I HAVE TO TELL THEM!!
SOPHIE'S ...
SOPHIE'S ...
TAP
TAP
TAP
TAP
PANT
PANT
TMP!!
...!!
!

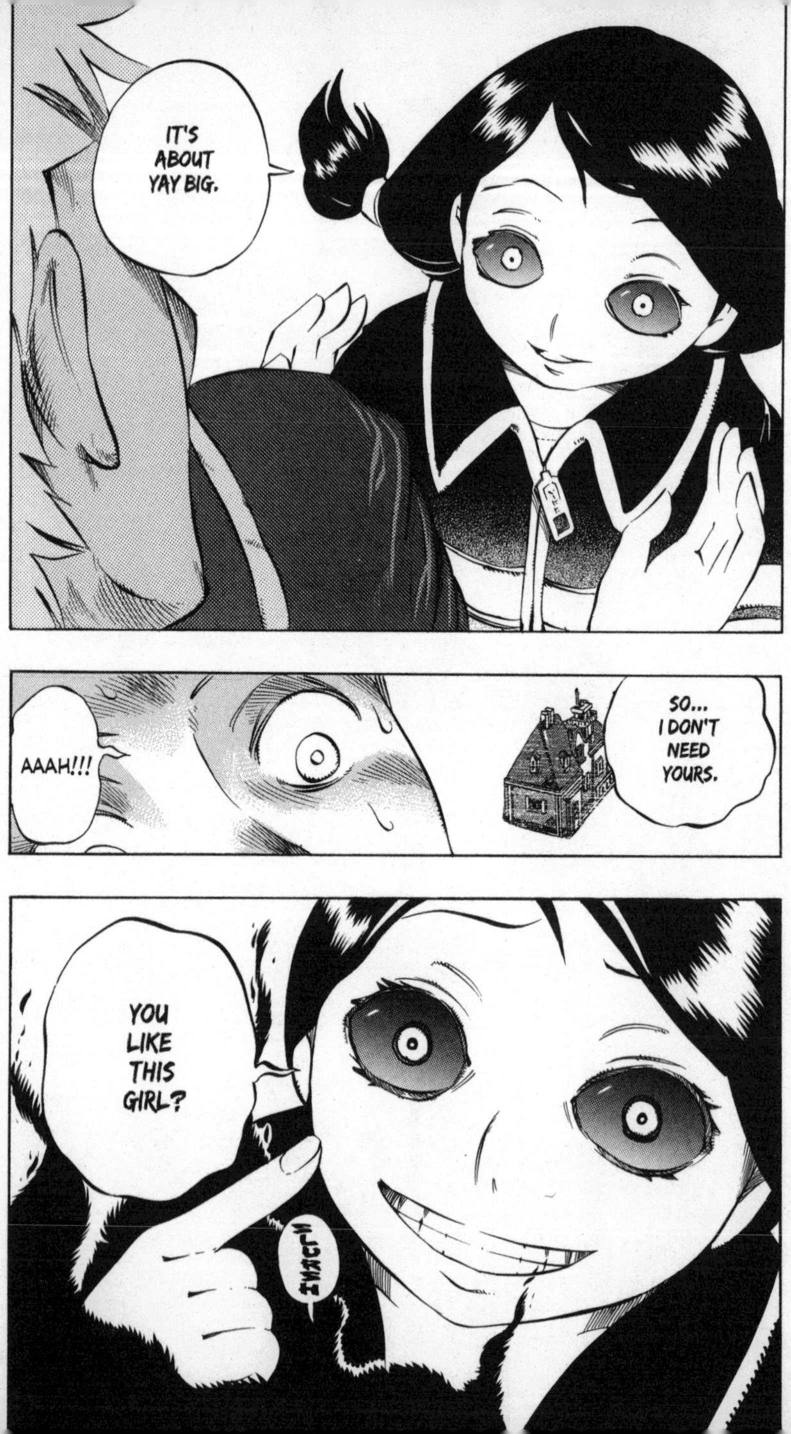
IT'S ABOUT YAY BIG.
SO... I DON'T NEED YOURS.
AAAH!!!
YOU LIKE THIS GIRL?

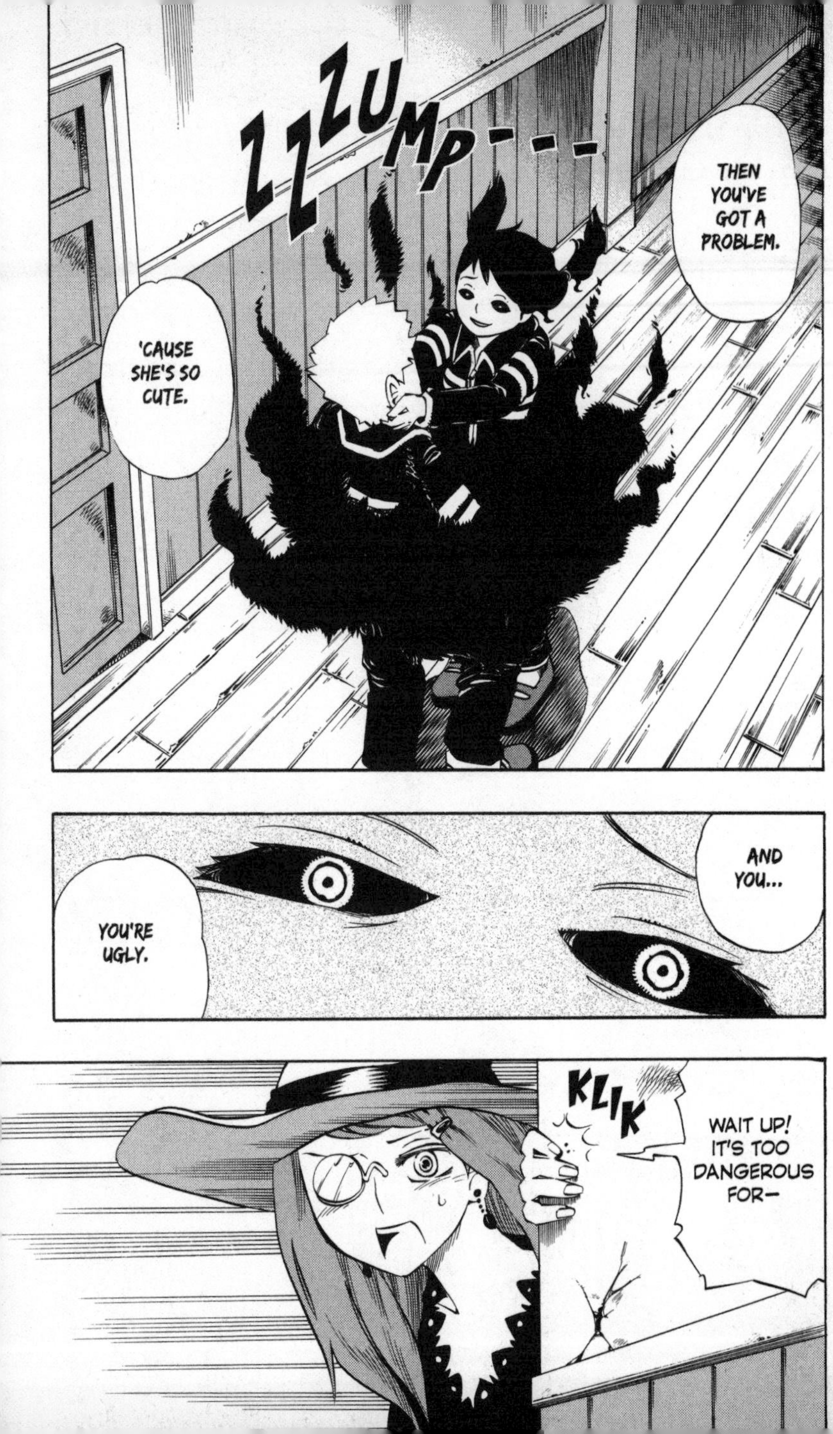
THEN YOU'VE GOT A PROBLEM.
ZZZUMP---
'CAUSE SHE'S SO CUTE.
AND YOU...
YOU'RE UGLY.
WAIT UP! IT'S TOO DANGEROUS FOR—
KLIK

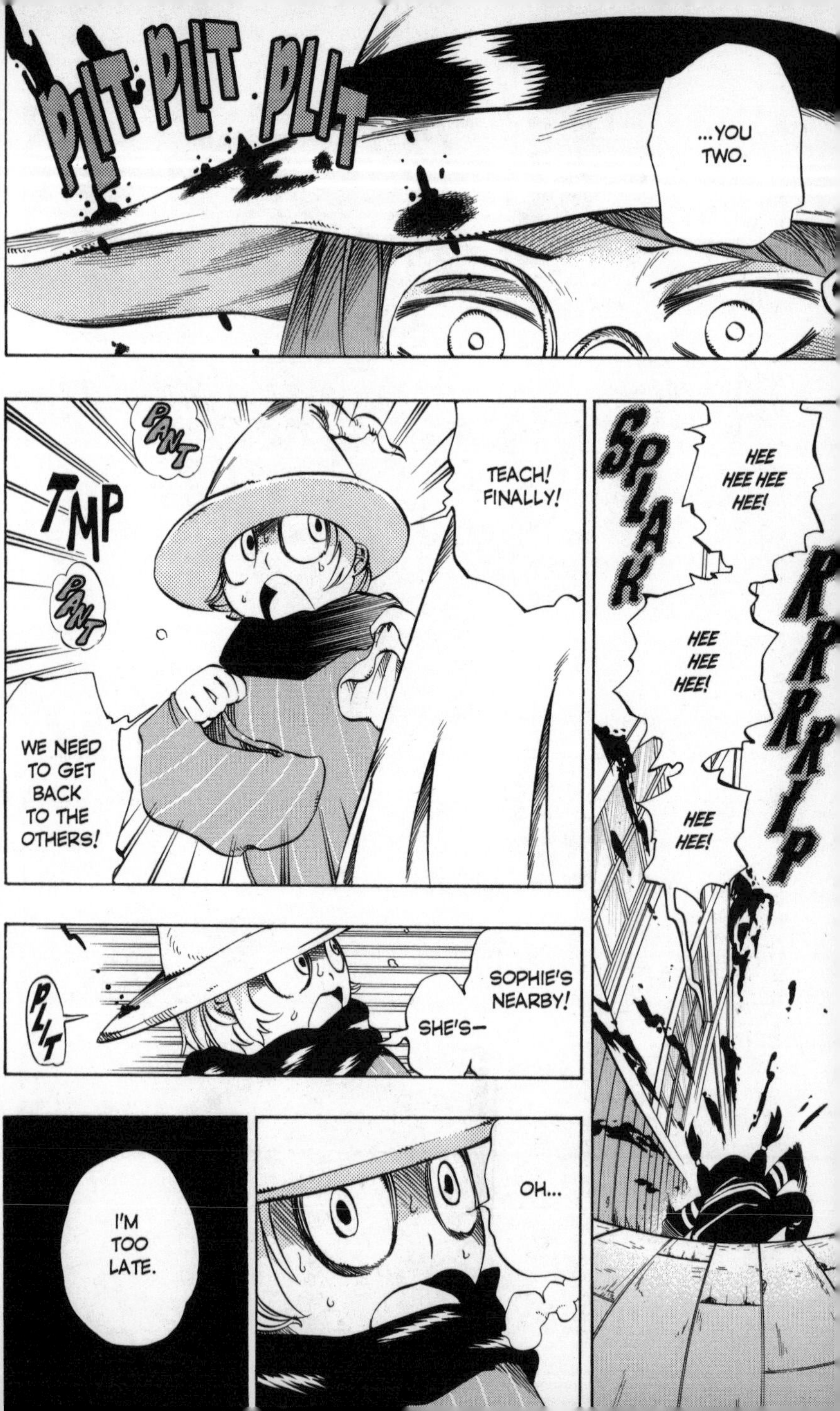
PLIT PLIT PLIT
...YOU TWO.
HEE HEE HEE HEE!
RRRRIP
SPLAK
HEE HEE HEE!
HEE HEE!
TEACH! FINALLY!
PANT
TMP
PANT
WE NEED TO GET BACK TO THE OTHERS!
SOPHIE'S NEARBY!
SHE'S—
PLIT
OH...
I'M TOO LATE.

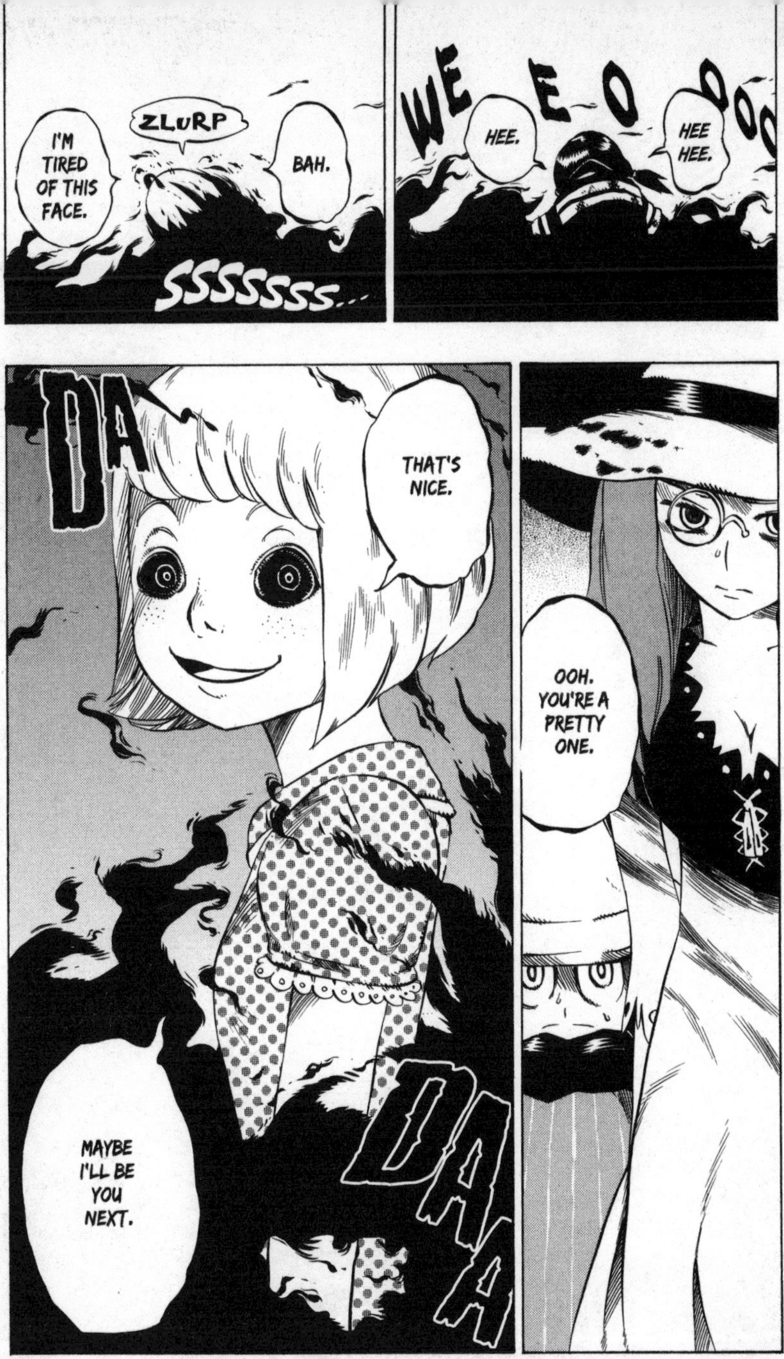
HEE HEE.
HEE.
WE E O OO
BAH.
ZLURP
I'M TIRED OF THIS FACE.
SSSSSSS...
OOH. YOU'RE A PRETTY ONE.
THAT'S NICE.
DA
MAYBE I'LL BE YOU NEXT.
DAA

THANKS FOR BUYING
FOUR WHOLE VOLUMES OF
MUHYO & ROJI! BRING
ON THE QUESTIONS!

Q: WHO DO YOU FIND THE
EASIEST TO DRAW?
—H.M., TOKYO

A: OH, OF COURSE, IT'S BIKO...
EXCEPT HER HAT IS
SURPRISINGLY... WELL,
MAYBE IT'S MUHYO! JUST,
THOSE EYES...IT'S TOUGH
GETTING THE RIGHT SHAPE...
I KNOW! ROJI!! BUT HIS
HAIR IS IMPOSSIBLE!!

AH HA HA HA. THEY'RE
ALL TOUGH...

ARTICLE 27
A RAY OF LIGHT

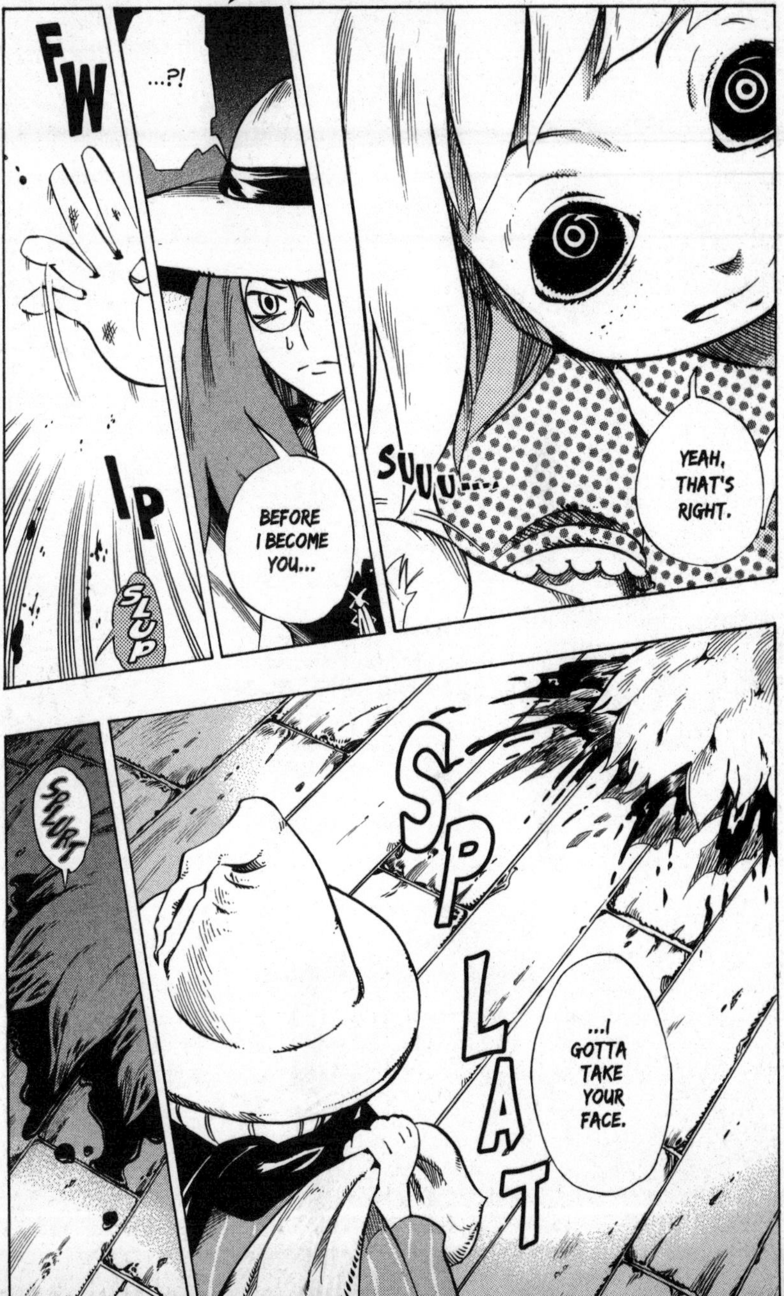
YEAH, THAT'S RIGHT.
SUUU...
...?!
BEFORE I BECOME YOU...
FWIP
SLUP
SPLAT
...I GOTTA TAKE YOUR FACE.
SPLURT

I-
IWAMOTO! !!

WH-
WHY?

BECAUSE.
JUST BECAUSE.

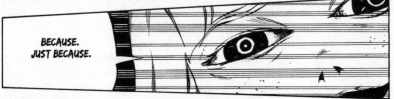

ARTICLE 27
A RAY OF LIGHT

CAN'T HAVE
TWO OF THE
SAME FACE
AROUND.

WE

EO OO...

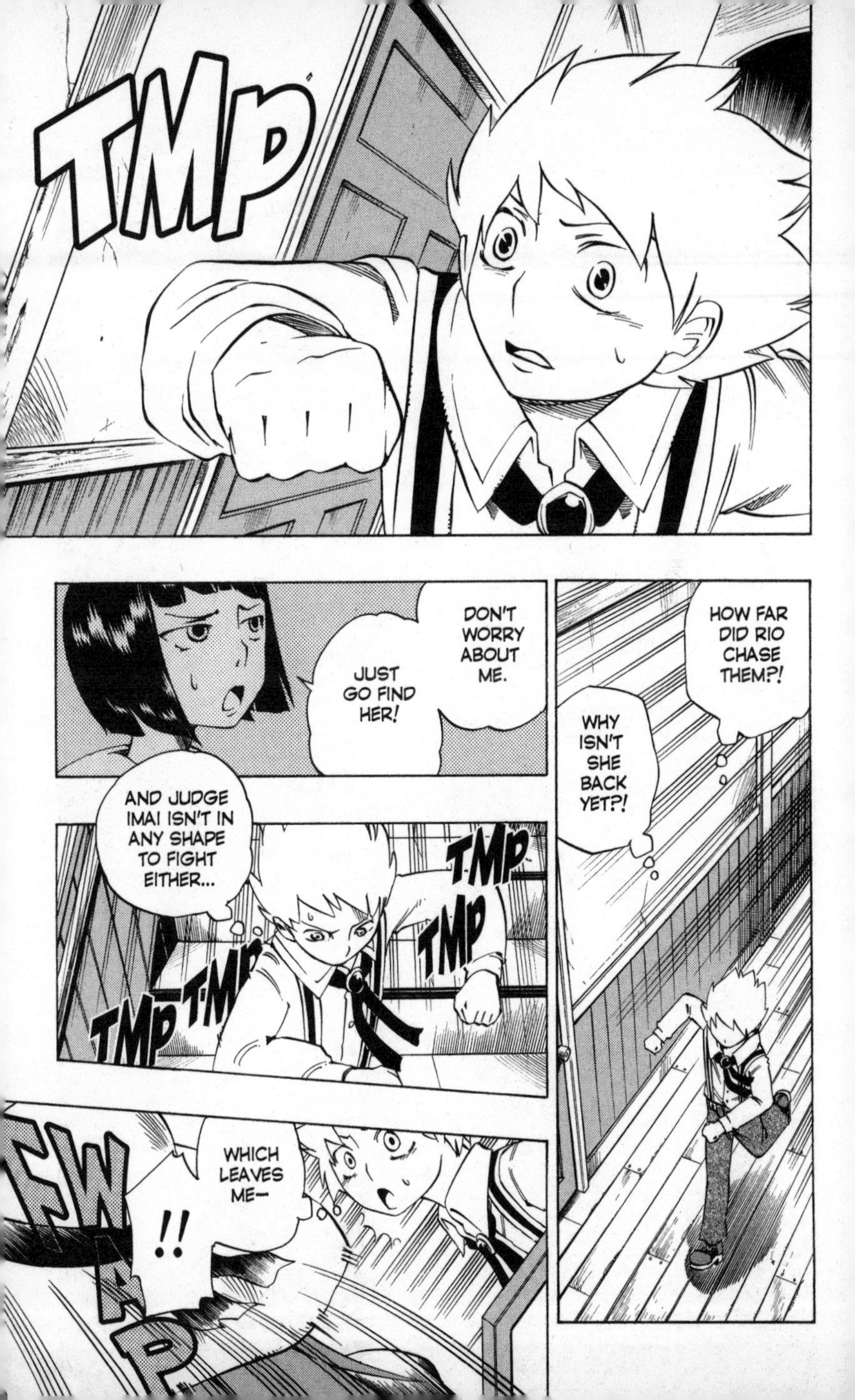
TMP
HOW FAR DID RIO CHASE THEM?!
WHY ISN'T SHE BACK YET?!
DON'T WORRY ABOUT ME.
JUST GO FIND HER!
AND JUDGE IMAI ISN'T IN ANY SHAPE TO FIGHT EITHER...
TMP
TMP
TMP
TMP
WHICH LEAVES ME—
!!
FWAP

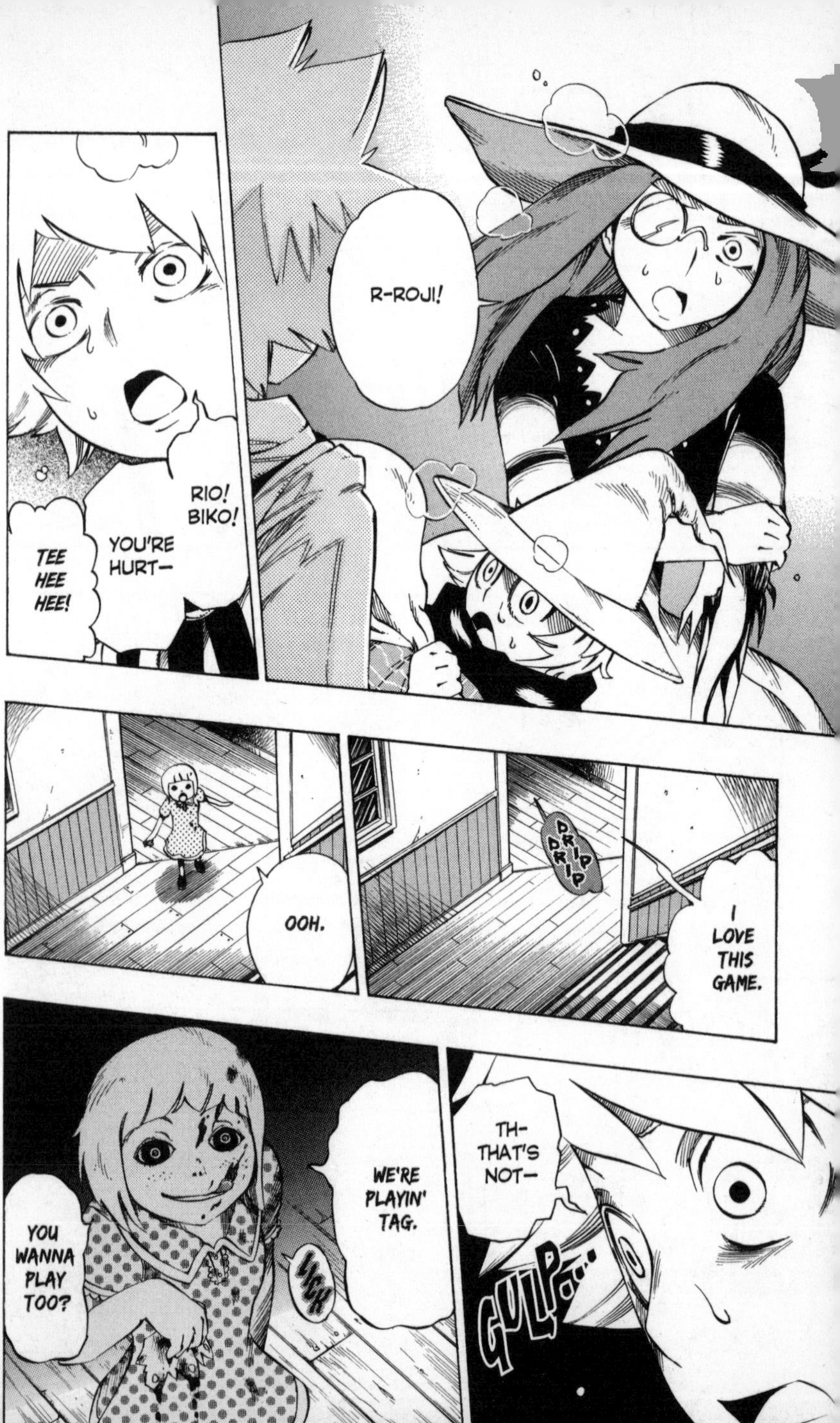
R-ROJI!
RIO! BIKO!
YOU'RE HURT—
TEE HEE HEE!
DRIP DRIP
I LOVE THIS GAME.
OOH.
TH- THAT'S NOT—
GULP...
WE'RE PLAYIN' TAG.
LICK
YOU WANNA PLAY TOO?

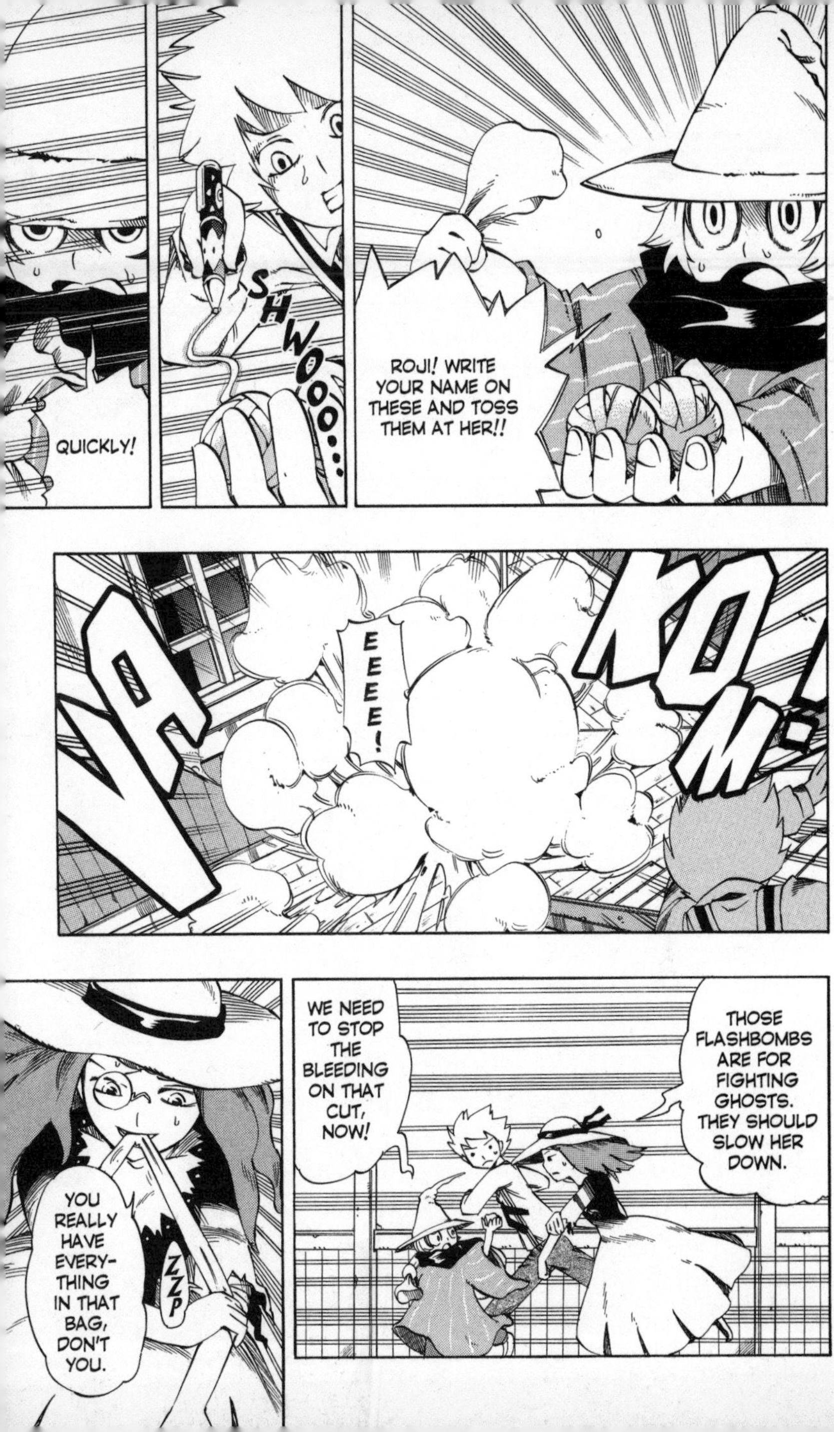
ROJI! WRITE YOUR NAME ON THESE AND TOSS THEM AT HER!!
SHWOOO...
QUICKLY!
EEEE!
THOSE FLASHBOMBS ARE FOR FIGHTING GHOSTS. THEY SHOULD SLOW HER DOWN.
WE NEED TO STOP THE BLEEDING ON THAT CUT, NOW!
YOU REALLY HAVE EVERY-THING IN THAT BAG, DON'T YOU.
ZZP

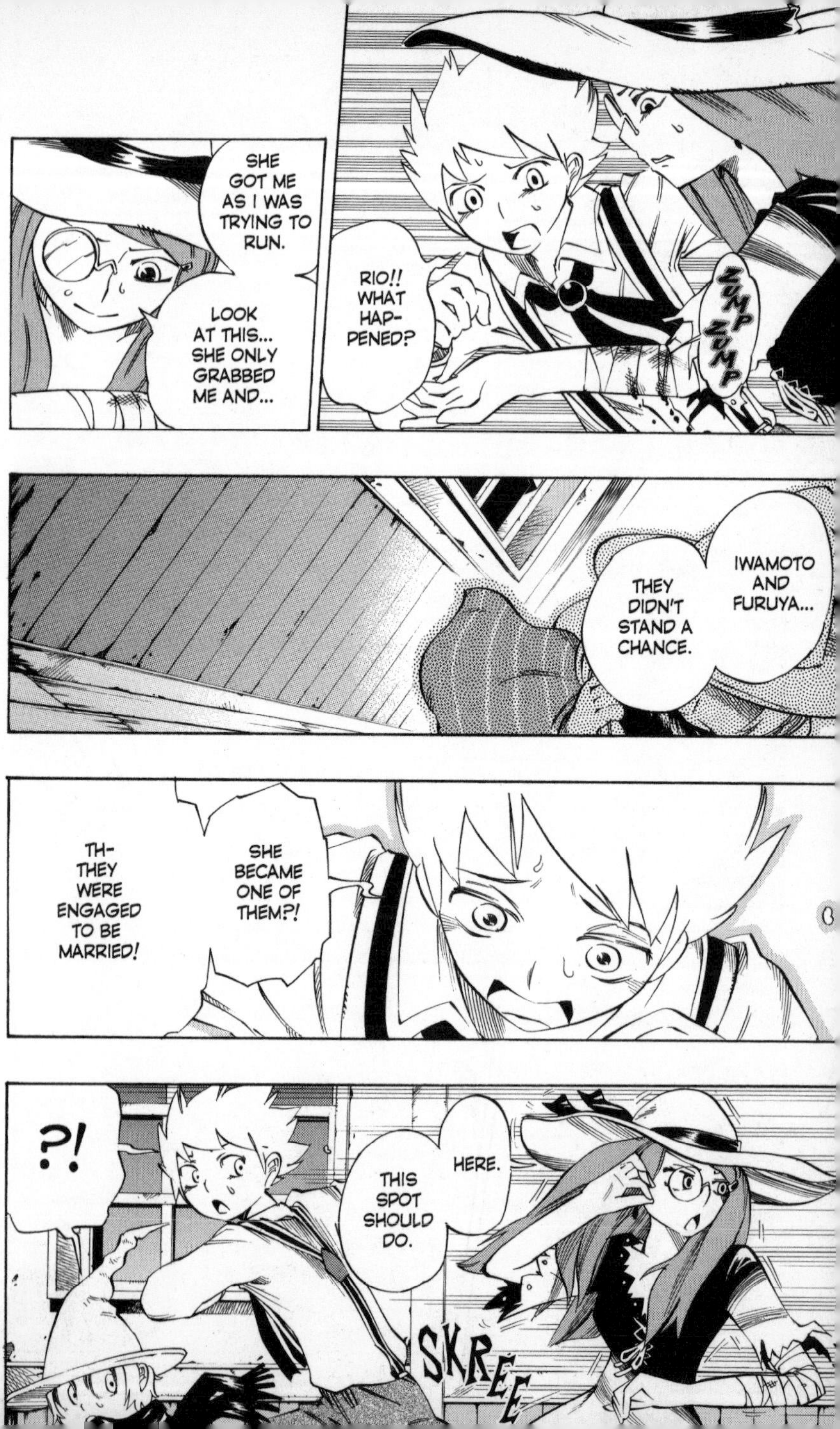
ZUMP ZUMP
RIO!! WHAT HAP-PENED?
SHE GOT ME AS I WAS TRYING TO RUN.
LOOK AT THIS... SHE ONLY GRABBED ME AND...
IWAMOTO AND FURUYA...
THEY DIDN'T STAND A CHANCE.
SHE BECAME ONE OF THEM?!
TH- THEY WERE ENGAGED TO BE MARRIED!
HERE.
THIS SPOT SHOULD DO.
?!
SKREE

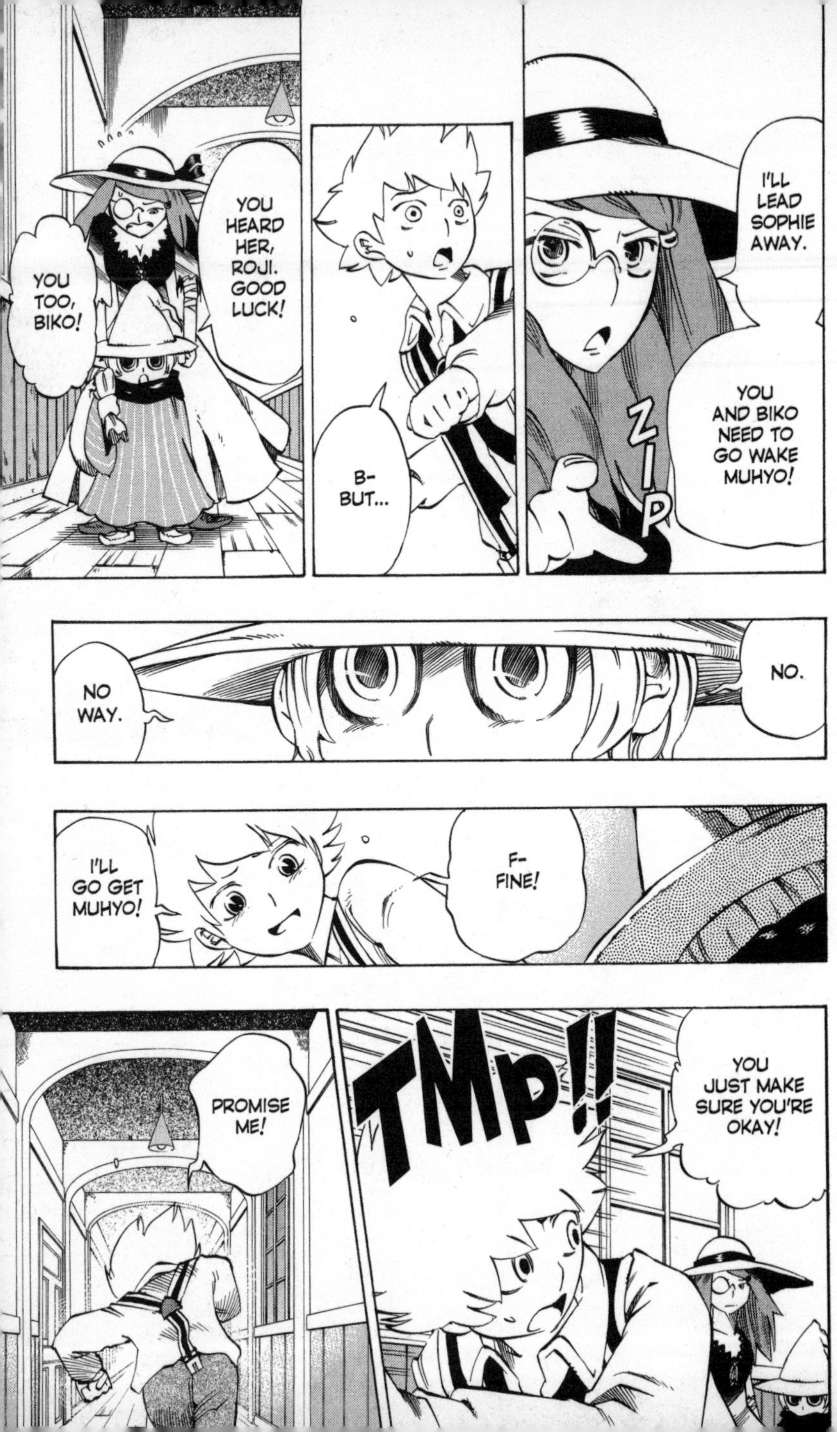
I'LL LEAD SOPHIE AWAY.
YOU AND BIKO NEED TO GO WAKE MUHYO!
ZIP
B-BUT...
YOU HEARD HER, ROJI. GOOD LUCK!
YOU TOO, BIKO!
NO.
NO WAY.
F-FINE!
I'LL GO GET MUHYO!
YOU JUST MAKE SURE YOU'RE OKAY!
TMP!!
PROMISE ME!

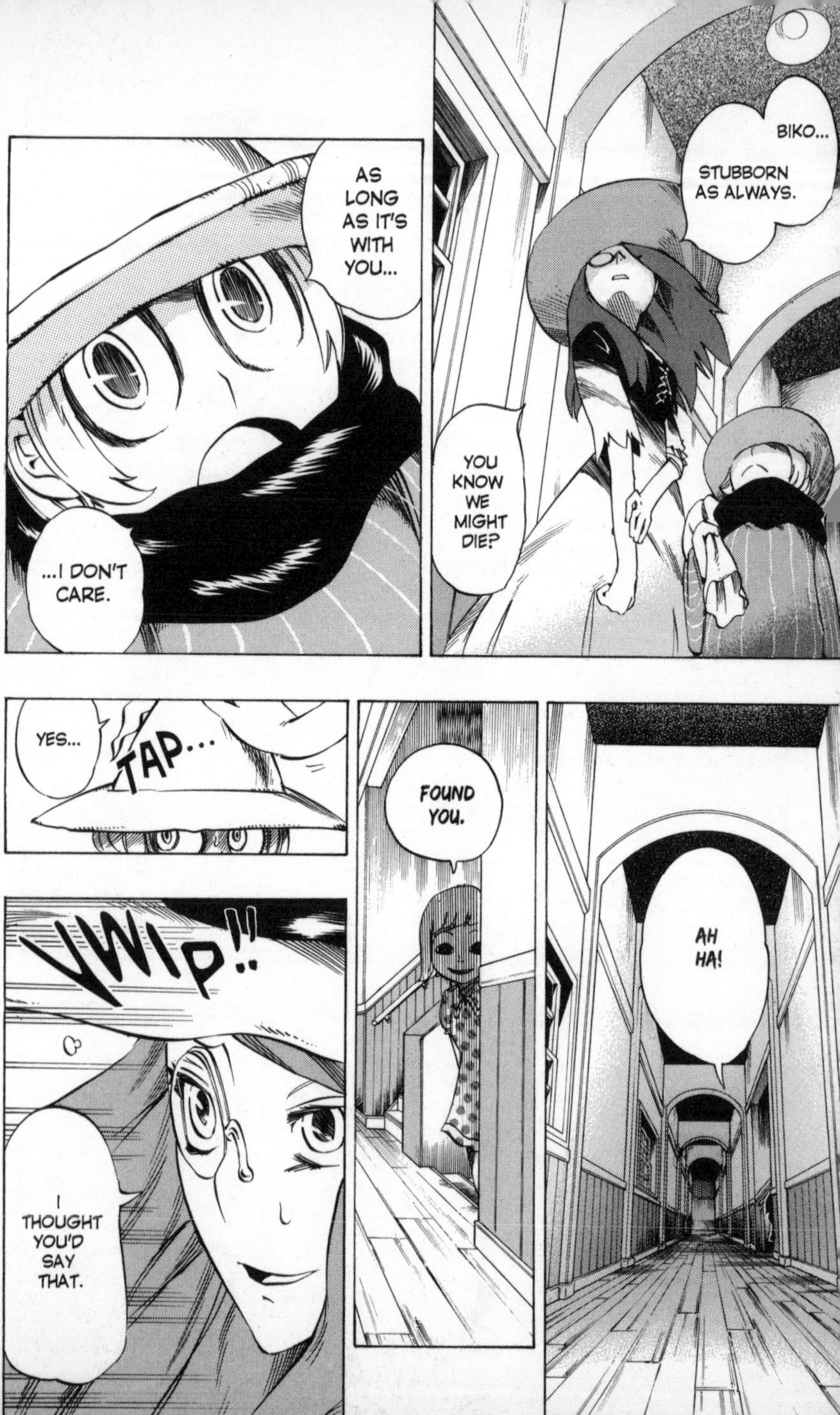
BIKO...
STUBBORN AS ALWAYS.
YOU KNOW WE MIGHT DIE?
AS LONG AS IT'S WITH YOU...
...I DON'T CARE.
AH HA!
FOUND YOU.
YES...
TAP...
VWIP!!
I THOUGHT YOU'D SAY THAT.

READ THIS WAY

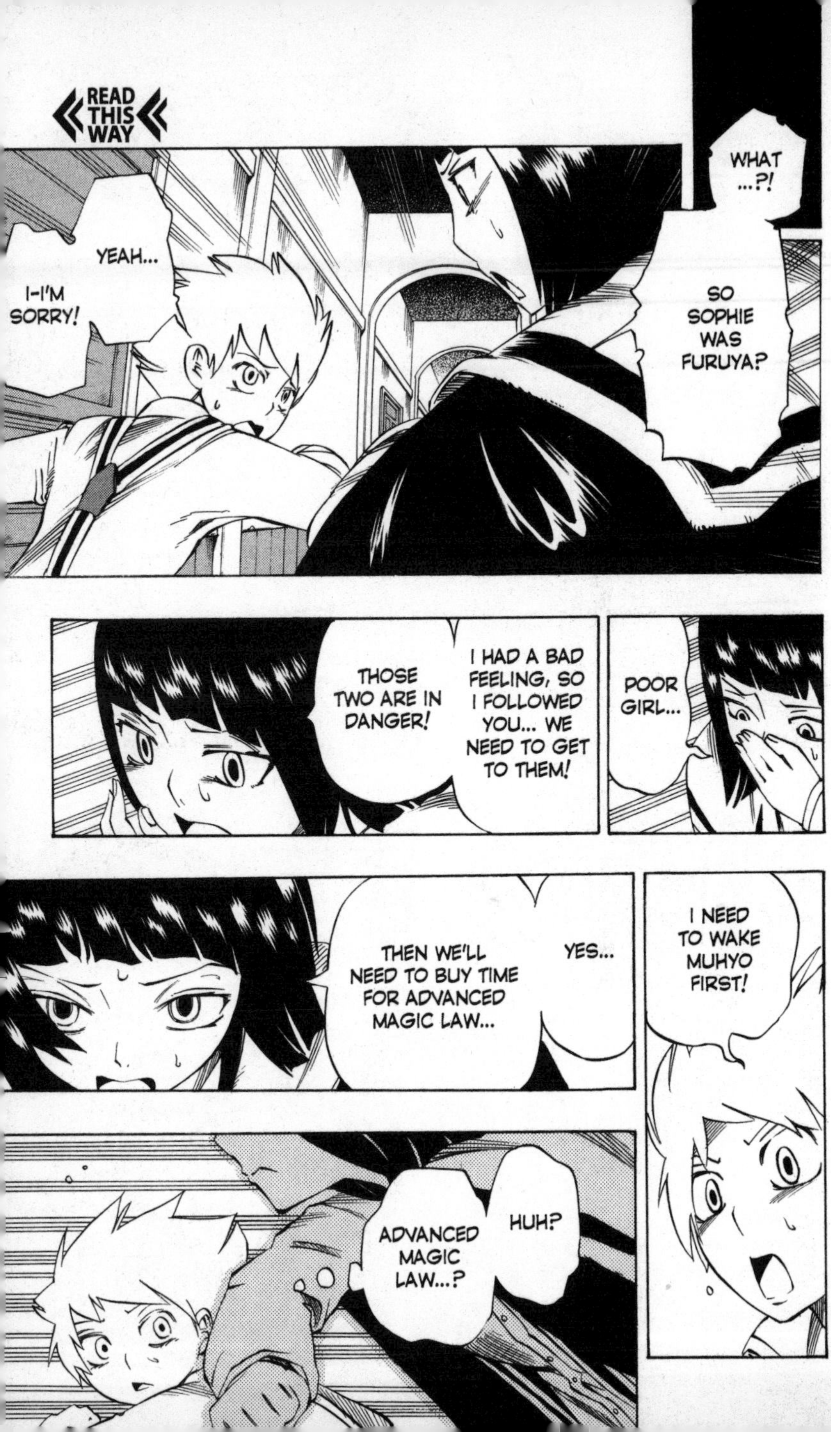
WHAT ...?!
SO SOPHIE WAS FURUYA?
YEAH...
I-I'M SORRY!
POOR GIRL...
I HAD A BAD FEELING, SO I FOLLOWED YOU... WE NEED TO GET TO THEM!
THOSE TWO ARE IN DANGER!
I NEED TO WAKE MUHYO FIRST!
YES...
THEN WE'LL NEED TO BUY TIME FOR ADVANCED MAGIC LAW...
HUH?
ADVANCED MAGIC LAW...?

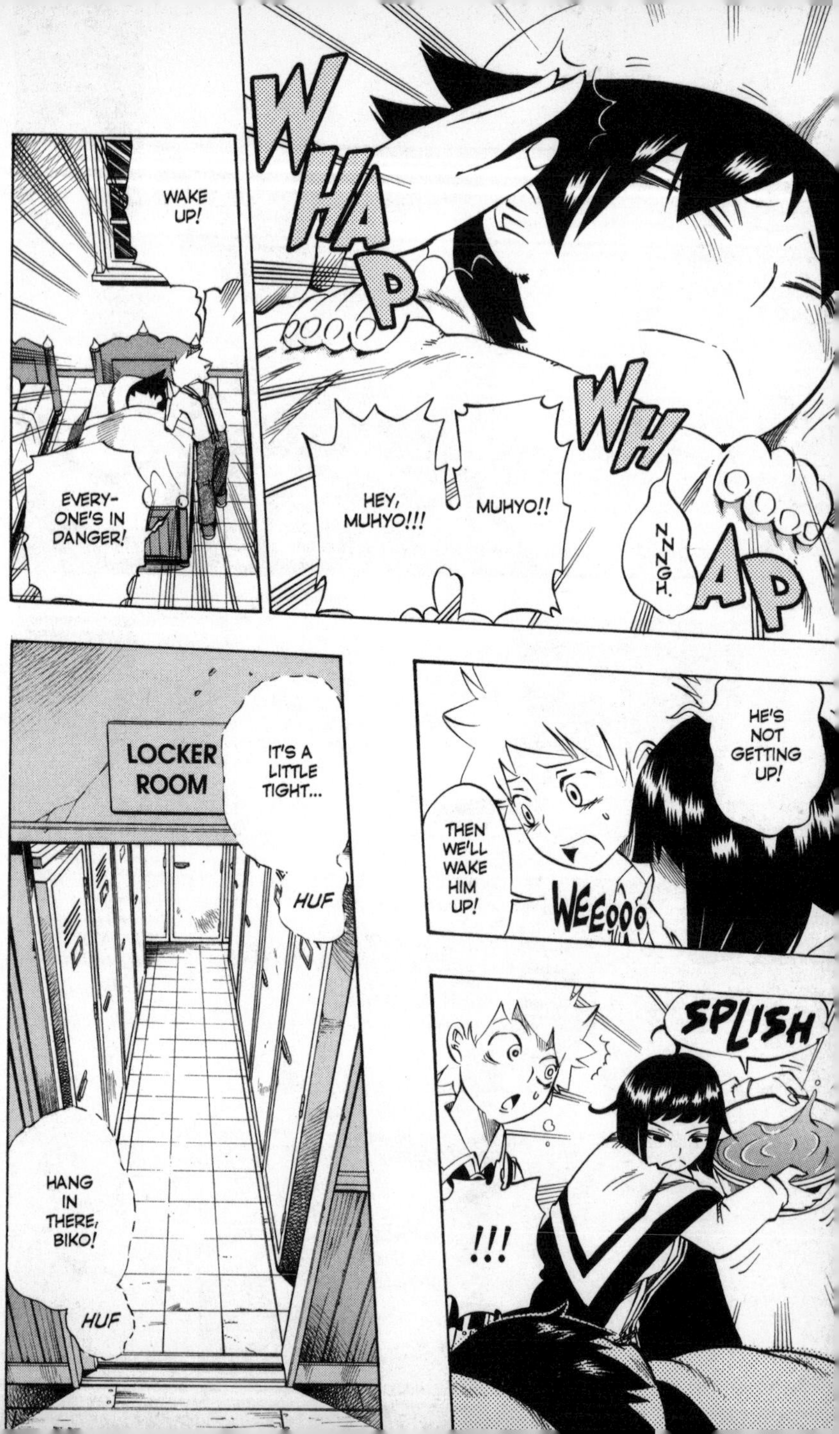
WHAP
WHAP
NNNGH.
MUHYO!!
HEY, MUHYO!!!
WAKE UP!
EVERY-ONE'S IN DANGER!
HE'S NOT GETTING UP!
THEN WE'LL WAKE HIM UP!
WEEOOO
SPLISH
!!!
LOCKER ROOM
IT'S A LITTLE TIGHT...
HUF
HANG IN THERE, BIKO!
HUF

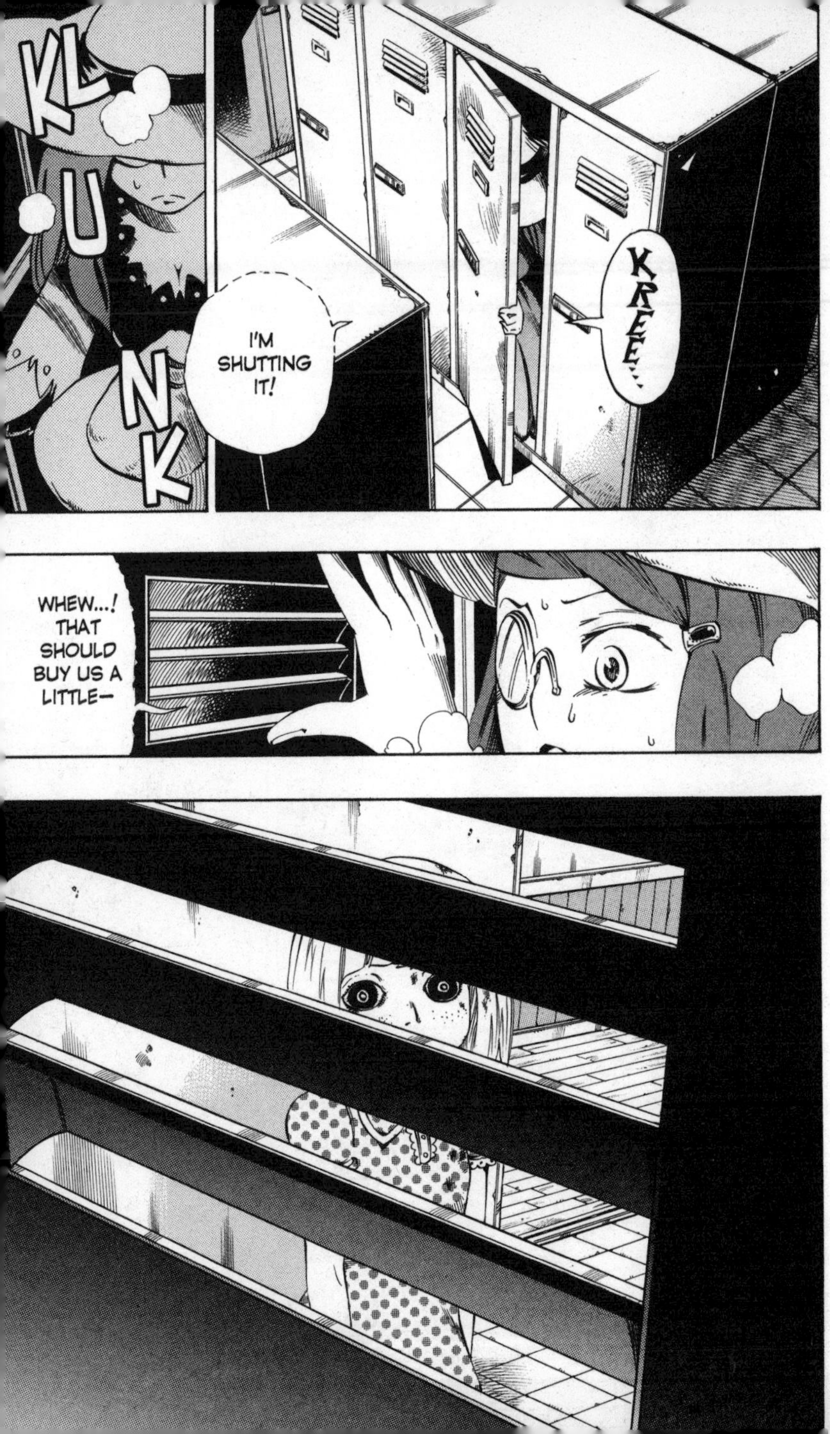
KREE...
I'M SHUTTING IT!
KLUNK
WHEW...! THAT SHOULD BUY US A LITTLE—

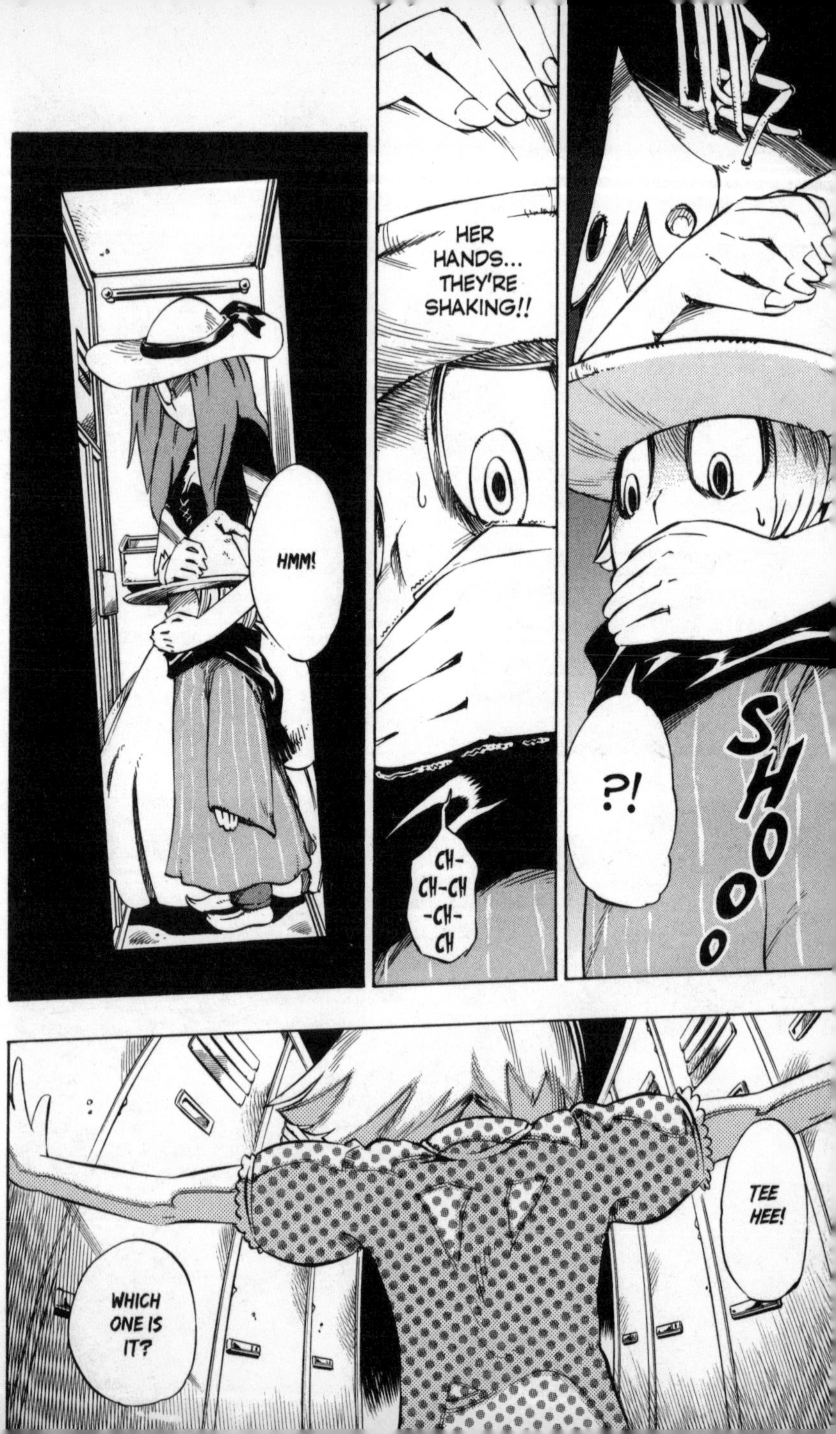
?!
SHOOOO
HER HANDS... THEY'RE SHAKING!!
CH-CH-CH-CH-CH
HMM!
TEE HEE!
WHICH ONE IS IT?

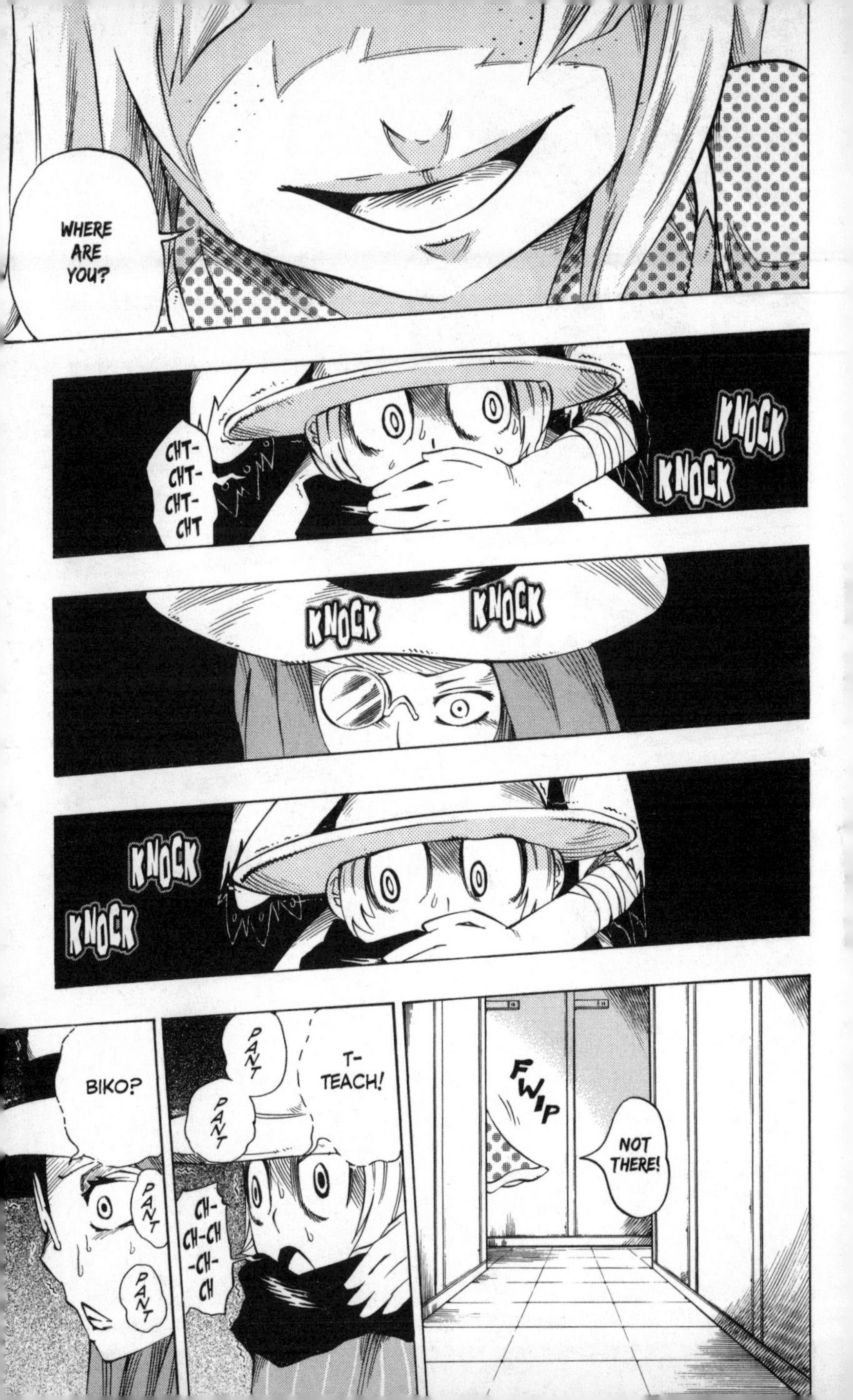
WHERE ARE YOU?
KNOCK
KNOCK
CHT-CHT-CHT-CHT
KNOCK
KNOCK
KNOCK
KNOCK
FWIP
NOT THERE!
T-TEACH!
PANT
PANT
CH-CH-CH-CH-CH
BIKO?
PANT
PANT

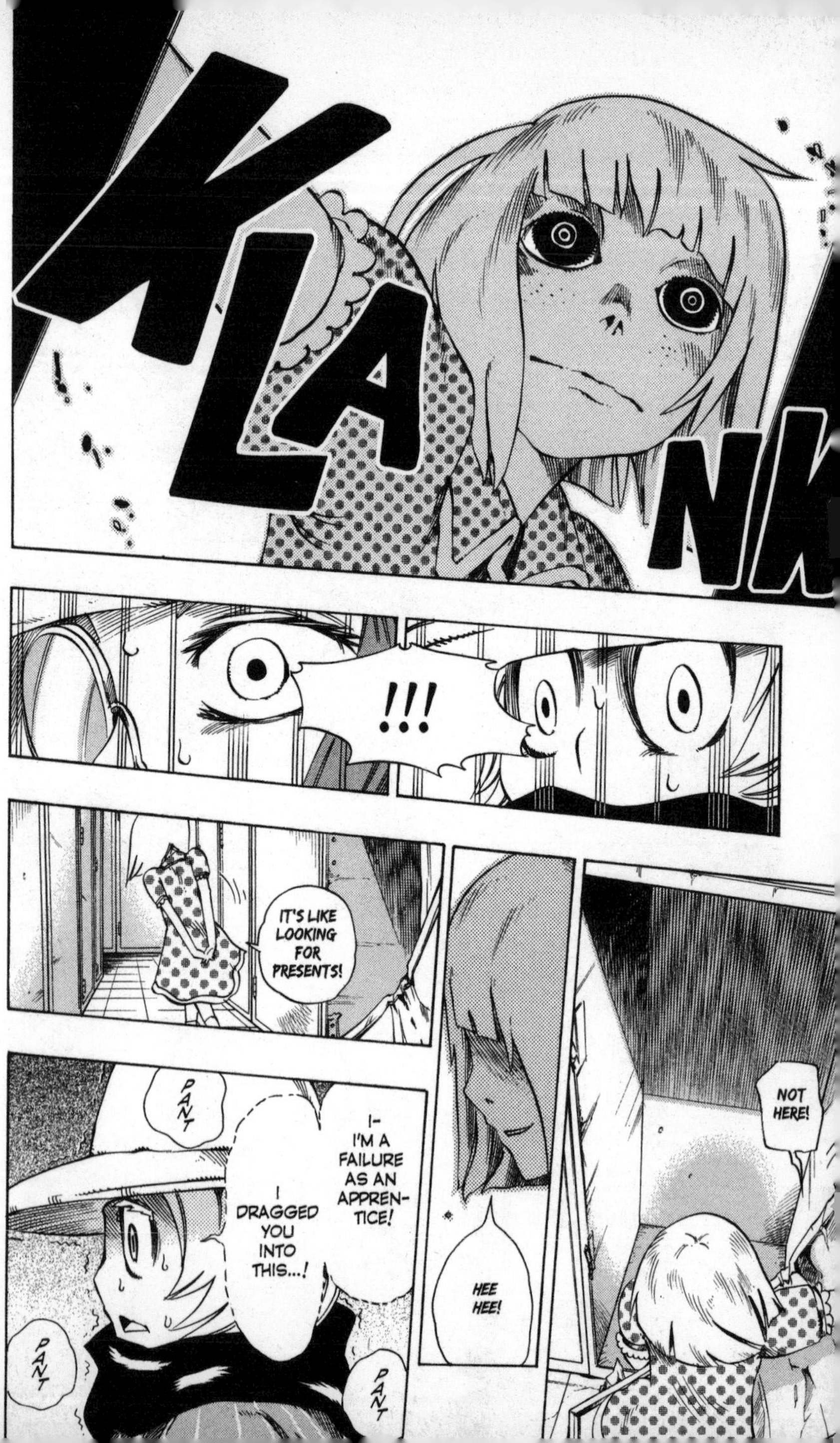
KLANK
!!!
NOT HERE!
HEE HEE!
IT'S LIKE LOOKING FOR PRESENTS!
I- I'M A FAILURE AS AN APPRENTICE!
PANT
I DRAGGED YOU INTO THIS...!
PANT
PANT

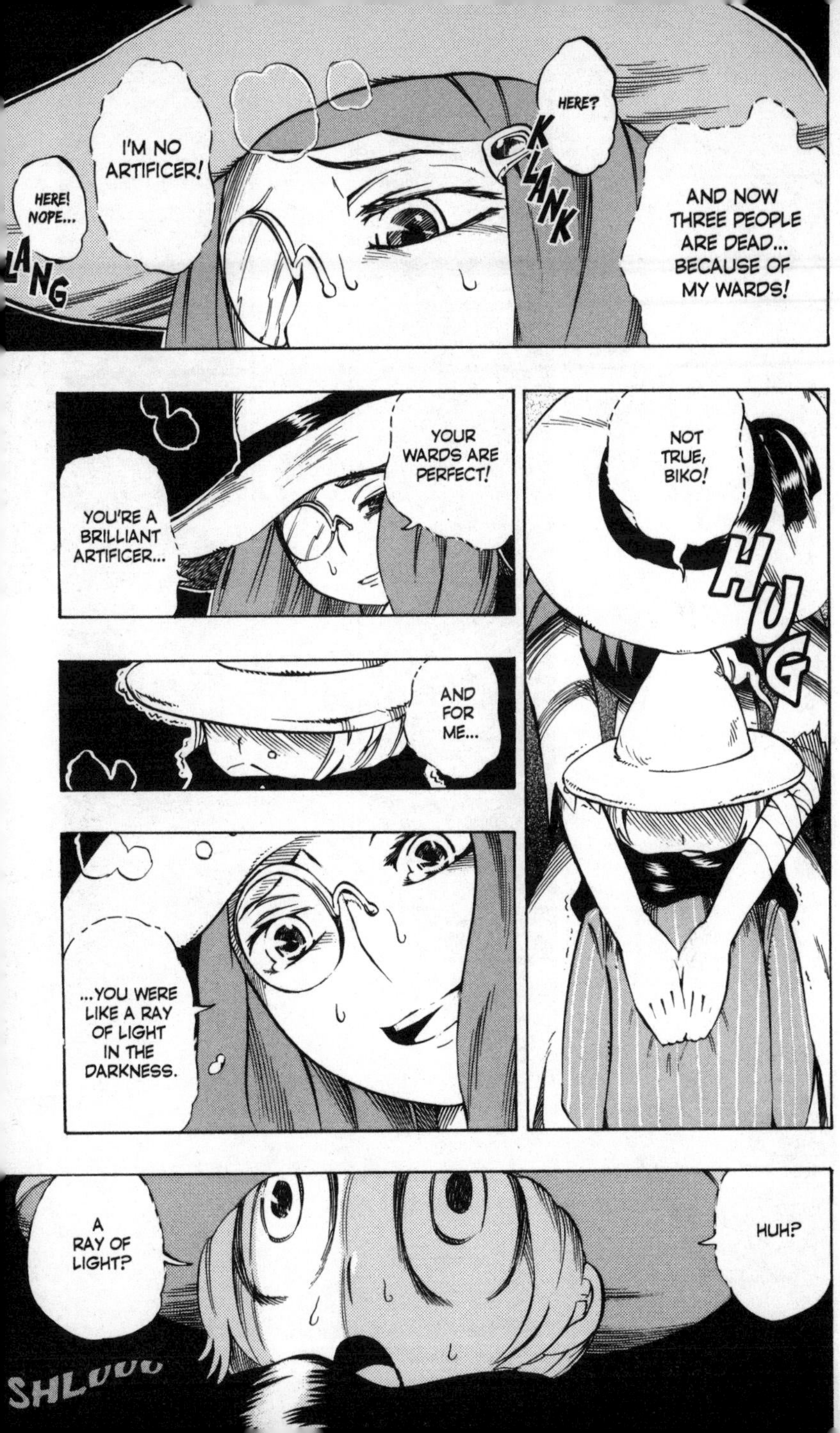
AND NOW THREE PEOPLE ARE DEAD... BECAUSE OF MY WARDS!
HERE?
KLANK
I'M NO ARTIFICER!
HERE! NOPE...
LANG
NOT TRUE, BIKO!
HUG
YOUR WARDS ARE PERFECT!
YOU'RE A BRILLIANT ARTIFICER...
AND FOR ME...
...YOU WERE LIKE A RAY OF LIGHT IN THE DARKNESS.
HUH?
A RAY OF LIGHT?
SHLUUU

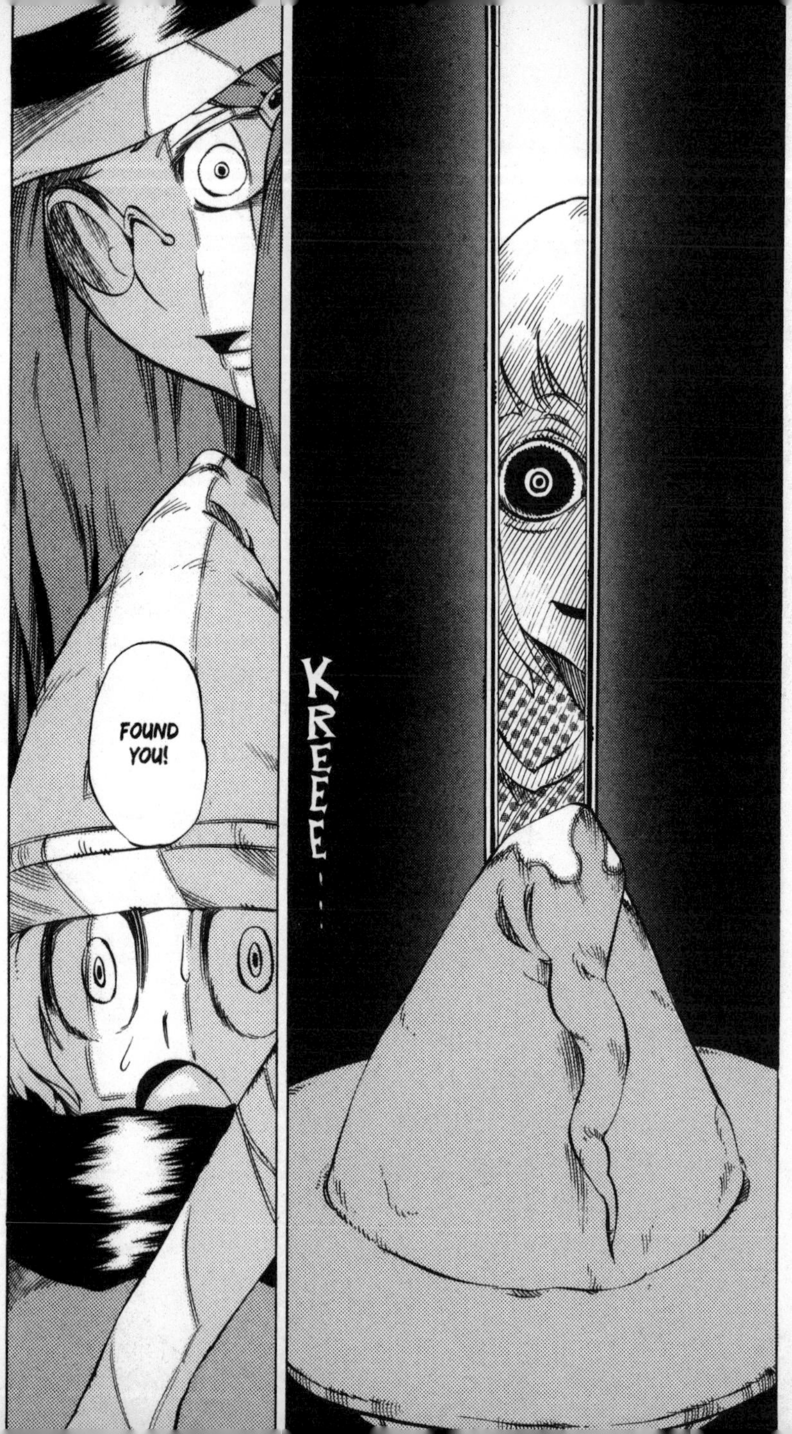
KREEEE...
FOUND YOU!

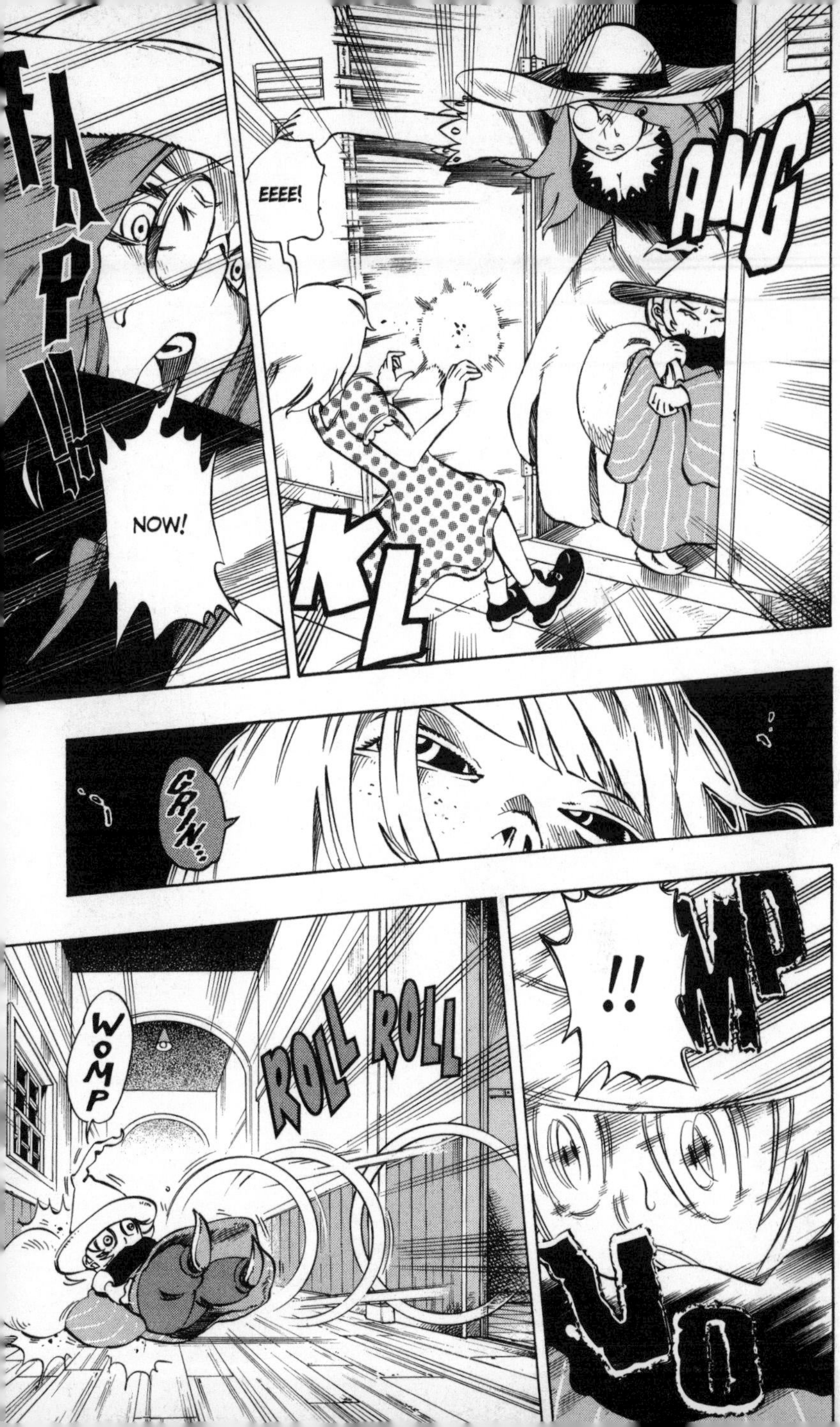
ANG
EEEE!
KL
FAP!!!
NOW!
GRIN...
!!
MP
VO
WOMP
ROLL ROLL

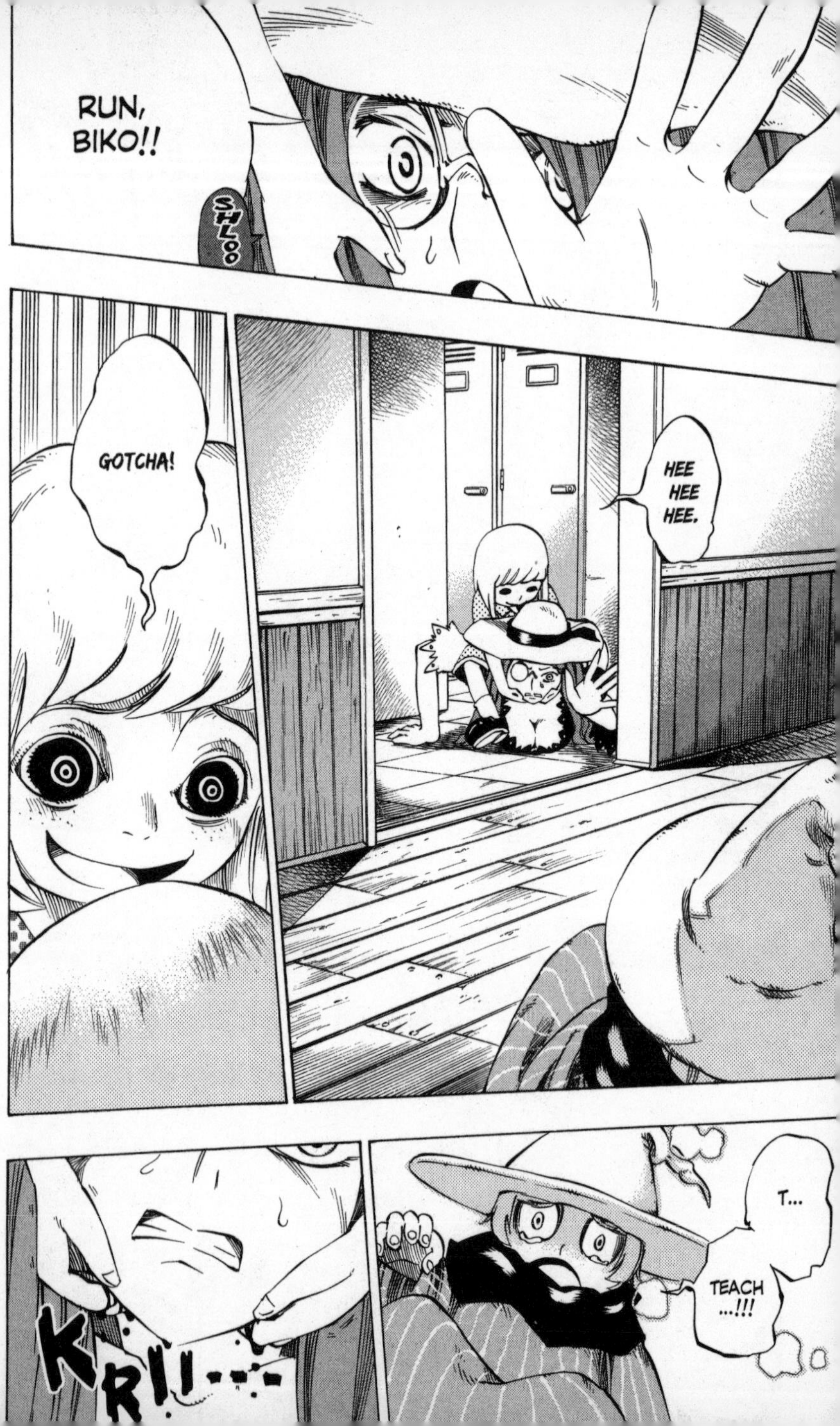
RUN, BIKO!!
SHLOO
HEE HEE HEE.
GOTCHA!
T...
TEACH ...!!!
KRI!...

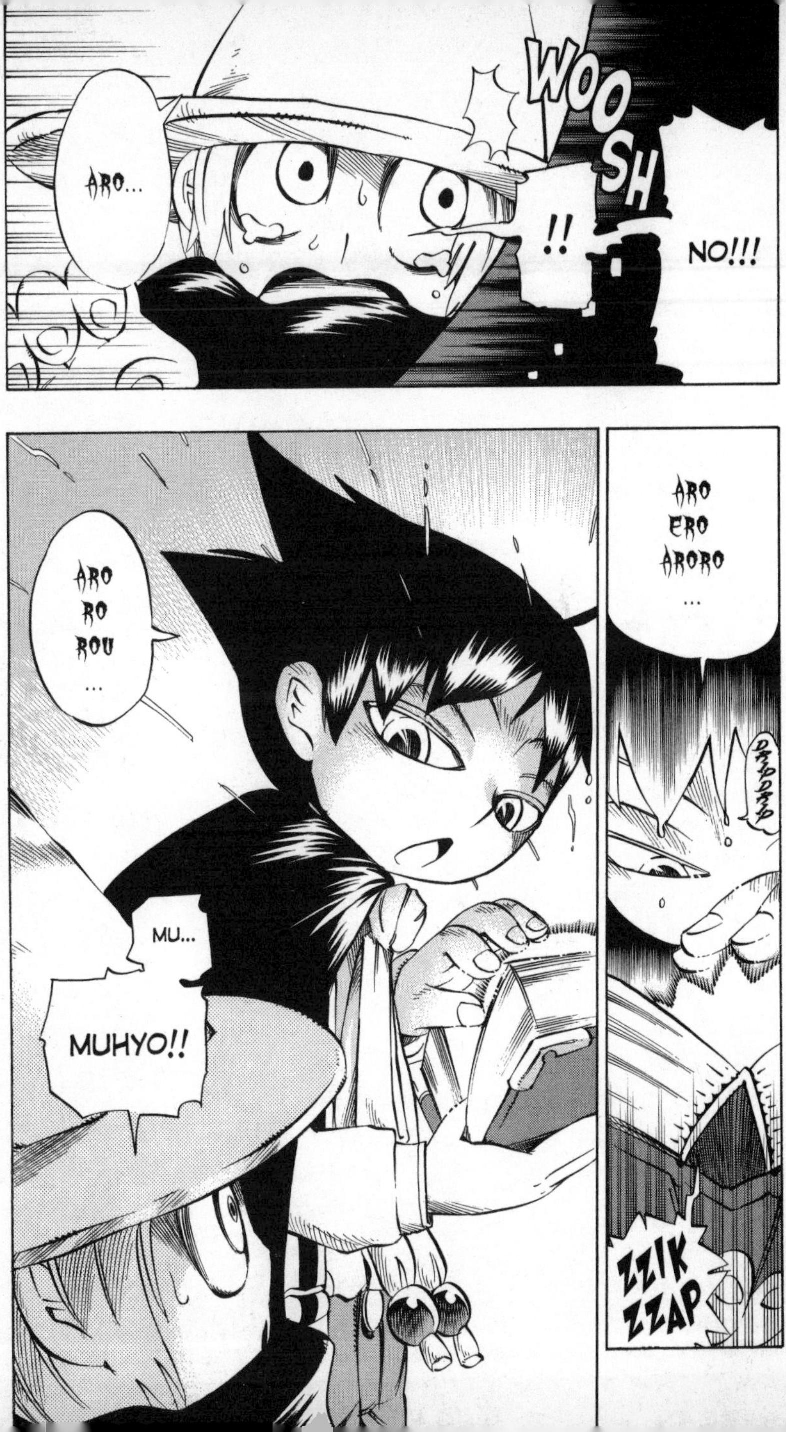
WOOSH
NO!!!
!!
ARO...
ARO ERO ARORO ...
ZZIK ZZAP
ARO RO ROU ...
MU...
MUHYO!!

Q: WHERE DID YOU COME UP WITH THE IDEA FOR MAGIC LAW?
—S.A. KANAGAWA PREFECTURE

A: HOW DID I, I WONDER... (LOOKS OFF INTO THE DISTANCE) HUH? WHAT'S THIS STABBING PAIN IN MY CHEST? THIS BURNING IN MY EYES! *SNIFF*... THE MONTHS IT TOOK TO COME UP WITH THIS IDEA...SO LONG, SO HARD... DAYS OF RUNNING, CHASING AFTER IDEAS ONLY TO COME UP EMPTY-HANDED. DAYS OF FUTILE STRUGGLING IN QUICK-SAND. I WALKED THE STREETS WHERE BOOKSELLERS PLIED THEIR WARES, SEARCHING FOR THE LOST LIGHT... IT... IT'S TOO MUCH. I CAN'T WRITE ABOUT THIS ANY MORE. MAYBE IN THE NEXT VOLUME. SOB.

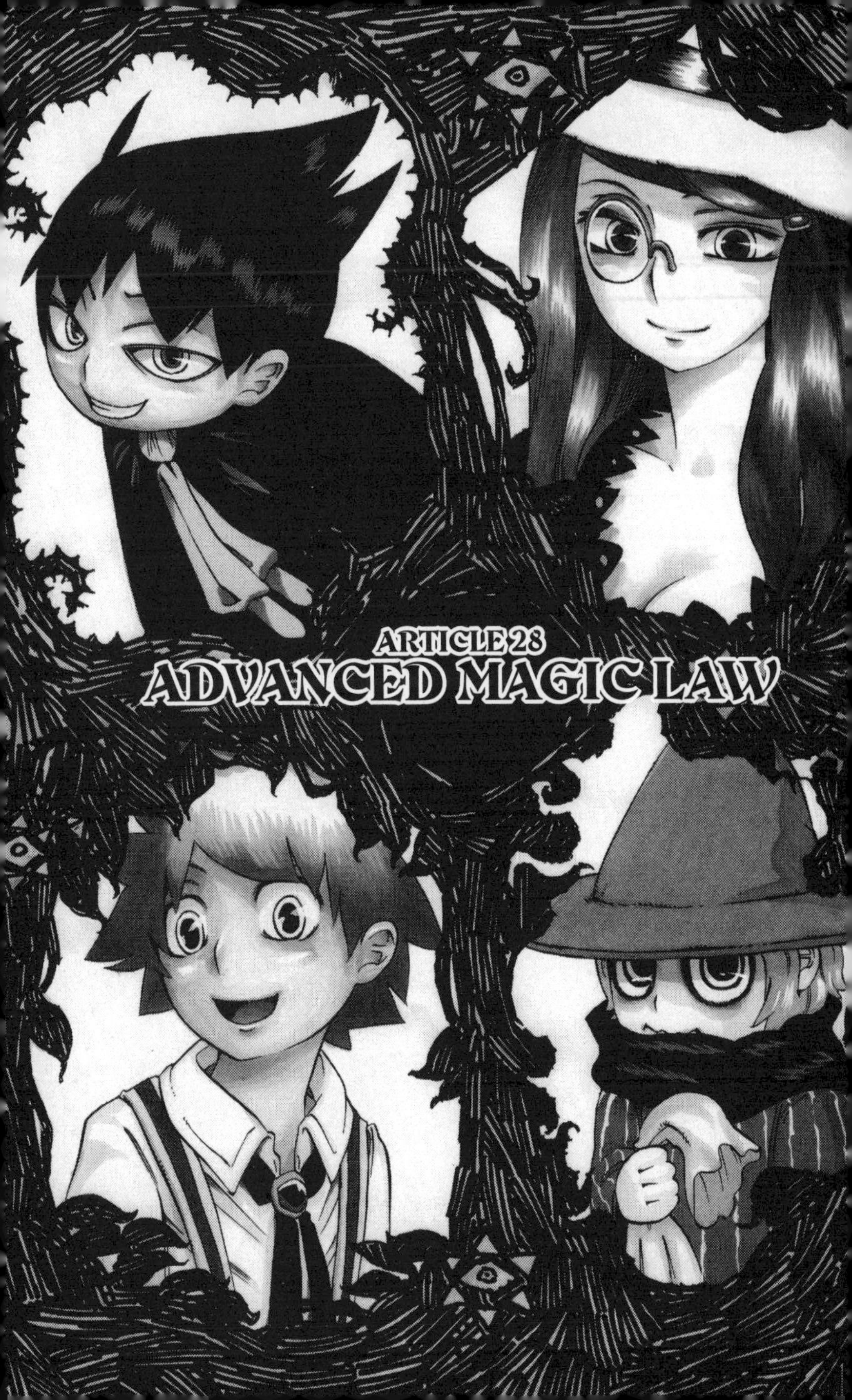
ARTICLE 28
ADVANCED MAGIC LAW

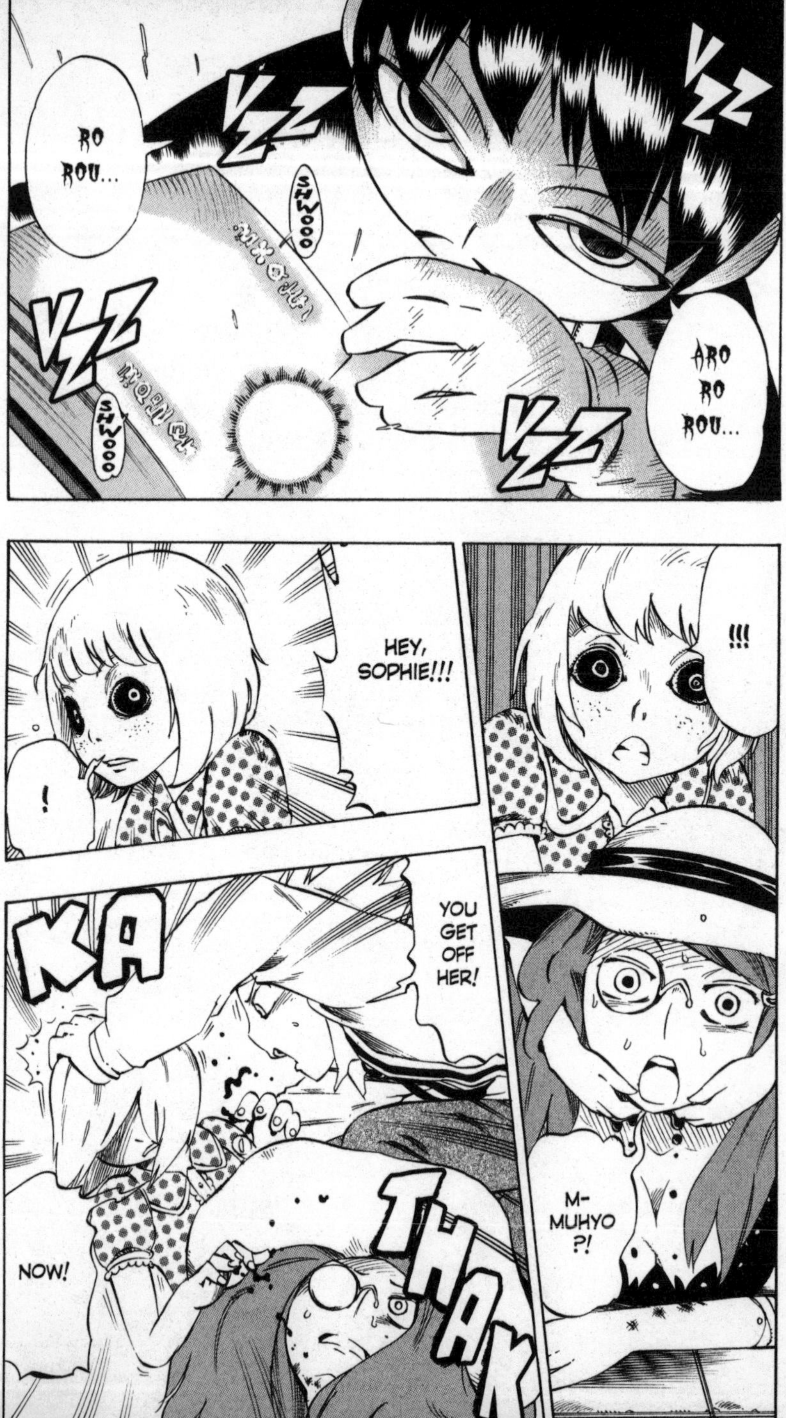
VZZ
ARO RO ROU...
VZZ
SHWOOO
VZZ
SHWOOO
VZZ
RO ROU...
!!!
HEY, SOPHIE!!!
!
M-MUHYO?!
YOU GET OFF HER!
KA
THAK
NOW!

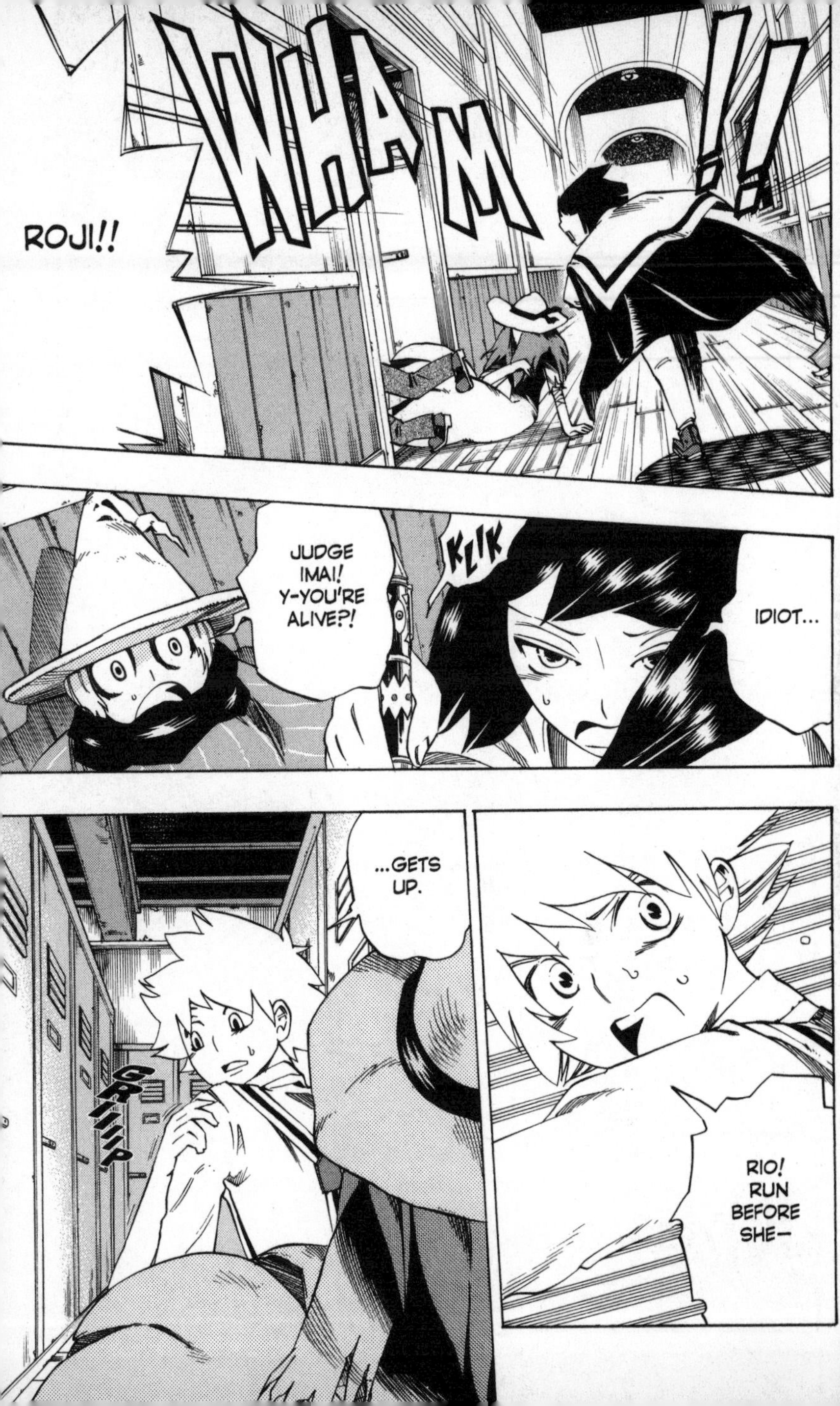
WHAM!!
ROJI!!
IDIOT...
KLIK
JUDGE IMAI! Y-YOU'RE ALIVE?!
RIO! RUN BEFORE SHE—
...GETS UP.
GRIIIIP

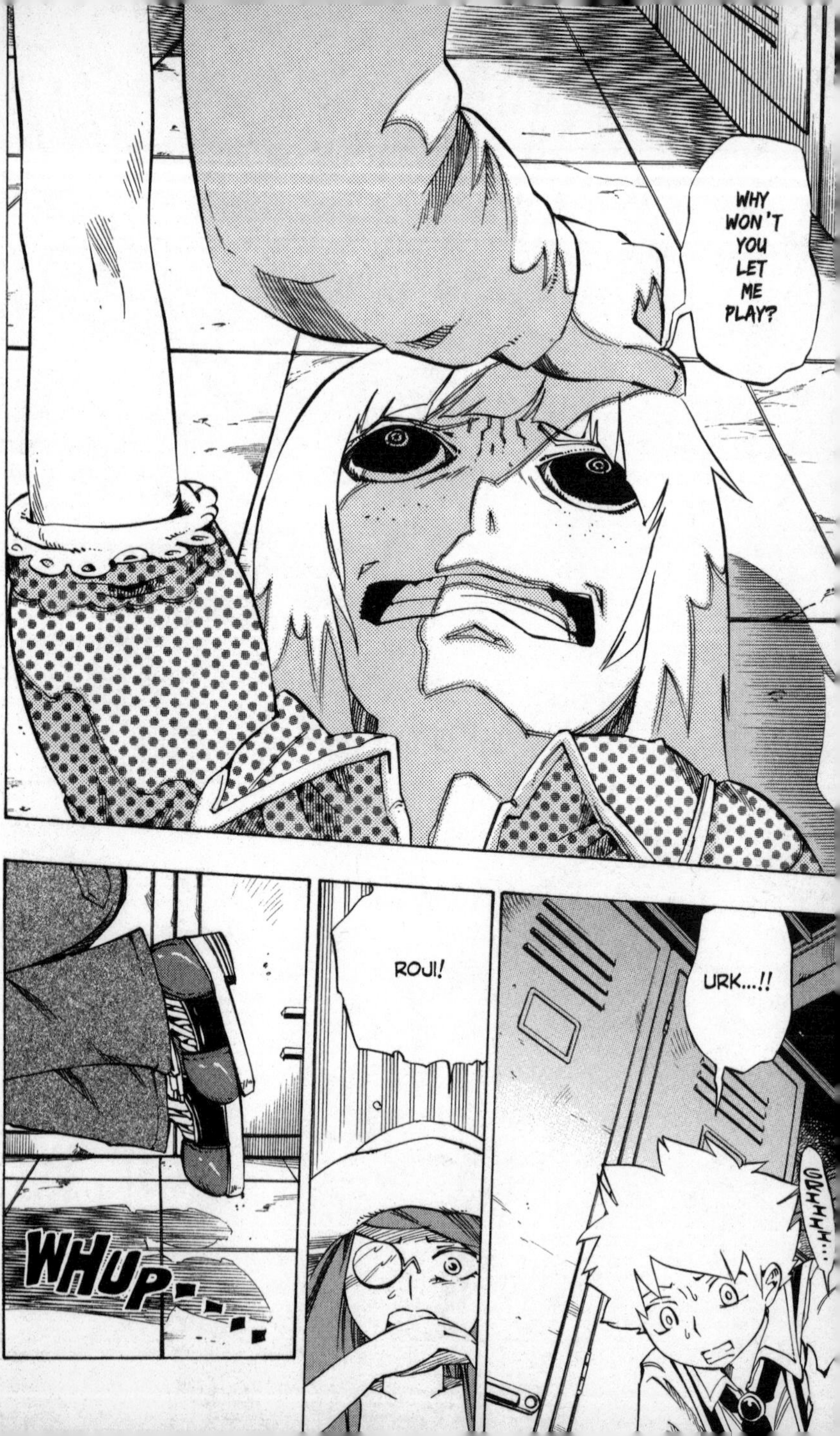
WHY WON'T YOU LET ME PLAY?
URK...!!
GRHHHH...
ROJI!
WHUP...

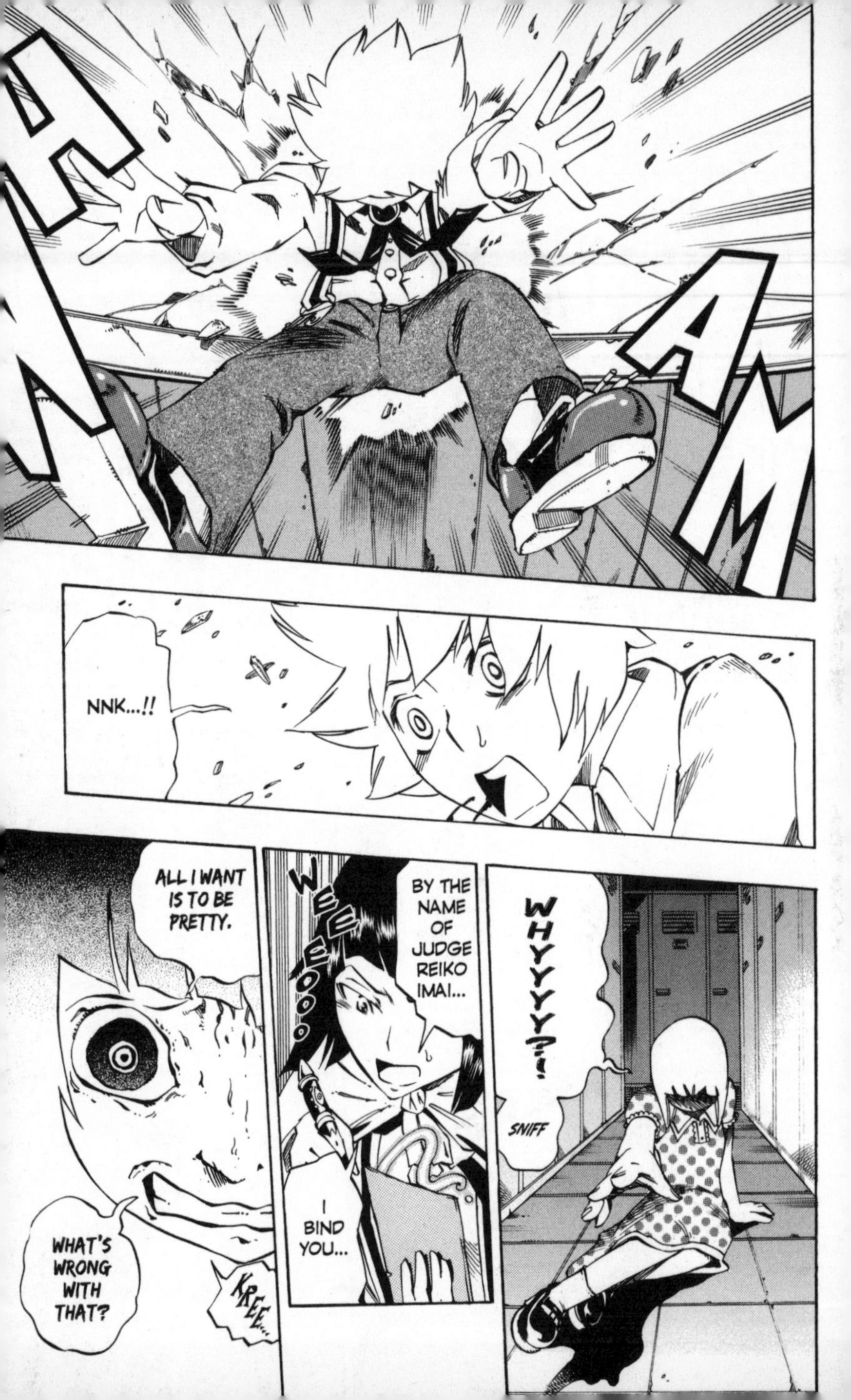
NNK...!!
WHYYYYY?!
SNIFF
BY THE NAME OF JUDGE REIKO IMAI...
WEEEOOOO
I BIND YOU...
ALL I WANT IS TO BE PRETTY.
WHAT'S WRONG WITH THAT?
KREE...

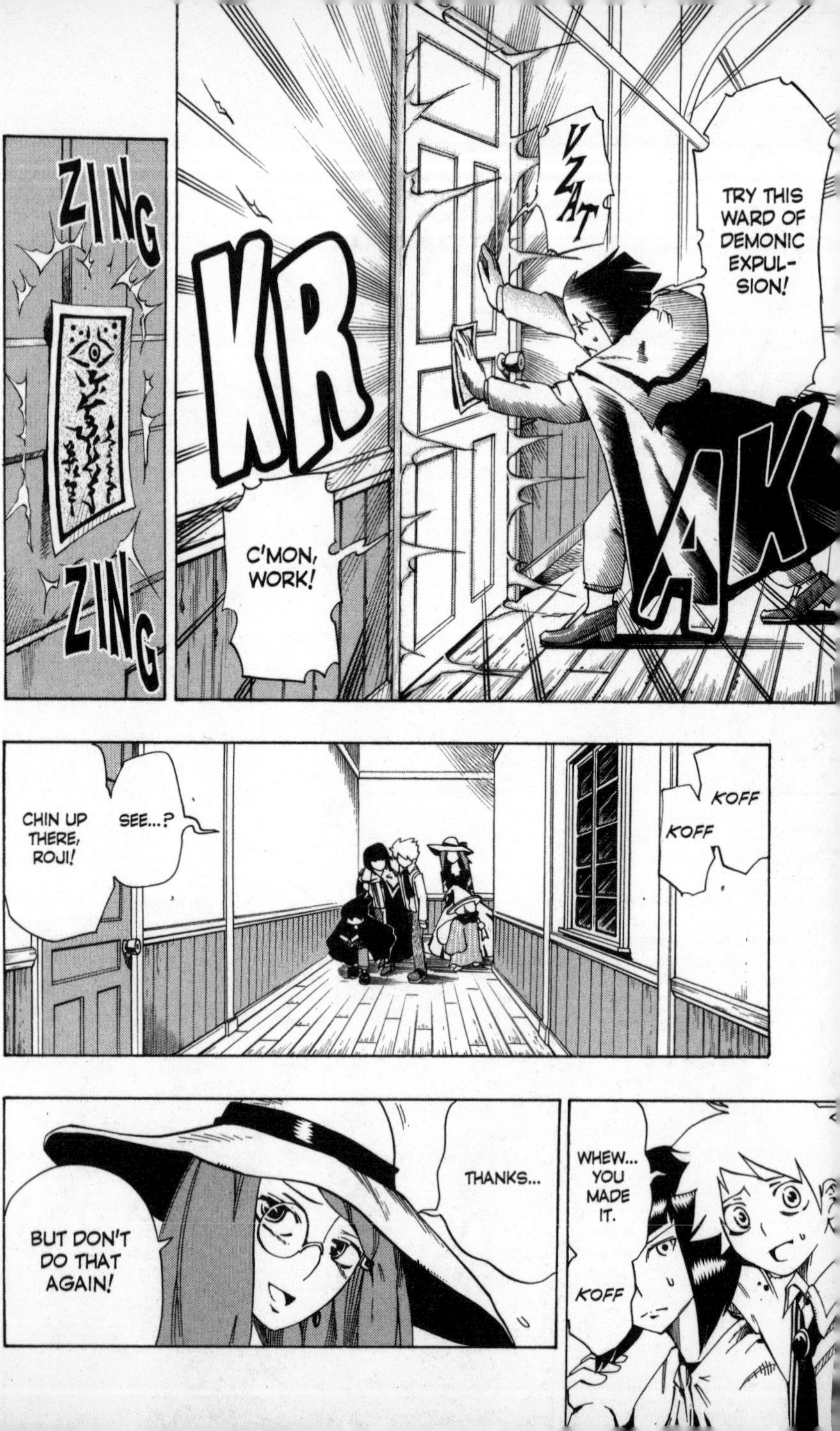
TRY THIS WARD OF DEMONIC EXPULSION!
VZAT
KR
AK
C'MON, WORK!
ZING
ZING
KOFF
KOFF
SEE...?
CHIN UP THERE, ROJI!
WHEW... YOU MADE IT.
KOFF
THANKS...
BUT DON'T DO THAT AGAIN!

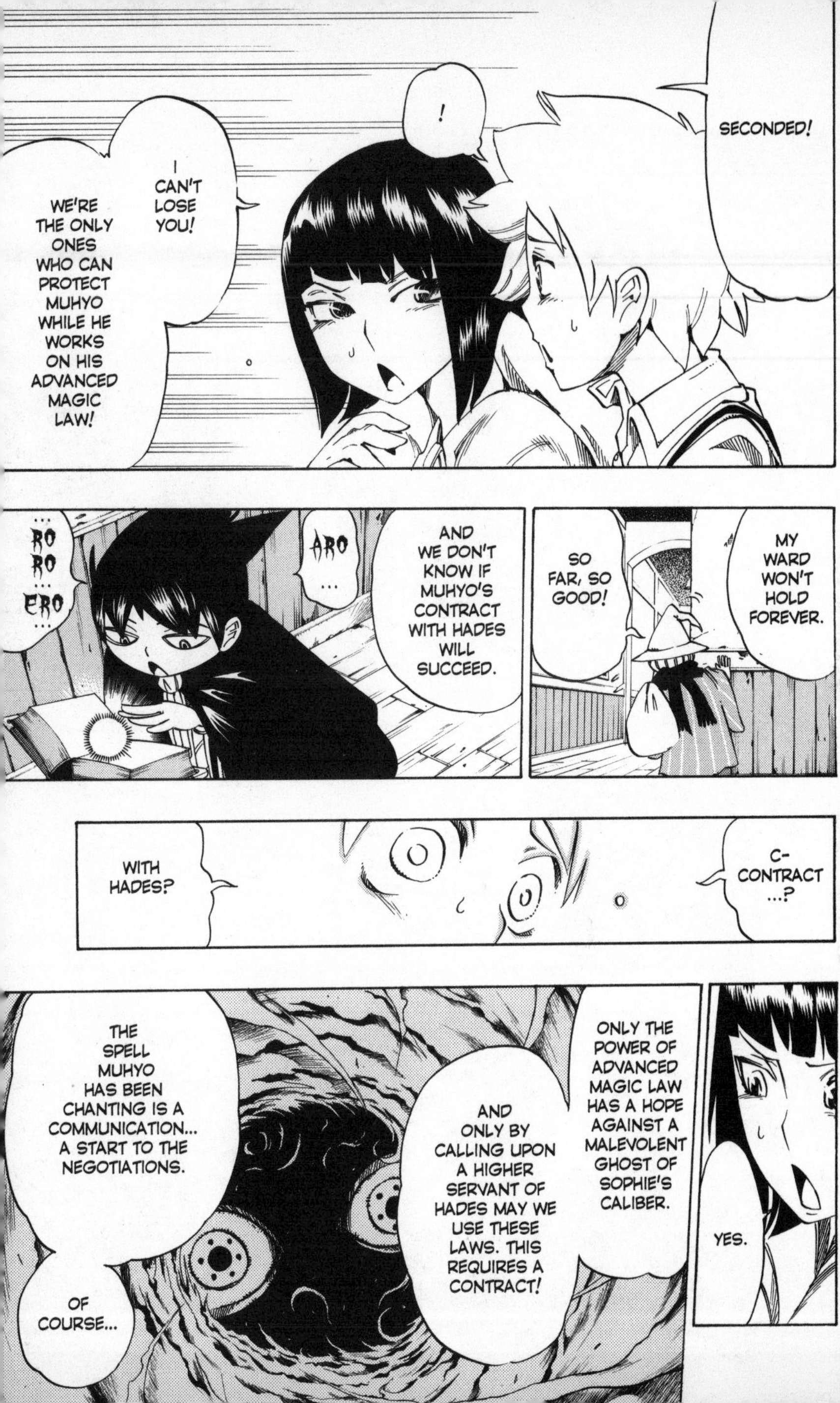
SECONDED!
!
I CAN'T LOSE YOU!
WE'RE THE ONLY ONES WHO CAN PROTECT MUHYO WHILE HE WORKS ON HIS ADVANCED MAGIC LAW!
MY WARD WON'T HOLD FOREVER.
SO FAR, SO GOOD!
AND WE DON'T KNOW IF MUHYO'S CONTRACT WITH HADES WILL SUCCEED.
ARO ...
...RO RO ... ERO ...
C-CONTRACT ...?
WITH HADES?
YES.
ONLY THE POWER OF ADVANCED MAGIC LAW HAS A HOPE AGAINST A MALEVOLENT GHOST OF SOPHIE'S CALIBER.
AND ONLY BY CALLING UPON A HIGHER SERVANT OF HADES MAY WE USE THESE LAWS. THIS REQUIRES A CONTRACT!
THE SPELL MUHYO HAS BEEN CHANTING IS A COMMUNICATION... A START TO THE NEGOTIATIONS.
OF COURSE...

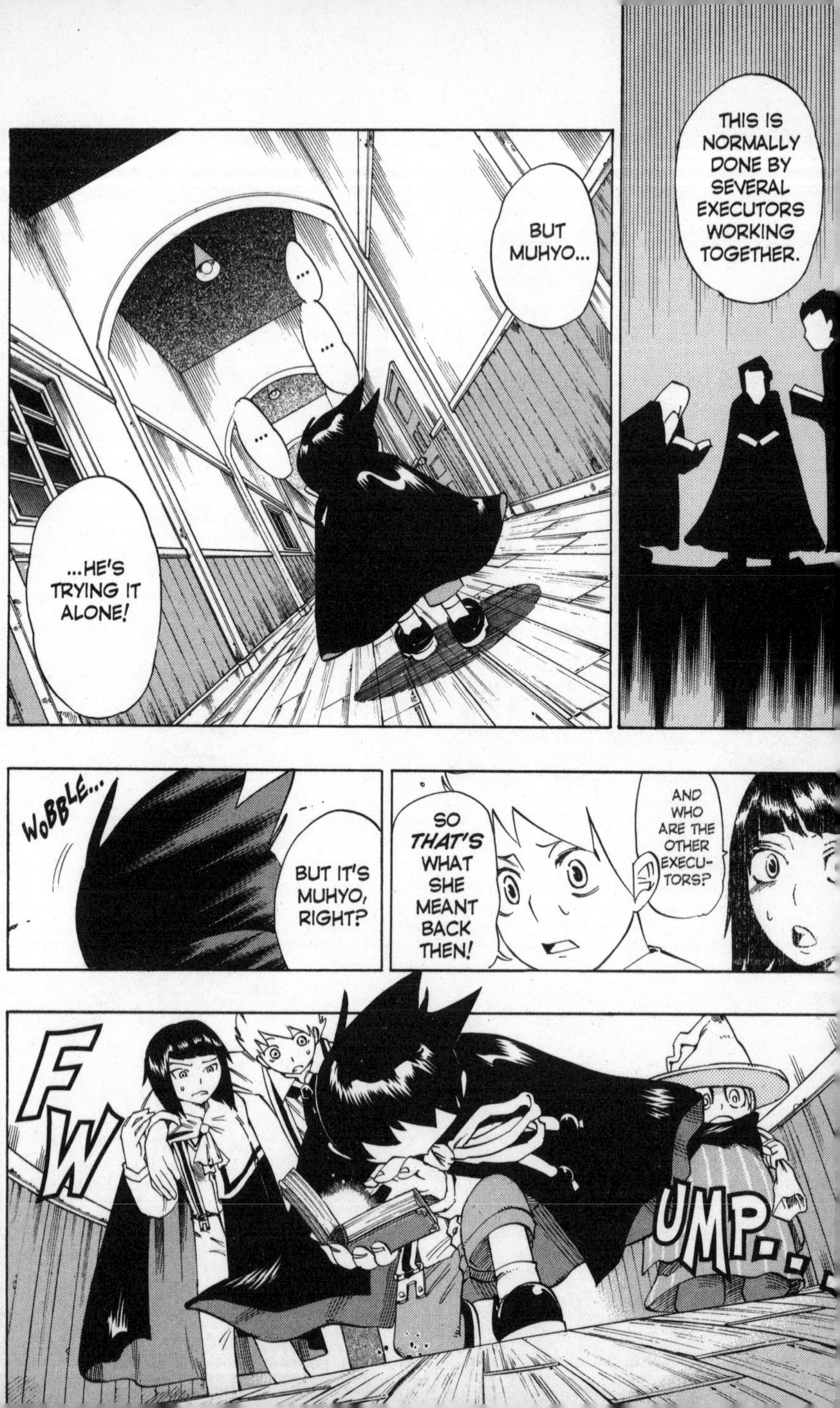
THIS IS NORMALLY DONE BY SEVERAL EXECUTORS WORKING TOGETHER.
BUT MUHYO...
...
...
...
...HE'S TRYING IT ALONE!
AND WHO ARE THE OTHER EXECUTORS?
SO *THAT'S* WHAT SHE MEANT BACK THEN!
BUT IT'S MUHYO, RIGHT?
WOBBLE...
FWUMP...

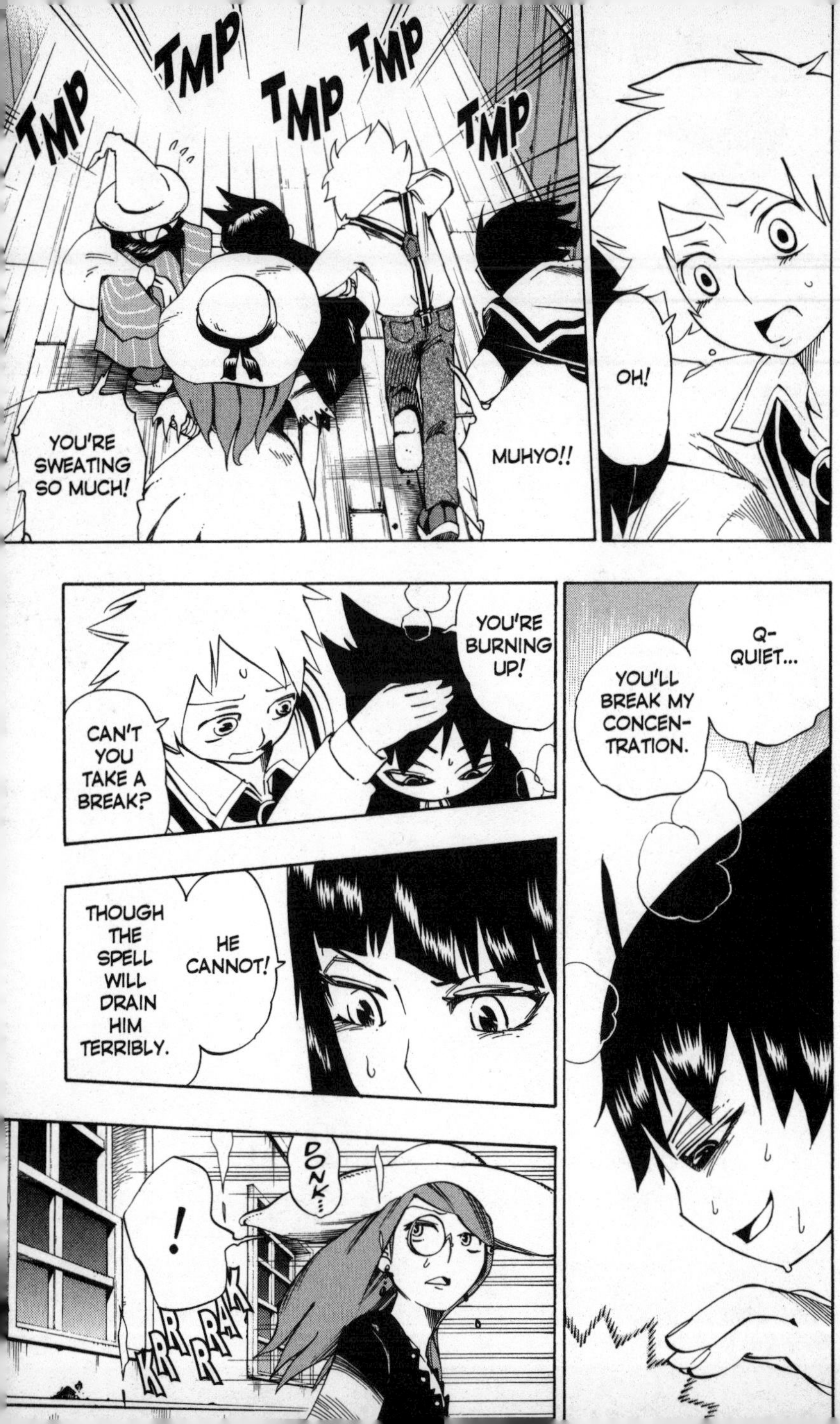
OH!
TMP
TMP
TMP
TMP
TMP
MUHYO!!
YOU'RE SWEATING SO MUCH!
YOU'RE BURNING UP!
CAN'T YOU TAKE A BREAK?
Q-QUIET...
YOU'LL BREAK MY CONCEN-TRATION.
HE CANNOT!
THOUGH THE SPELL WILL DRAIN HIM TERRIBLY.
DONK...
!
KRR RAK

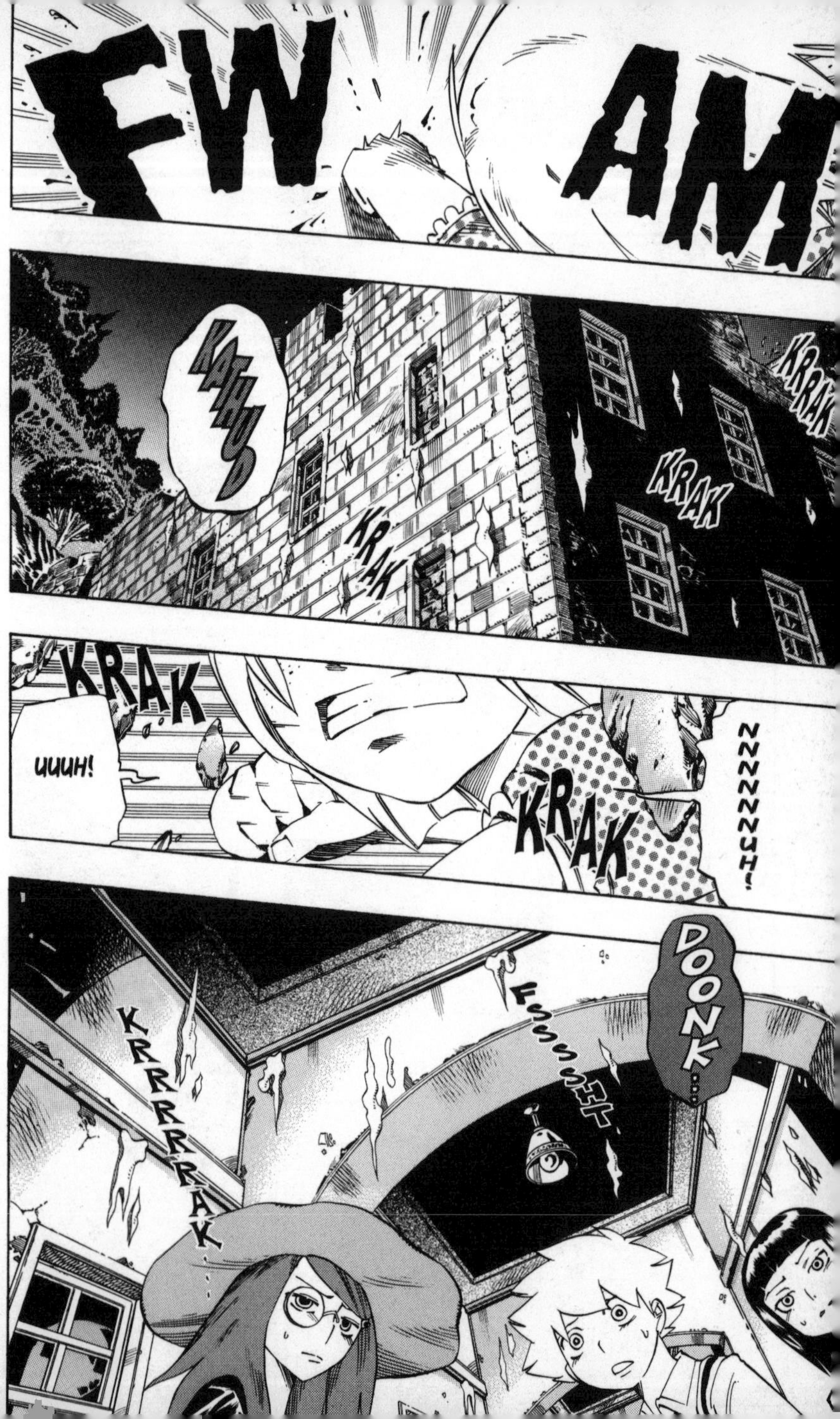
FW AM
KRRAK
KRAK
KATHUD
KRAK
NNNNNNNUH!
KRAK
KRAK
uuuh!
DOONK...
FSSSSHT
KRRRRRRAK...

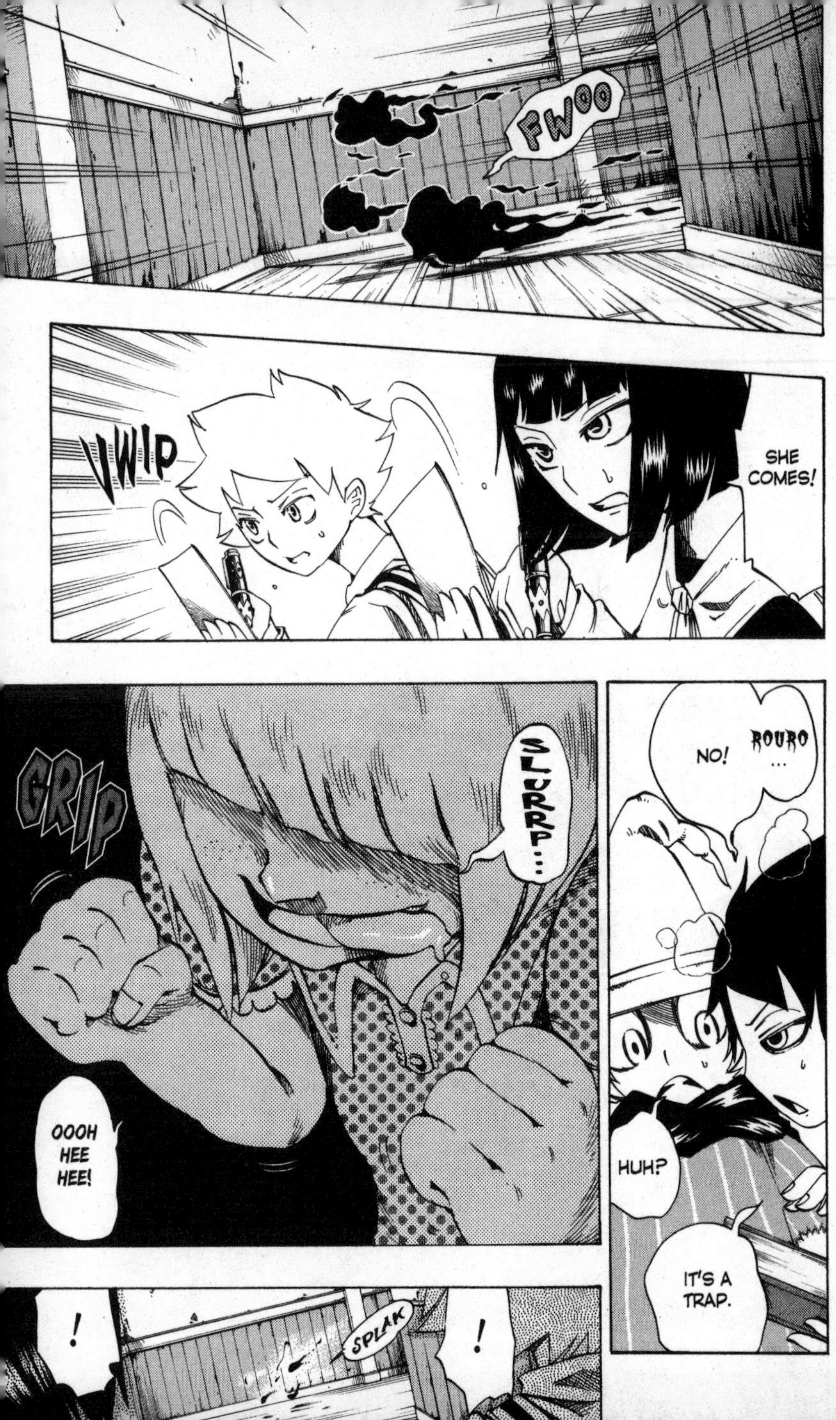
FWOO
SHE COMES!
VWIP
ROURO ...
NO!
HUH?
IT'S A TRAP.
SLURRP...
GRIP
OOOH HEE HEE!
!
SPLAK
!

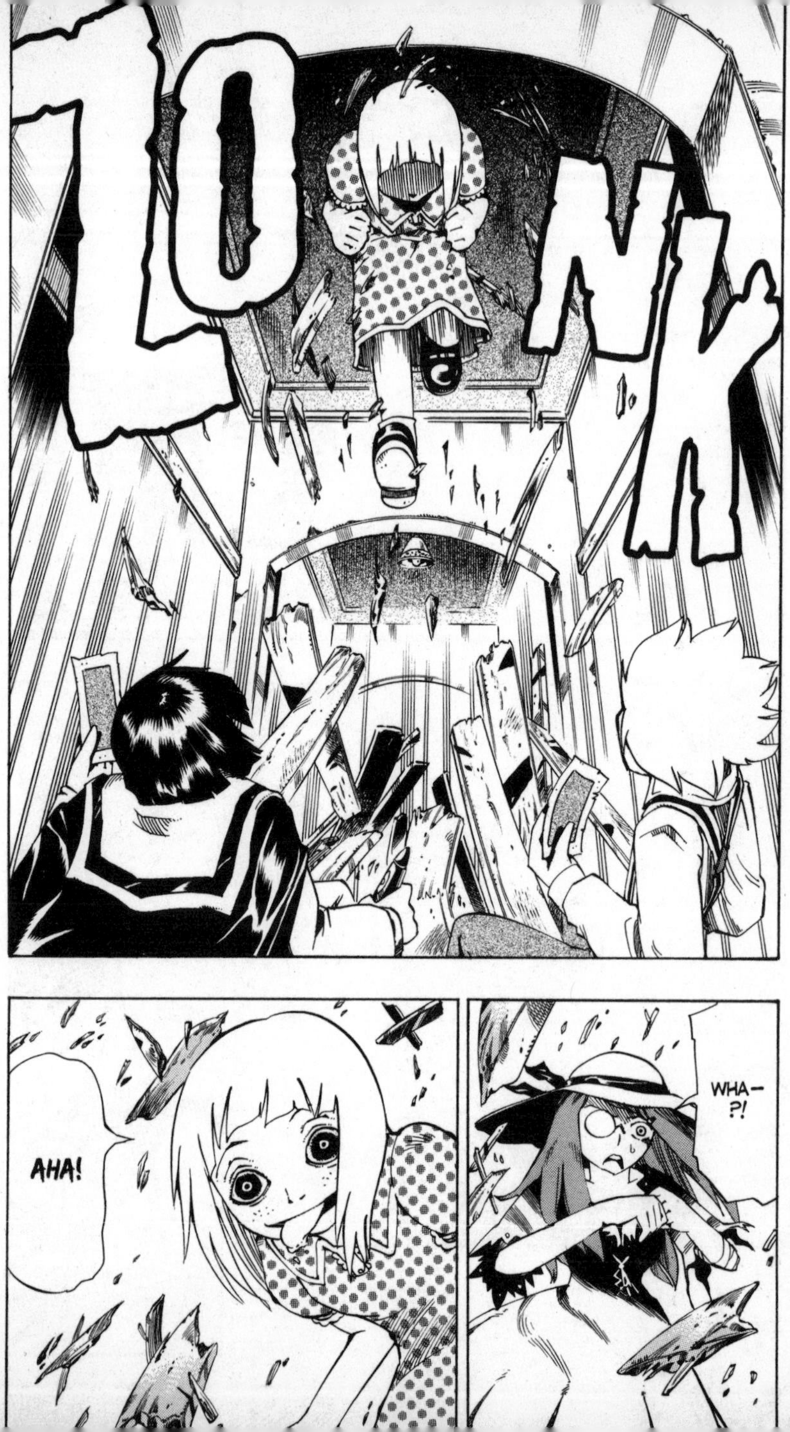
ZOONK
WHA—
?!
AHA!

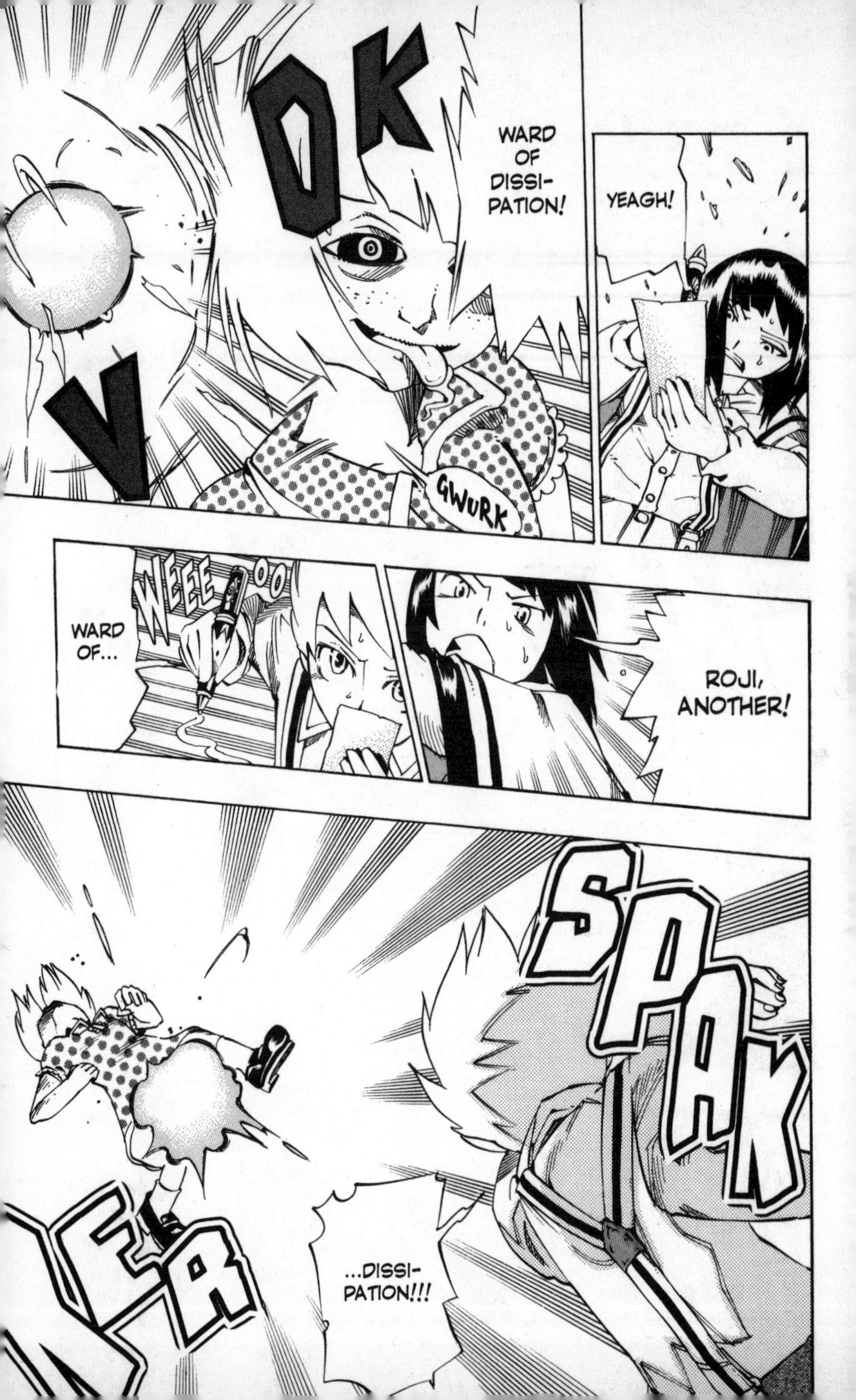
YEAGH!
WARD OF DISSI-PATION!
OK
V
GWURK
ROJI, ANOTHER!
WARD OF...
WEEE
SPAK
...DISSI-PATION!!!

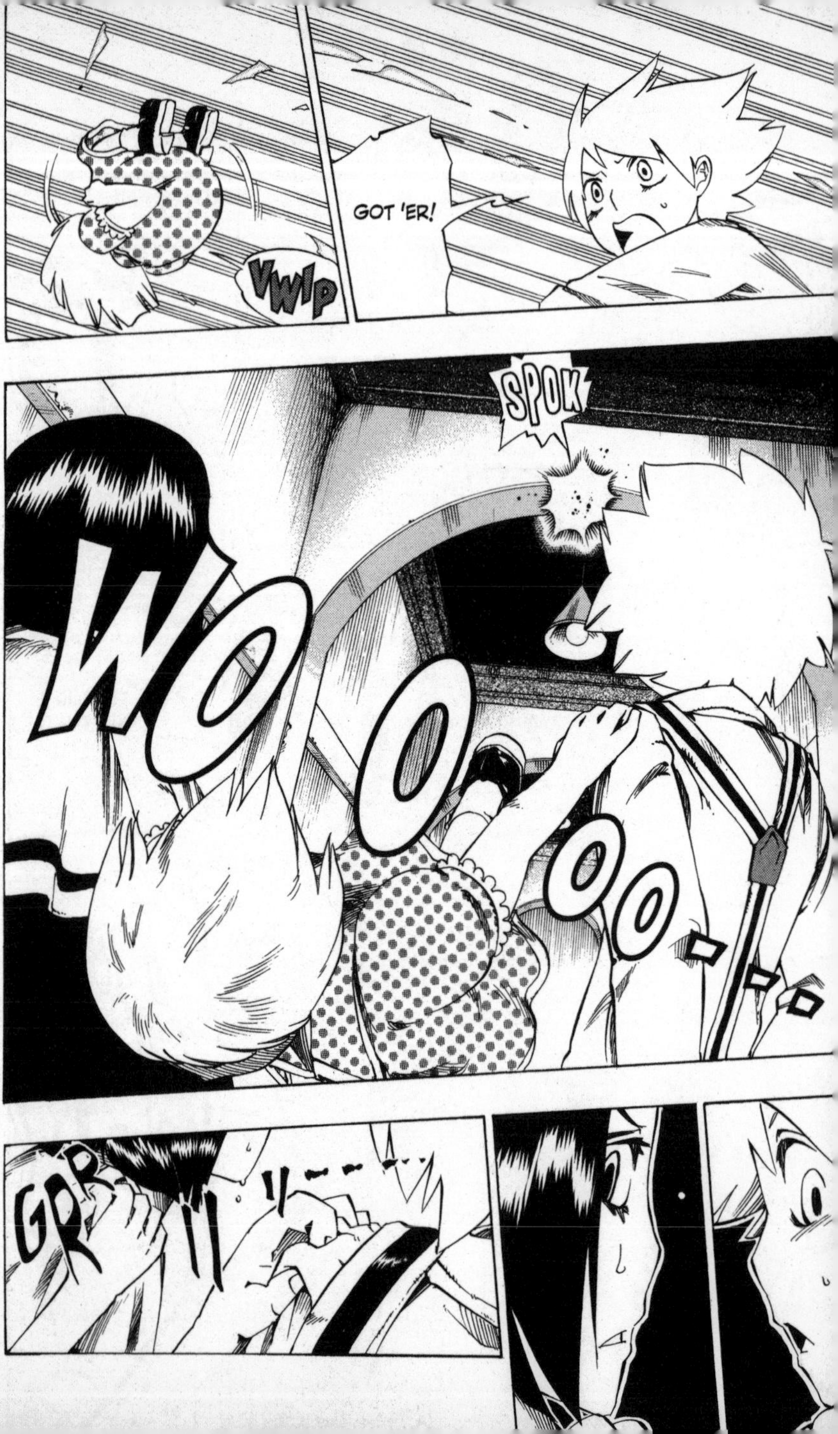
GOT 'ER!
VWIP
SPOK
WOOOOO
GRR

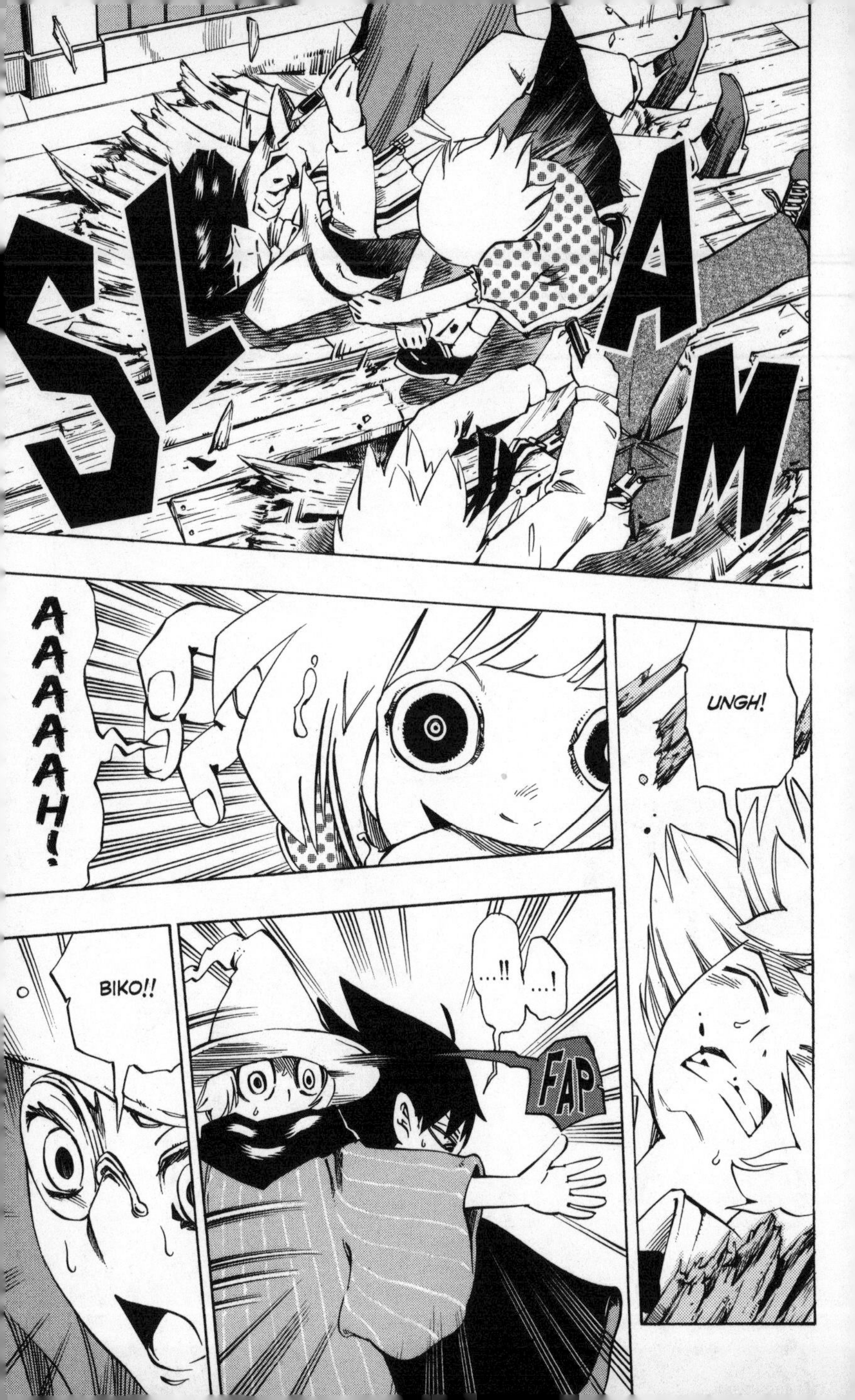
SLAM
UNGH!
AAAAAAH!
...!
...!!
FAP
BIKO!!

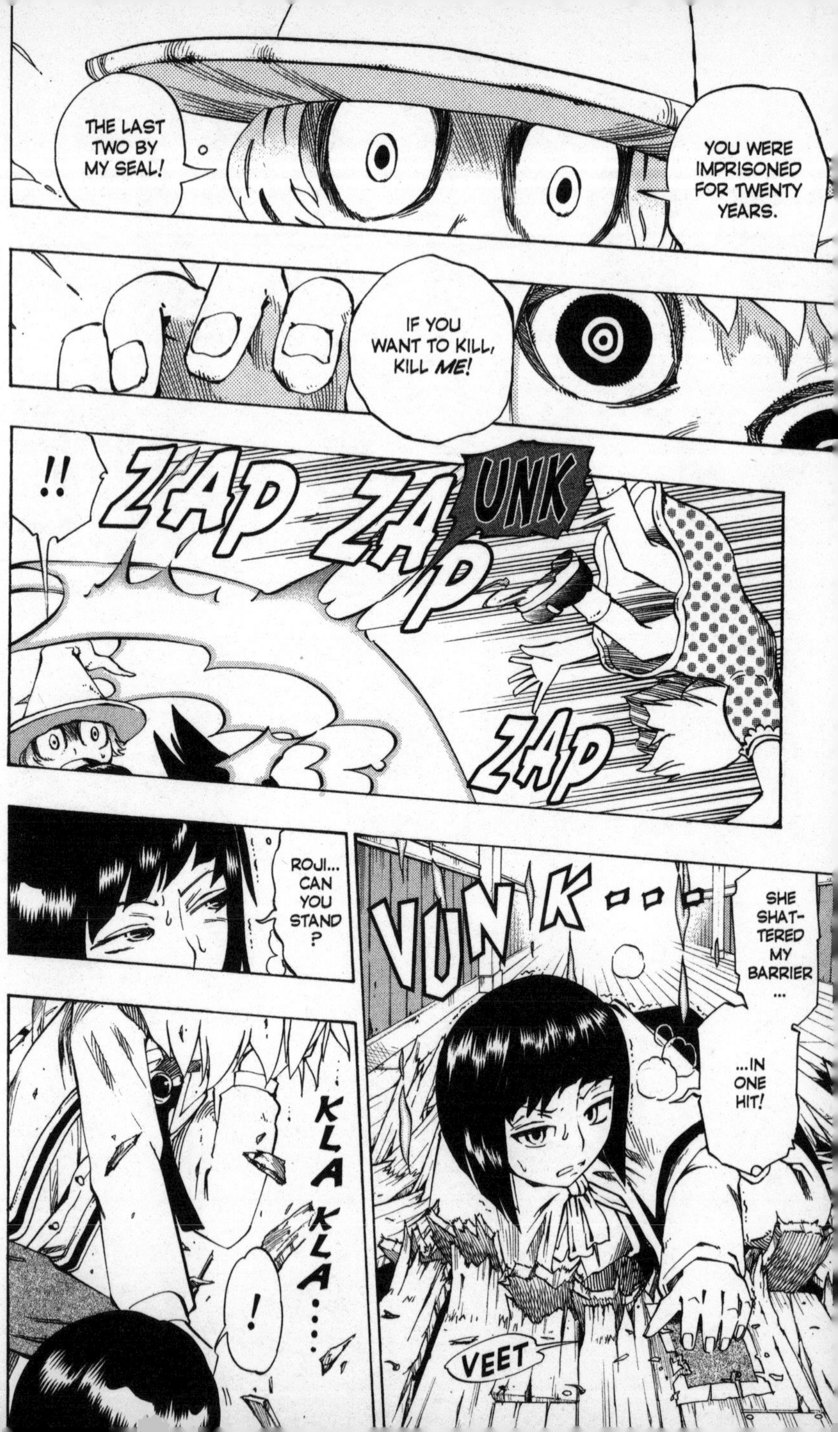
YOU WERE IMPRISONED FOR TWENTY YEARS.
THE LAST TWO BY MY SEAL!
IF YOU WANT TO KILL, KILL ME!
ZAP
ZAP
UNK
ZAP
!!
VUNK...
SHE SHATTERED MY BARRIER...
...IN ONE HIT!
VEET
ROJI... CAN YOU STAND?
KLA KLA....
!

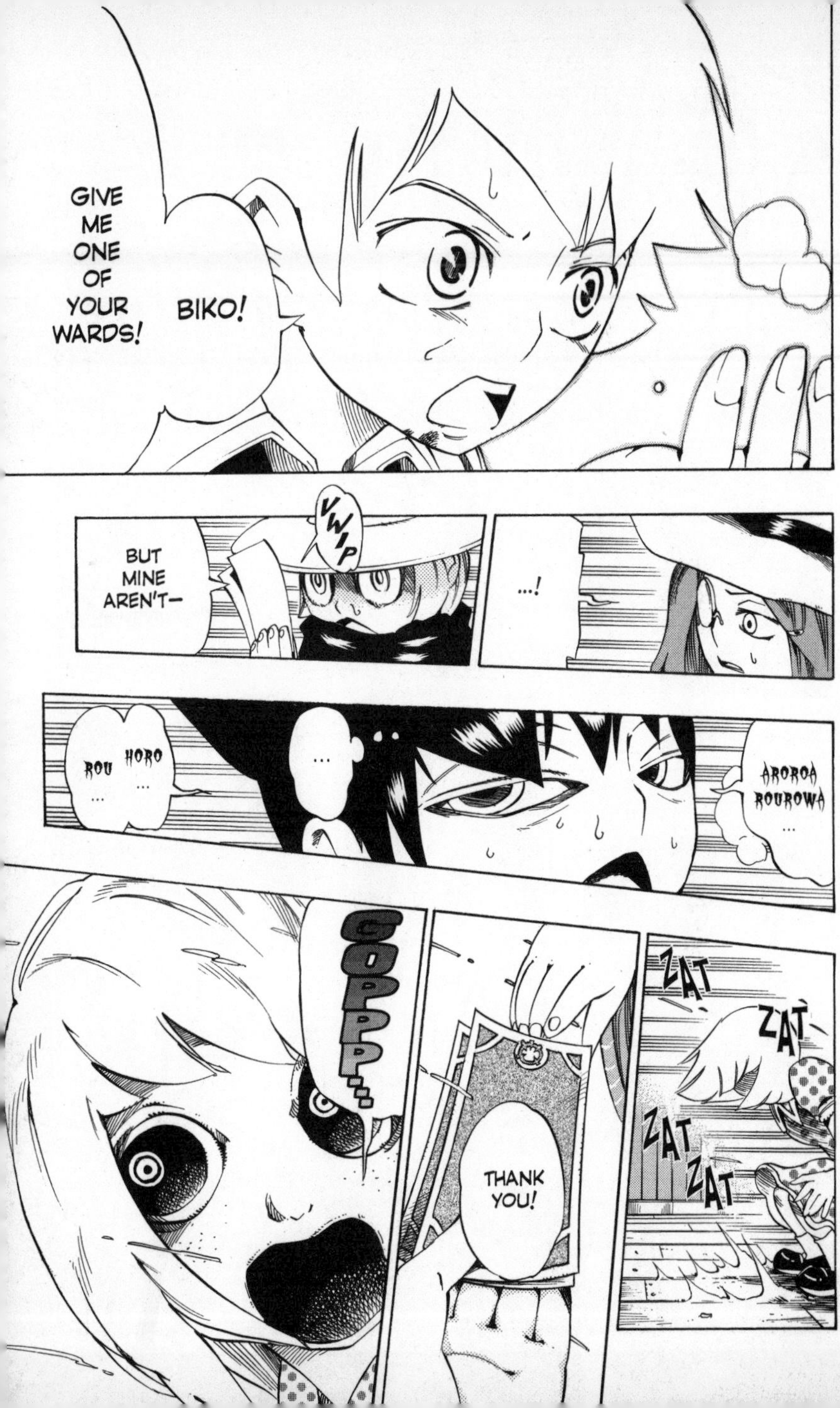
BIKO!
GIVE ME ONE OF YOUR WARDS!
...!
VWIP
BUT MINE AREN'T—
ARORA ROUROWA ...
...
ROU ... HORO ...
ZAT
ZAT
ZAT
ZAT
THANK YOU!
GOPPP...

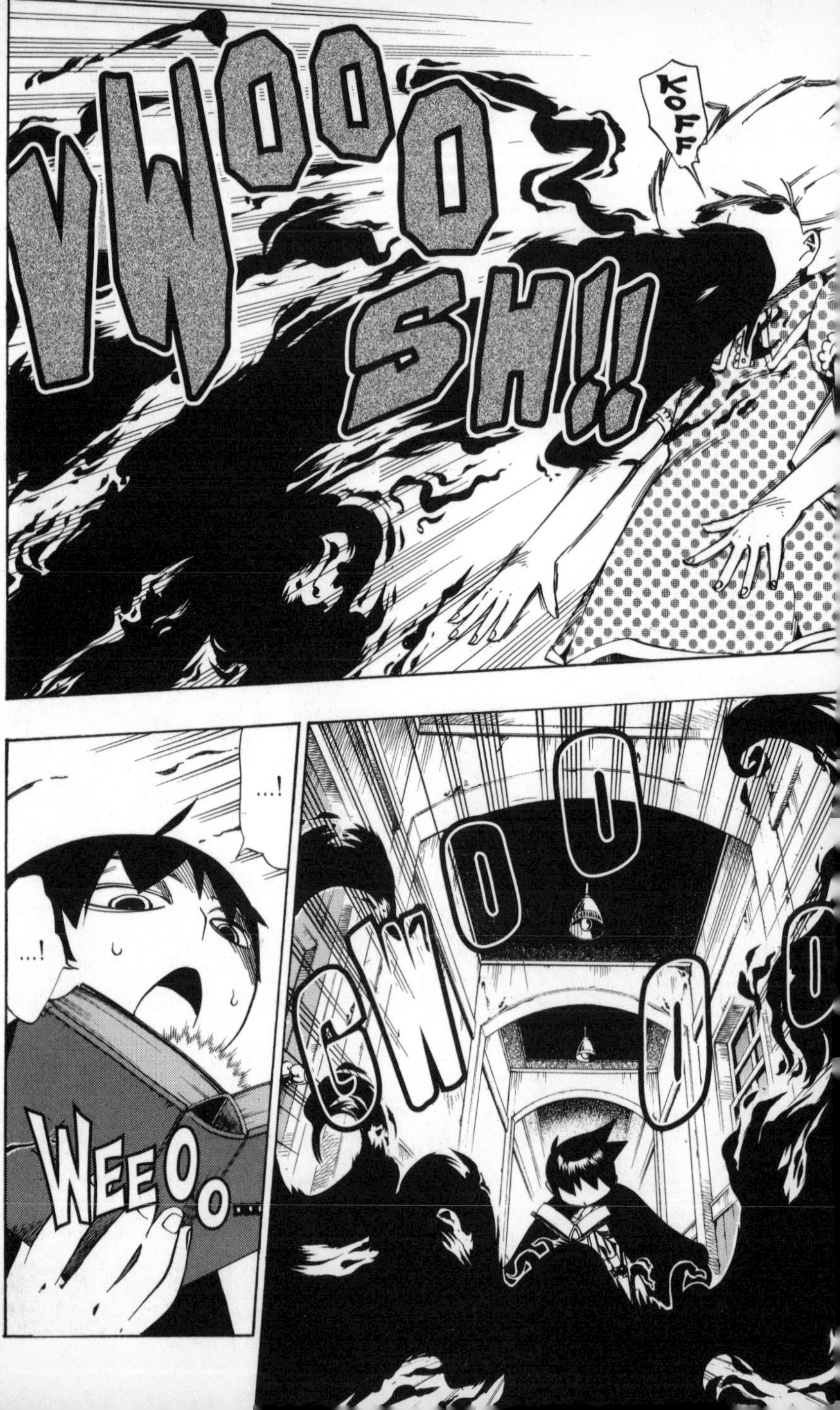
KOFF
VWOOOSH!!
GWOOOOOO
...!
...!
WEEOo...

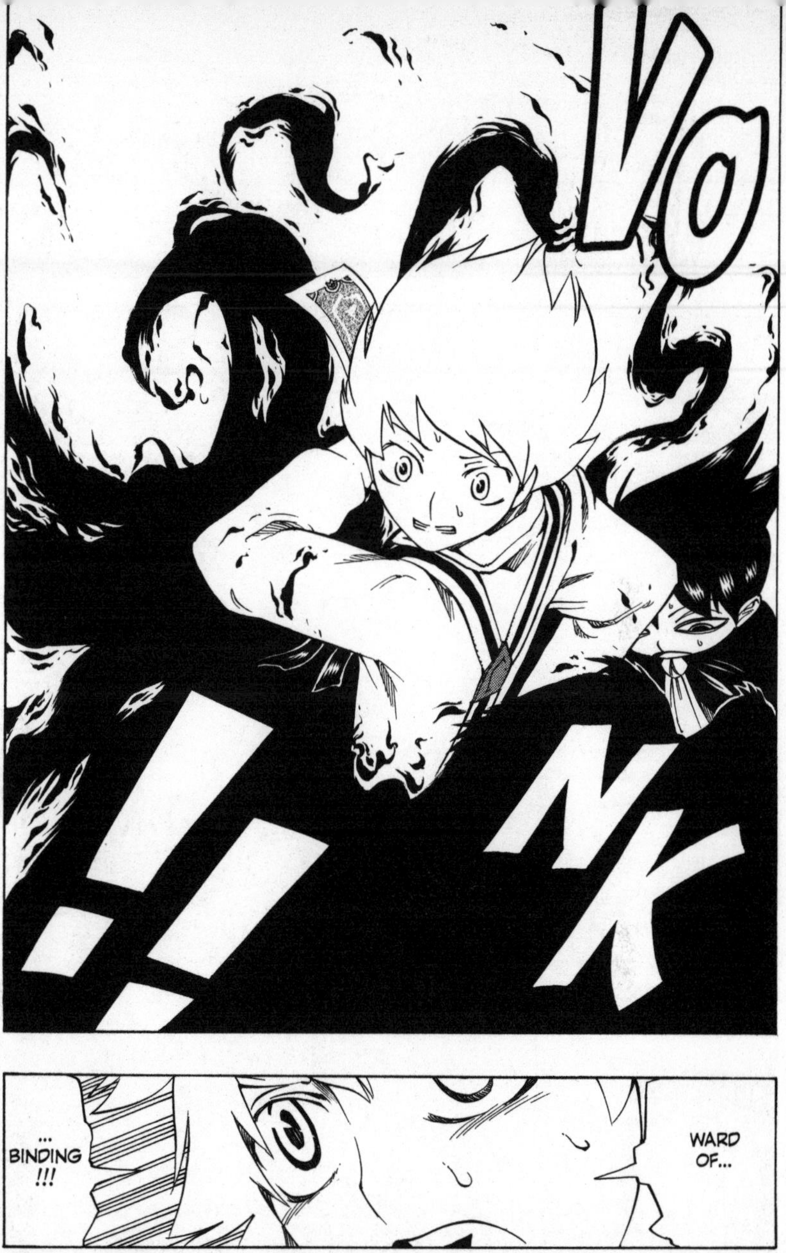
VO
NK!!
WARD OF...
...BINDING!!!

I'LL PROTECT MUHYO!

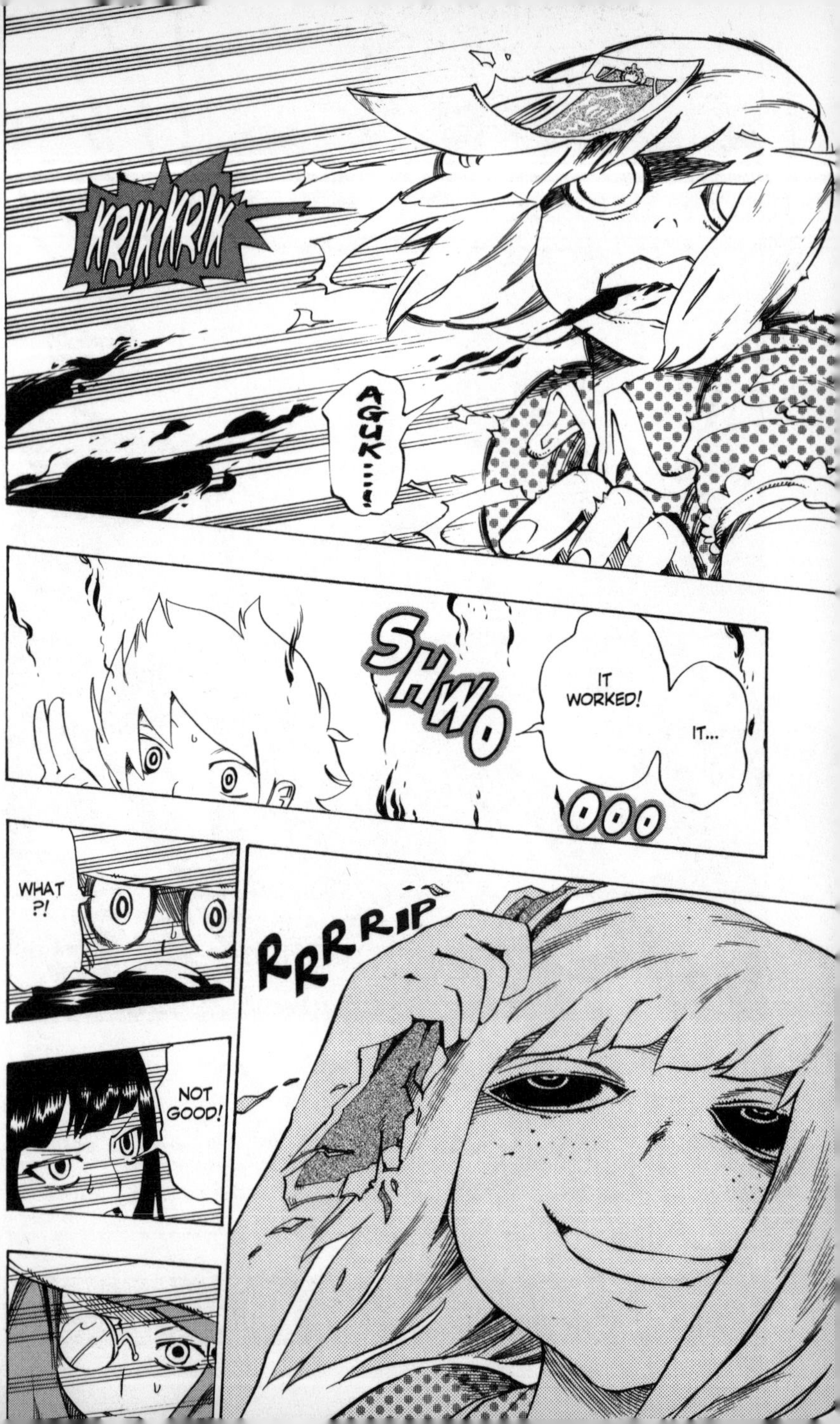
KRIK KRIK
AGUK...!!
SHWOOOO
IT WORKED!
IT...
RRRRIP
WHAT?!
NOT GOOD!

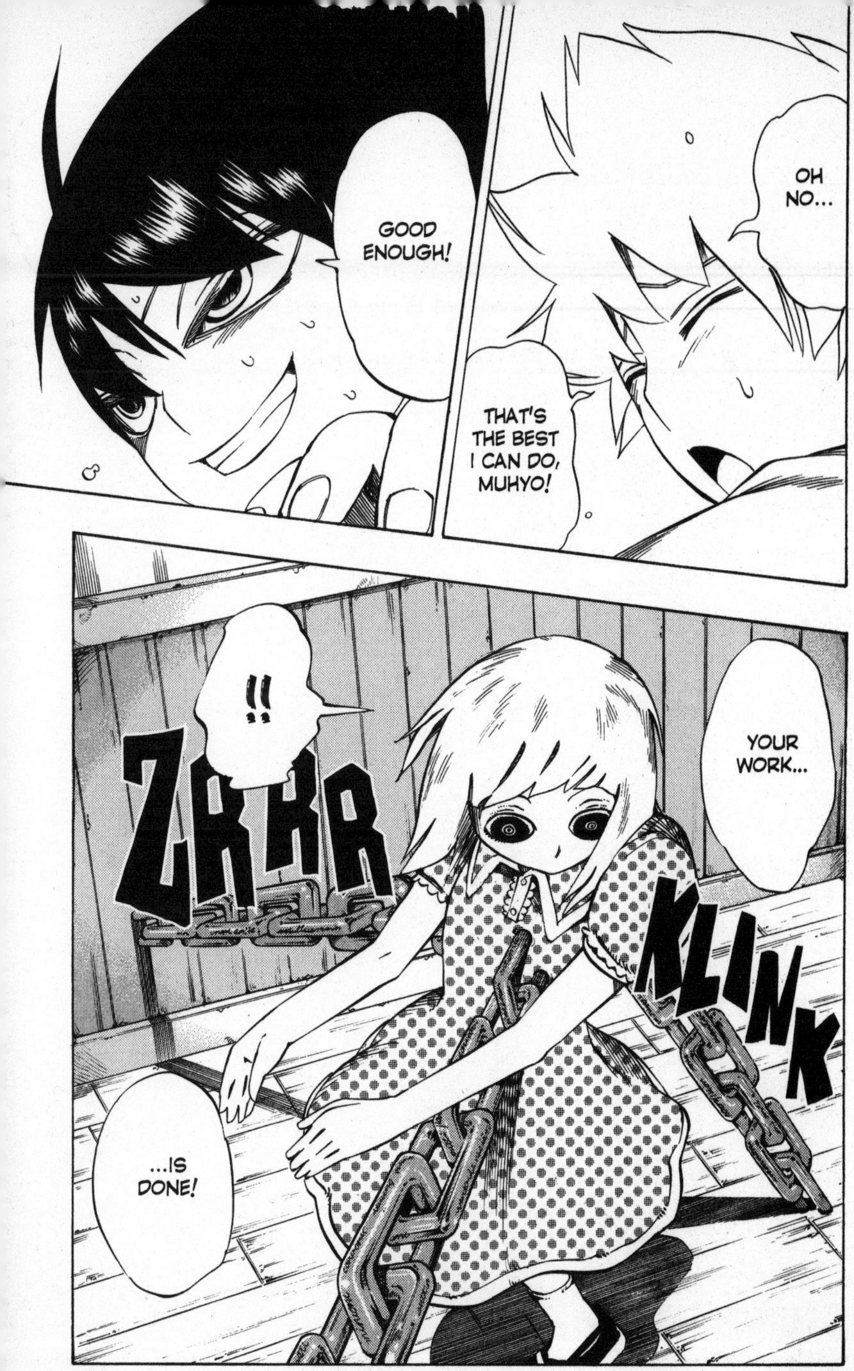
OH NO...
THAT'S THE BEST I CAN DO, MUHYO!
GOOD ENOUGH!
YOUR WORK...
KLINK
!!
ZRRR
...IS DONE!

REIKO IMAI
BIRTHDAY: FEBRUARY 10
HEIGHT: 164 CM
LIKES: MILK
      CHEESE (ALL DAIRY PRODUCTS)
      PICKLED FOOD (ESPECIALLY PICKLED ONIONS!)

TALENTS: MEMORIZATION (AND RECITATION)
        KENDO (5 DAN, REALLY GOOD)

NOT GOOD WITH: ASTROLOGY
              (DISTURBS HER, SO SHE AVOIDS IT)

ARTICLE 29
SAD TIMES AHEAD

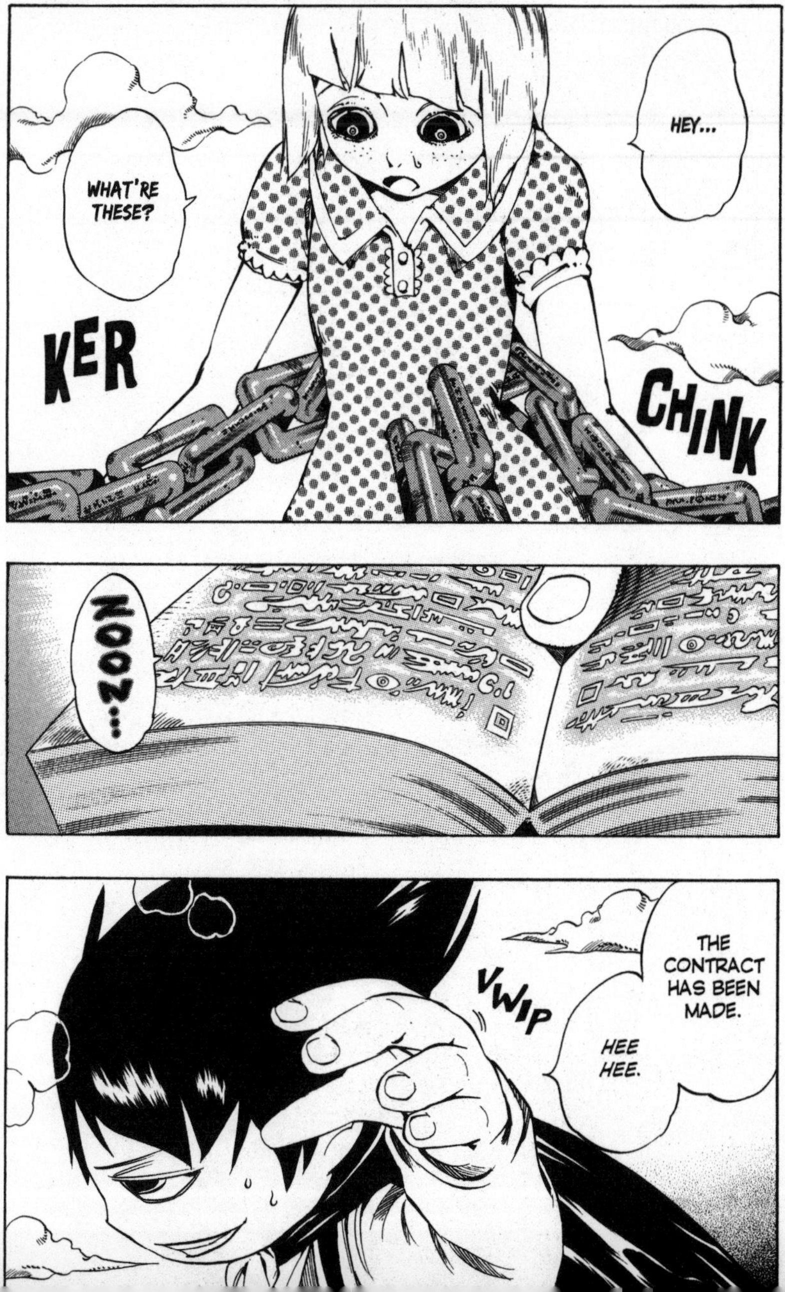
HEY...
WHAT'RE THESE?
KER
CHINK
ZOON...
THE CONTRACT HAS BEEN MADE.
HEE HEE.
VWIP

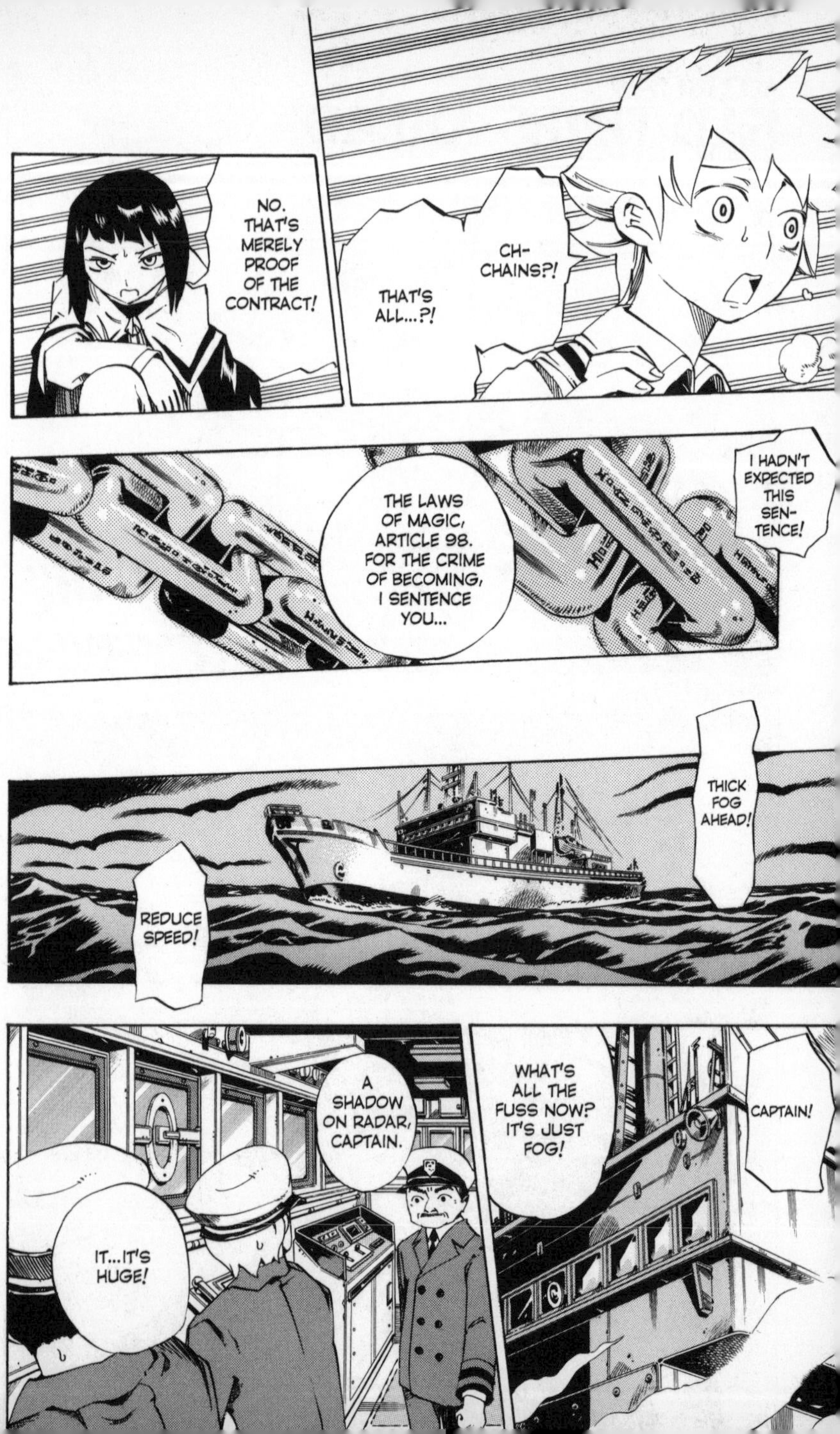
CH- CHAINS?!
THAT'S ALL...?!
NO. THAT'S MERELY PROOF OF THE CONTRACT!
I HADN'T EXPECTED THIS SEN- TENCE!
THE LAWS OF MAGIC, ARTICLE 98. FOR THE CRIME OF BECOMING, I SENTENCE YOU...
THICK FOG AHEAD!
REDUCE SPEED!
CAPTAIN!
WHAT'S ALL THE FUSS NOW? IT'S JUST FOG!
A SHADOW ON RADAR, CAPTAIN.
IT...IT'S HUGE!

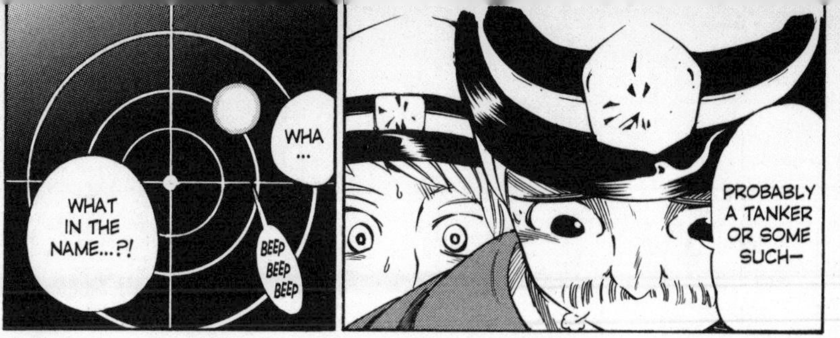
PROBABLY A TANKER OR SOME SUCH—
WHA ...
WHAT IN THE NAME...?!
BEEP BEEP BEEP

ARTICLE 29
SAD TIMES AHEAD

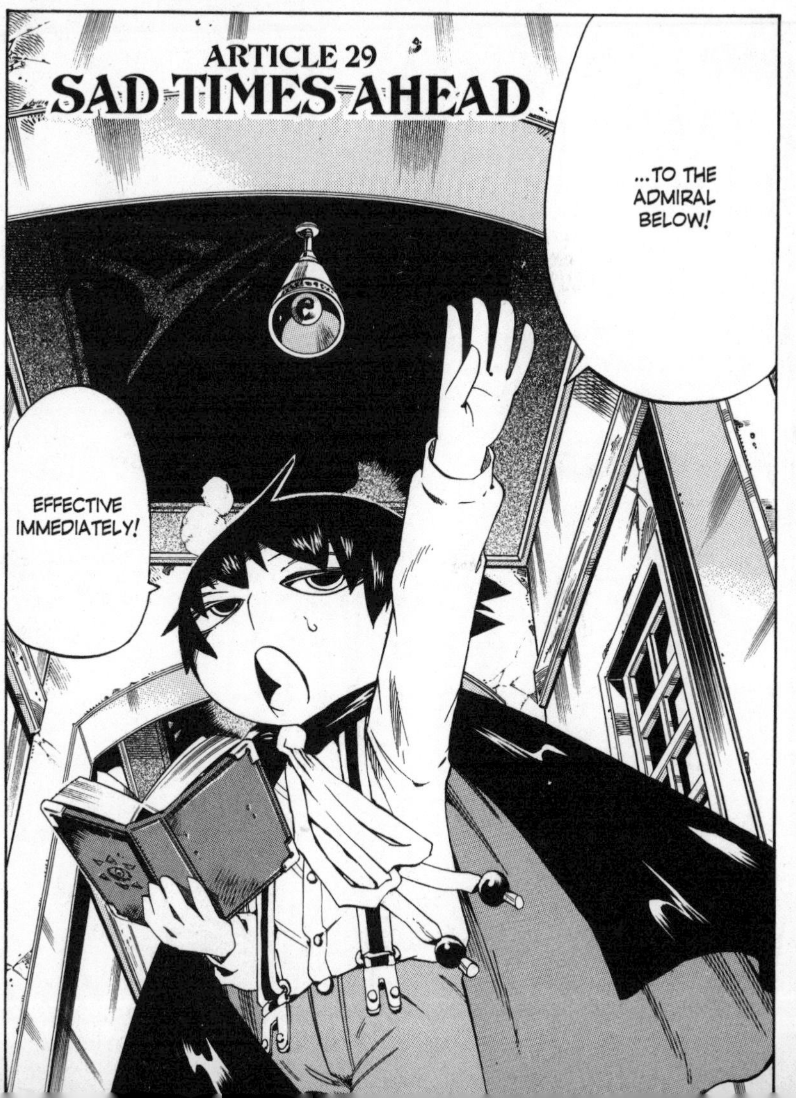
...TO THE ADMIRAL BELOW!
EFFECTIVE IMMEDIATELY!

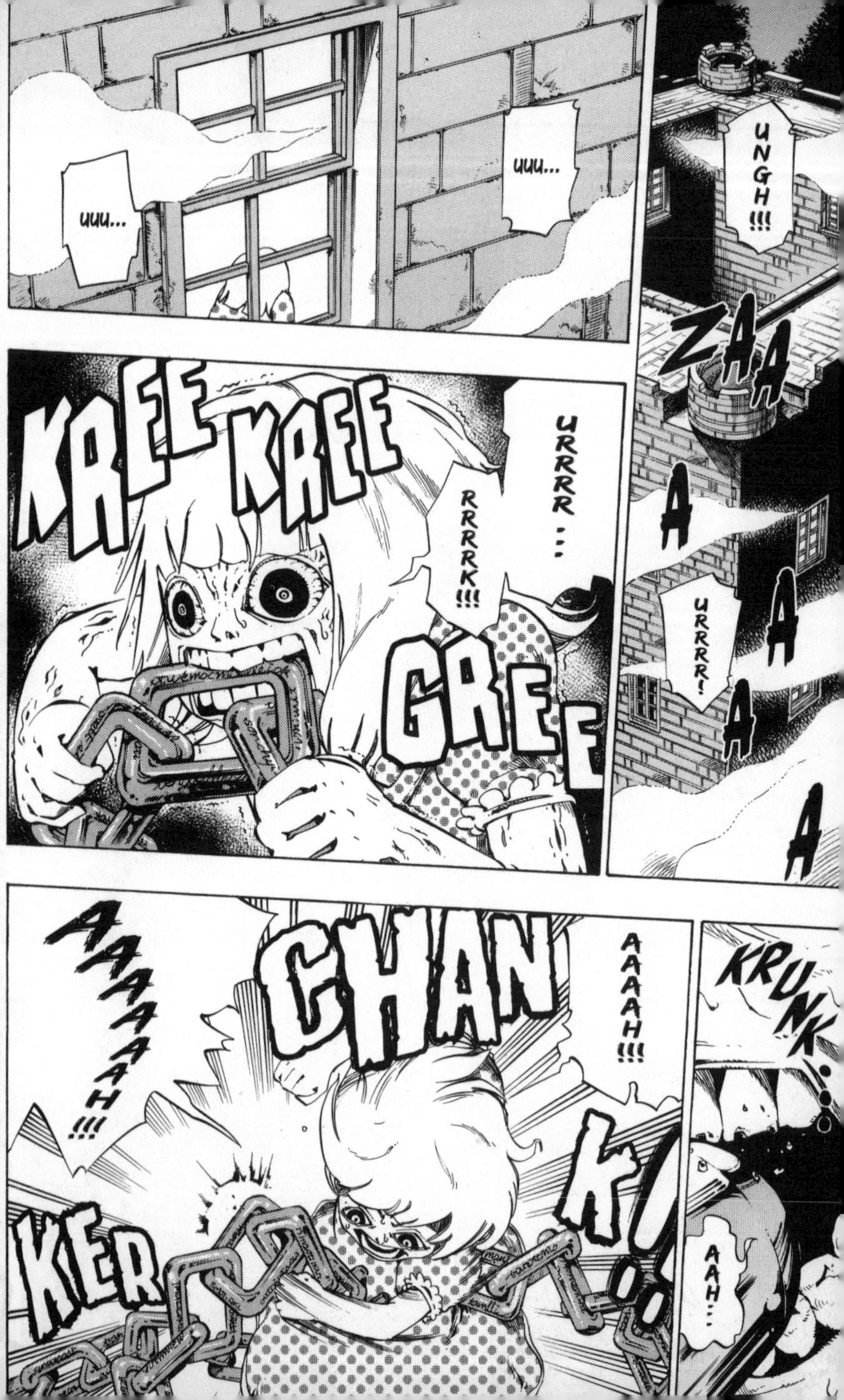
UNGH!!!
ZAAAAAAA
URRRR!
uuu...
uuu...
URRRR...
RRRRK!!!
GREE
KREE KREE
KRUNK...
AAH...
AAAAH!!!
KER CHANK!
AAAAAAAAH!!!

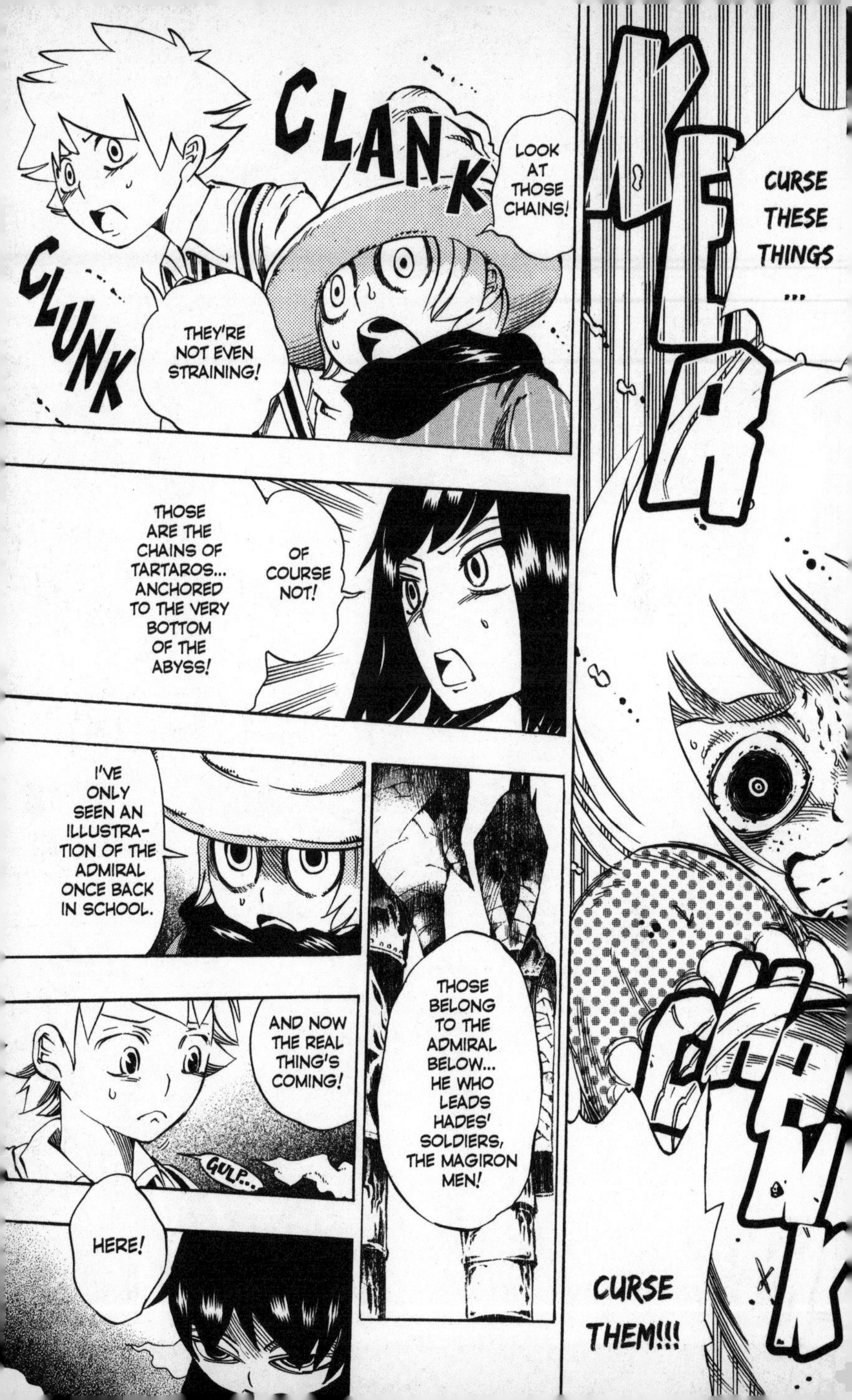
CURSE THESE THINGS...
CURSE THEM!!!
CLANK
LOOK AT THOSE CHAINS!
CLUNK
THEY'RE NOT EVEN STRAINING!
OF COURSE NOT!
THOSE ARE THE CHAINS OF TARTAROS... ANCHORED TO THE VERY BOTTOM OF THE ABYSS!
THOSE BELONG TO THE ADMIRAL BELOW... HE WHO LEADS HADES' SOLDIERS, THE MAGIRON MEN!
I'VE ONLY SEEN AN ILLUSTRATION OF THE ADMIRAL ONCE BACK IN SCHOOL.
AND NOW THE REAL THING'S COMING!
GULP...
HERE!

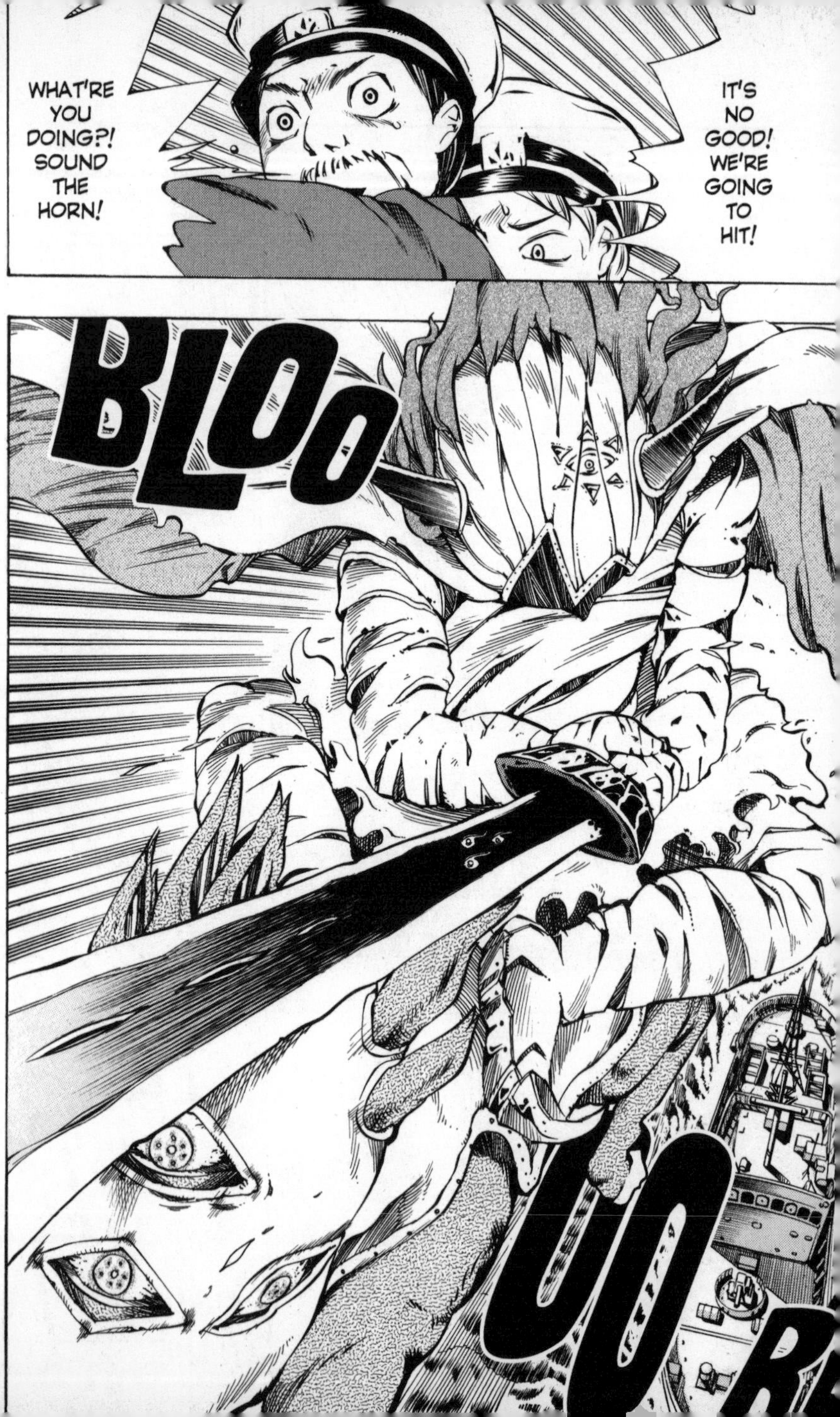
IT'S NO GOOD! WE'RE GOING TO HIT!
WHAT'RE YOU DOING?! SOUND THE HORN!
BLOO
OOR

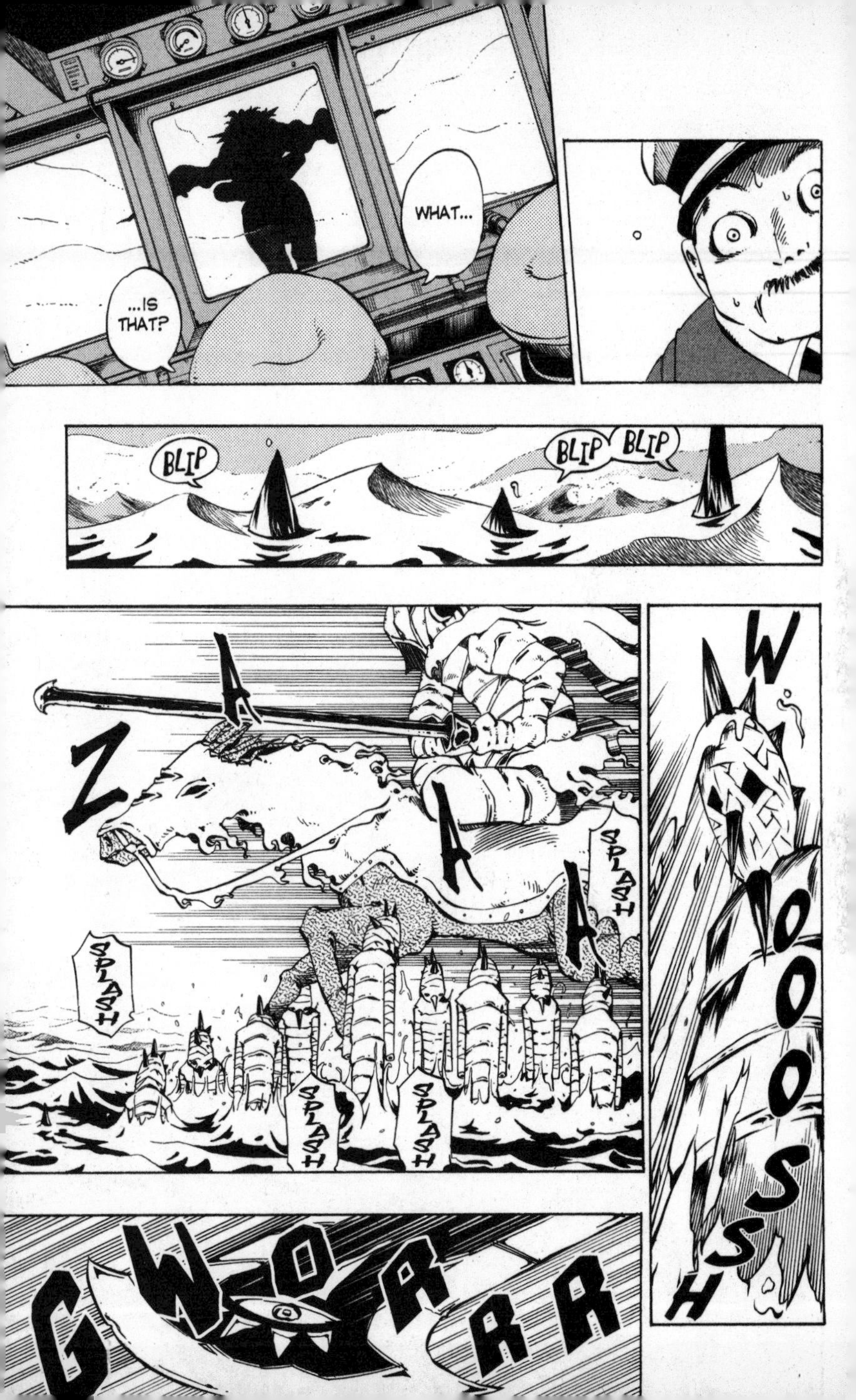
WHAT...
...IS THAT?
BLIP
BLIP
BLIP
WOOOOSSH
ZAAAA
SPLASH
SPLASH
SPLASH
SPLASH
GWORRR

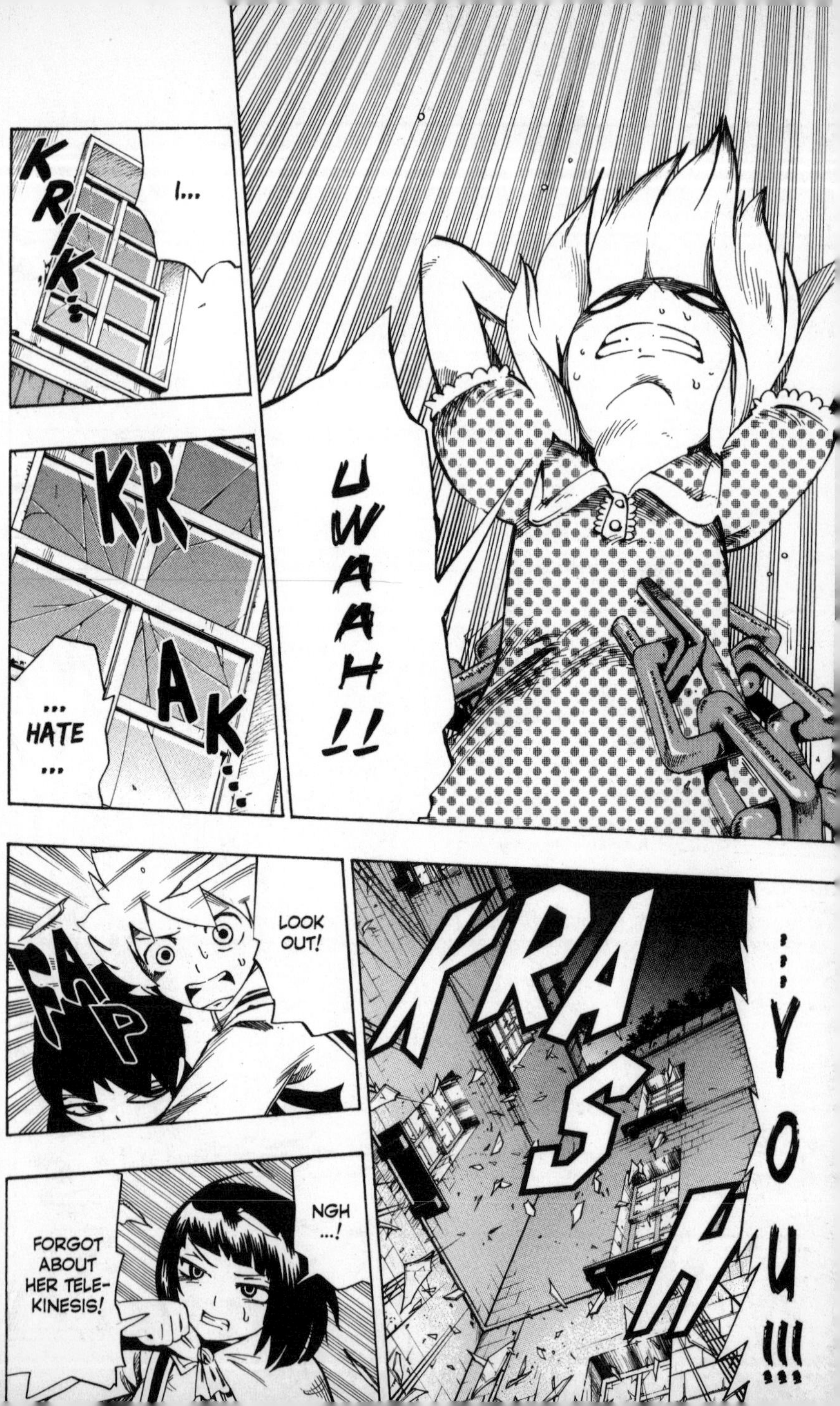
UWAAAH!!
KRIK
I...
KRAK
...HATE...
KRASH
...YOU!!!
LOOK OUT!
FAP
NGH...!
FORGOT ABOUT HER TELE-KINESIS!

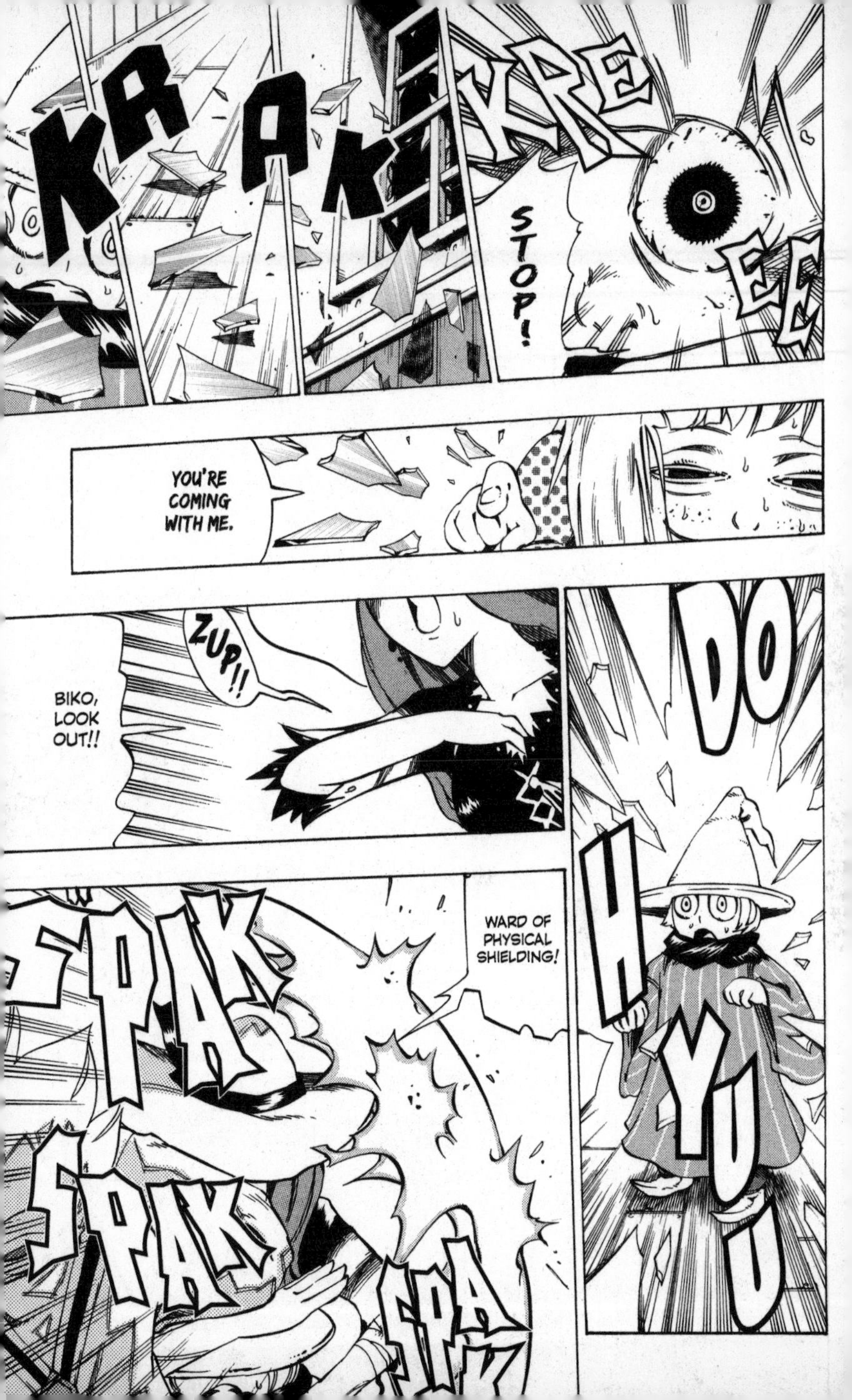
KRAKKREEE
STOP!
YOU'RE COMING WITH ME.
DOHYUU
BIKO, LOOK OUT!!
ZUP!!
WARD OF PHYSICAL SHIELDING!
SPAK
SPAK
SPA

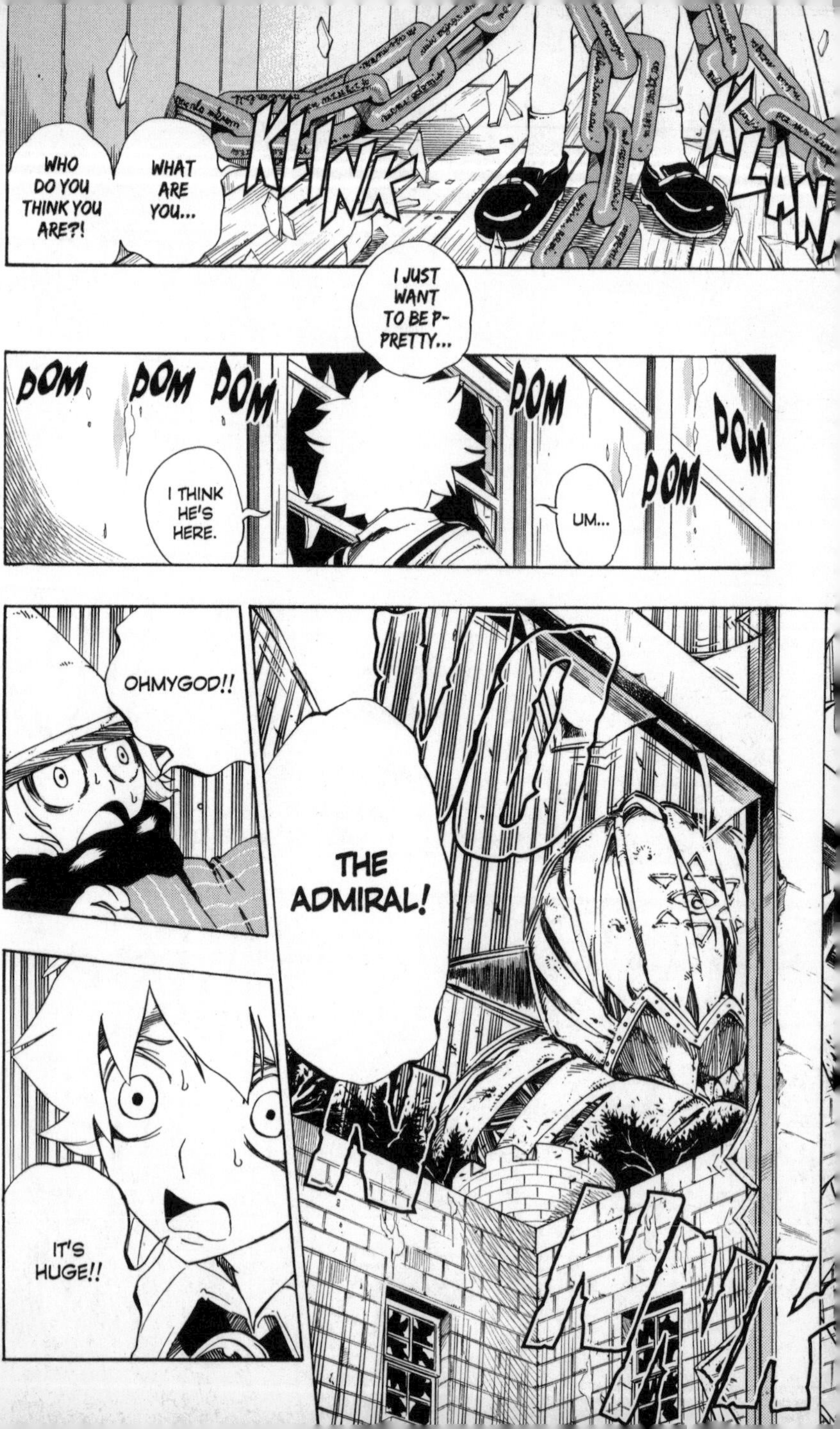
KLAN
KLINK
WHAT ARE YOU...
WHO DO YOU THINK YOU ARE?!
I JUST WANT TO BE P-PRETTY...
DOM
DOM
DOM
UM...
DOM DOM DOM
I THINK HE'S HERE.
THE ADMIRAL!
OHMYGOD!!
IT'S HUGE!!

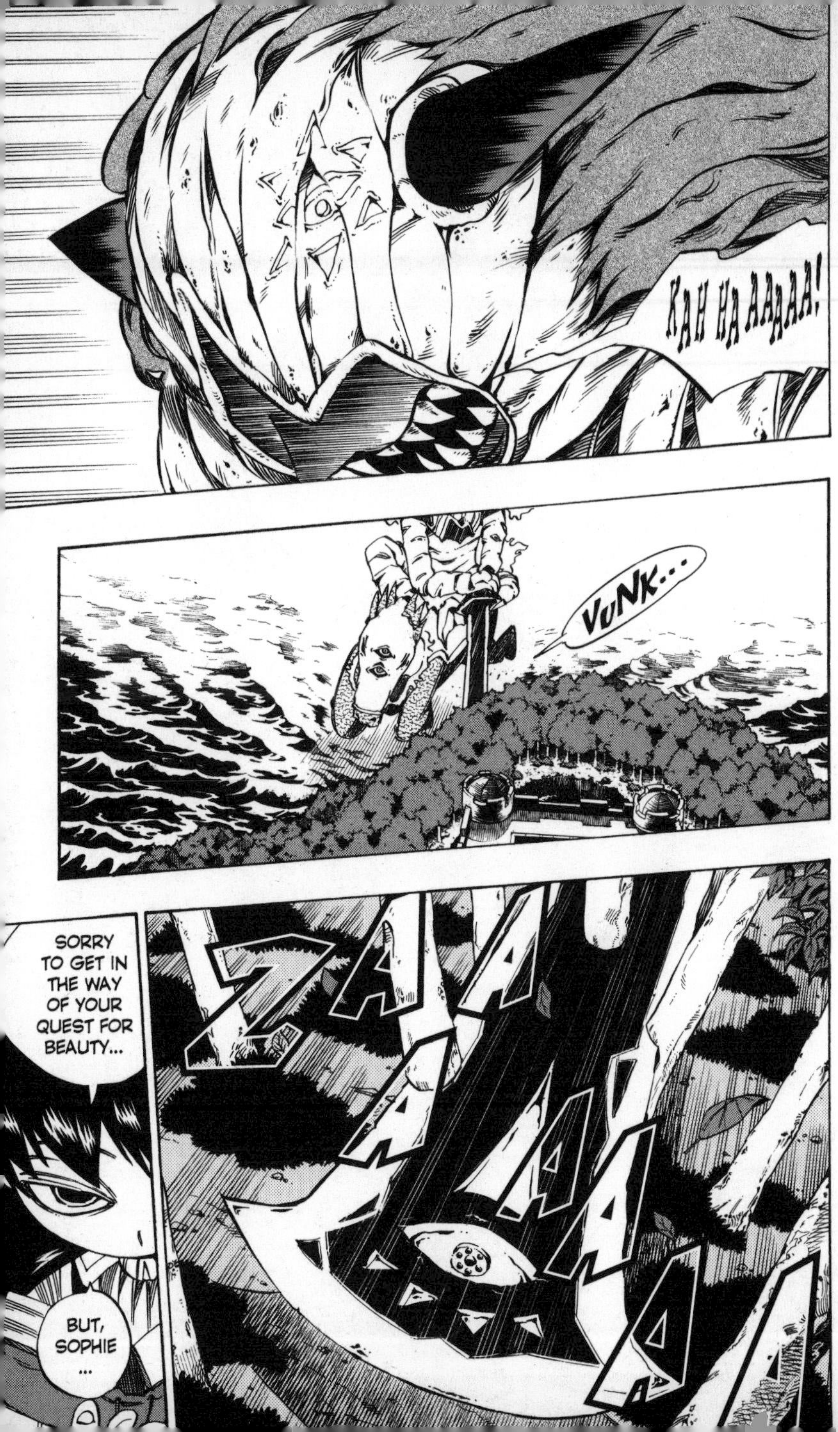
KAH HA AAAAAA!
VUNK...
ZAAAAAAA
SORRY TO GET IN THE WAY OF YOUR QUEST FOR BEAUTY...
BUT, SOPHIE...

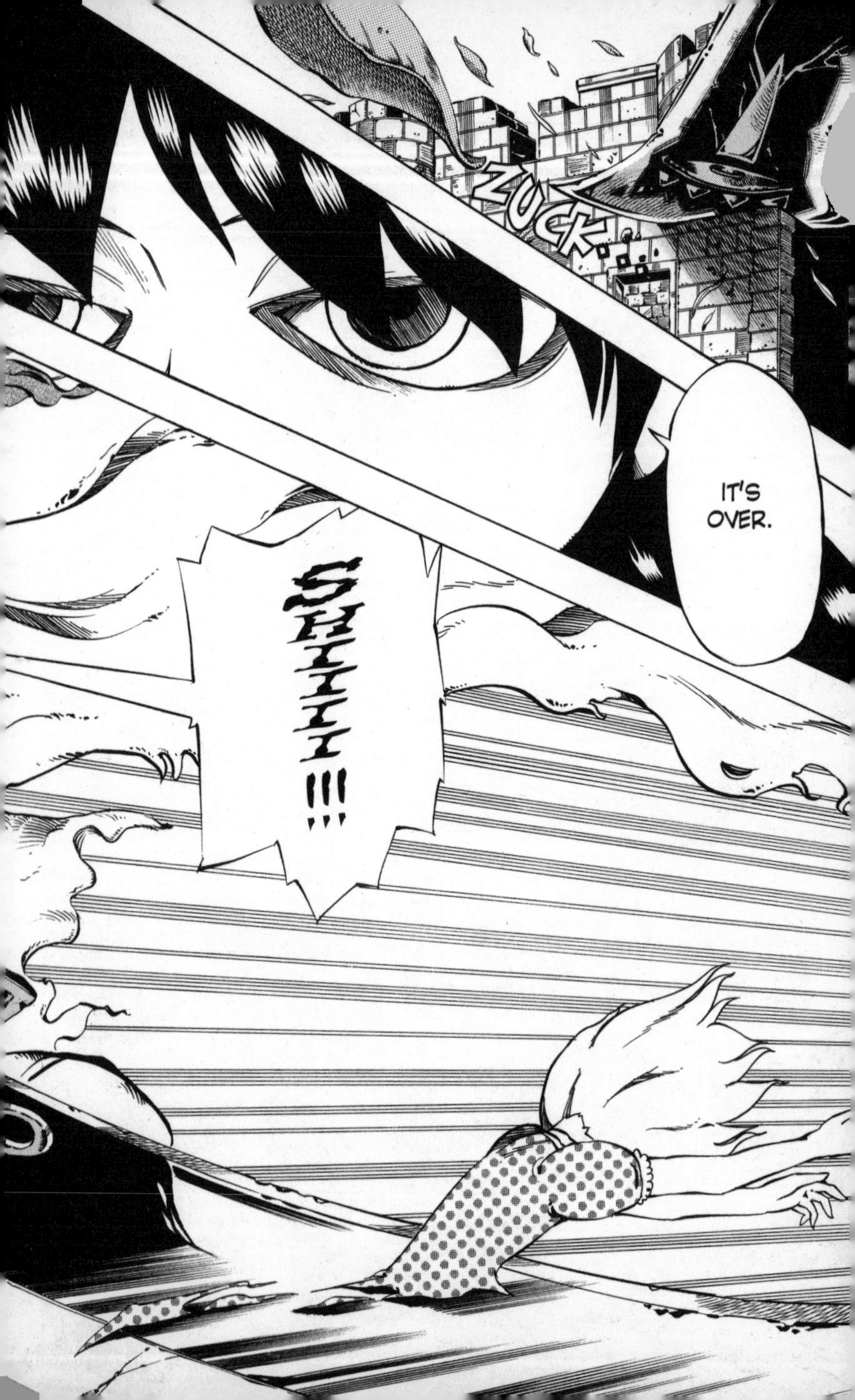
ZUCK
IT'S OVER.
SHIIIII!!!

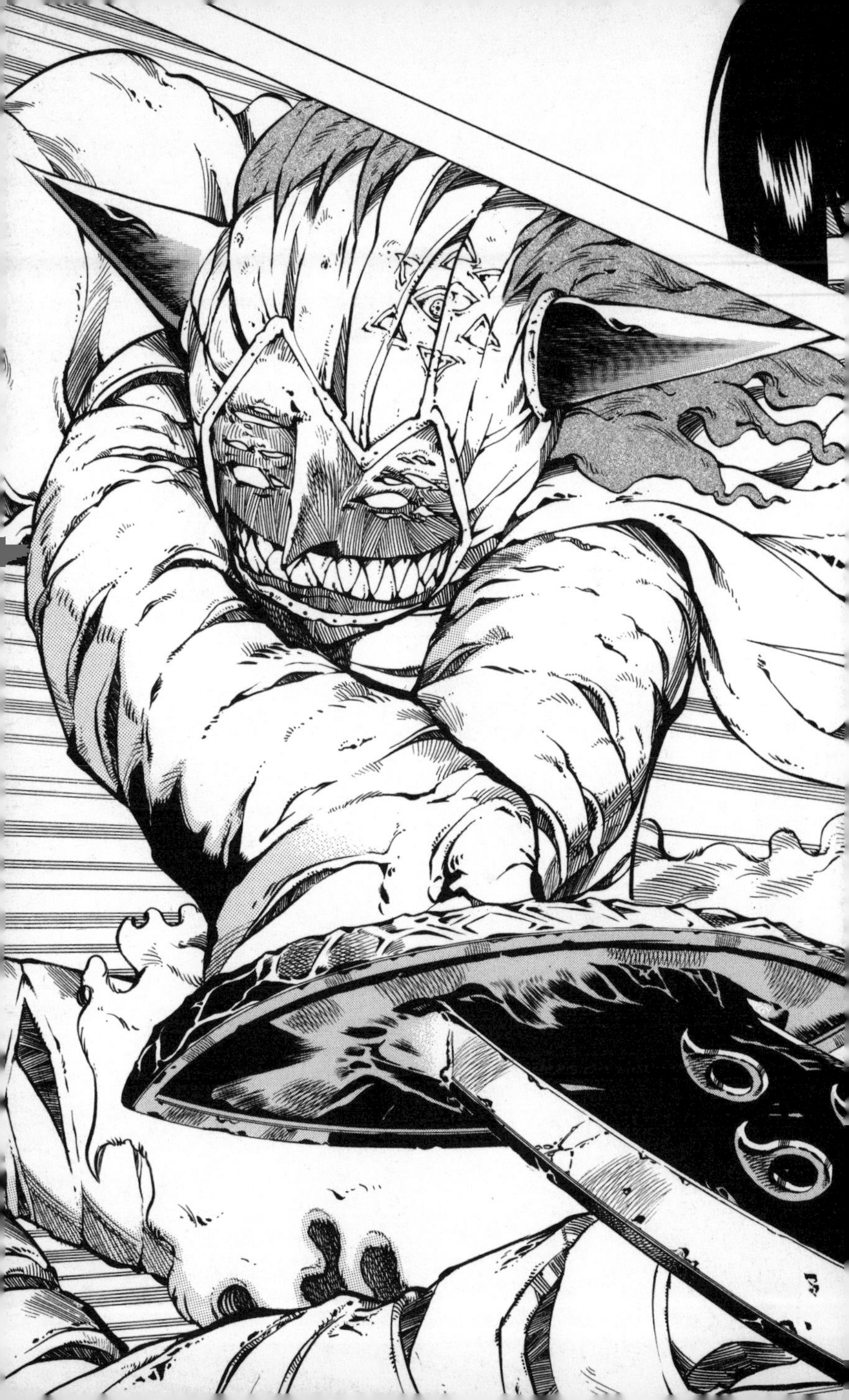

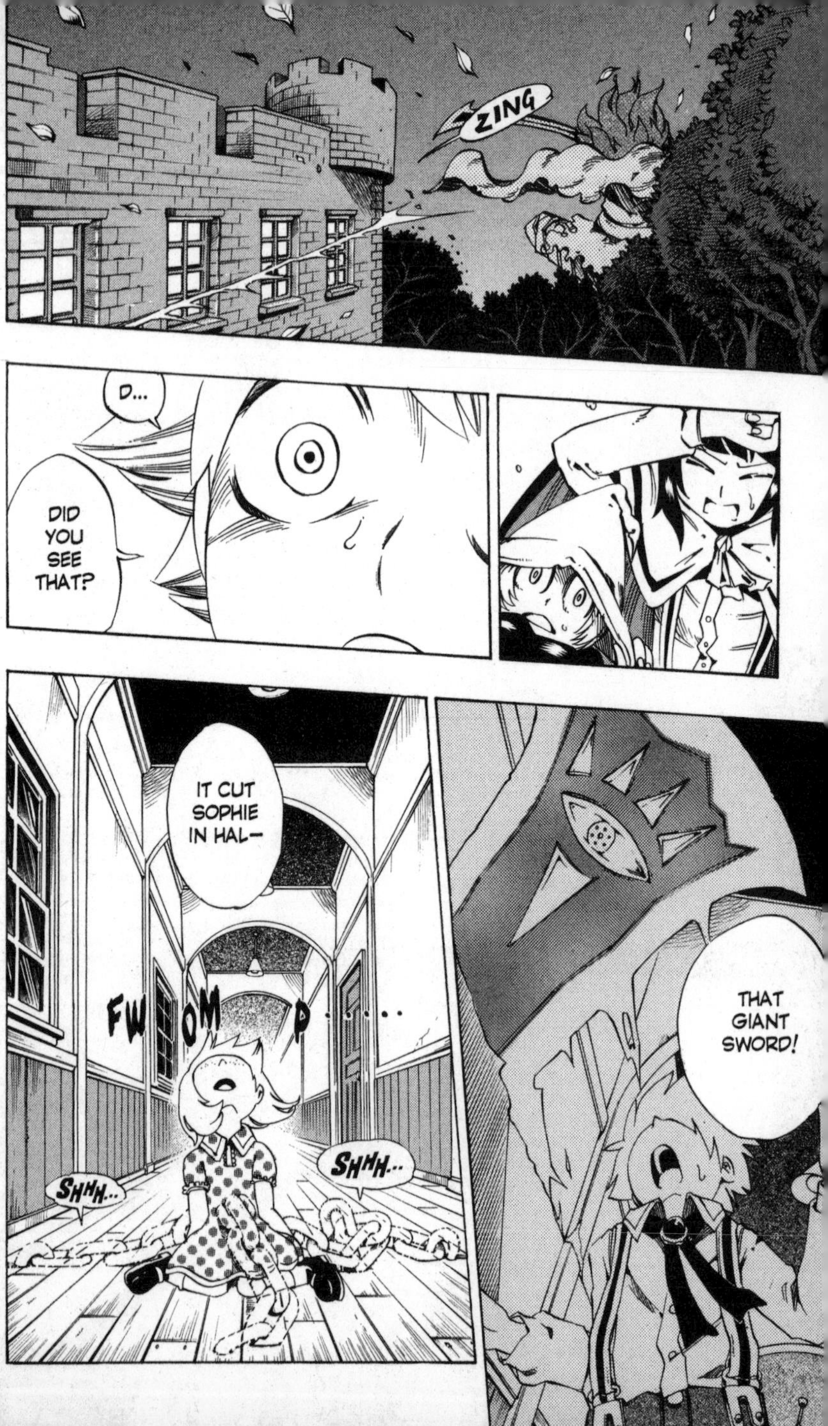
ZING
D...
DID YOU SEE THAT?
THAT GIANT SWORD!
IT CUT SOPHIE IN HAL—
FWOMP......
SHHH...
SHHH...

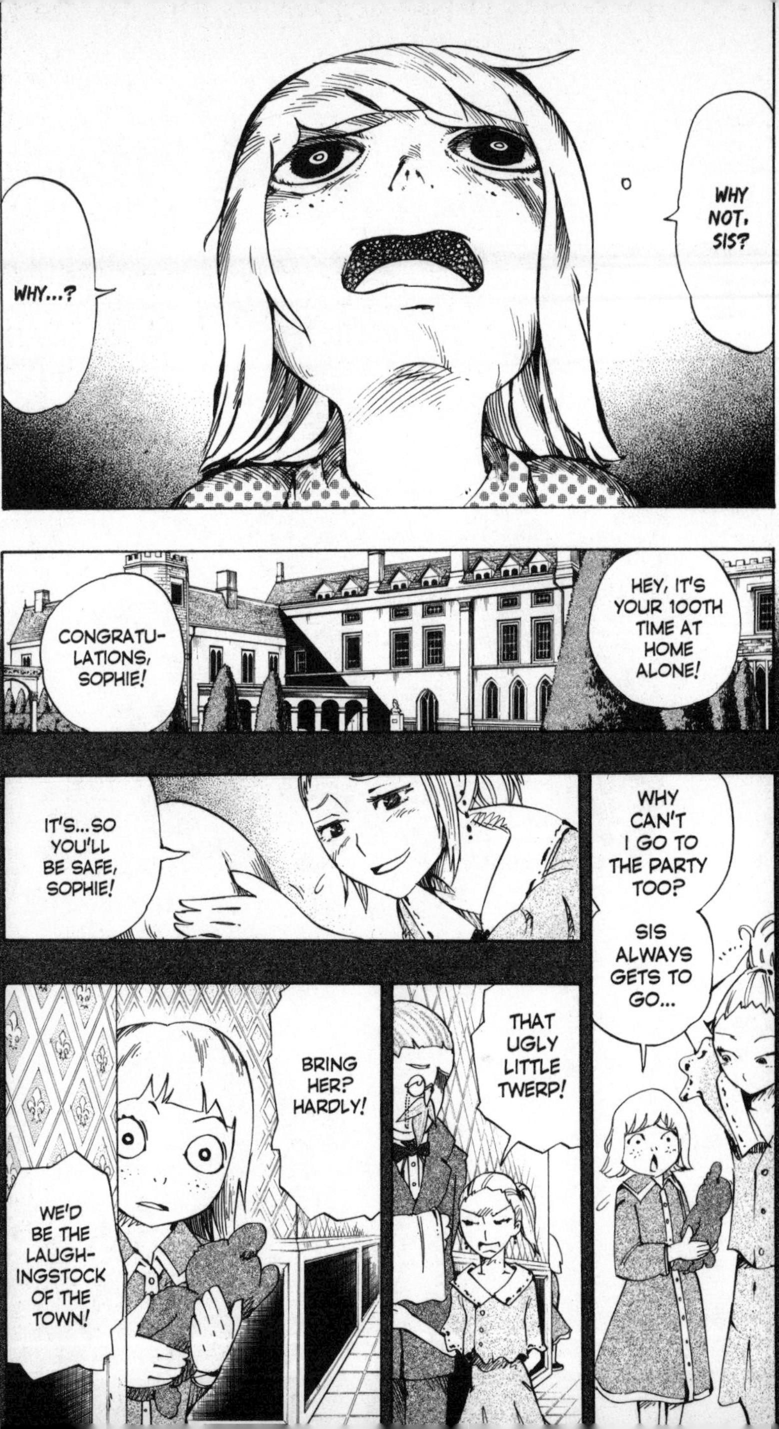
WHY NOT, SIS?
WHY...?
HEY, IT'S YOUR 100TH TIME AT HOME ALONE!
CONGRATU-LATIONS, SOPHIE!
WHY CAN'T I GO TO THE PARTY TOO?
SIS ALWAYS GETS TO GO...
...
IT'S...SO YOU'LL BE SAFE, SOPHIE!
THAT UGLY LITTLE TWERP!
BRING HER? HARDLY!
WE'D BE THE LAUGH-INGSTOCK OF THE TOWN!

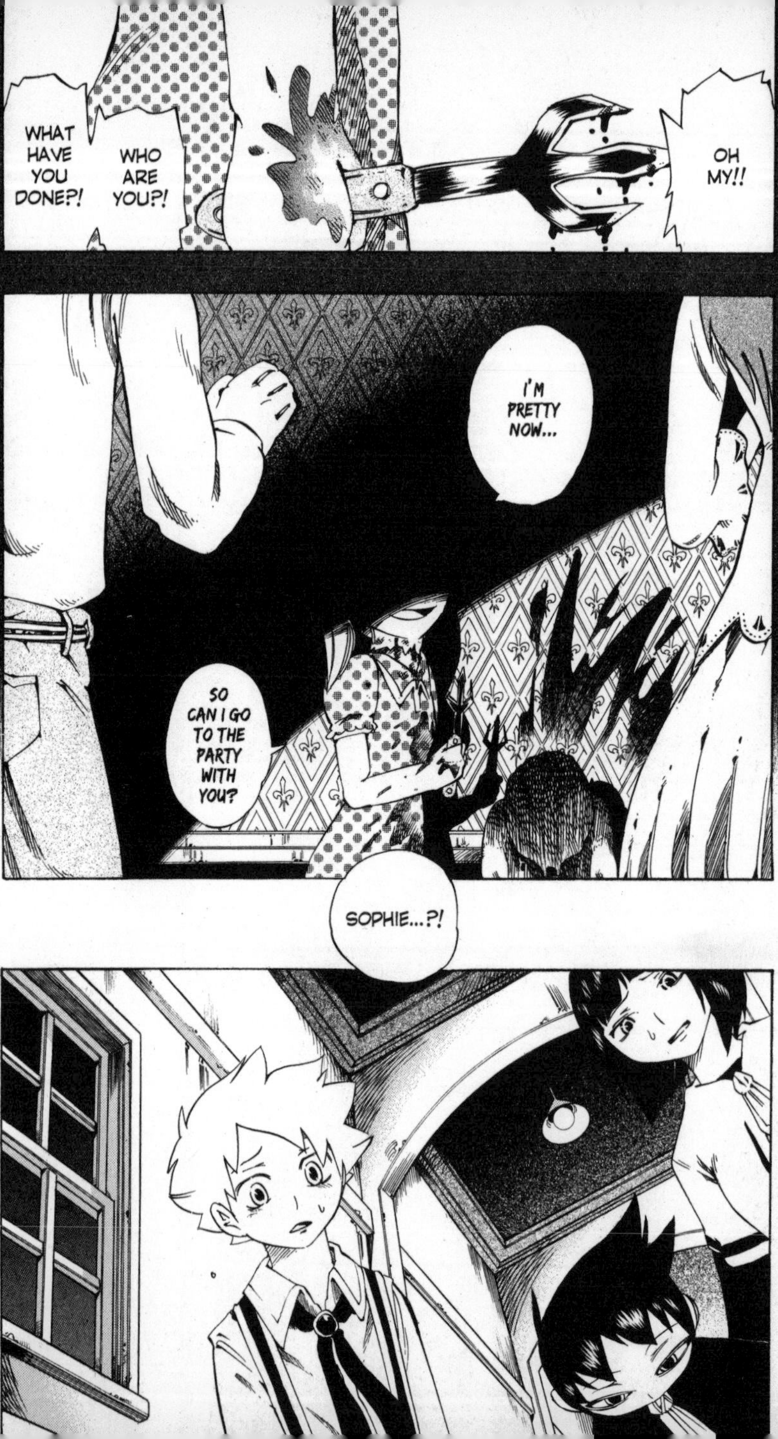
OH MY!!
WHO ARE YOU?!
WHAT HAVE YOU DONE?!
I'M PRETTY NOW...
SO CAN I GO TO THE PARTY WITH YOU?
SOPHIE...?!

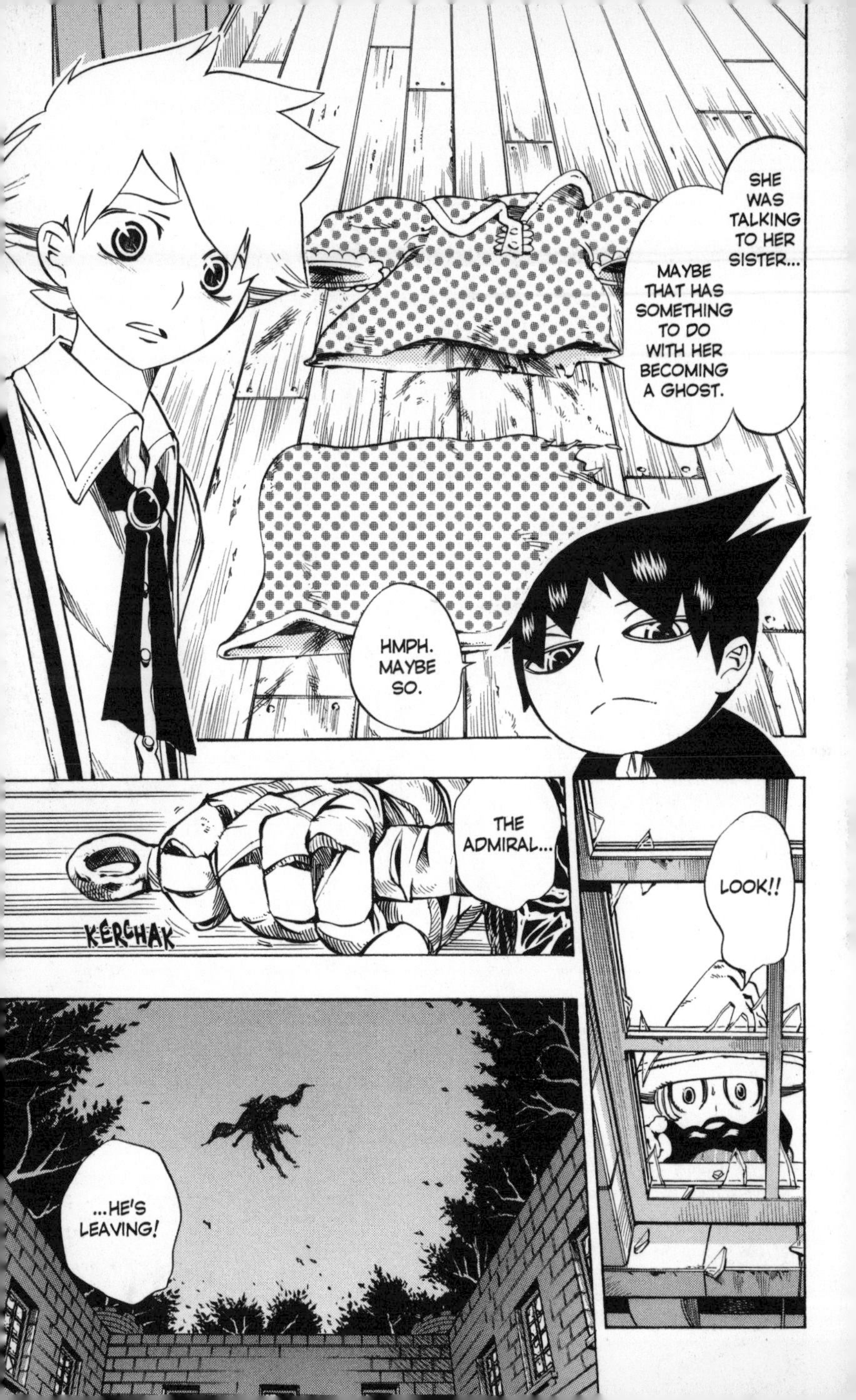
SHE WAS TALKING TO HER SISTER...
MAYBE THAT HAS SOMETHING TO DO WITH HER BECOMING A GHOST.
HMPH. MAYBE SO.
LOOK!!
THE ADMIRAL...
KERCHAK
...HE'S LEAVING!

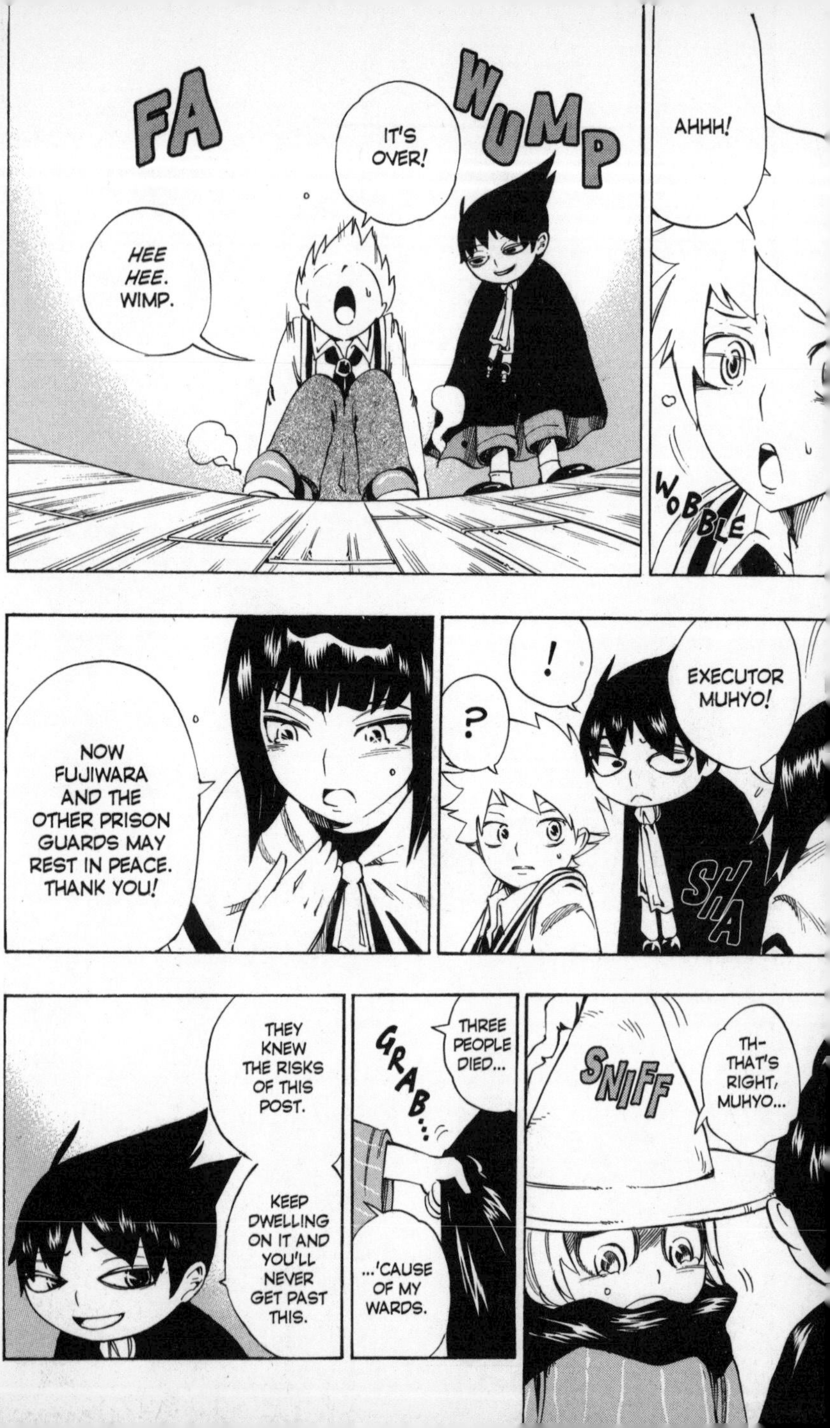
AHHH!
WOBBLE
FAWUMP
IT'S OVER!
HEE HEE. WIMP.
EXECUTOR MUHYO!
!
?
SHA
NOW FUJIWARA AND THE OTHER PRISON GUARDS MAY REST IN PEACE. THANK YOU!
TH- THAT'S RIGHT, MUHYO...
SNIFF
THREE PEOPLE DIED...
GRAB...
...'CAUSE OF MY WARDS.
THEY KNEW THE RISKS OF THIS POST.
KEEP DWELLING ON IT AND YOU'LL NEVER GET PAST THIS.

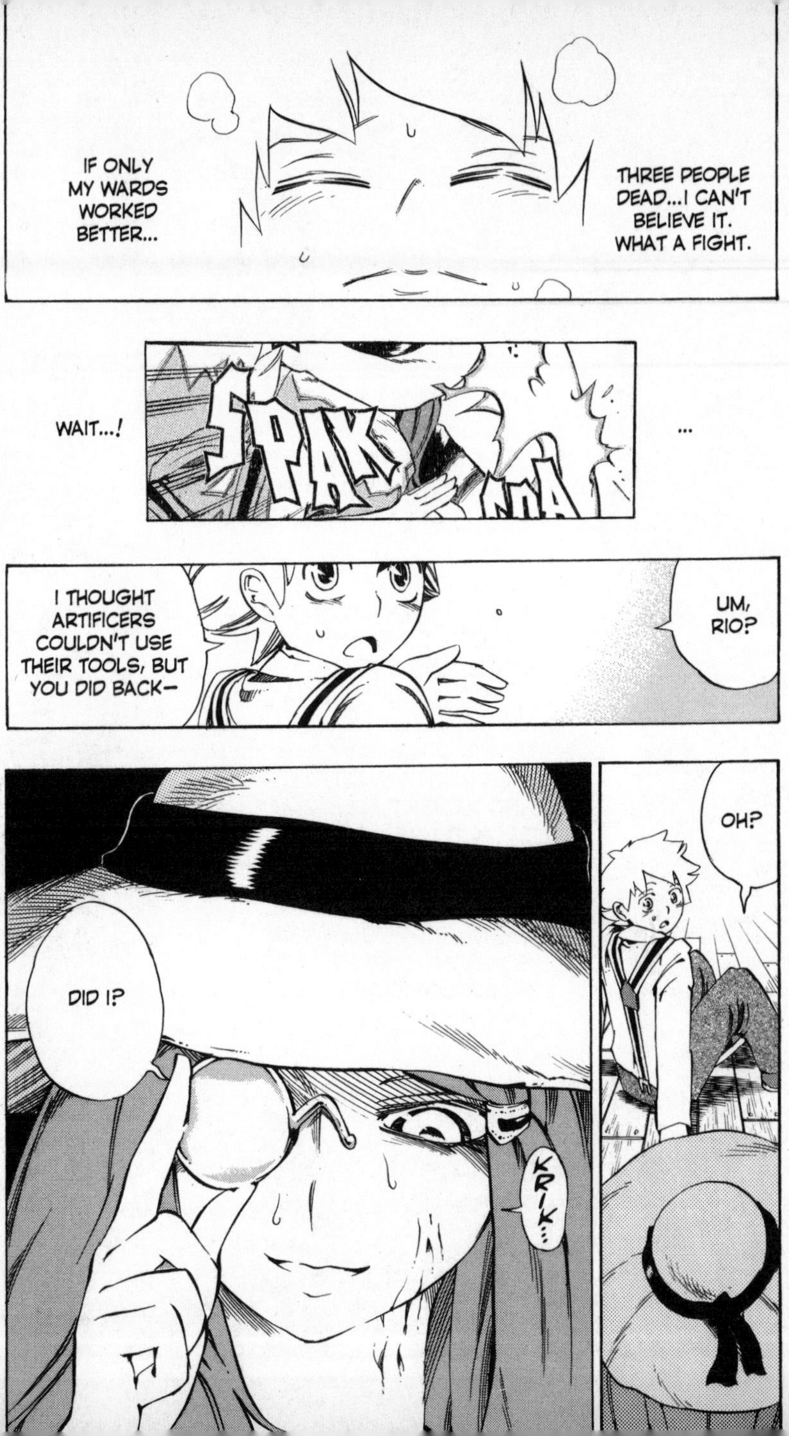
THREE PEOPLE DEAD...I CAN'T BELIEVE IT. WHAT A FIGHT.
IF ONLY MY WARDS WORKED BETTER...
...
SPAK
WAIT...!
UM, RIO?
I THOUGHT ARTIFICERS COULDN'T USE THEIR TOOLS, BUT YOU DID BACK—
OH?
DID I?
KRIK...

Q: WHAT MADE YOU WANT TO
   BECOME A MANGA ARTIST?
   –K.Y. FROM AICHI PREFECTURE

A: BECAUSE THERE WAS A
   STORY I WANTED TO DRAW.
   I'D BEEN DRAWING MANGA
   SINCE 2ND GRADE, AND WHILE
   I LOST TRACK OF WHAT I WAS
   DOING EVERY NOW AND THEN,
   MY HEAD HAS ALWAYS BEEN
   FILLED WITH WILD FANTASIES
   AND ADVENTURE. "WHAT IF I
   TOOK THESE CHARACTERS AND
   MADE THEM DO THIS...HAH!")

   ...YOU GET THE IDEA. BUT
   SERIOUSLY, YOU THINK
   SOMEONE LIKE ME COULD
   GET A JOB DOING
   ANYTHING ELSE?

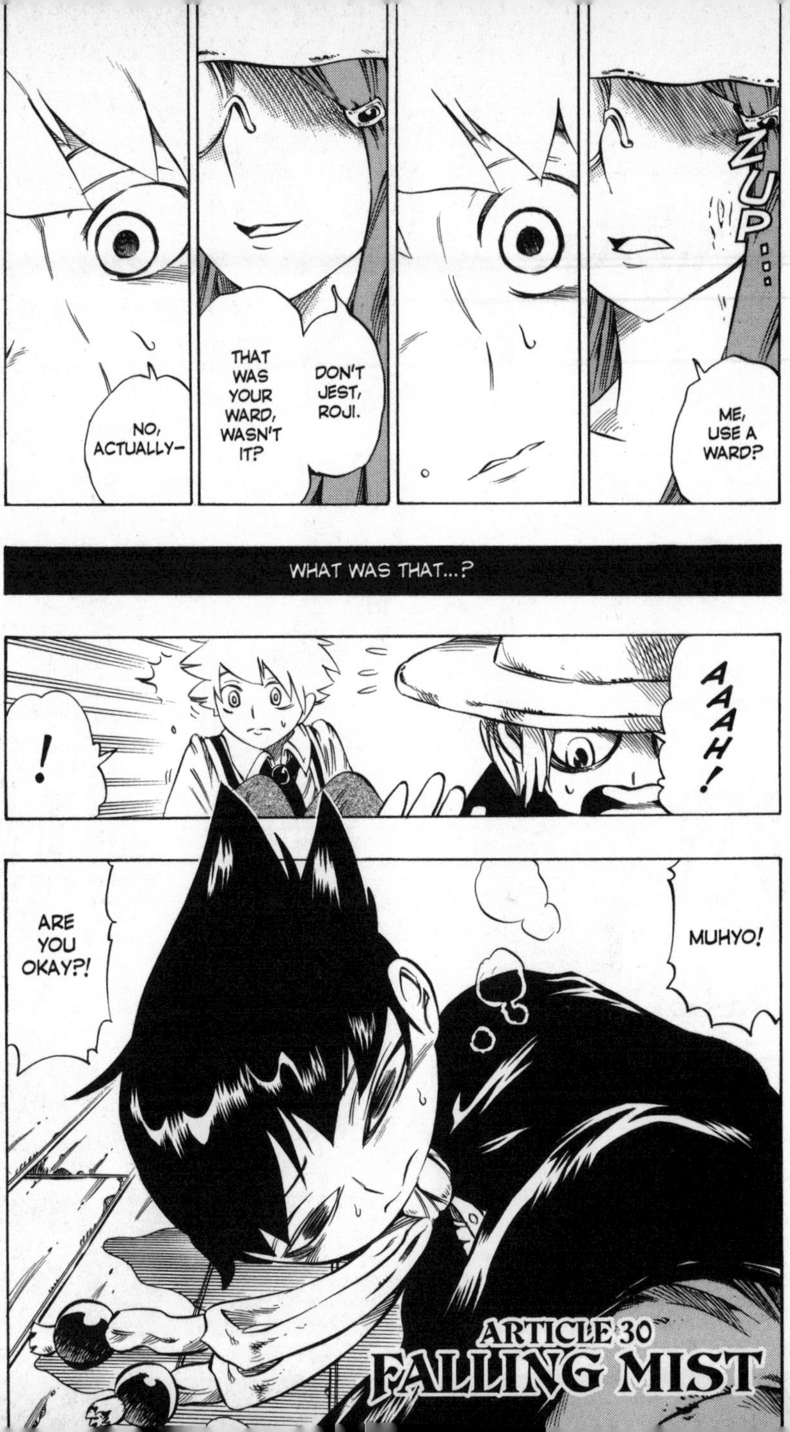
ZUP...
ME, USE A WARD?
DON'T JEST, ROJI.
THAT WAS YOUR WARD, WASN'T IT?
NO, ACTUALLY-
WHAT WAS THAT...?
AAAH!
!
MUHYO!
ARE YOU OKAY?!
ARTICLE 30
FALLING MIST

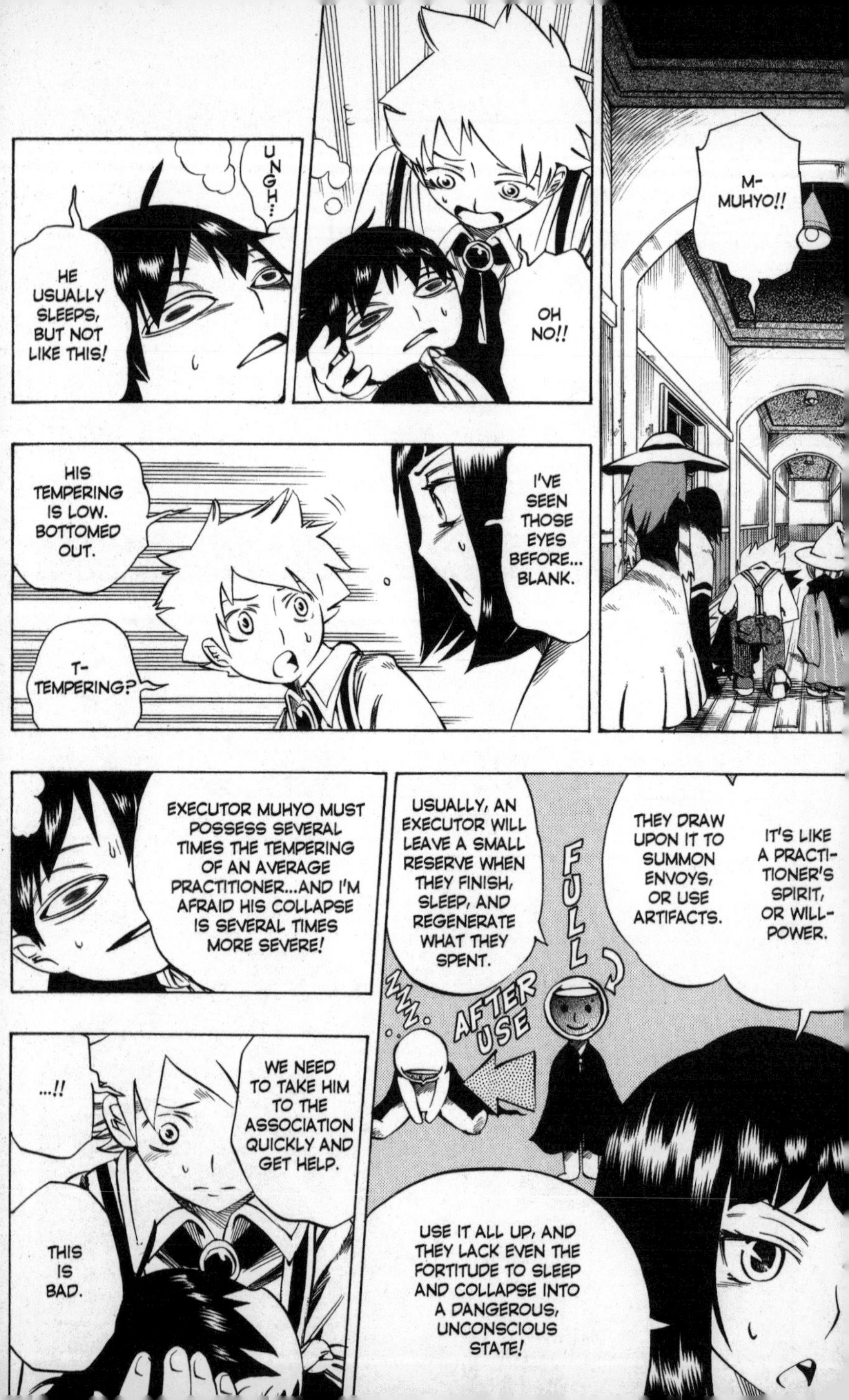
M-
MUHYO!!
OH NO!!
UNGH...
HE USUALLY SLEEPS, BUT NOT LIKE THIS!
I'VE SEEN THOSE EYES BEFORE... BLANK.
HIS TEMPERING IS LOW. BOTTOMED OUT.
T-TEMPERING?
IT'S LIKE A PRACTITIONER'S SPIRIT, OR WILL-POWER.
THEY DRAW UPON IT TO SUMMON ENVOYS, OR USE ARTIFACTS.
USUALLY, AN EXECUTOR WILL LEAVE A SMALL RESERVE WHEN THEY FINISH, SLEEP, AND REGENERATE WHAT THEY SPENT.
FULL
AFTER USE
MMM...
USE IT ALL UP, AND THEY LACK EVEN THE FORTITUDE TO SLEEP AND COLLAPSE INTO A DANGEROUS, UNCONSCIOUS STATE!
EXECUTOR MUHYO MUST POSSESS SEVERAL TIMES THE TEMPERING OF AN AVERAGE PRACTITIONER...AND I'M AFRAID HIS COLLAPSE IS SEVERAL TIMES MORE SEVERE!
WE NEED TO TAKE HIM TO THE ASSOCIATION QUICKLY AND GET HELP.
...!!
THIS IS BAD.

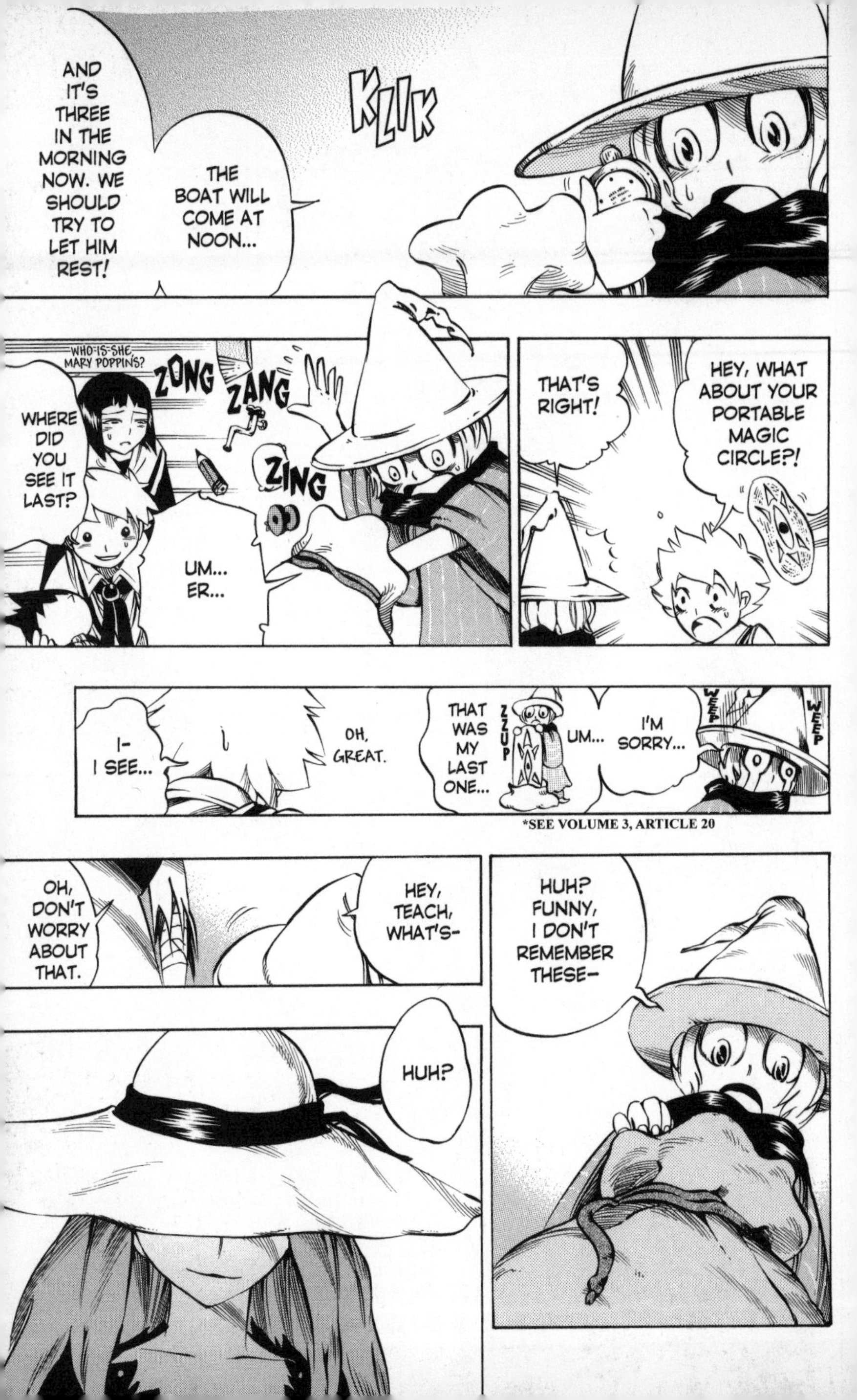
KLIK
THE BOAT WILL COME AT NOON...
AND IT'S THREE IN THE MORNING NOW. WE SHOULD TRY TO LET HIM REST!
HEY, WHAT ABOUT YOUR PORTABLE MAGIC CIRCLE?!
THAT'S RIGHT!
ZANG
ZING
ZONG
UM... ER...
WHERE DID YOU SEE IT LAST?
WHO-IS-SHE, MARY POPPINS?
WEEP
WEEP
I'M SORRY...
UM...
ZZUP
THAT WAS MY LAST ONE...
OH, GREAT.
I- I SEE...
HUH? FUNNY, I DON'T REMEMBER THESE-
HEY, TEACH, WHAT'S-
OH, DON'T WORRY ABOUT THAT.
HUH?
*SEE VOLUME 3, ARTICLE 20

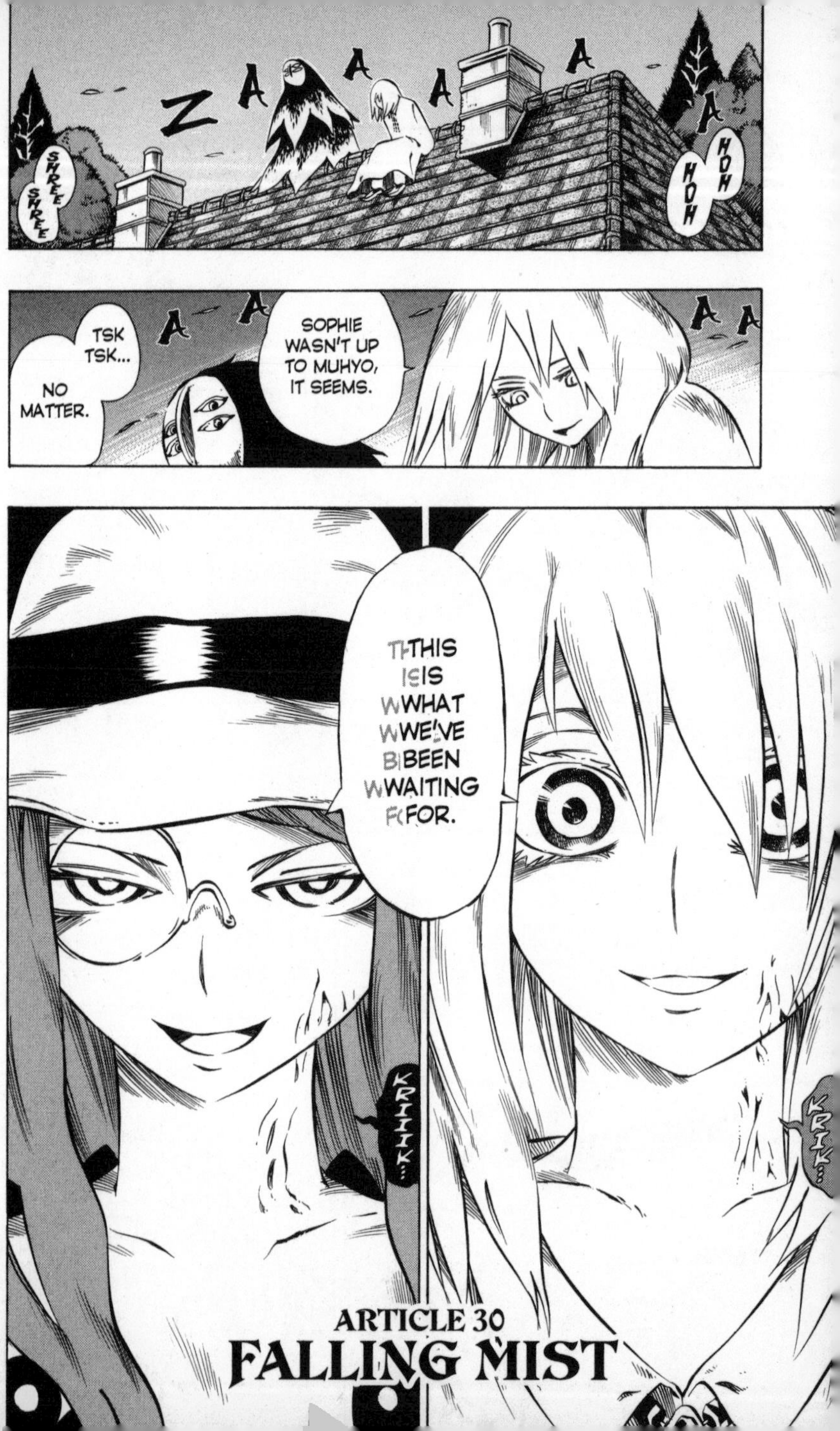
HOH HOH
ZAAAAA
SHREE SHREE
SOPHIE WASN'T UP TO MUHYO, IT SEEMS.
TSK TSK...
NO MATTER.
AA
T-THIS I-IS W-WHAT W-WE'VE B-BEEN W-WAITING F-FOR.
KRIK...
KRIIIK...

ARTICLE 30
FALLING MIST

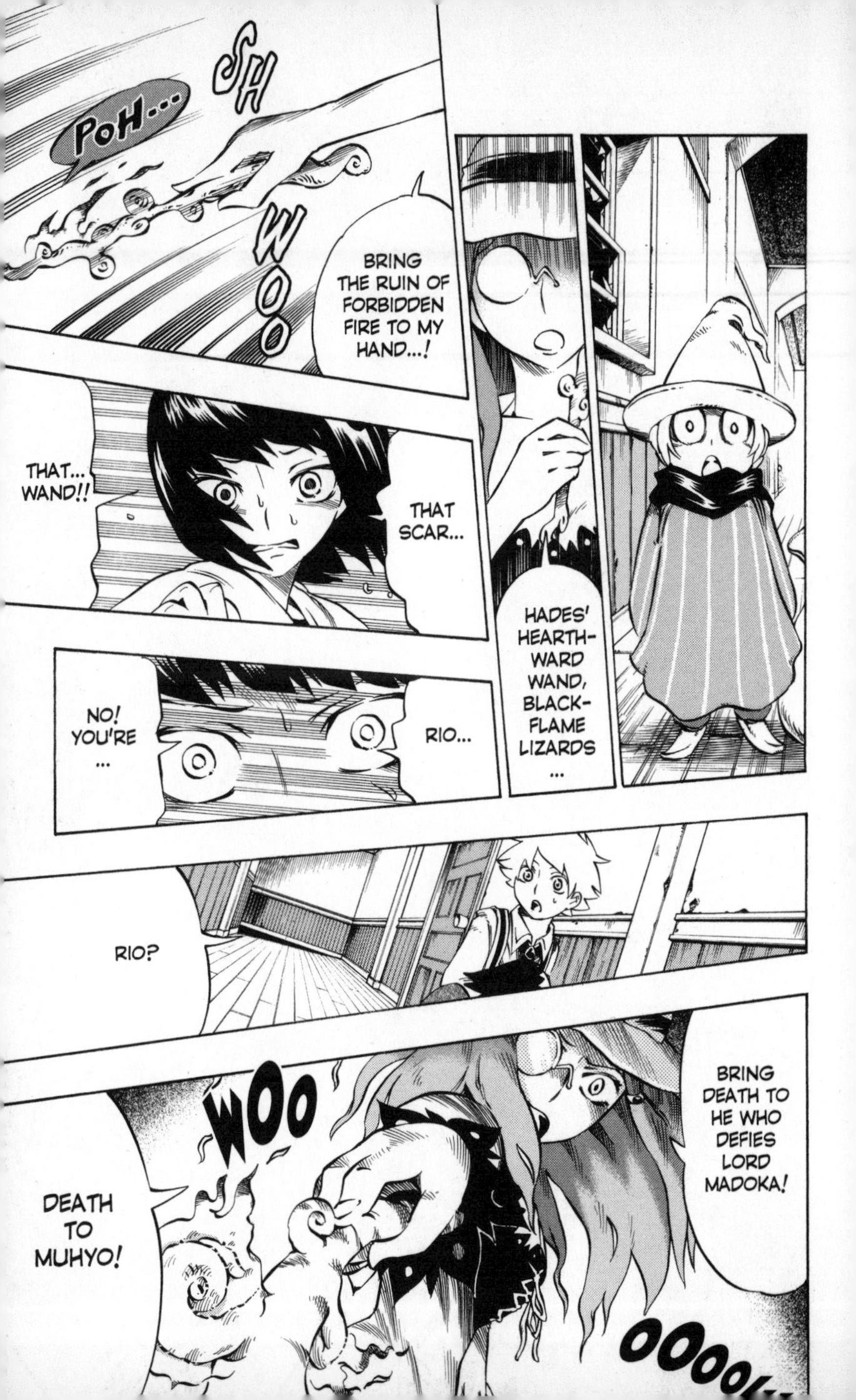
HADES' HEARTH-WARD WAND, BLACK-FLAME LIZARDS ...
SHWOOO
BRING THE RUIN OF FORBIDDEN FIRE TO MY HAND...!
POH...
THAT SCAR...
THAT... WAND!!
RIO...
NO! YOU'RE ...
RIO?
BRING DEATH TO HE WHO DEFIES LORD MADOKA!
WOO
DEATH TO MUHYO!
OOOO!!

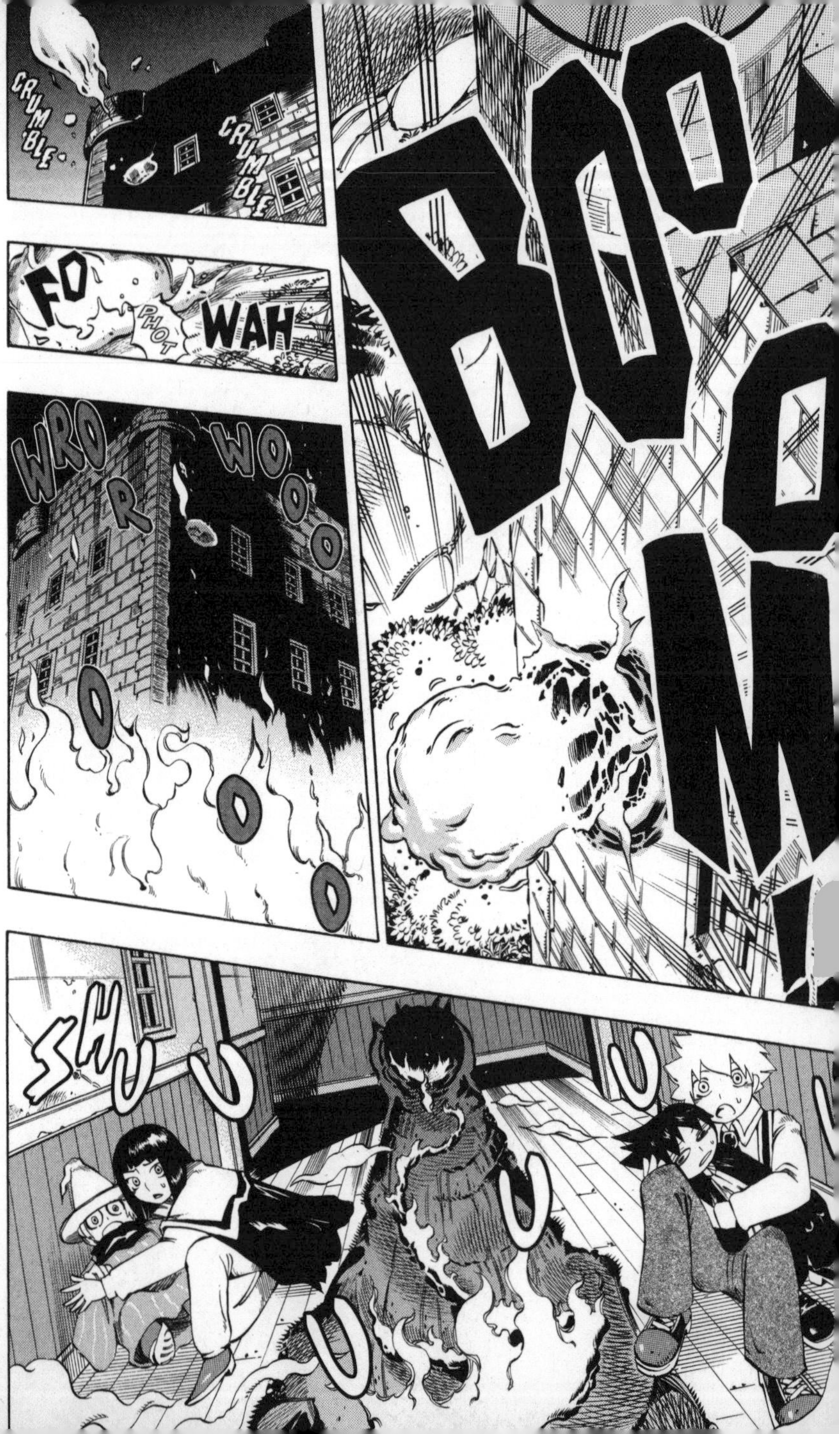
BOOOM
CRUMBLE CRUMBLE
CRUMBLE
FO
PHOT
WAH
WOOOO
WROR
SHUUU

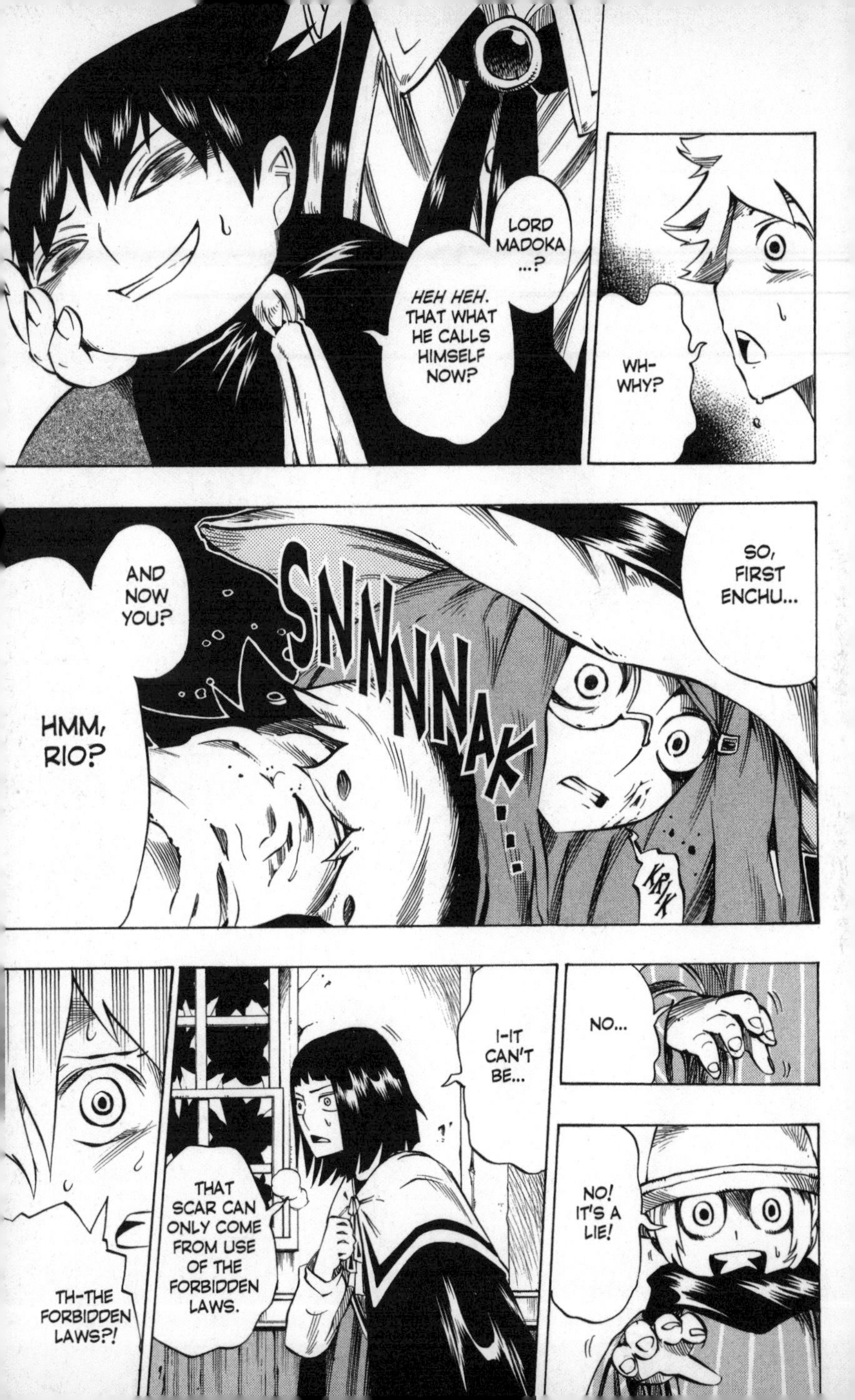
WH-WHY?
LORD MADOKA ...?
HEH HEH. THAT WHAT HE CALLS HIMSELF NOW?
SO, FIRST ENCHU...
AND NOW YOU?
SNNNNNAK...
HMM, RIO?
KRIK
NO...
NO! IT'S A LIE!
I-IT CAN'T BE...
THAT SCAR CAN ONLY COME FROM USE OF THE FORBIDDEN LAWS.
TH-THE FORBIDDEN LAWS?!

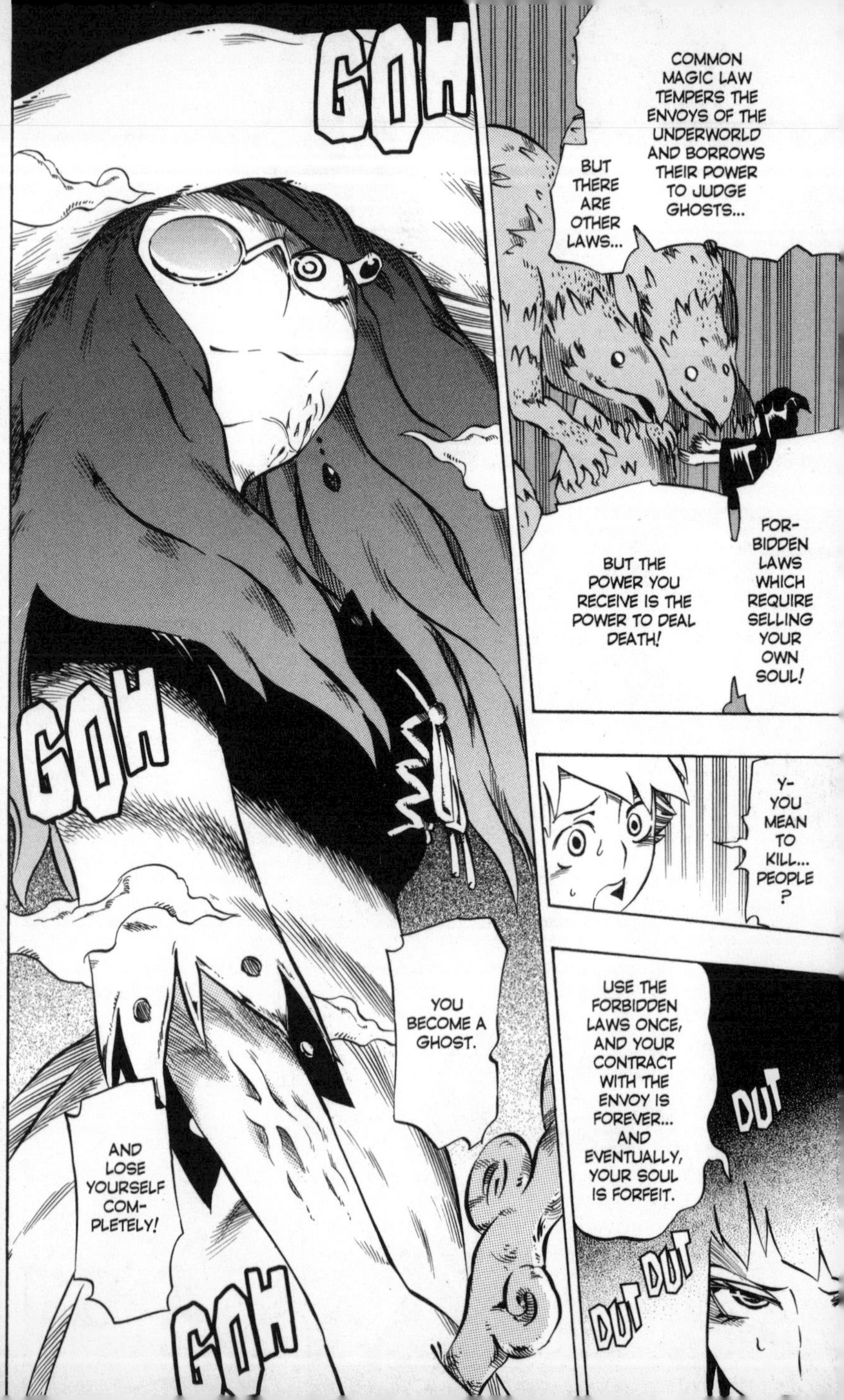
COMMON MAGIC LAW TEMPERS THE ENVOYS OF THE UNDERWORLD AND BORROWS THEIR POWER TO JUDGE GHOSTS...
BUT THERE ARE OTHER LAWS...
FOR-BIDDEN LAWS WHICH REQUIRE SELLING YOUR OWN SOUL!
BUT THE POWER YOU RECEIVE IS THE POWER TO DEAL DEATH!
Y-YOU MEAN TO KILL... PEOPLE?
USE THE FORBIDDEN LAWS ONCE, AND YOUR CONTRACT WITH THE ENVOY IS FOREVER... AND EVENTUALLY, YOUR SOUL IS FORFEIT.
DUT
DUT DUT DUT
GOH
GOH
YOU BECOME A GHOST.
AND LOSE YOURSELF COM-PLETELY!
GOH

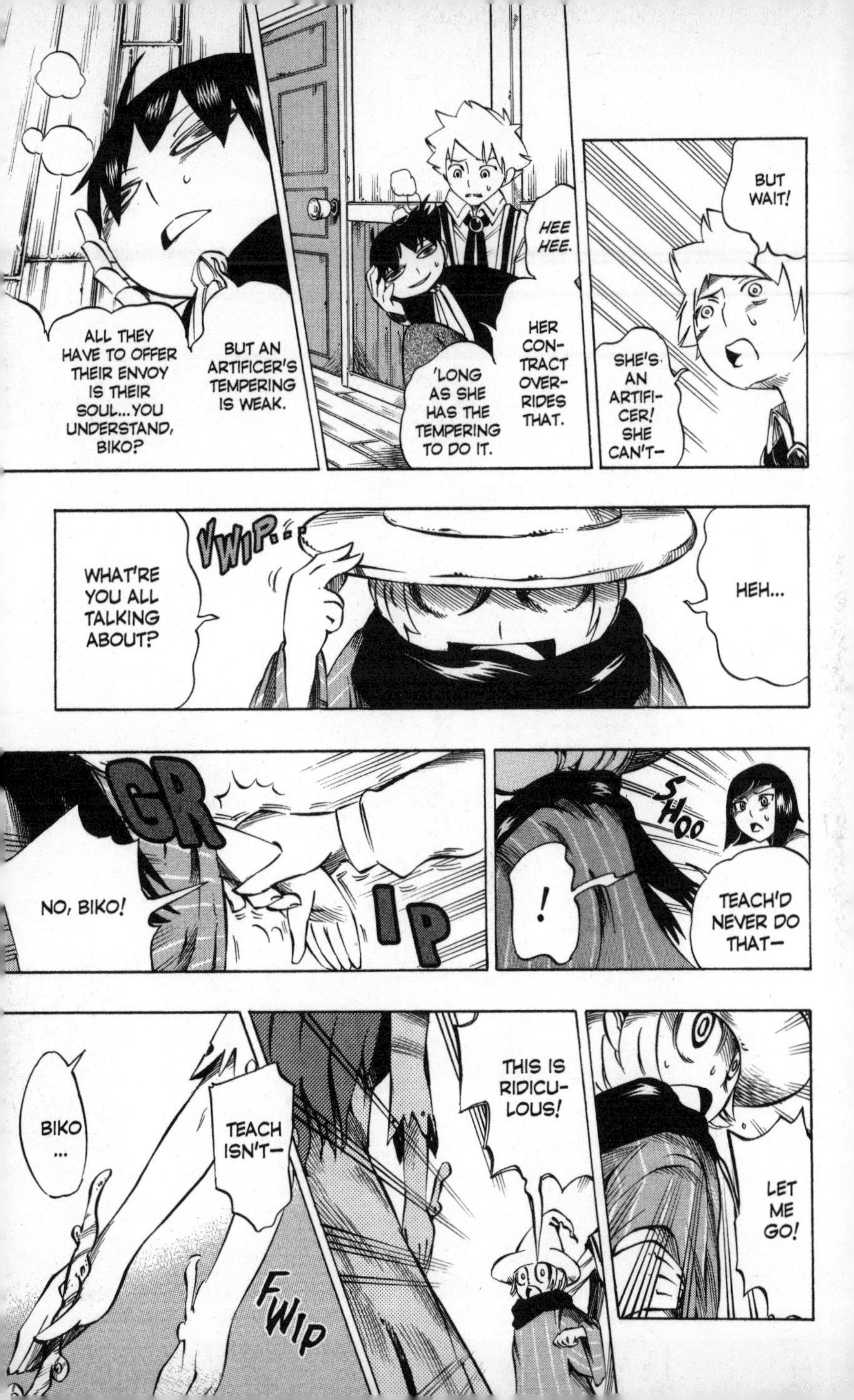
BUT WAIT!
SHE'S AN ARTIFICER! SHE CAN'T—
HEE HEE.
HER CONTRACT OVERRIDES THAT.
'LONG AS SHE HAS THE TEMPERING TO DO IT.
BUT AN ARTIFICER'S TEMPERING IS WEAK.
ALL THEY HAVE TO OFFER THEIR ENVOY IS THEIR SOUL...YOU UNDERSTAND, BIKO?
HEH...
VWIP...
WHAT'RE YOU ALL TALKING ABOUT?
SHOO
!
TEACH'D NEVER DO THAT—
GR
IP
NO, BIKO!
LET ME GO!
THIS IS RIDICULOUS!
TEACH ISN'T—
FWIP
BIKO ...

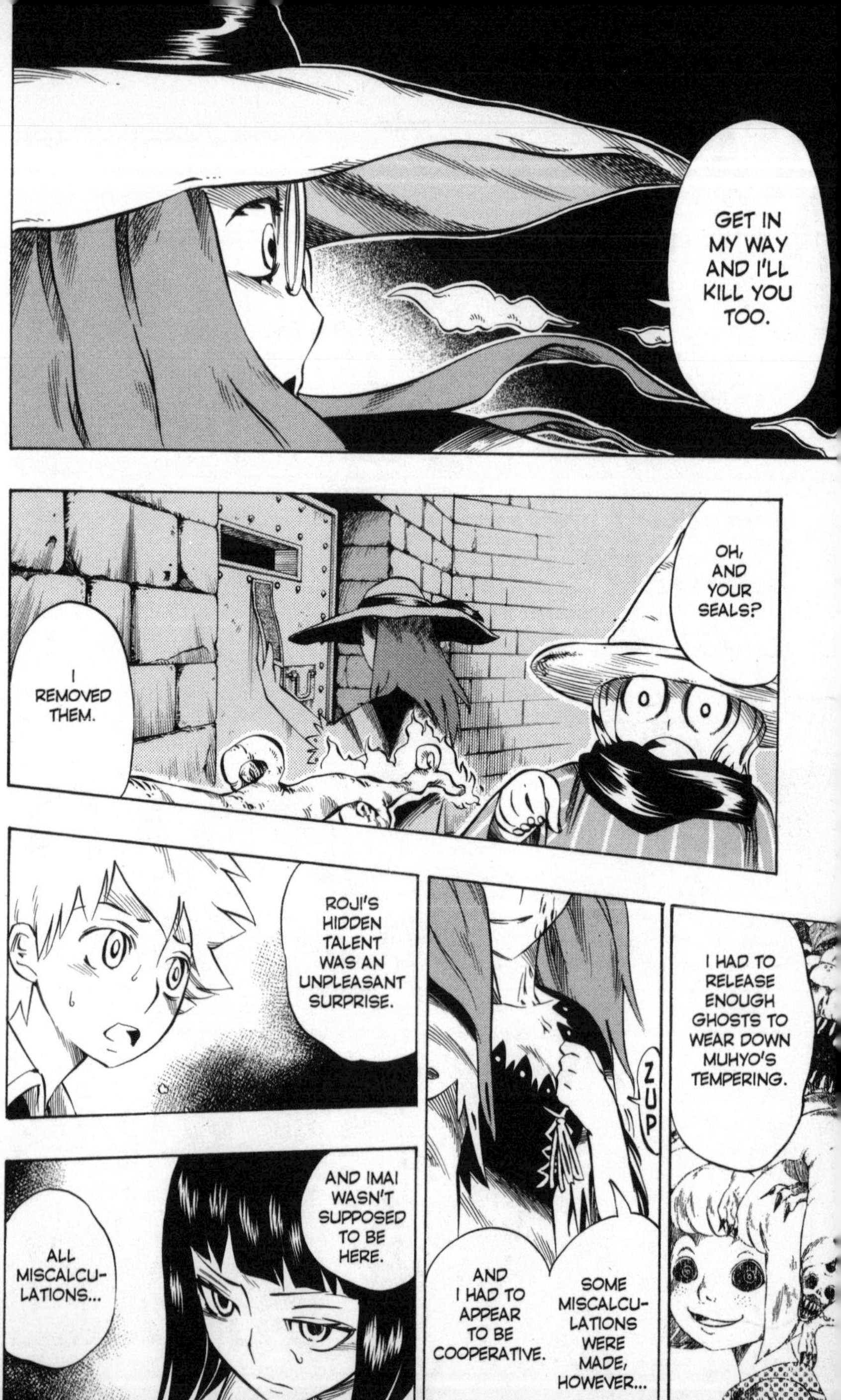
GET IN MY WAY AND I'LL KILL YOU TOO.
OH, AND YOUR SEALS?
I REMOVED THEM.
I HAD TO RELEASE ENOUGH GHOSTS TO WEAR DOWN MUHYO'S TEMPERING.
ZUP
SOME MISCALCULATIONS WERE MADE, HOWEVER...
AND I HAD TO APPEAR TO BE COOPERATIVE.
ROJI'S HIDDEN TALENT WAS AN UNPLEASANT SURPRISE.
AND IMAI WASN'T SUPPOSED TO BE HERE.
ALL MISCALCULATIONS...

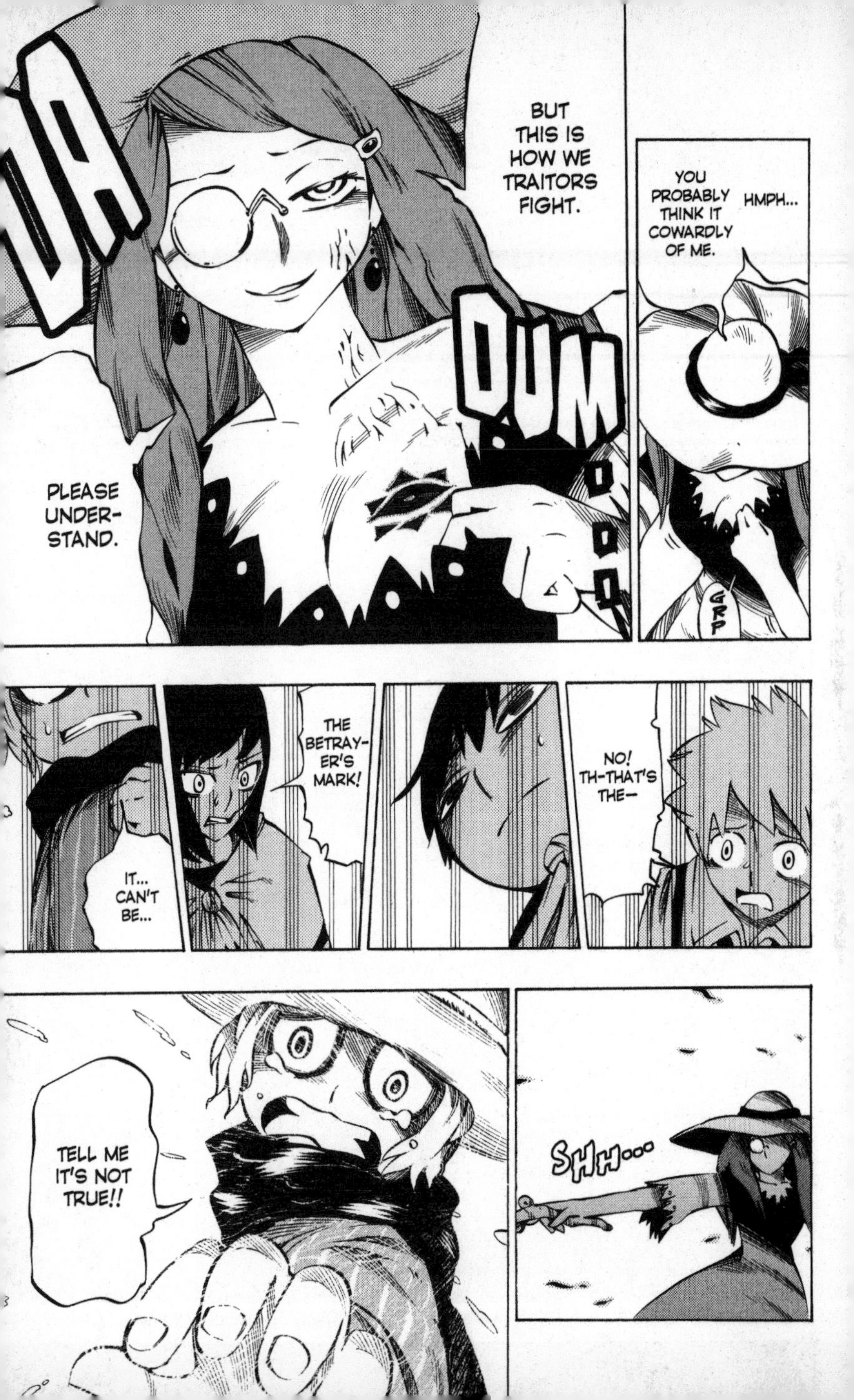
HMPH...
YOU PROBABLY THINK IT COWARDLY OF ME.
GRP
BUT THIS IS HOW WE TRAITORS FIGHT.
DUM
DA
PLEASE UNDER-STAND.
NO! TH-THAT'S THE—
THE BETRAY-ER'S MARK!
IT... CAN'T BE...
SHHooo
TELL ME IT'S NOT TRUE!!

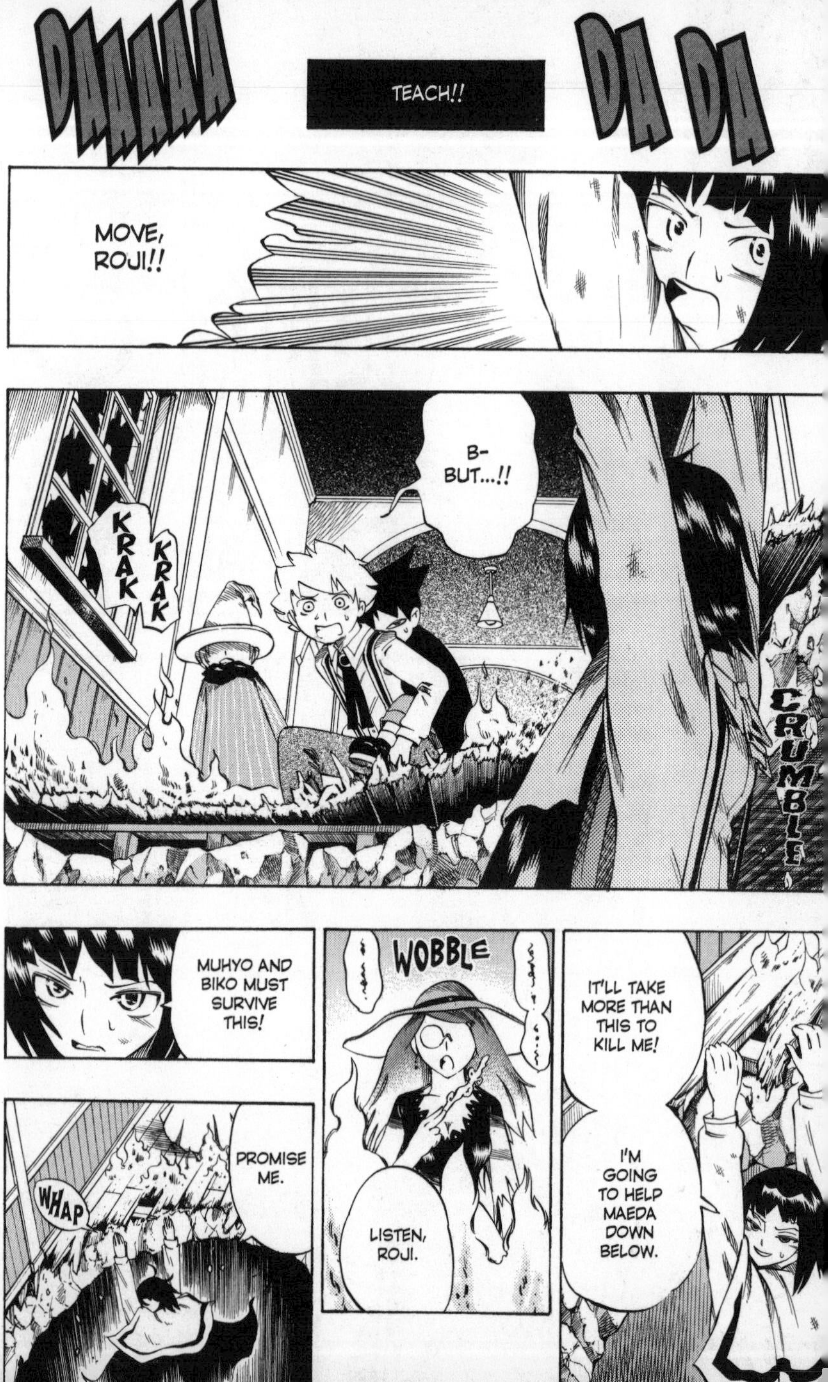
DAAAAA DA DA
TEACH!!
MOVE, ROJI!!
B- BUT...!!
CRUMBLE
KRAK KRAK
IT'LL TAKE MORE THAN THIS TO KILL ME!
I'M GOING TO HELP MAEDA DOWN BELOW.
WOBBLE
LISTEN, ROJI.
MUHYO AND BIKO MUST SURVIVE THIS!
PROMISE ME.
WHAP

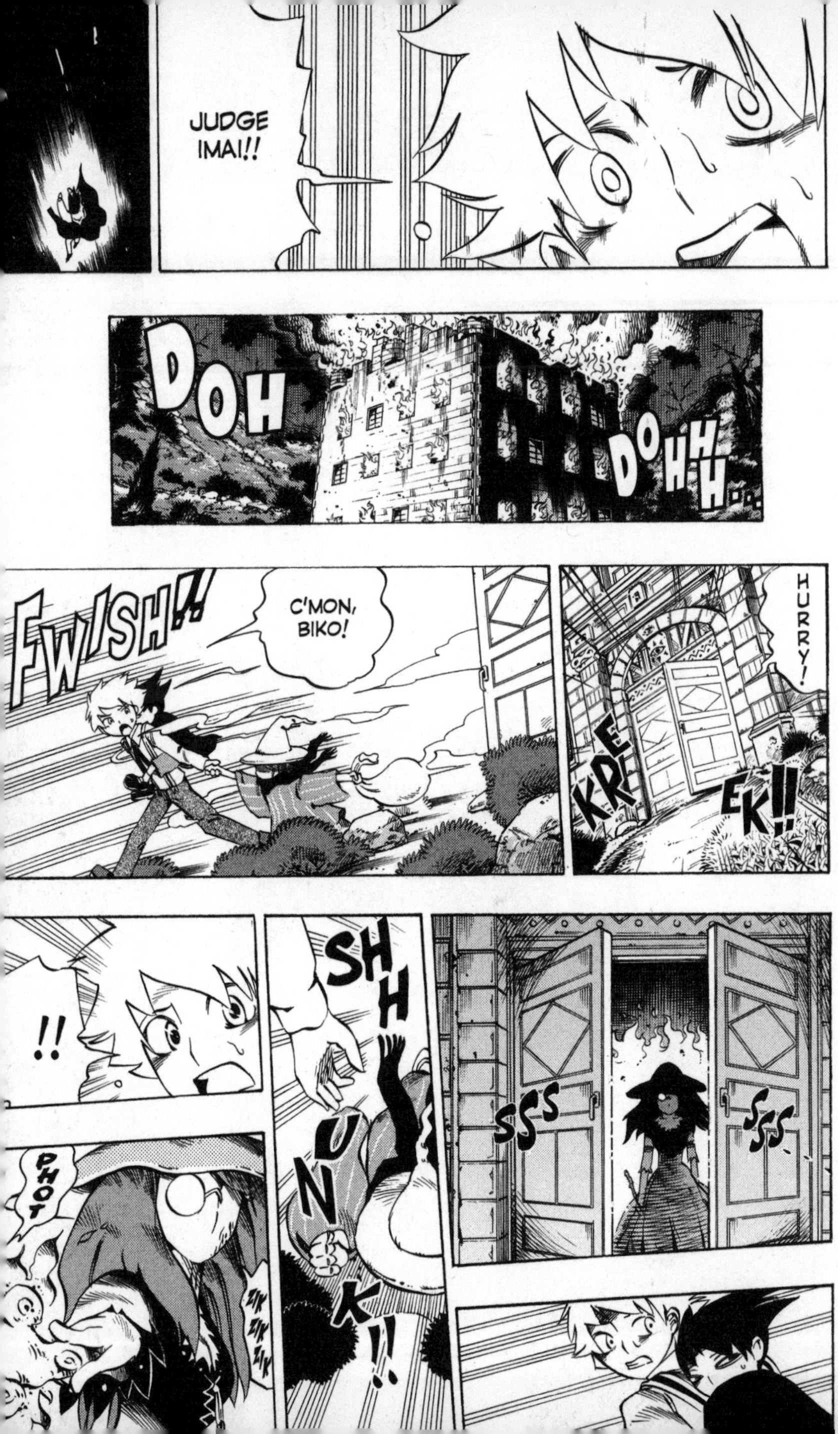
JUDGE IMAI!!
DOH
DOHHH...
HURRY!
KREEEK!!
C'MON, BIKO!
FWISH!!
SSS
SSS
SHHUNK!!
!!
PHOT
ZIK ZIK ZIK

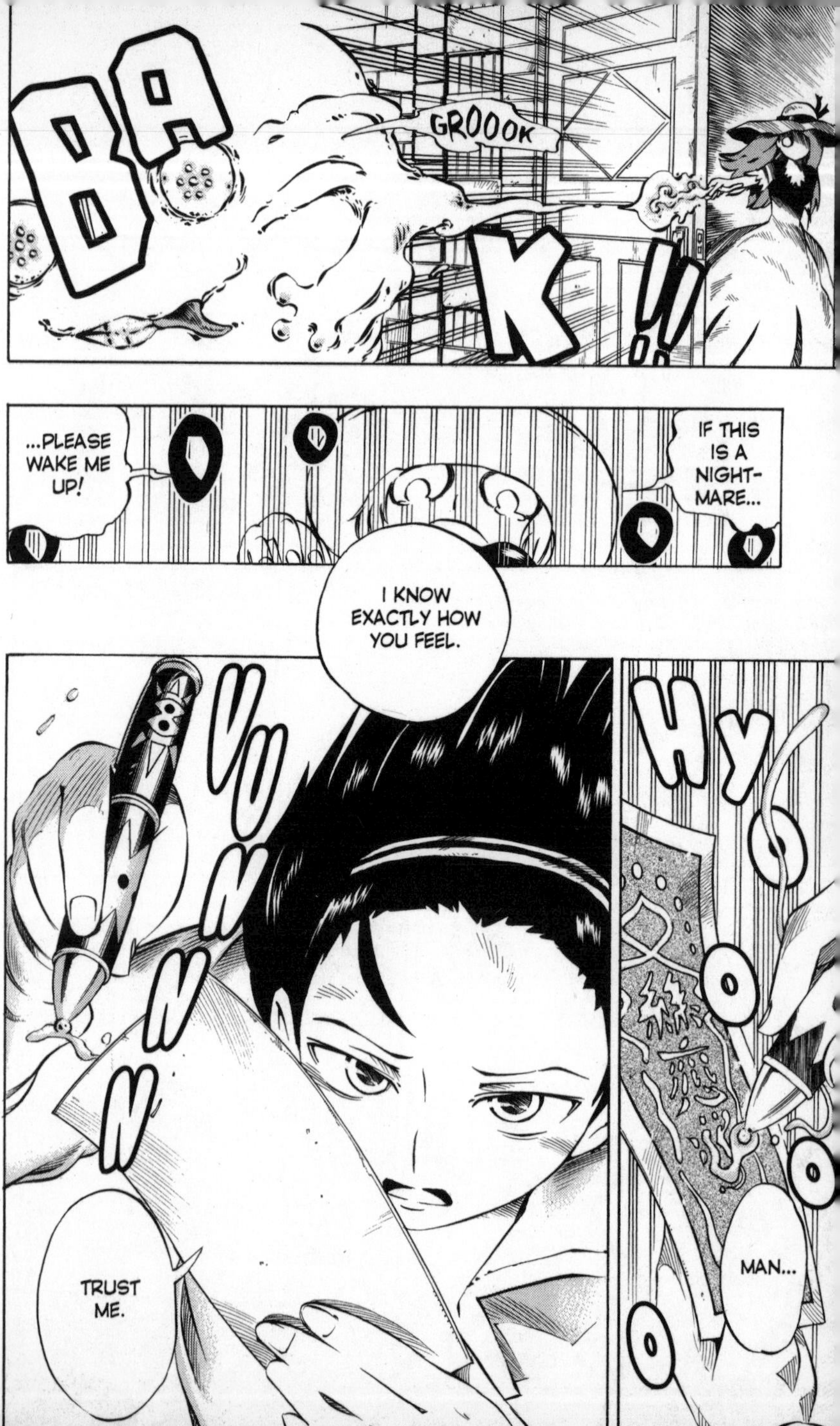
GROOOK
BAKT!!
IF THIS IS A NIGHTMARE...
...PLEASE WAKE ME UP!
I KNOW EXACTLY HOW YOU FEEL.
HYOOO
MAN...
VUUNNNN
TRUST ME.

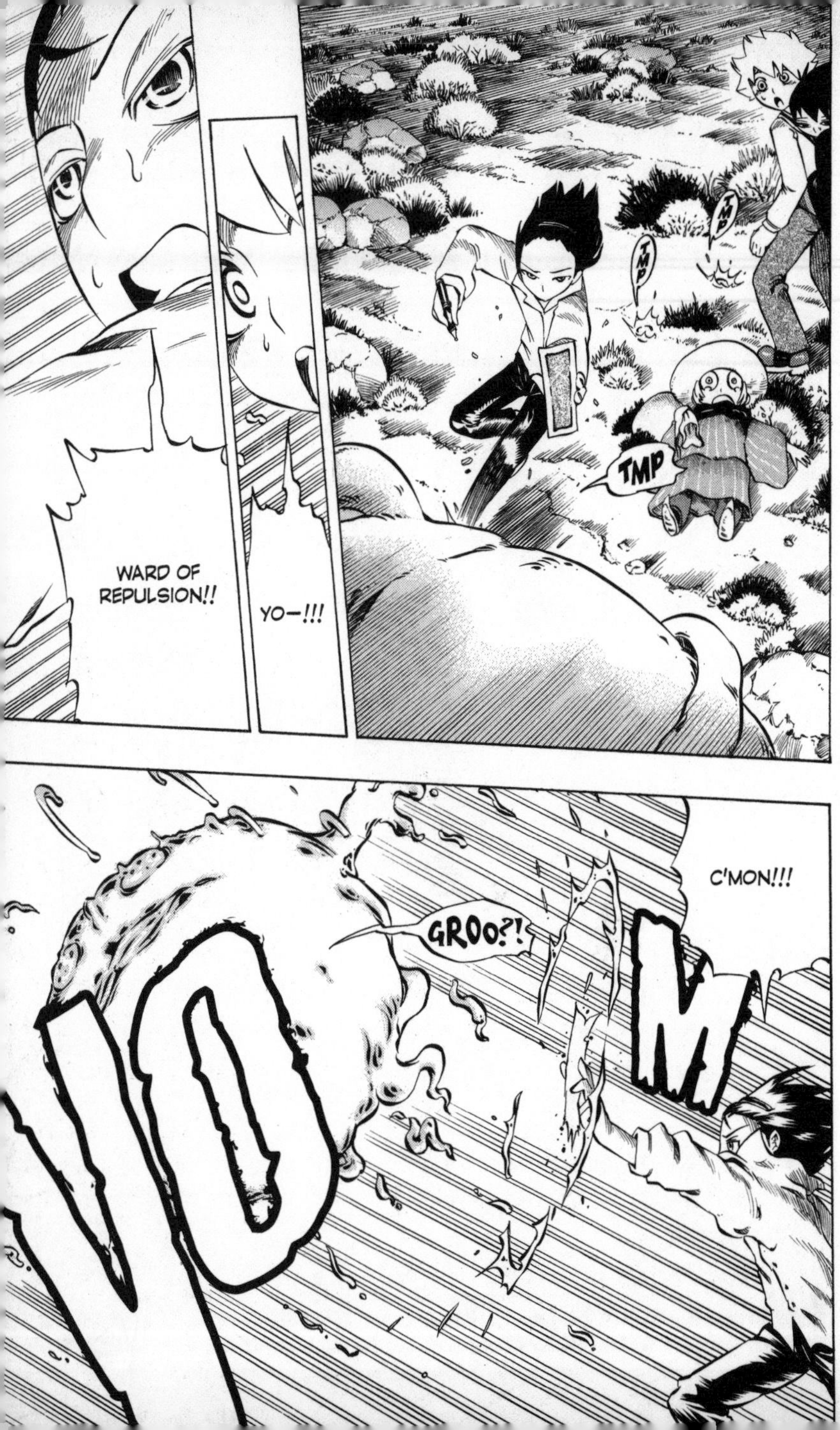
TMP
TMP
TMP
YO—!!!
WARD OF REPULSION!!
C'MON!!!
GROO?!
VOM

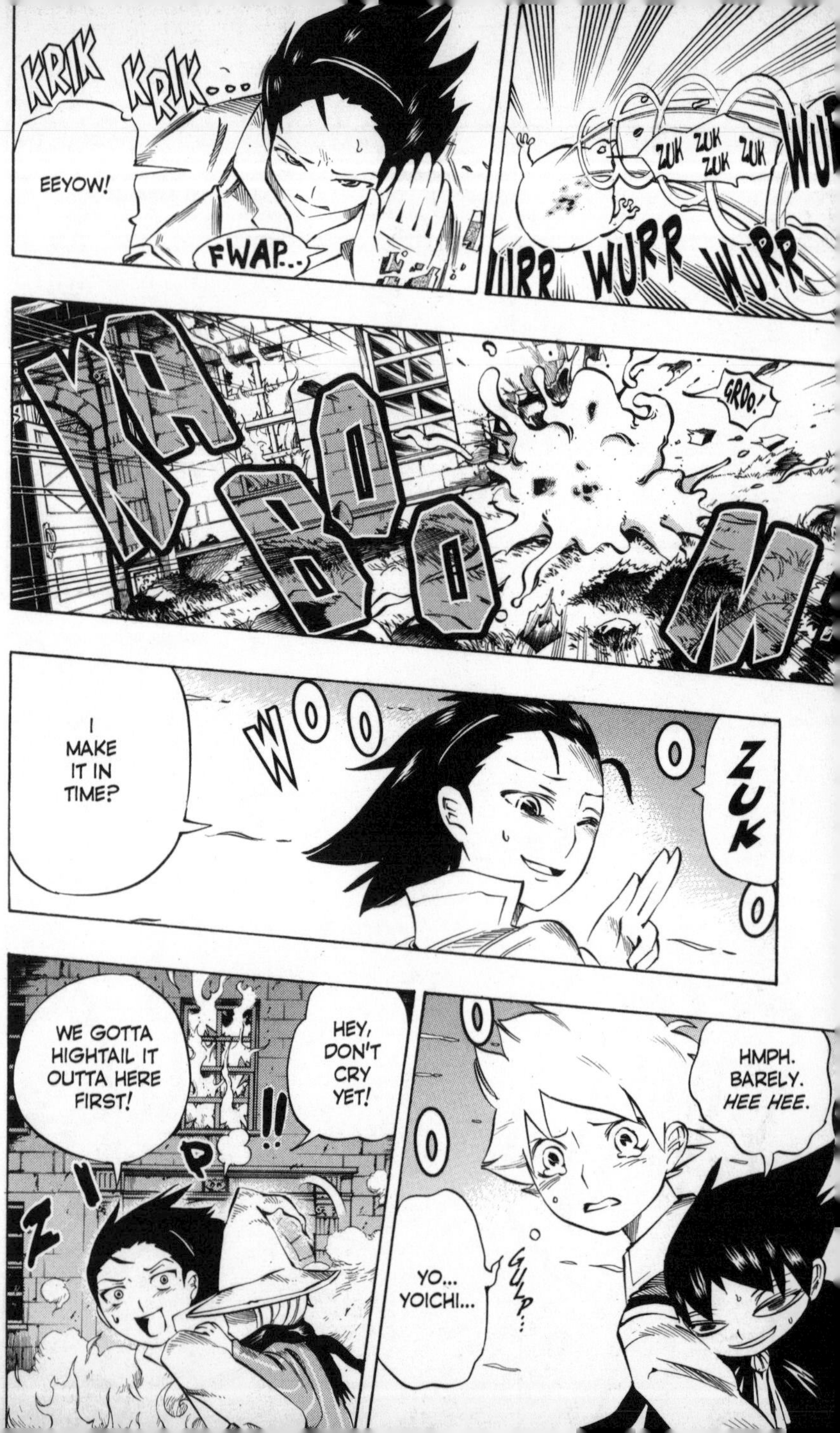
ZUK ZUK ZUK ZUK
WURR WURR WURR WURR
KRIK KRIK...
EEYOW!
FWAP...
GROO!
KABOOM
WOOOOO
ZUK
I MAKE IT IN TIME?
HMPH. BARELY. HEE HEE.
YO... YOICHI...
GULP...
HEY, DON'T CRY YET!
!!
WE GOTTA HIGHTAIL IT OUTTA HERE FIRST!
ZIP

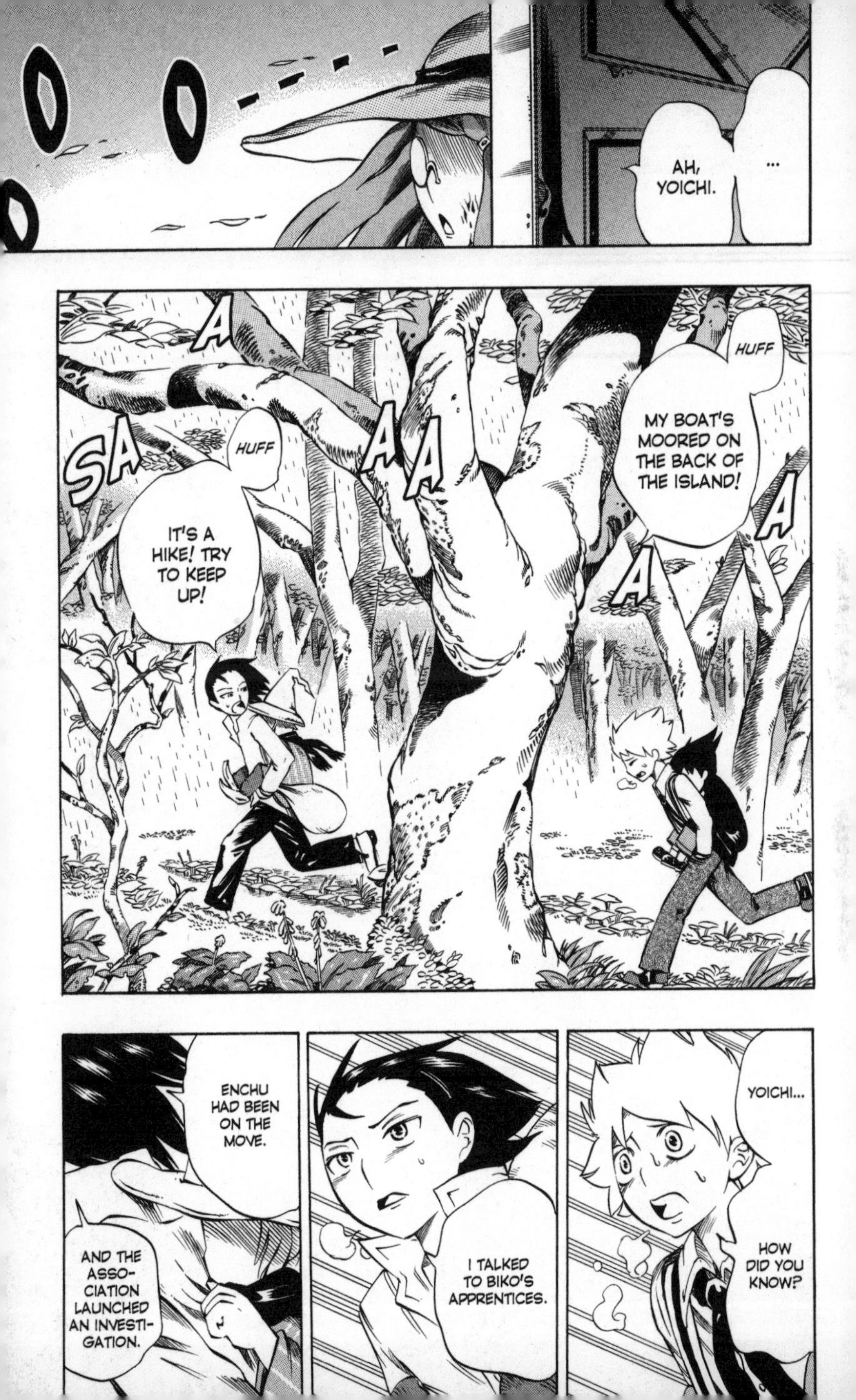
...
AH, YOICHI.
HUFF
MY BOAT'S MOORED ON THE BACK OF THE ISLAND!
A
A
AA
A
SA
HUFF
IT'S A HIKE! TRY TO KEEP UP!
YOICHI...
HOW DID YOU KNOW?
I TALKED TO BIKO'S APPRENTICES.
ENCHU HAD BEEN ON THE MOVE.
AND THE ASSO-CIATION LAUNCHED AN INVESTI-GATION.

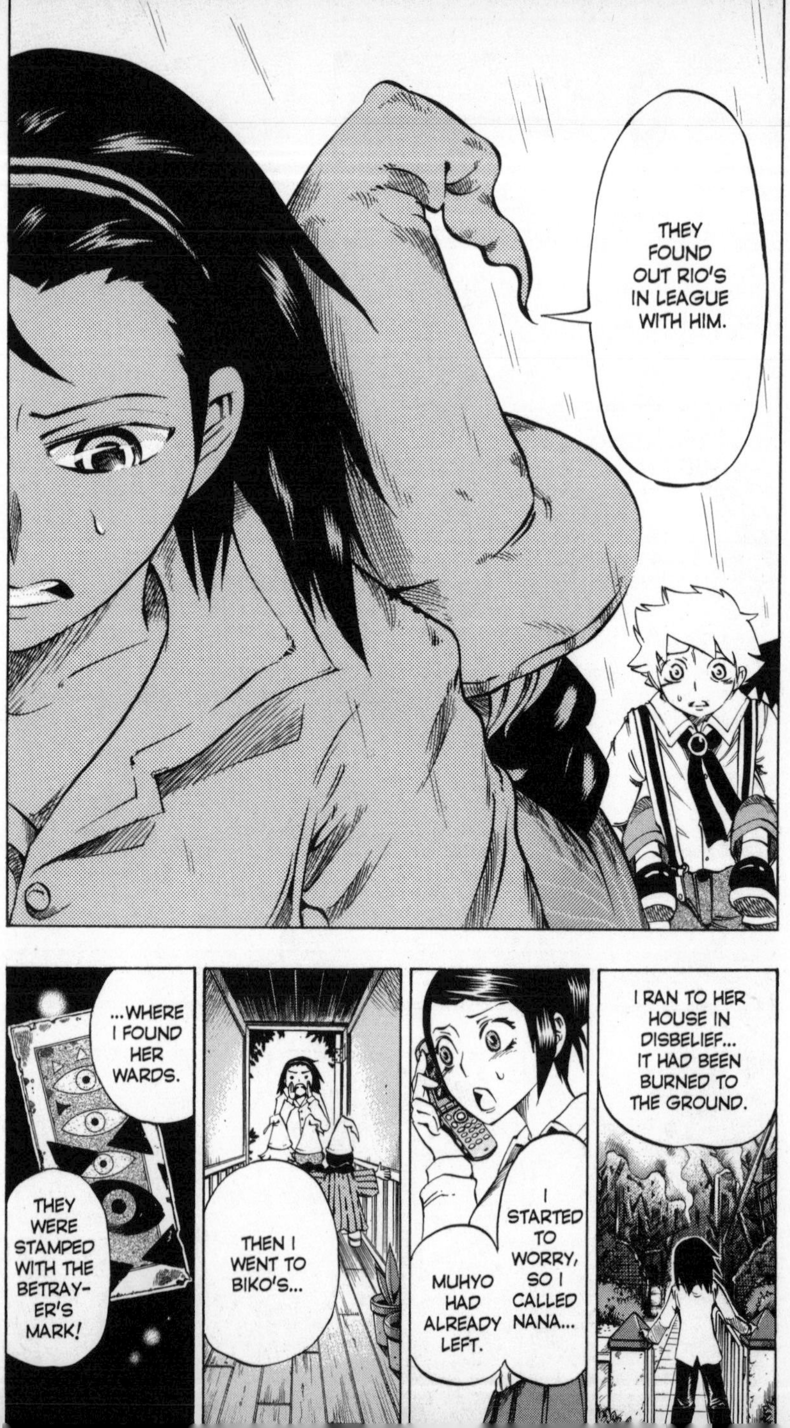
THEY FOUND OUT RIO'S IN LEAGUE WITH HIM.
I RAN TO HER HOUSE IN DISBELIEF... IT HAD BEEN BURNED TO THE GROUND.
I STARTED TO WORRY, SO I CALLED NANA...
MUHYO HAD ALREADY LEFT.
THEN I WENT TO BIKO'S...
...WHERE I FOUND HER WARDS.
THEY WERE STAMPED WITH THE BETRAY-ER'S MARK!

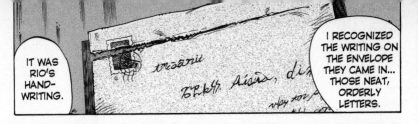

I RECOGNIZED THE WRITING ON THE ENVELOPE THEY CAME IN... THOSE NEAT, ORDERLY LETTERS.

IT WAS RIO'S HANDWRITING.

SAAAAAA

K-KINDA COLD...

THE RAIN...

IT'S RAINING.

YEAH, IT IS...

IT CAN'T BE.

IT CAN'T!!

I DON'T BELIEVE IT.

Q: HOW DO YOU ABBREVIATE
   THE TITLE OF YOUR MANGA?
   -N.S. FROM HYOGO
    PREFECTURE

A: I GET THIS QUESTION
   A LOT. SEEMS LIKE
   EVERYONE HAS THEIR OWN
   VERSION... "MUHYO ROJI"
   IS THE MOST POPULAR.
   SOME PEOPLE JUST CALL
   IT "MAGIC LAW" OR EVEN
   "BURMUHYO." (GET IT?
   BUREAU... MUHYO...) BY
   THE WAY, MY EDITOR AND
   I JUST CALL IT "MUHYO."

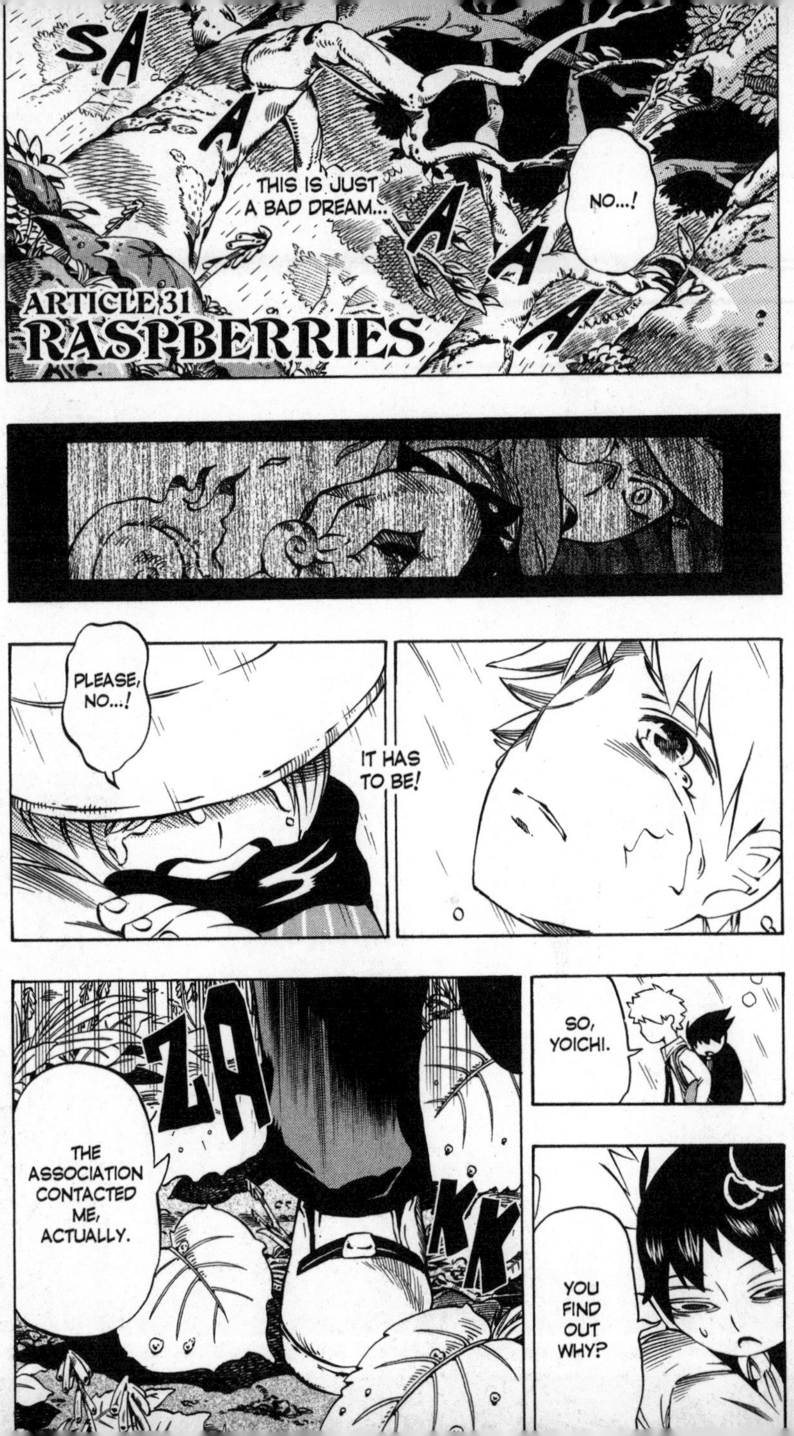
SAAAAAA
NO...!
THIS IS JUST A BAD DREAM...
ARTICLE 31 RASPBERRIES
PLEASE, NO...!
IT HAS TO BE!
SO, YOICHI.
YOU FIND OUT WHY?
ZAKK
THE ASSOCIATION CONTACTED ME, ACTUALLY.

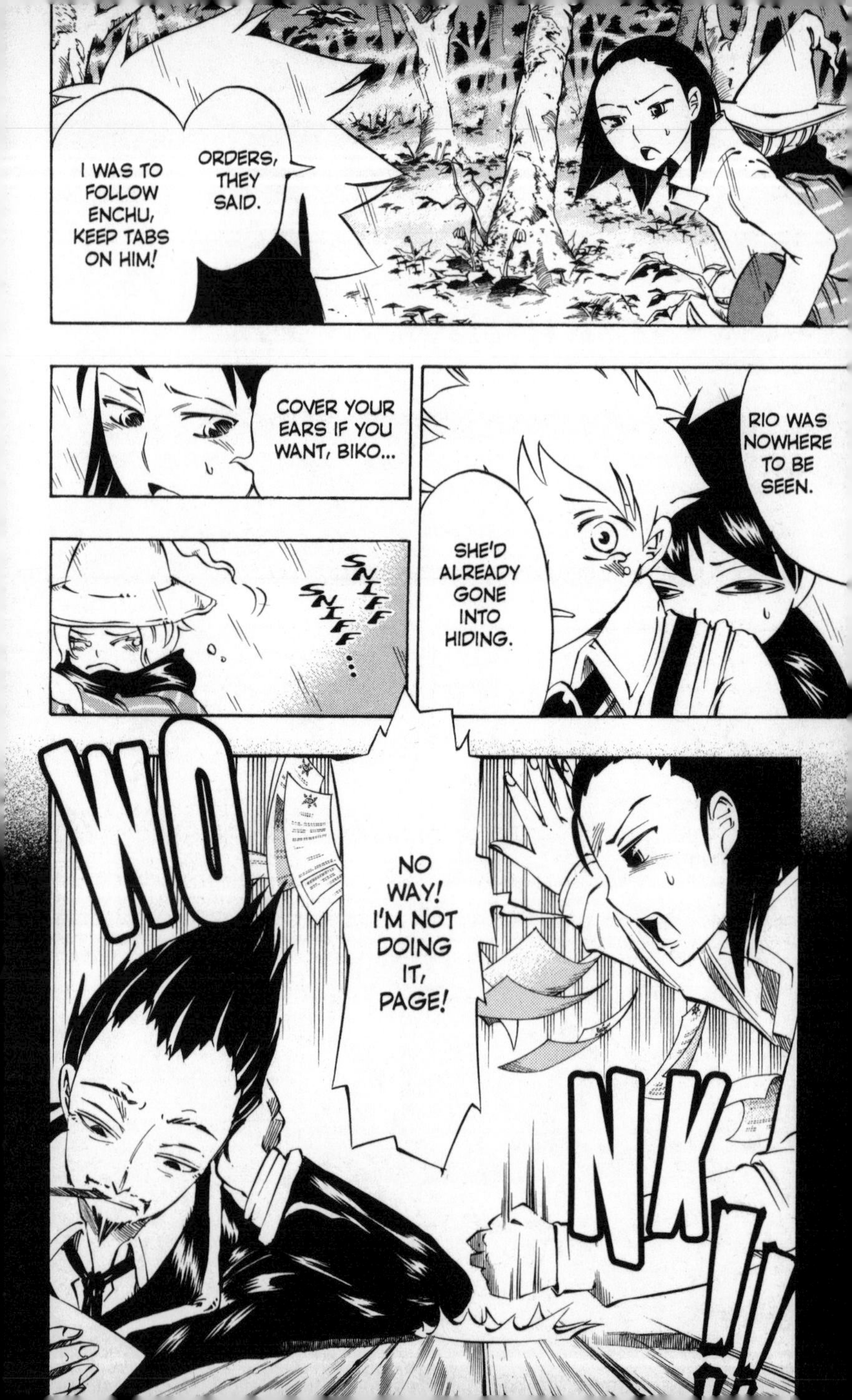
ORDERS, THEY SAID.
I WAS TO FOLLOW ENCHU, KEEP TABS ON HIM!
RIO WAS NOWHERE TO BE SEEN.
SHE'D ALREADY GONE INTO HIDING.
COVER YOUR EARS IF YOU WANT, BIKO...
SNIFF SNIFF...
NO WAY! I'M NOT DOING IT, PAGE!
WONK!!

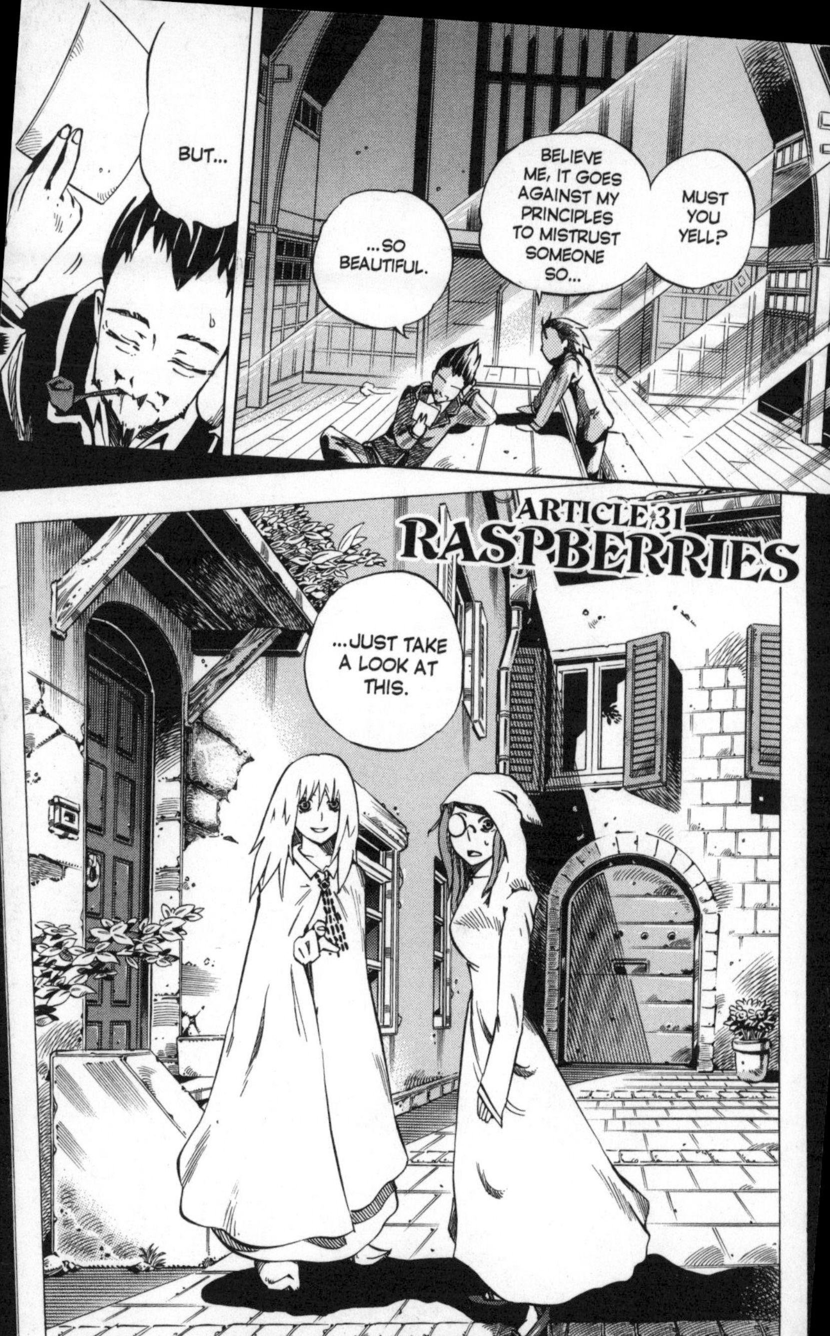
MUST YOU YELL?
BELIEVE ME, IT GOES AGAINST MY PRINCIPLES TO MISTRUST SOMEONE SO...
...SO BEAUTIFUL.
BUT...
ARTICLE 31
RASPBERRIES
...JUST TAKE A LOOK AT THIS.

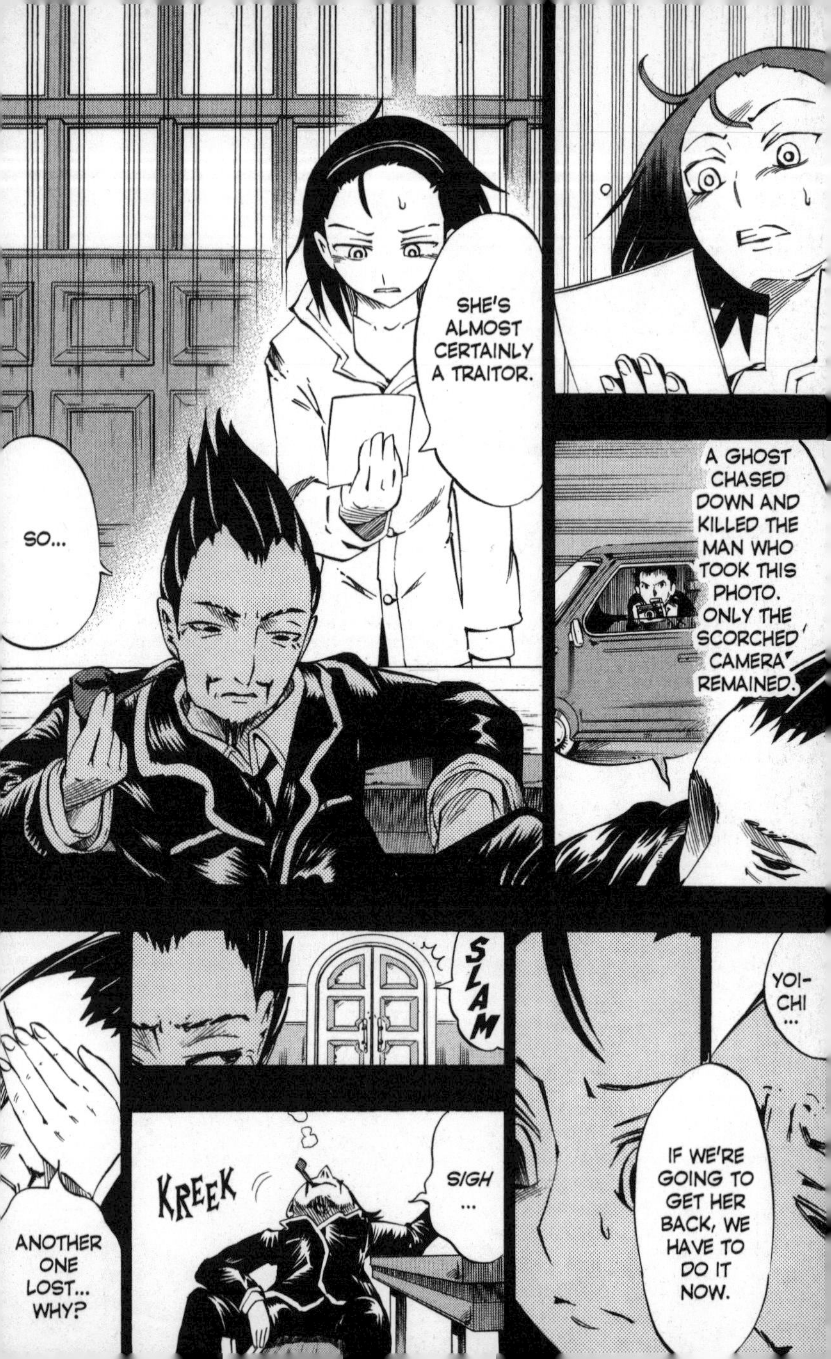
A GHOST CHASED DOWN AND KILLED THE MAN WHO TOOK THIS PHOTO. ONLY THE SCORCHED CAMERA REMAINED.
SHE'S ALMOST CERTAINLY A TRAITOR.
SO...
YOI-CHI...
IF WE'RE GOING TO GET HER BACK, WE HAVE TO DO IT NOW.
SLAM
SIGH...
KREEK
ANOTHER ONE LOST... WHY?

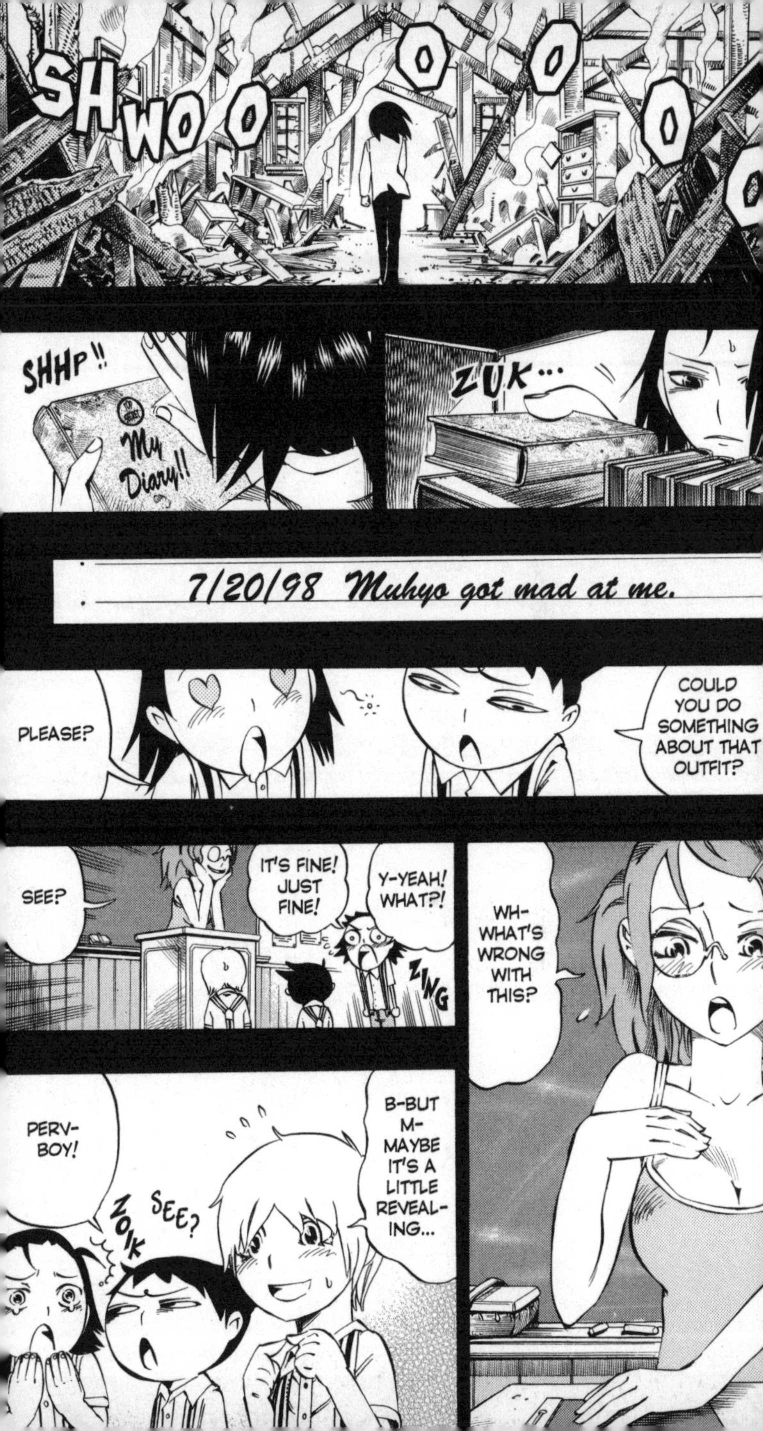
SHWOOOOOO
ZUK...
SHHP!!
My Diary!!
7/20/98 Muhyo got mad at me.
COULD YOU DO SOMETHING ABOUT THAT OUTFIT?
PLEASE?
WH-WHAT'S WRONG WITH THIS?
Y-YEAH! WHAT?!
IT'S FINE! JUST FINE!
SEE?
ZING
B-BUT M-MAYBE IT'S A LITTLE REVEAL-ING...
SEE?
NOIK
PERV-BOY!

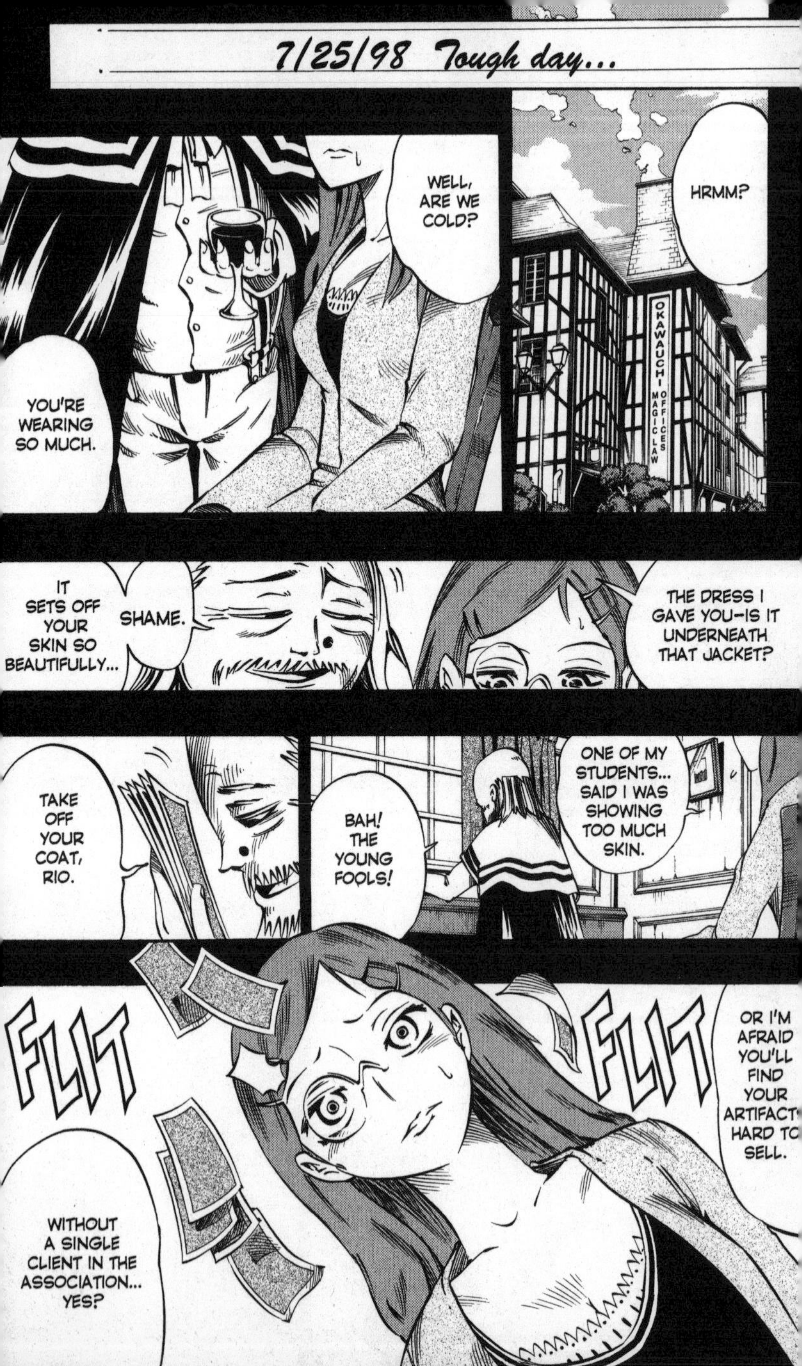
7/25/98 Tough day...
HRMM?
OKAWAUCHI MAGIC LAW OFFICES
WELL, ARE WE COLD?
YOU'RE WEARING SO MUCH.
THE DRESS I GAVE YOU—IS IT UNDERNEATH THAT JACKET?
SHAME.
IT SETS OFF YOUR SKIN SO BEAUTIFULLY...
ONE OF MY STUDENTS... SAID I WAS SHOWING TOO MUCH SKIN.
BAH! THE YOUNG FOOLS!
TAKE OFF YOUR COAT, RIO.
OR I'M AFRAID YOU'LL FIND YOUR ARTIFACTS HARD TO SELL.
FLIT
FLIT
WITHOUT A SINGLE CLIENT IN THE ASSOCIATION... YES?

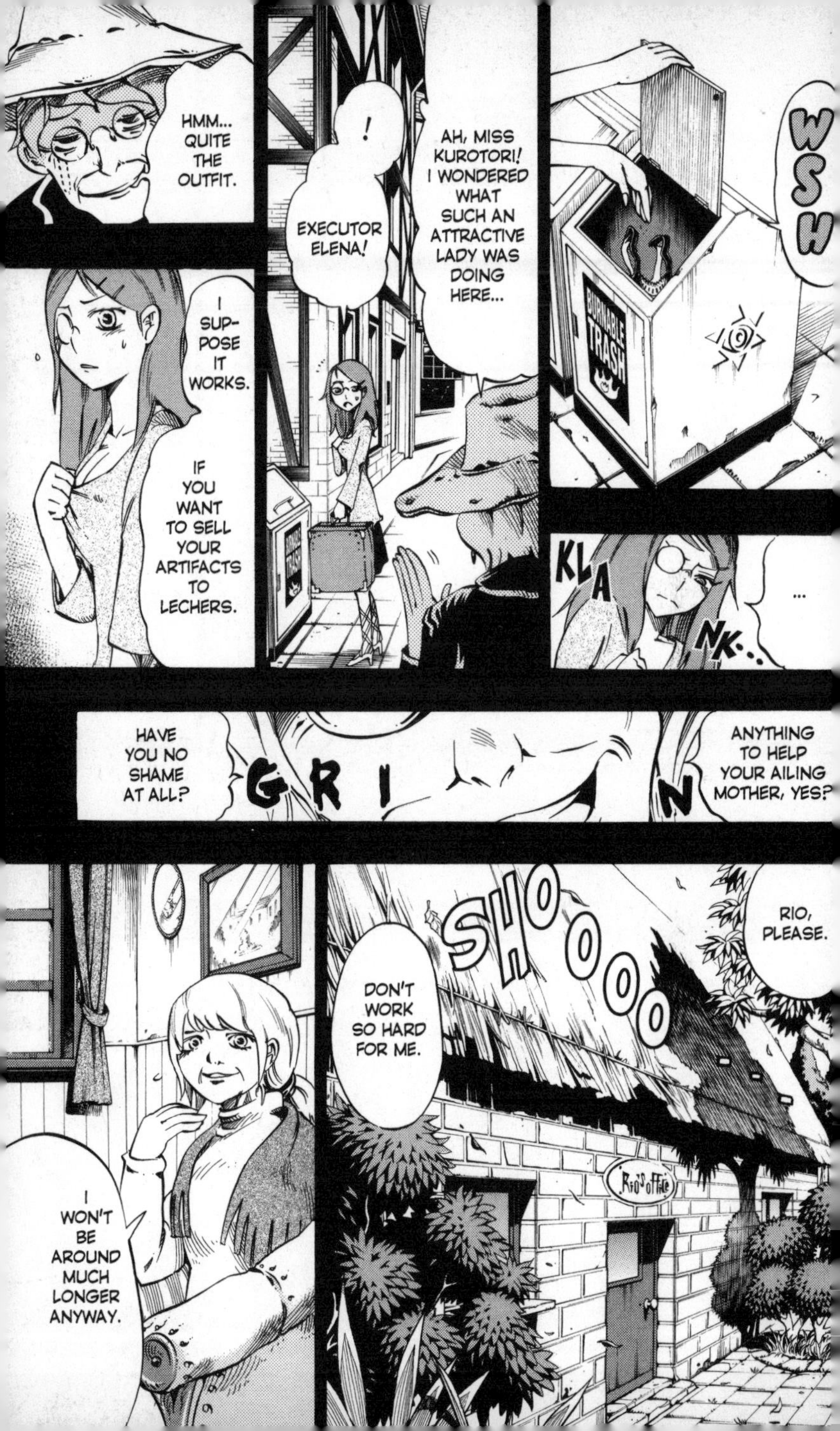
WSH
BURNABLE TRASH
KLANK...
...
AH, MISS KUROTORI! I WONDERED WHAT SUCH AN ATTRACTIVE LADY WAS DOING HERE...
!
EXECUTOR ELENA!
HMM... QUITE THE OUTFIT.
I SUPPOSE IT WORKS.
IF YOU WANT TO SELL YOUR ARTIFACTS TO LECHERS.
ANYTHING TO HELP YOUR AILING MOTHER, YES?
GRIN
HAVE YOU NO SHAME AT ALL?
SHOOOO
RIO, PLEASE.
DON'T WORK SO HARD FOR ME.
I WON'T BE AROUND MUCH LONGER ANYWAY.

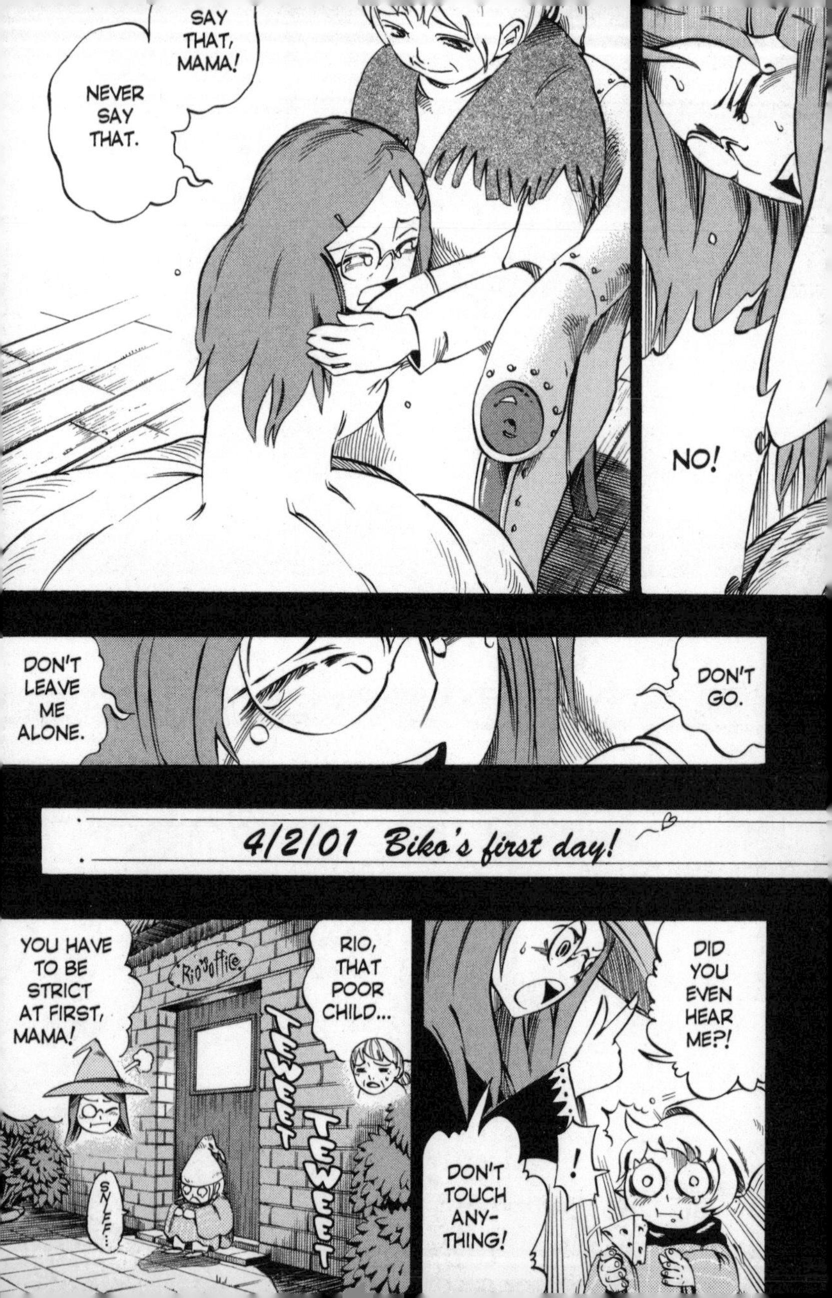
NO!
SAY THAT, MAMA!
NEVER SAY THAT.
DON'T GO.
DON'T LEAVE ME ALONE.
4/2/01 Biko's first day!
DID YOU EVEN HEAR ME?!
!
DON'T TOUCH ANY-THING!
RIO, THAT POOR CHILD...
TEWEET
TEWEET
YOU HAVE TO BE STRICT AT FIRST, MAMA!
Rio's office
SNIFF...

3/4/03 Biko passed her licensing exam...

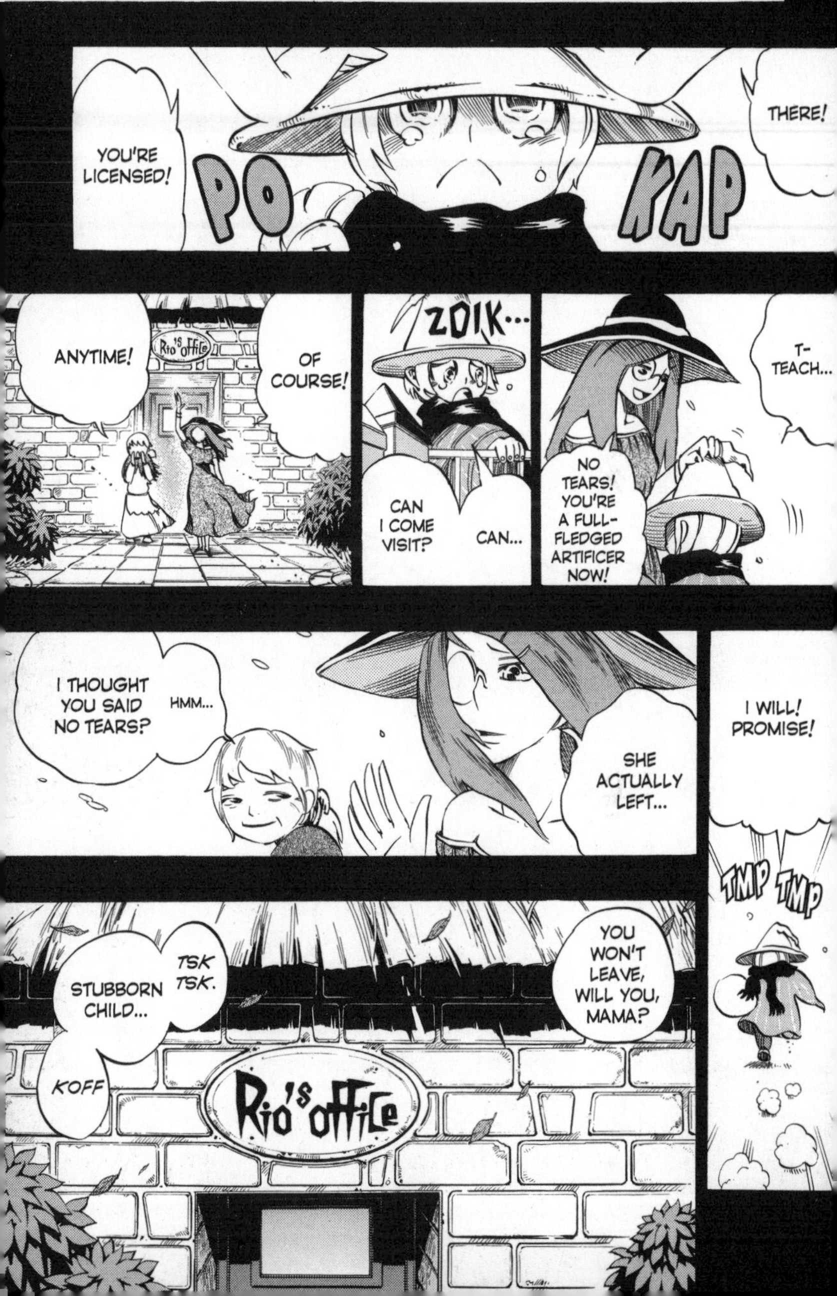
THERE!
KAP
PO
YOU'RE LICENSED!
T-TEACH...
NO TEARS! YOU'RE A FULL-FLEDGED ARTIFICER NOW!
ZOIK...
CAN...
CAN I COME VISIT?
OF COURSE!
ANYTIME!
Rio's office
I WILL! PROMISE!
TMP TMP
SHE ACTUALLY LEFT...
HMM...
I THOUGHT YOU SAID NO TEARS?
YOU WON'T LEAVE, WILL YOU, MAMA?
TSK TSK.
STUBBORN CHILD...
KOFF
Rio's office

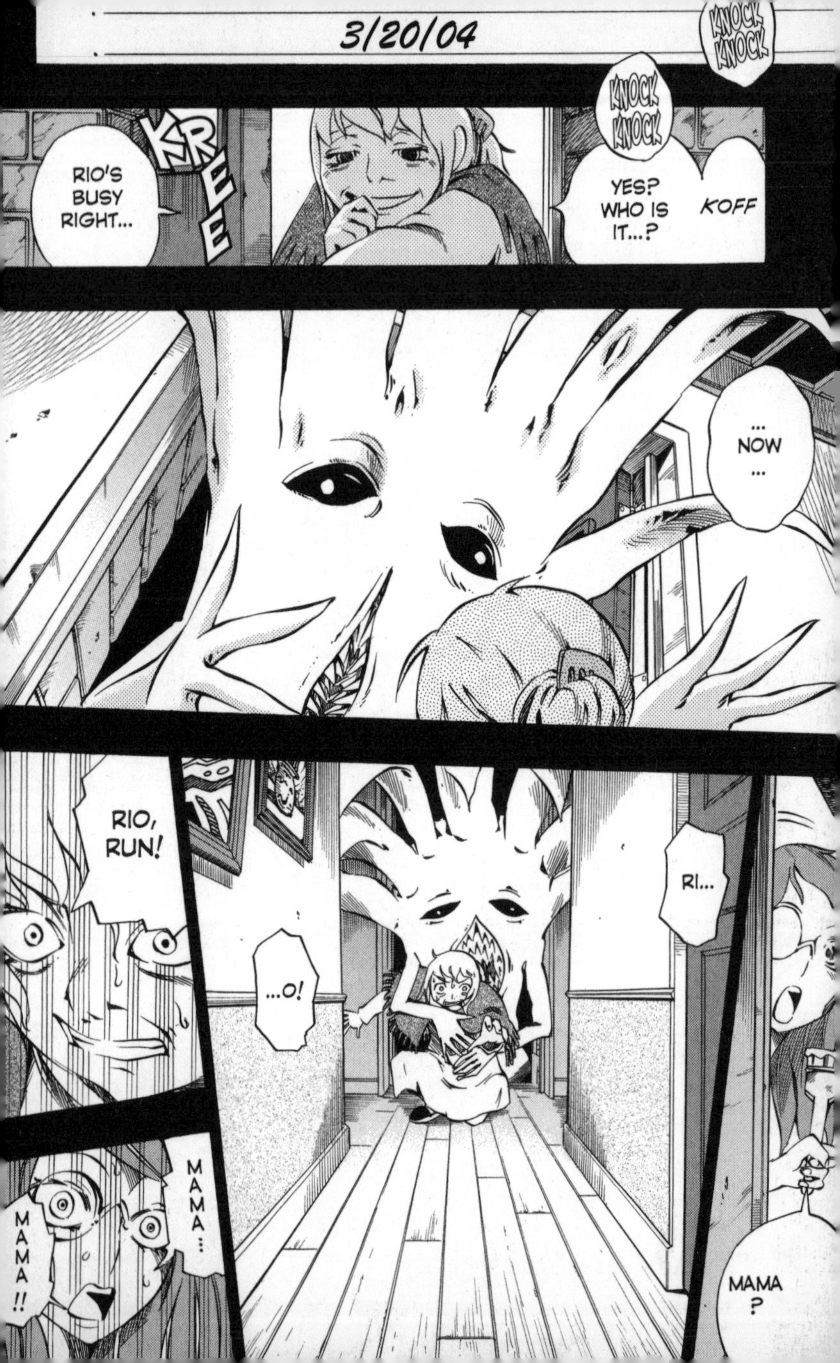

3/20/04
KNOCK KNOCK
KNOCK KNOCK
YES? WHO IS IT...?
KOFF
KREE
RIO'S BUSY RIGHT...
... NOW ...
RI...
MAMA ?
...O!
RIO, RUN!
MAMA...
MAMA!!

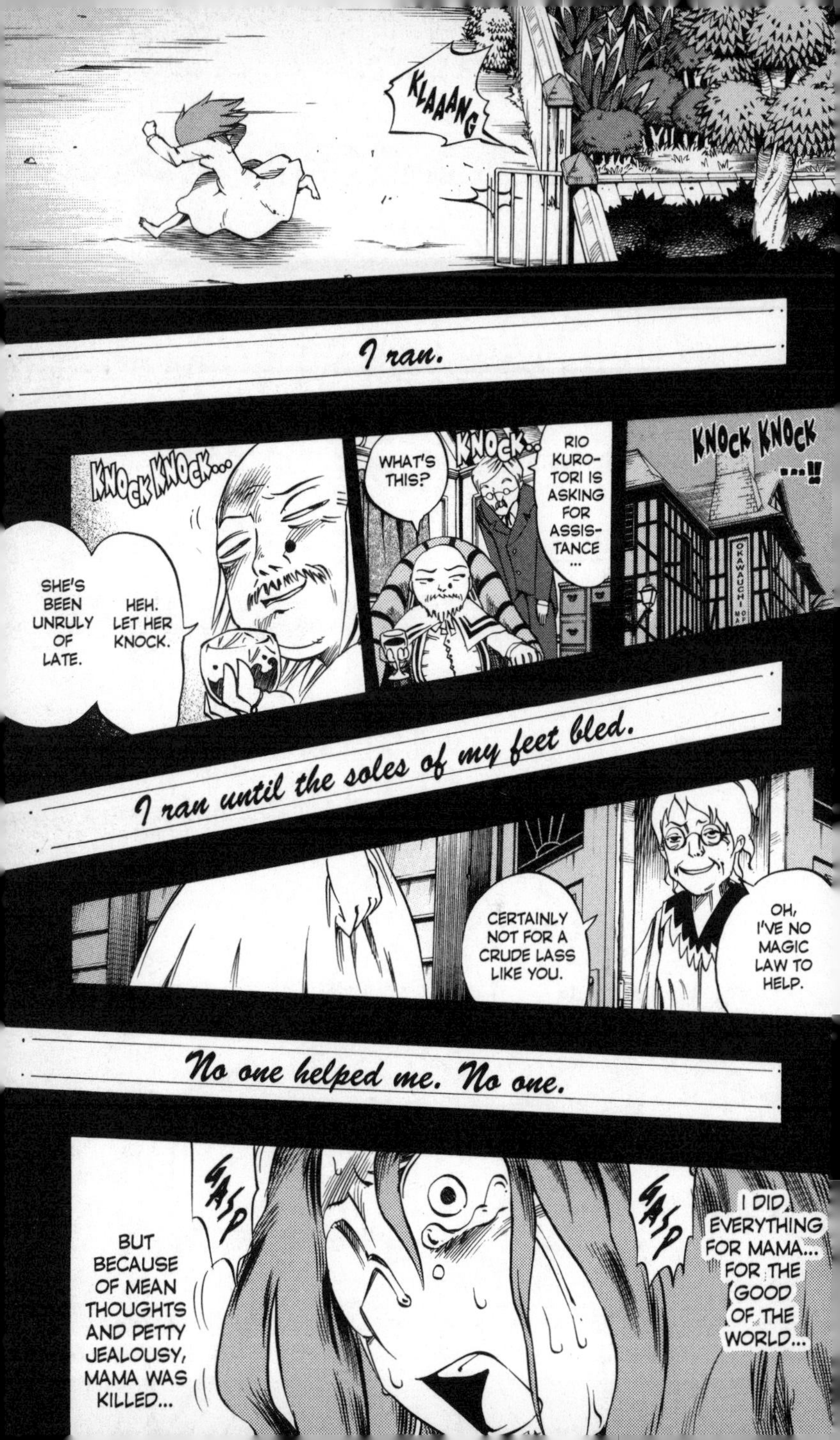

KLAAANG
I ran.
KNOCK KNOCK ...!!
KNOCK..
RIO KUROTORI IS ASKING FOR ASSISTANCE ...
WHAT'S THIS?
KNOCK KNOCK...
HEH. LET HER KNOCK.
SHE'S BEEN UNRULY OF LATE.
I ran until the soles of my feet bled.
OH, I'VE NO MAGIC LAW TO HELP.
CERTAINLY NOT FOR A CRUDE LASS LIKE YOU.
No one helped me. No one.
I DID EVERYTHING FOR MAMA... FOR THE GOOD OF THE WORLD...
GASP
GASP
BUT BECAUSE OF MEAN THOUGHTS AND PETTY JEALOUSY, MAMA WAS KILLED...

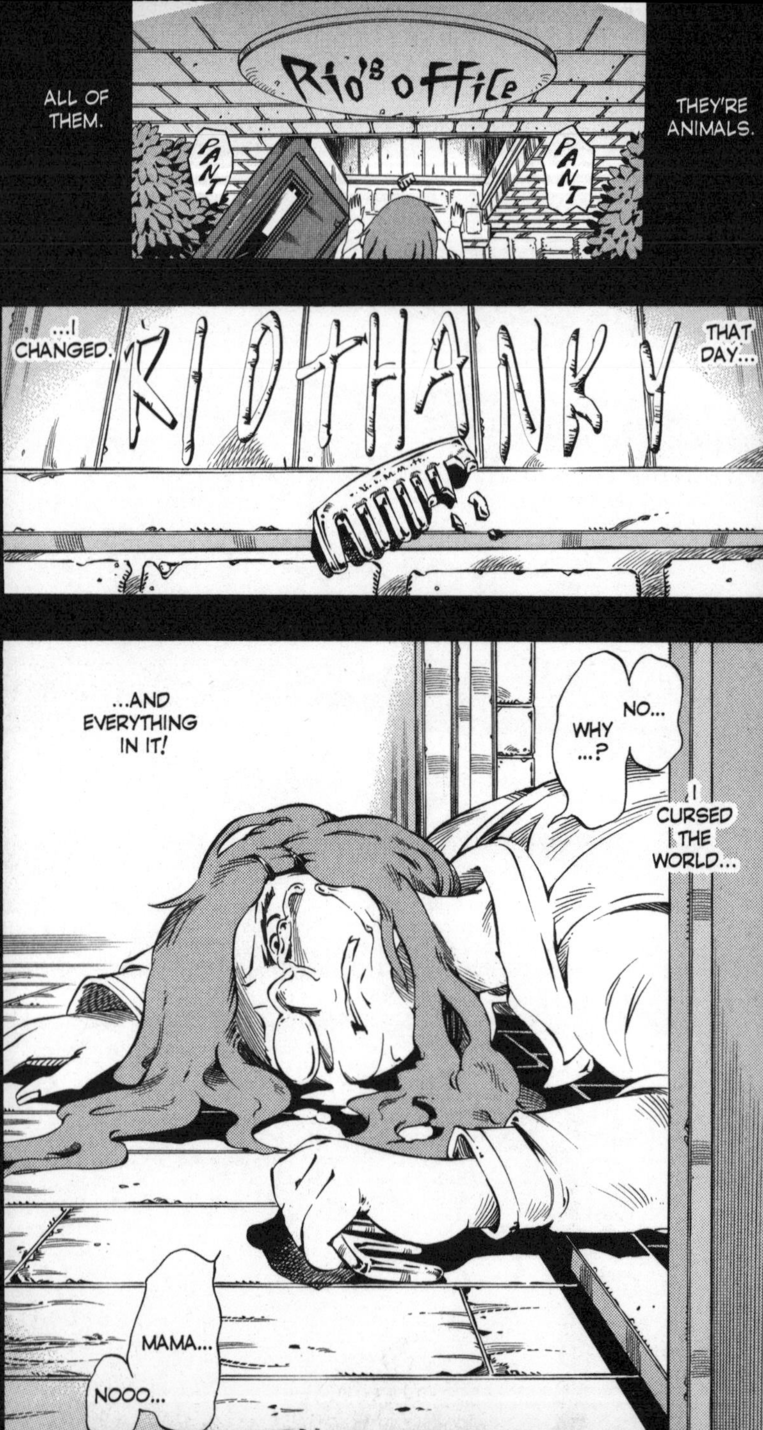
THEY'RE ANIMALS.
PANT
PANT
Rio's office
ALL OF THEM.
THAT DAY...
...I CHANGED.
NO...
WHY ...?
I CURSED THE WORLD...
...AND EVERYTHING IN IT!
MAMA...
NOOO...

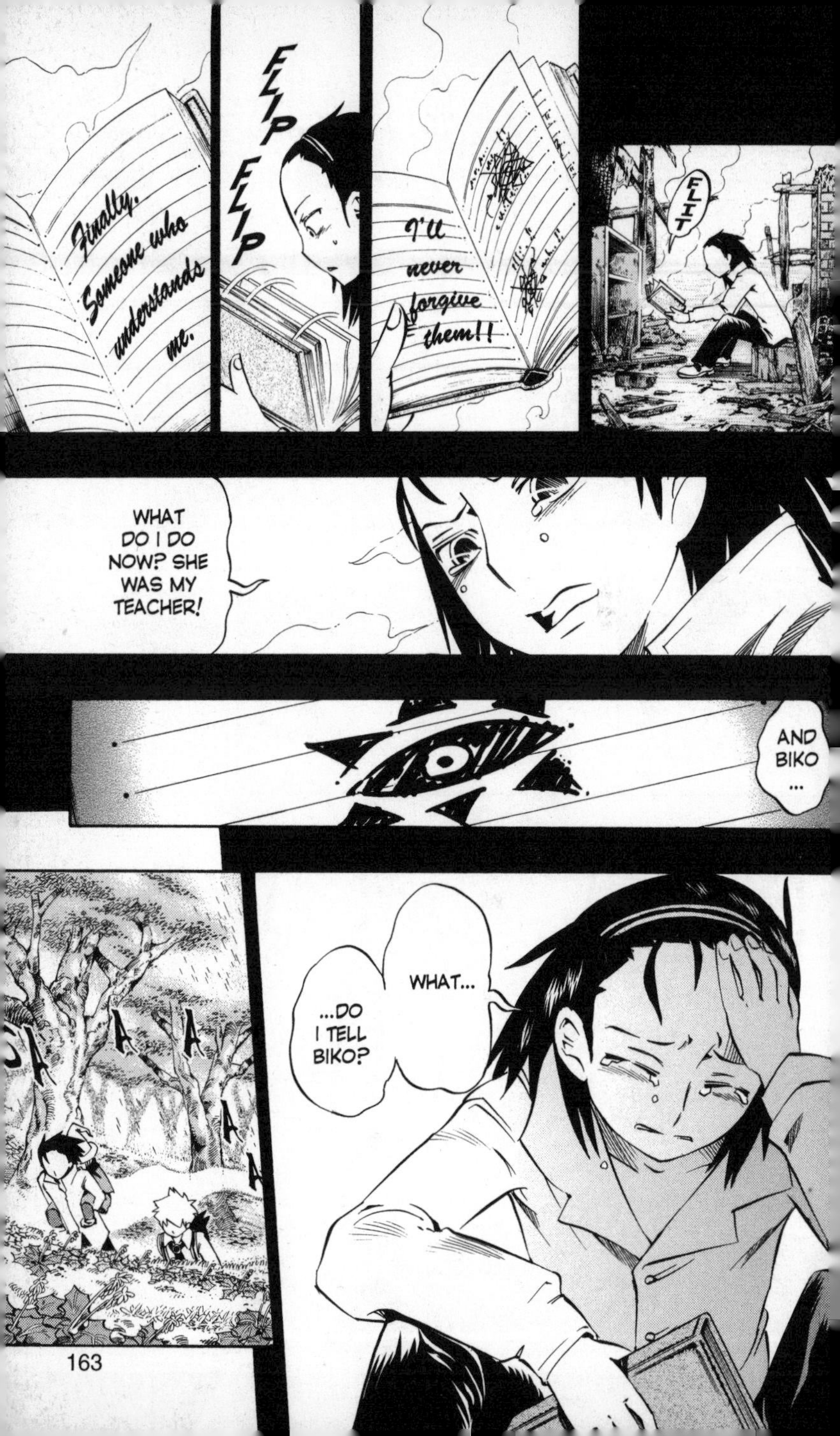
FLIT
I'll never forgive them!!
FLIP FLIP
Finally. Someone who understands me.
WHAT DO I DO NOW? SHE WAS MY TEACHER!
AND BIKO ...
WHAT...
...DO I TELL BIKO?

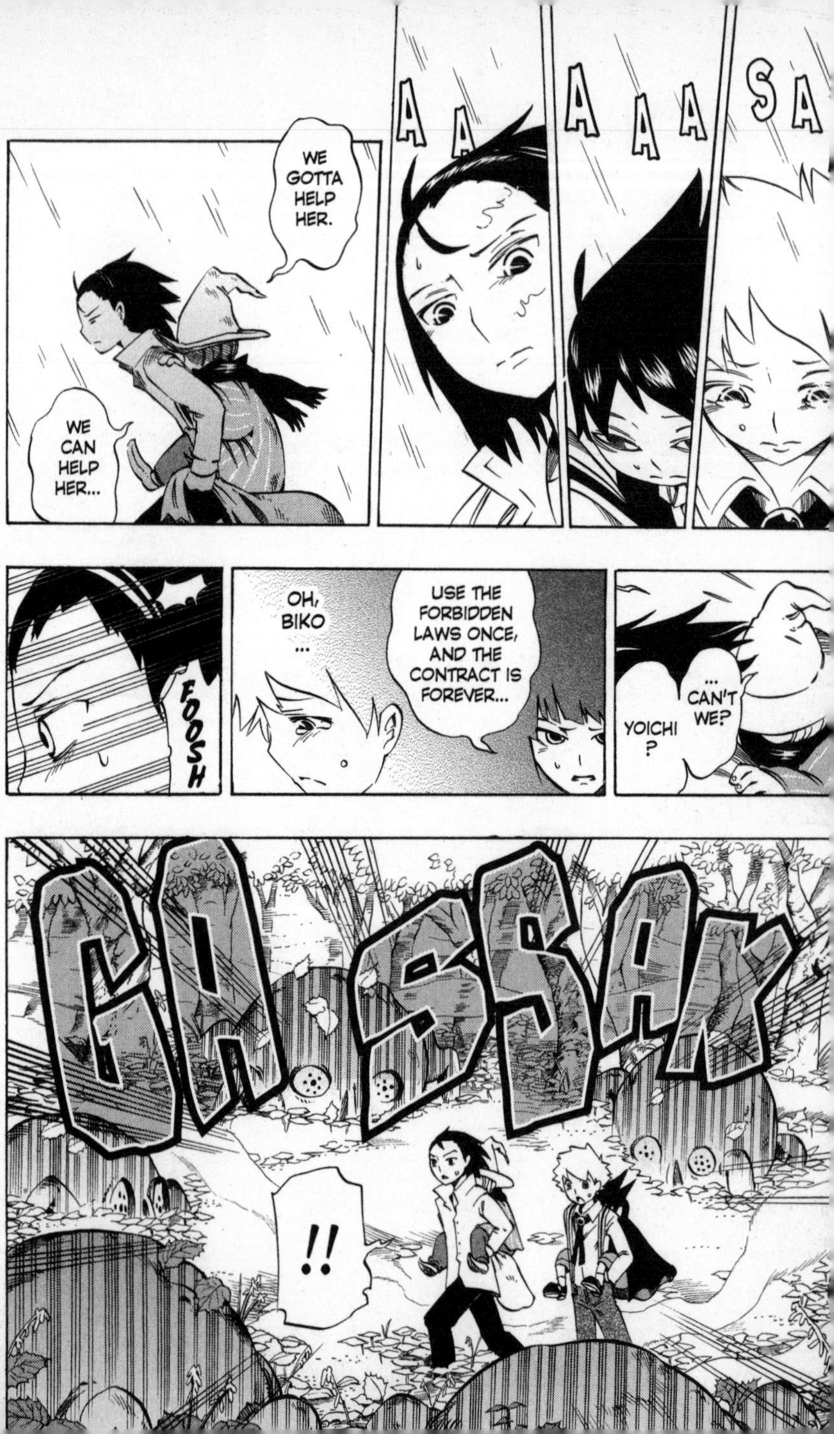
SA
A A
A A
WE GOTTA HELP HER.
WE CAN HELP HER...
... CAN'T WE?
YOICHI ?
USE THE FORBIDDEN LAWS ONCE, AND THE CONTRACT IS FOREVER...
OH, BIKO ...
FOOSH
CA-SSAK
!!

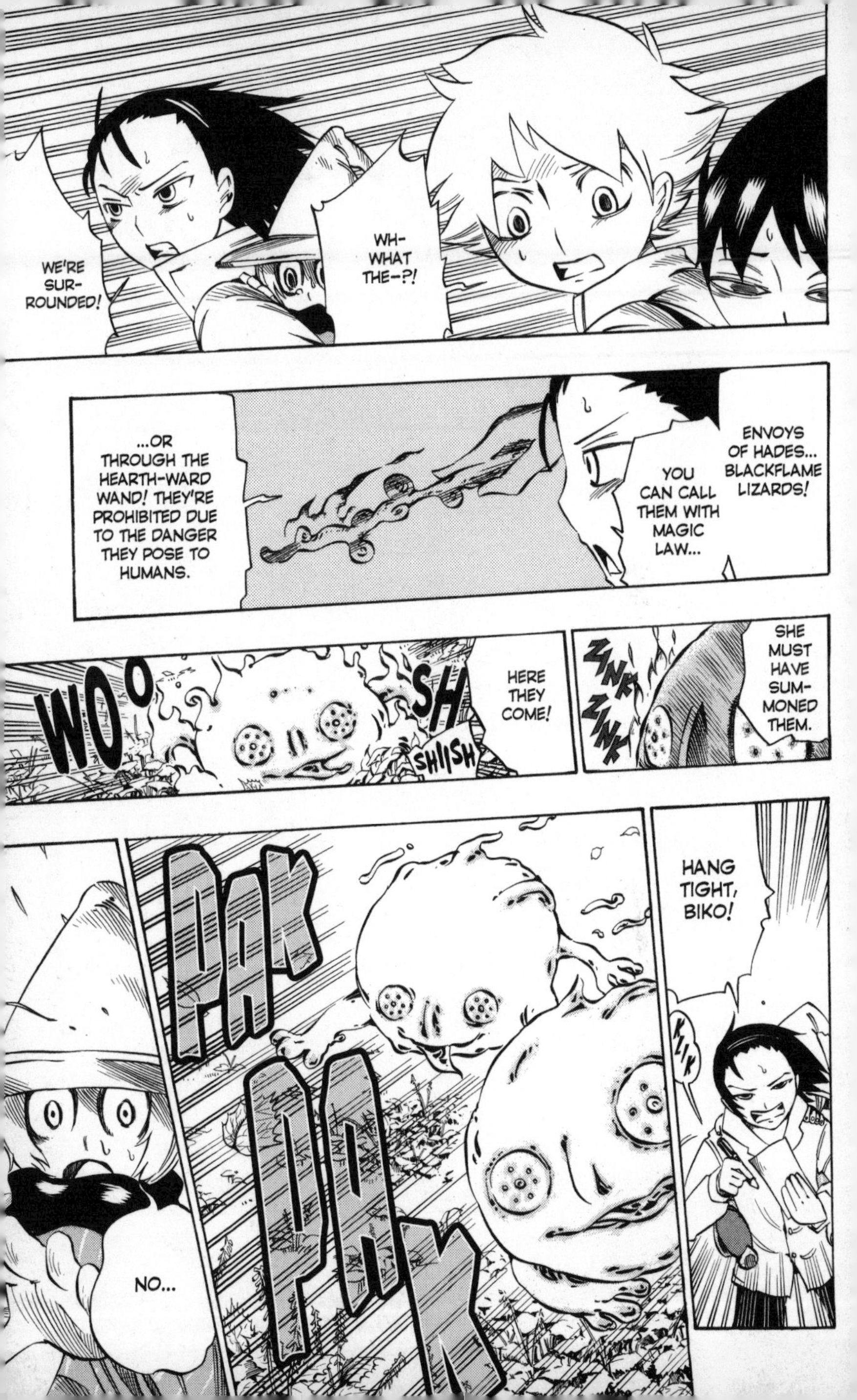
WH-WHAT THE-?!
WE'RE SUR-ROUNDED!
ENVOYS OF HADES... BLACKFLAME LIZARDS!
YOU CAN CALL THEM WITH MAGIC LAW...
...OR THROUGH THE HEARTH-WARD WAND! THEY'RE PROHIBITED DUE TO THE DANGER THEY POSE TO HUMANS.
SHE MUST HAVE SUM-MONED THEM.
ZINK ZINK
HERE THEY COME!
SH
SHIISH
WOO
HANG TIGHT, BIKO!
KLIK
PAK
PAK
NO...

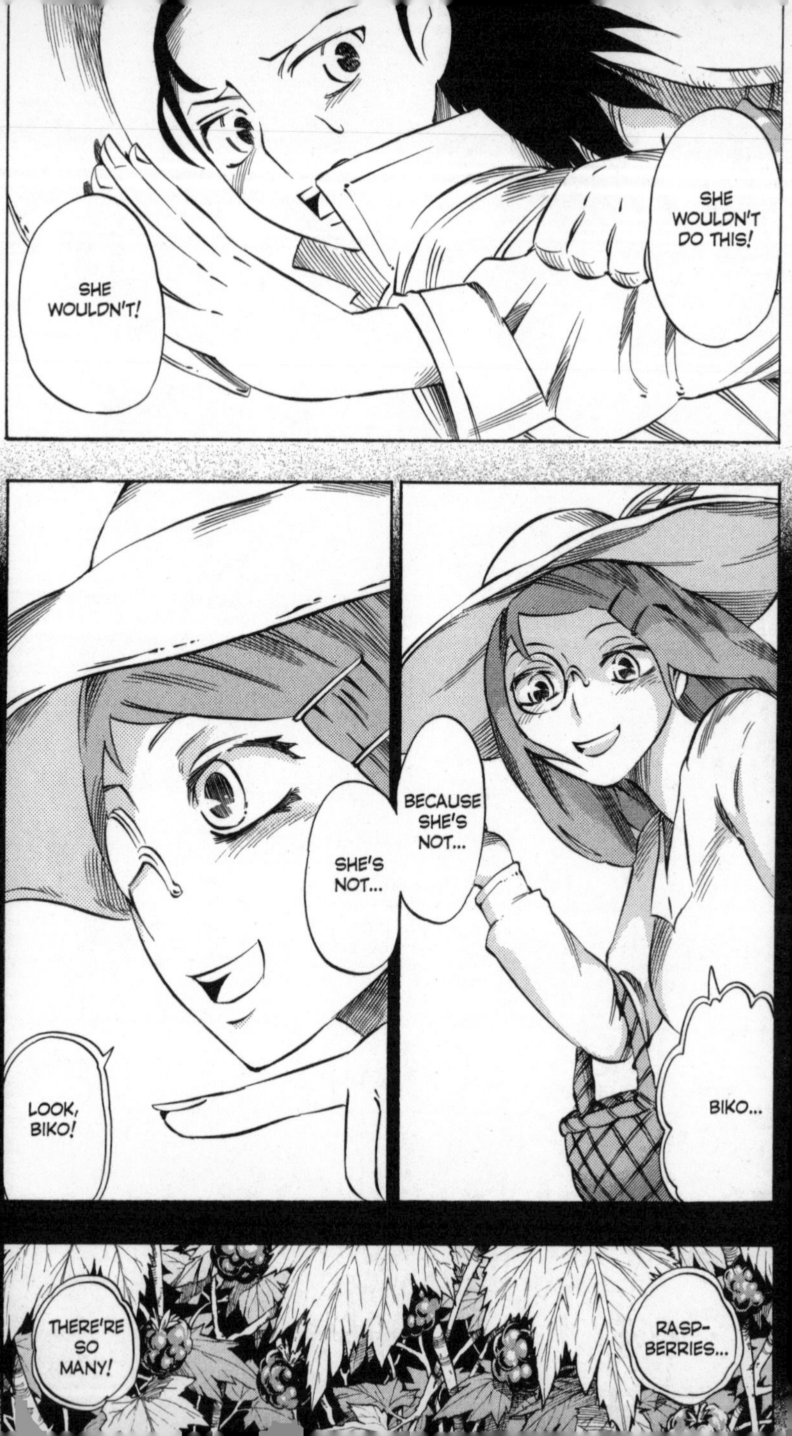
SHE WOULDN'T DO THIS!
SHE WOULDN'T!
BECAUSE SHE'S NOT...
BIKO...
SHE'S NOT...
LOOK, BIKO!
RASP-BERRIES...
THERE'RE SO MANY!

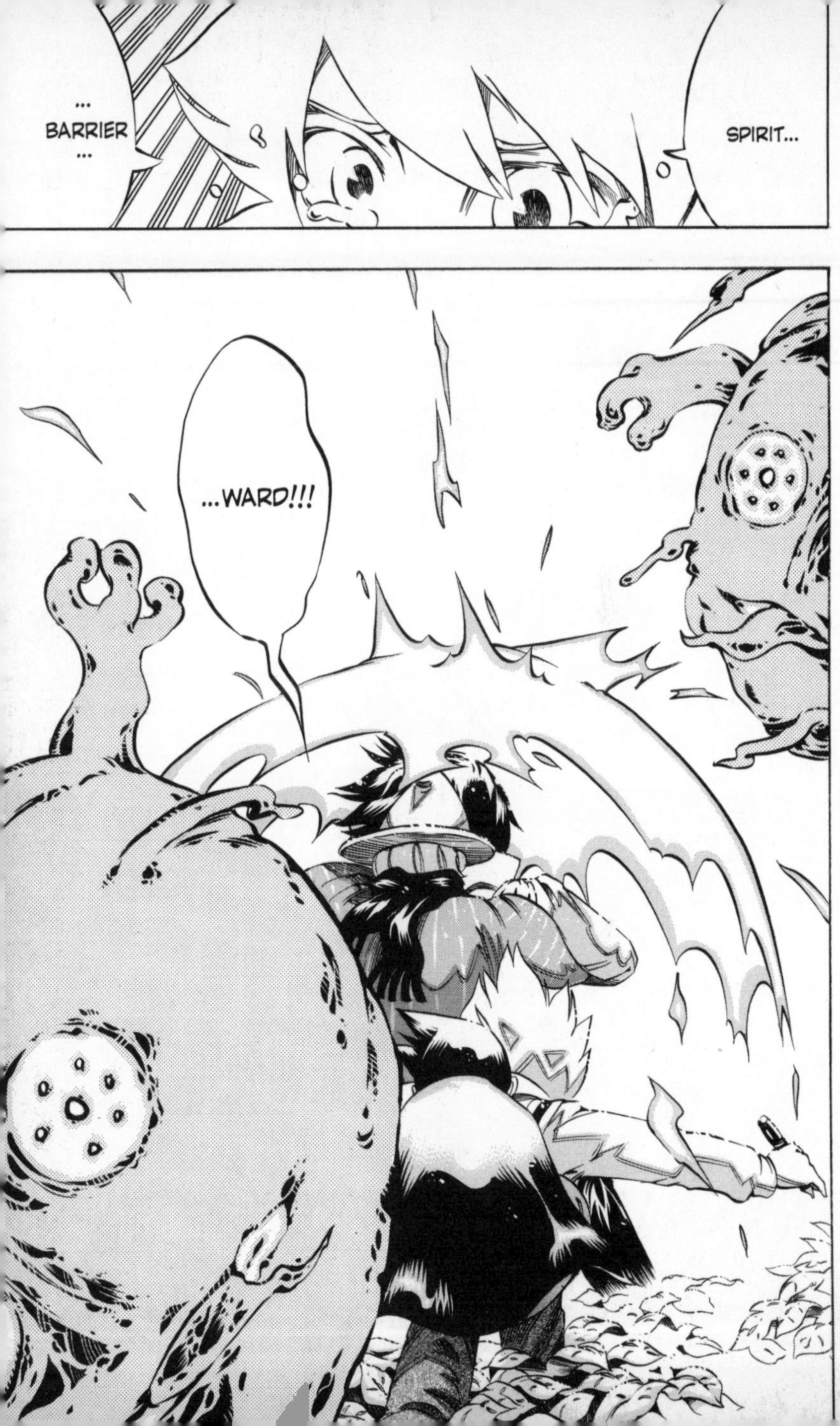
SPIRIT...
... BARRIER ...
...WARD!!!

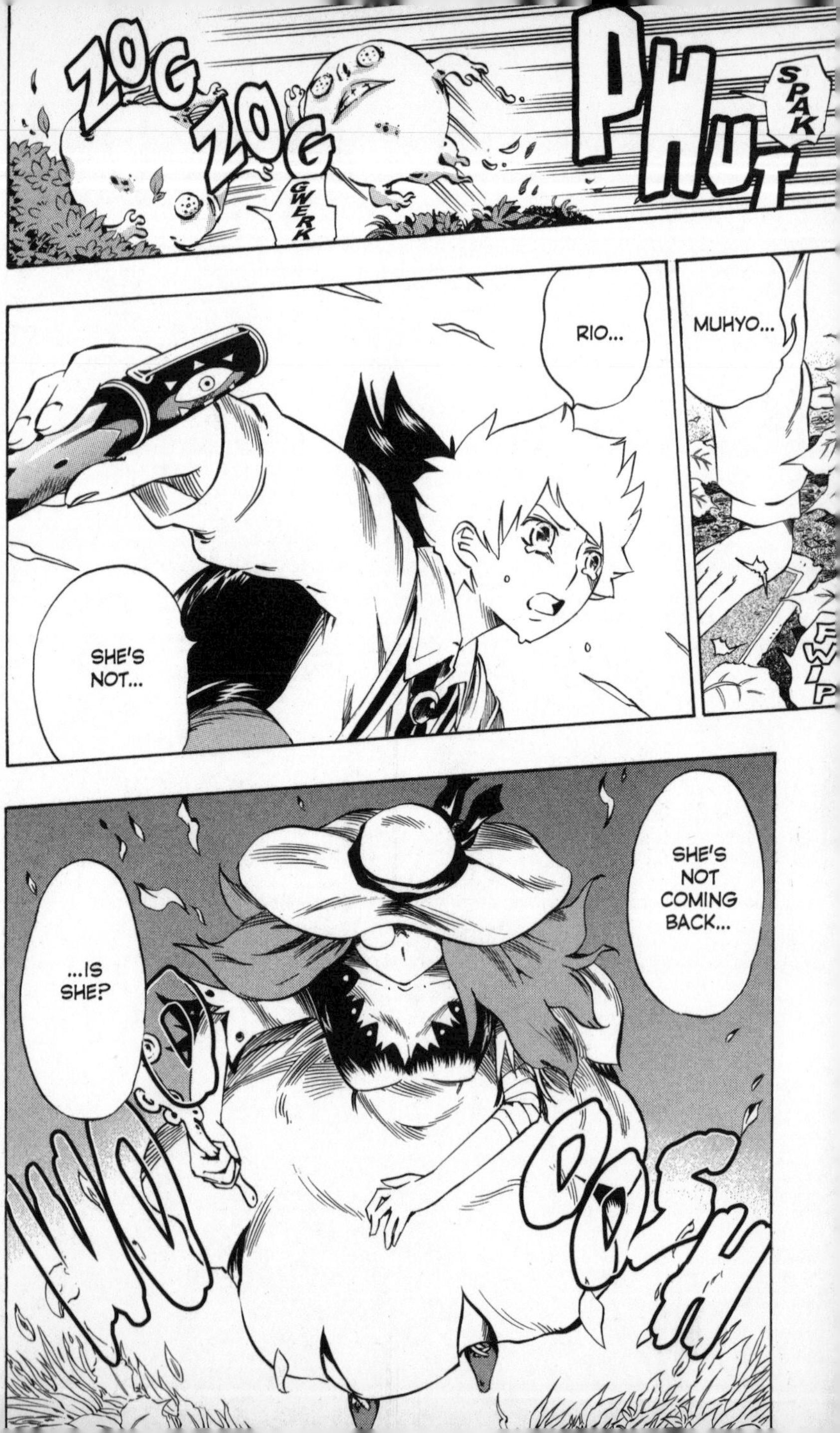
PHUT
SPAK
ZOG ZOG
GWERK
MUHYO...
FWIP
RIO...
SHE'S NOT...
SHE'S NOT COMING BACK...
...IS SHE?

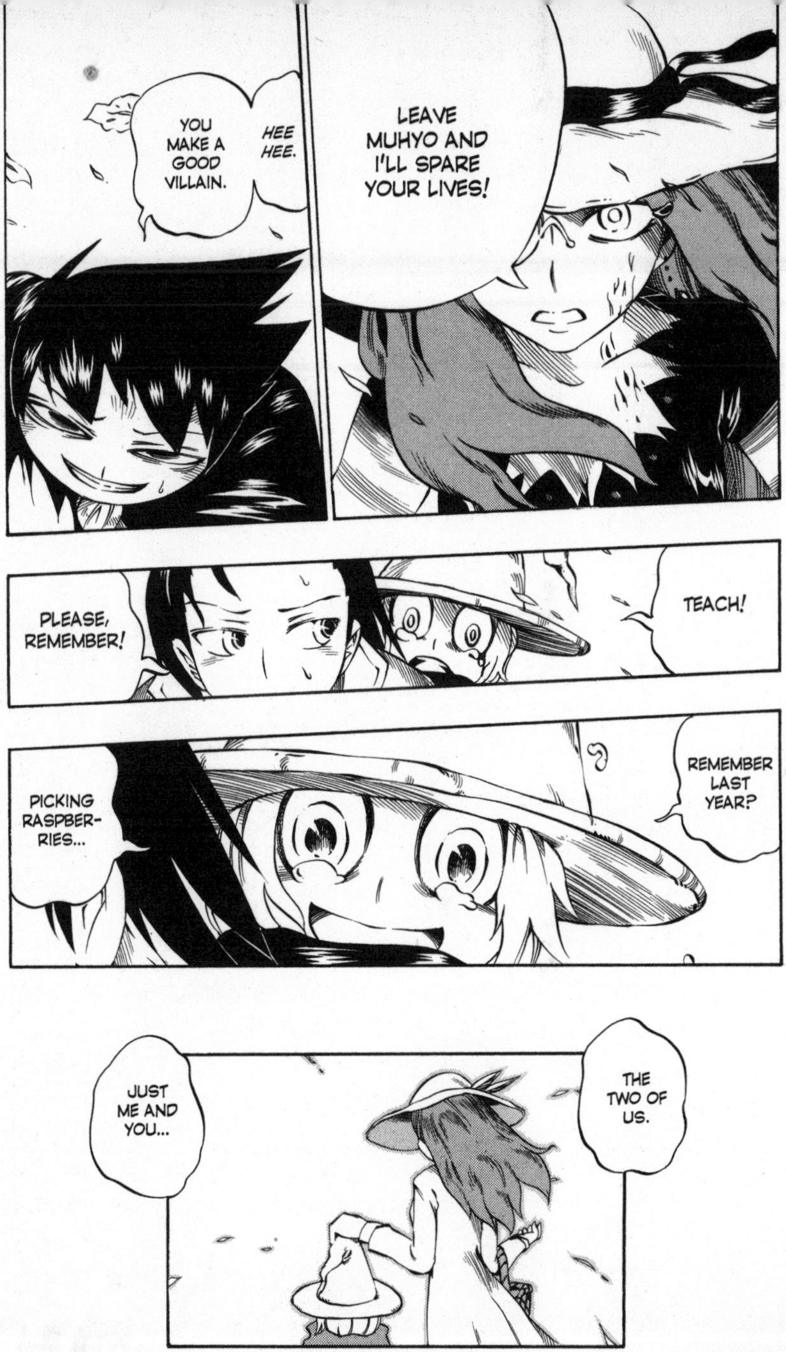
LEAVE MUHYO AND I'LL SPARE YOUR LIVES!
HEE HEE.
YOU MAKE A GOOD VILLAIN.
TEACH!
PLEASE, REMEMBER!
REMEMBER LAST YEAR?
PICKING RASPBERRIES...
THE TWO OF US.
JUST ME AND YOU...

— A DAY IN BIKO'S OFFICE ② —

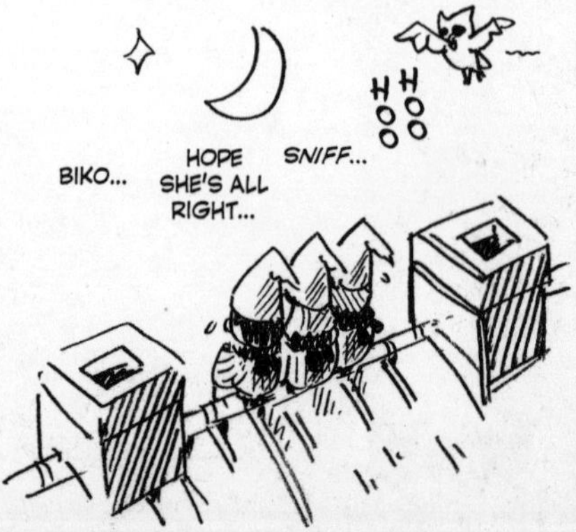
HOO HOO
SNIFF...
HOPE SHE'S ALL RIGHT...
BIKO...

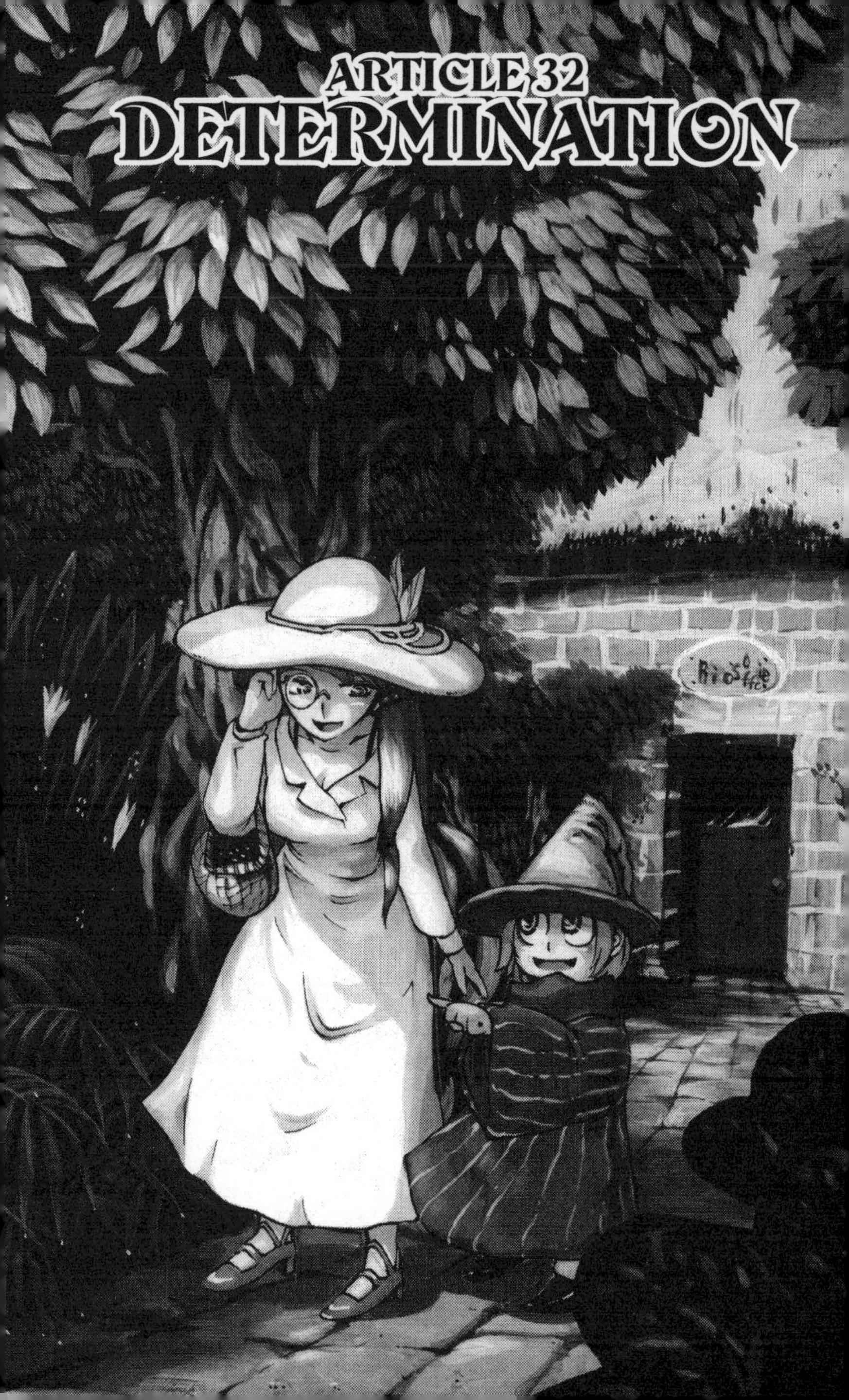
ARTICLE 32
DETERMINATION

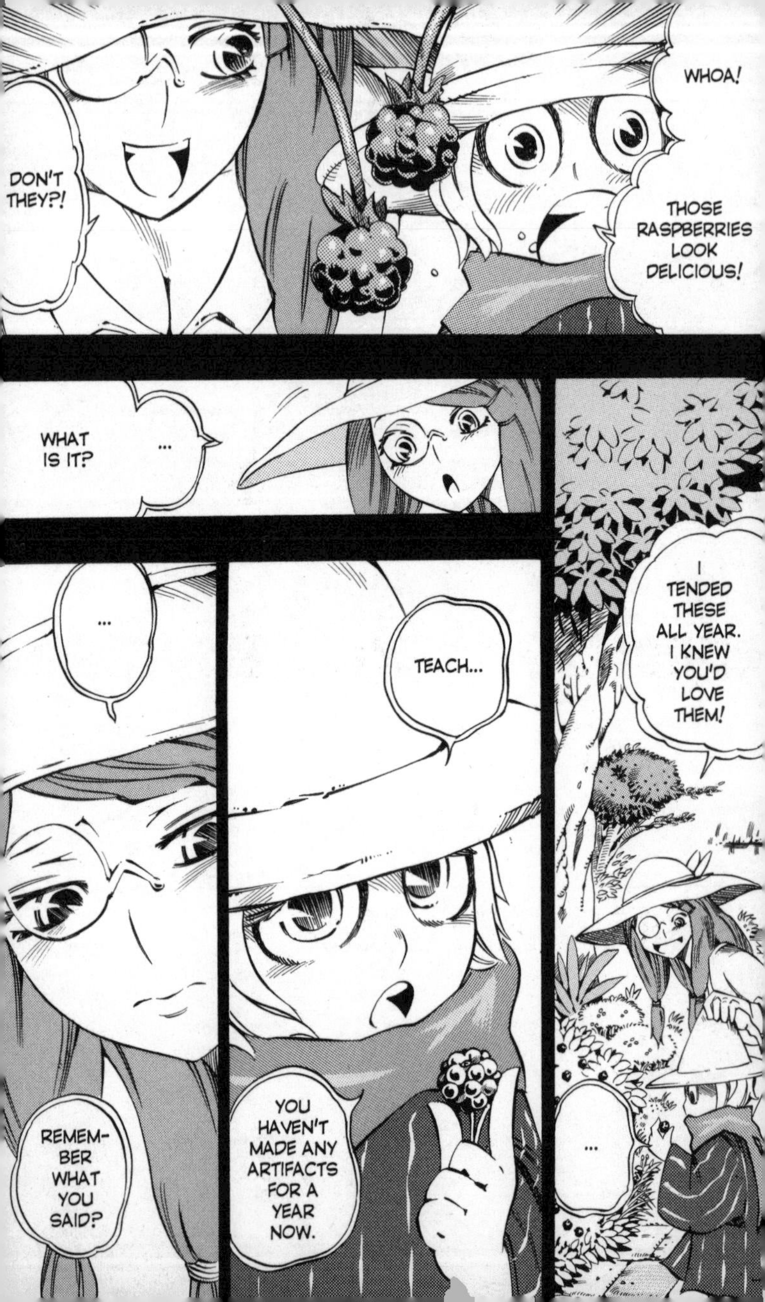
WHOA!
THOSE RASPBERRIES LOOK DELICIOUS!
DON'T THEY?!
I TENDED THESE ALL YEAR. I KNEW YOU'D LOVE THEM!
...
...
WHAT IS IT?
TEACH...
YOU HAVEN'T MADE ANY ARTIFACTS FOR A YEAR NOW.
...
REMEMBER WHAT YOU SAID?

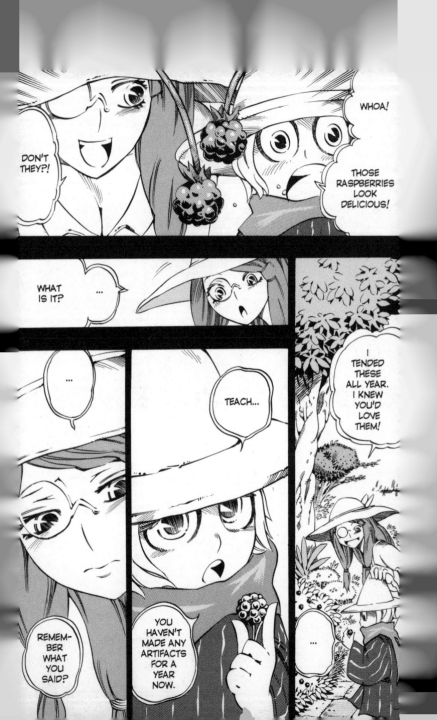

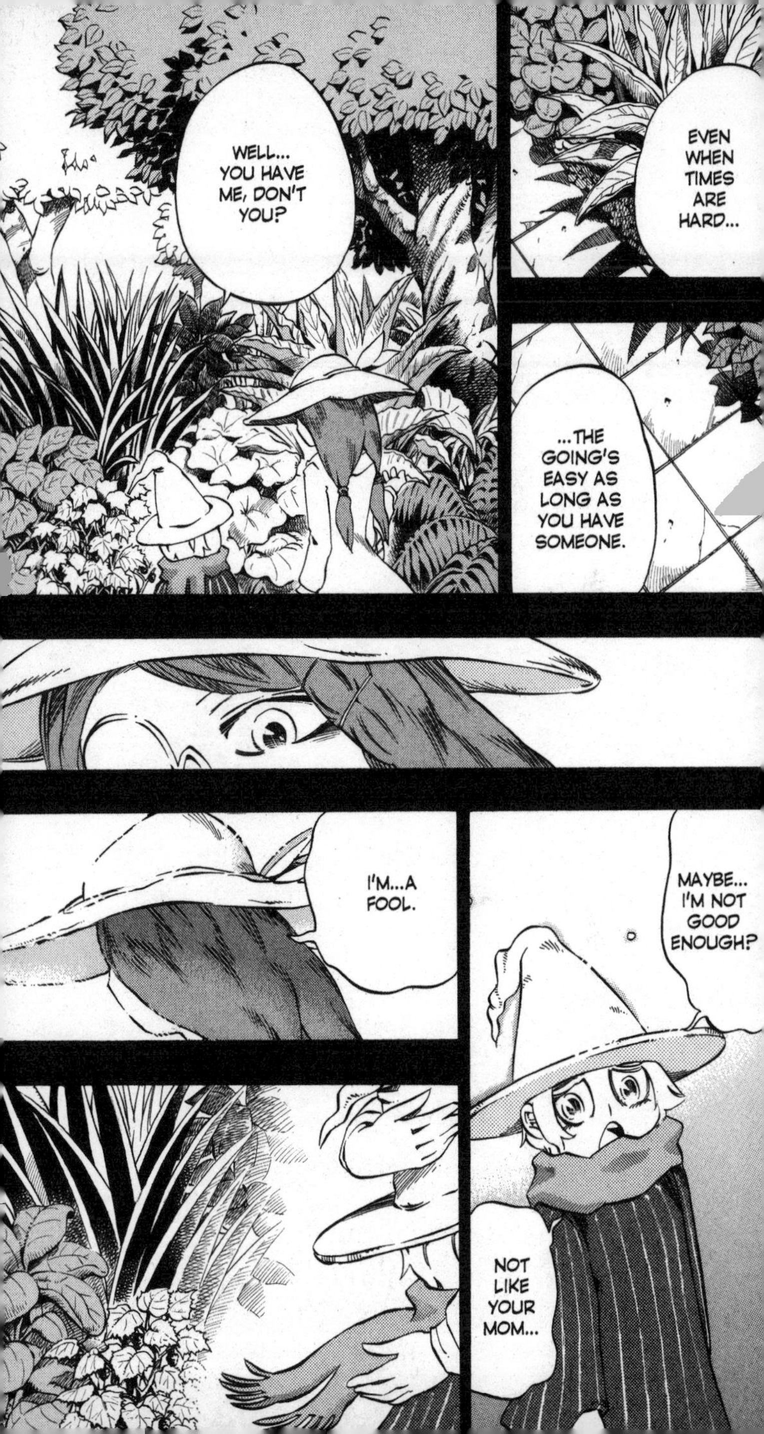
EVEN WHEN TIMES ARE HARD...
...THE GOING'S EASY AS LONG AS YOU HAVE SOMEONE.
WELL... YOU HAVE ME, DON'T YOU?
MAYBE... I'M NOT GOOD ENOUGH?
NOT LIKE YOUR MOM...
I'M...A FOOL.

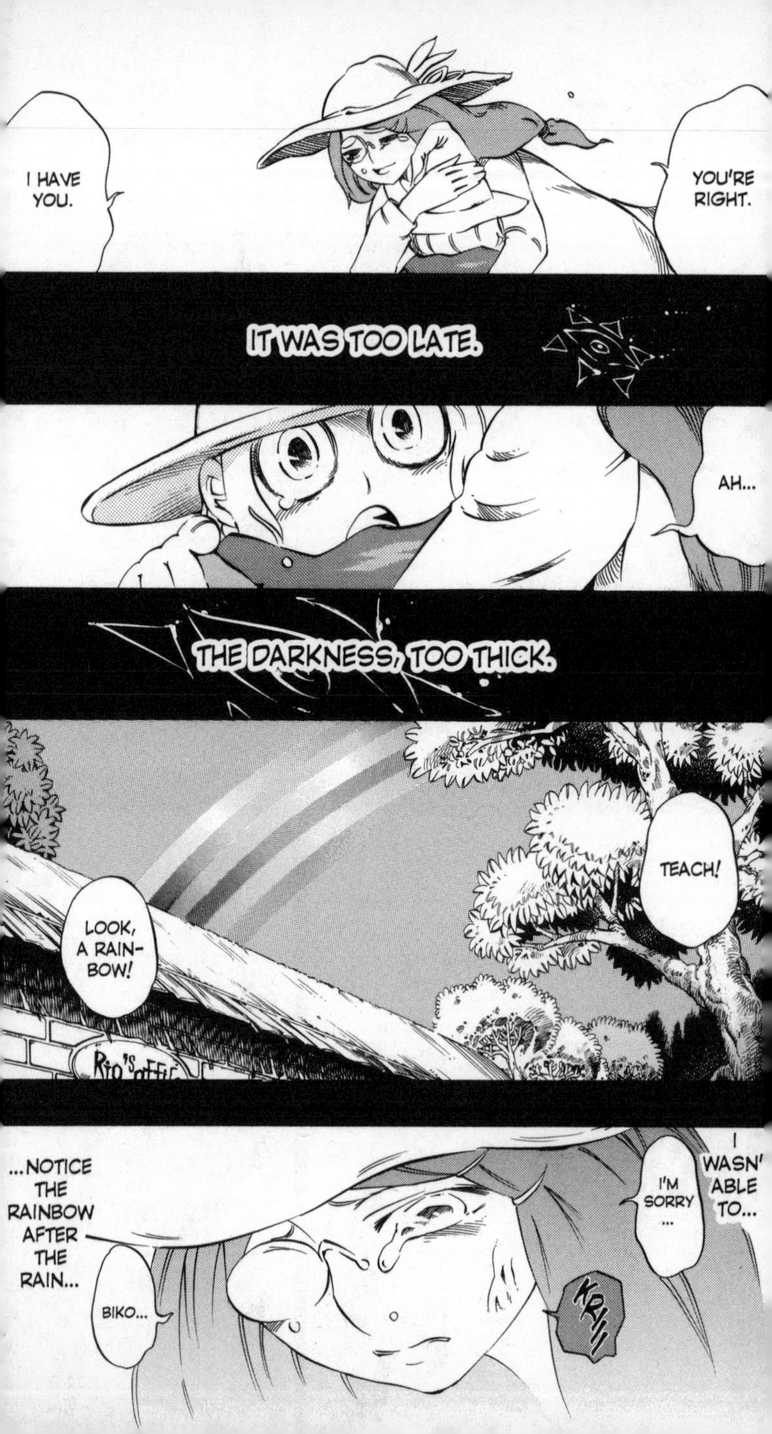
YOU'RE RIGHT.
I HAVE YOU.
IT WAS TOO LATE.
AH...
THE DARKNESS, TOO THICK.
TEACH!
LOOK, A RAIN-BOW!
I WASN' ABLE TO...
I'M SORRY...
...NOTICE THE RAINBOW AFTER THE RAIN...
KRIII
BIKO...

READ THIS WAY

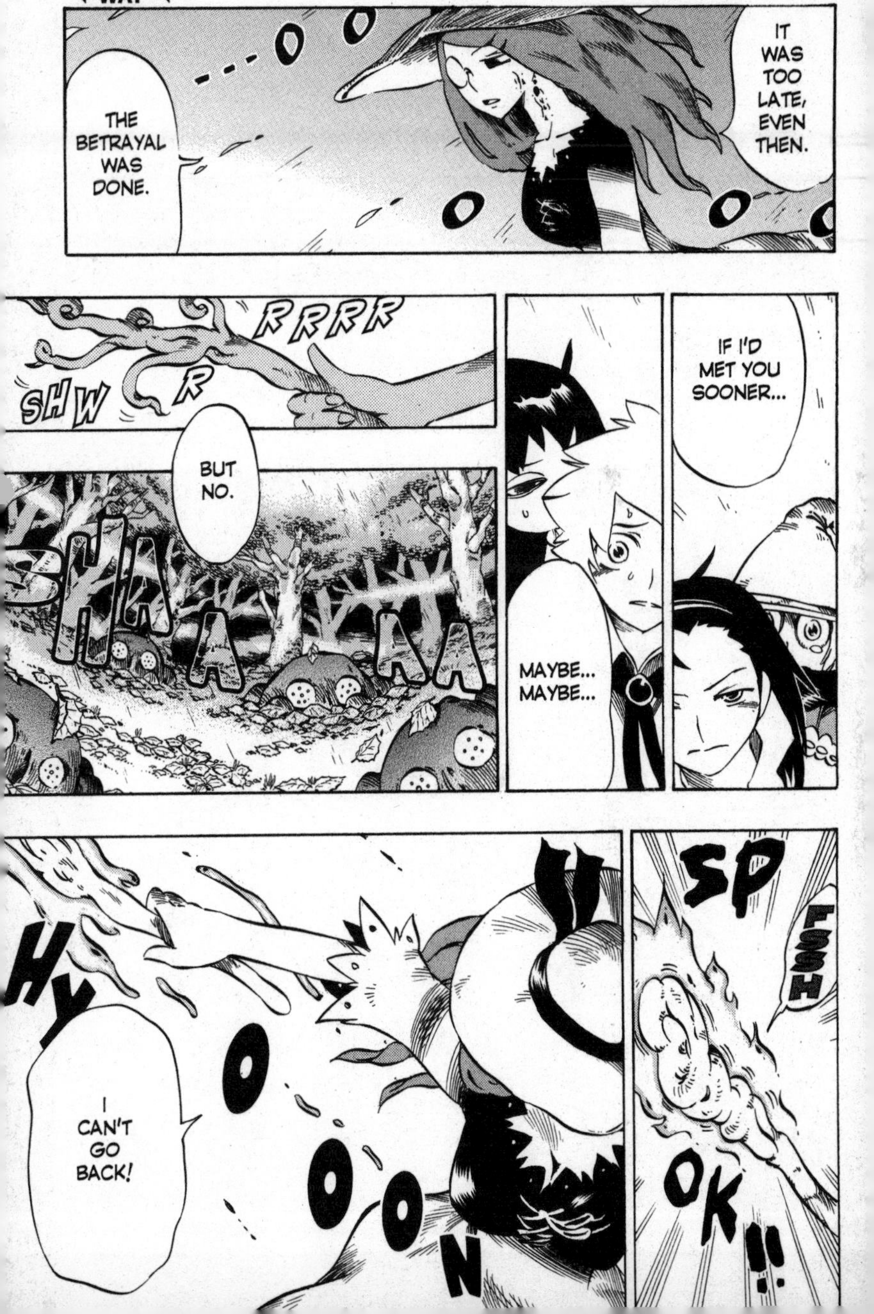
IT WAS TOO LATE, EVEN THEN.
...OO
THE BETRAYAL WAS DONE.
OOO
IF I'D MET YOU SOONER...
MAYBE... MAYBE...
RRRRR
SHW R
BUT NO.
SHAAAA
SP
FSSH
OK!!
HYOOOON
I CAN'T GO BACK!

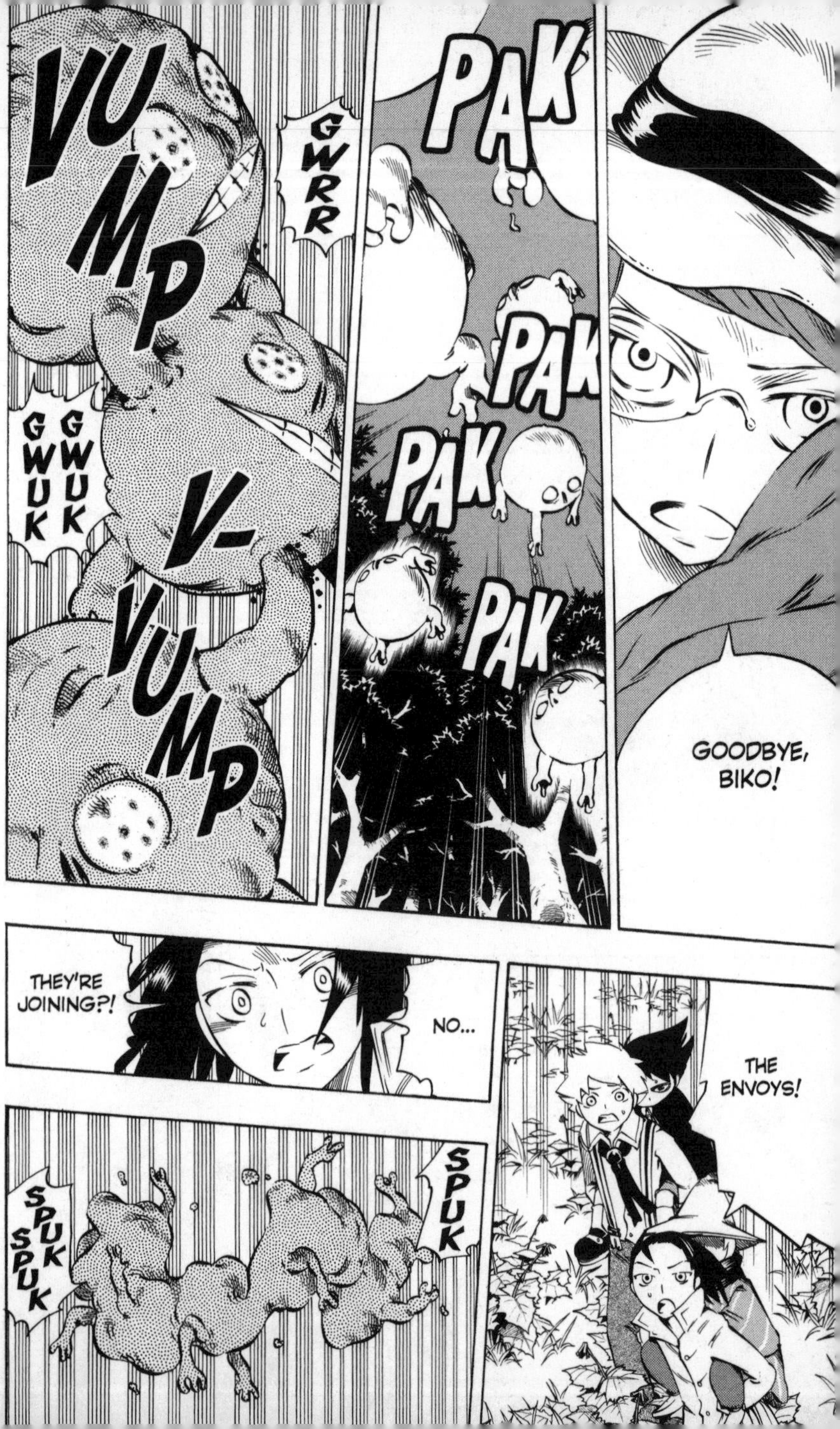
GOODBYE, BIKO!
PAK
PAK
PAK
PAK
GWRR
VUMP
GWUK GWUK
V-VUMP
THE ENVOYS!
THEY'RE JOINING?!
NO...
SPUK
SPUK SPUK

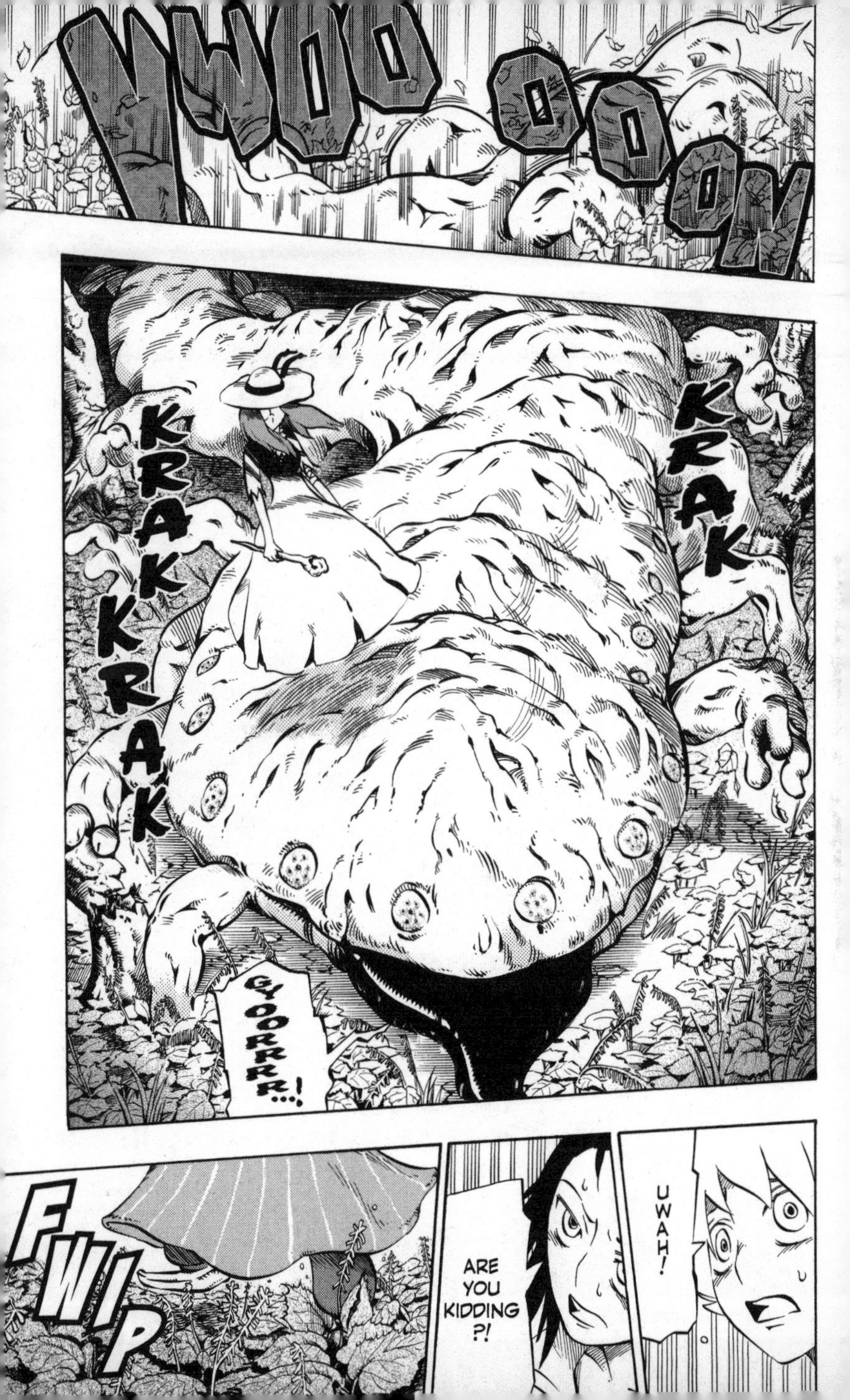
WWOOOOOM
KRAK
KRAKKRAK
GYOORRR...!
UWAH!
ARE YOU KIDDING ?!
FWIP

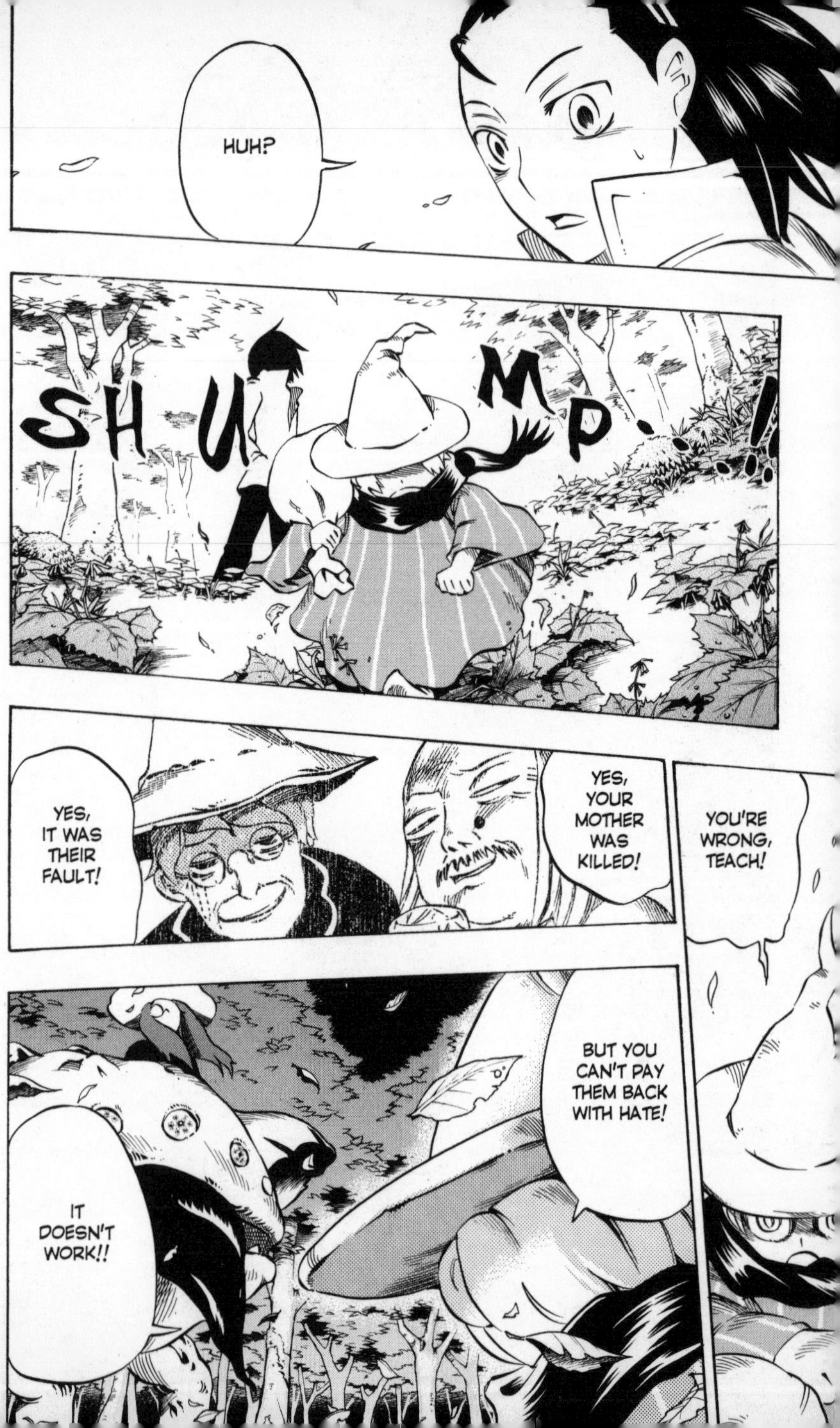
HUH?
SHUMP!!
YOU'RE WRONG, TEACH!
YES, YOUR MOTHER WAS KILLED!
YES, IT WAS THEIR FAULT!
BUT YOU CAN'T PAY THEM BACK WITH HATE!
IT DOESN'T WORK!!

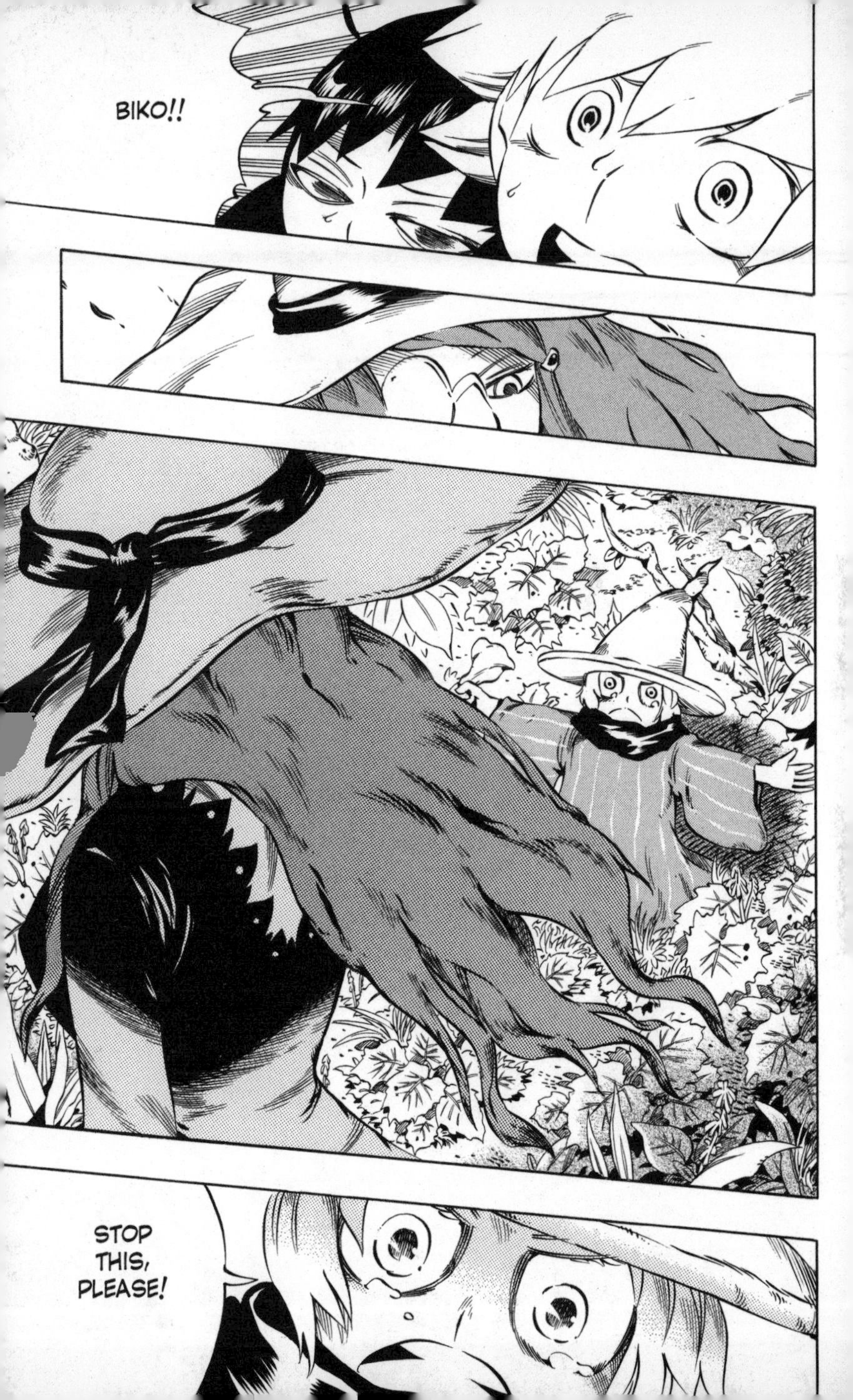
BIKO!!
STOP THIS, PLEASE!

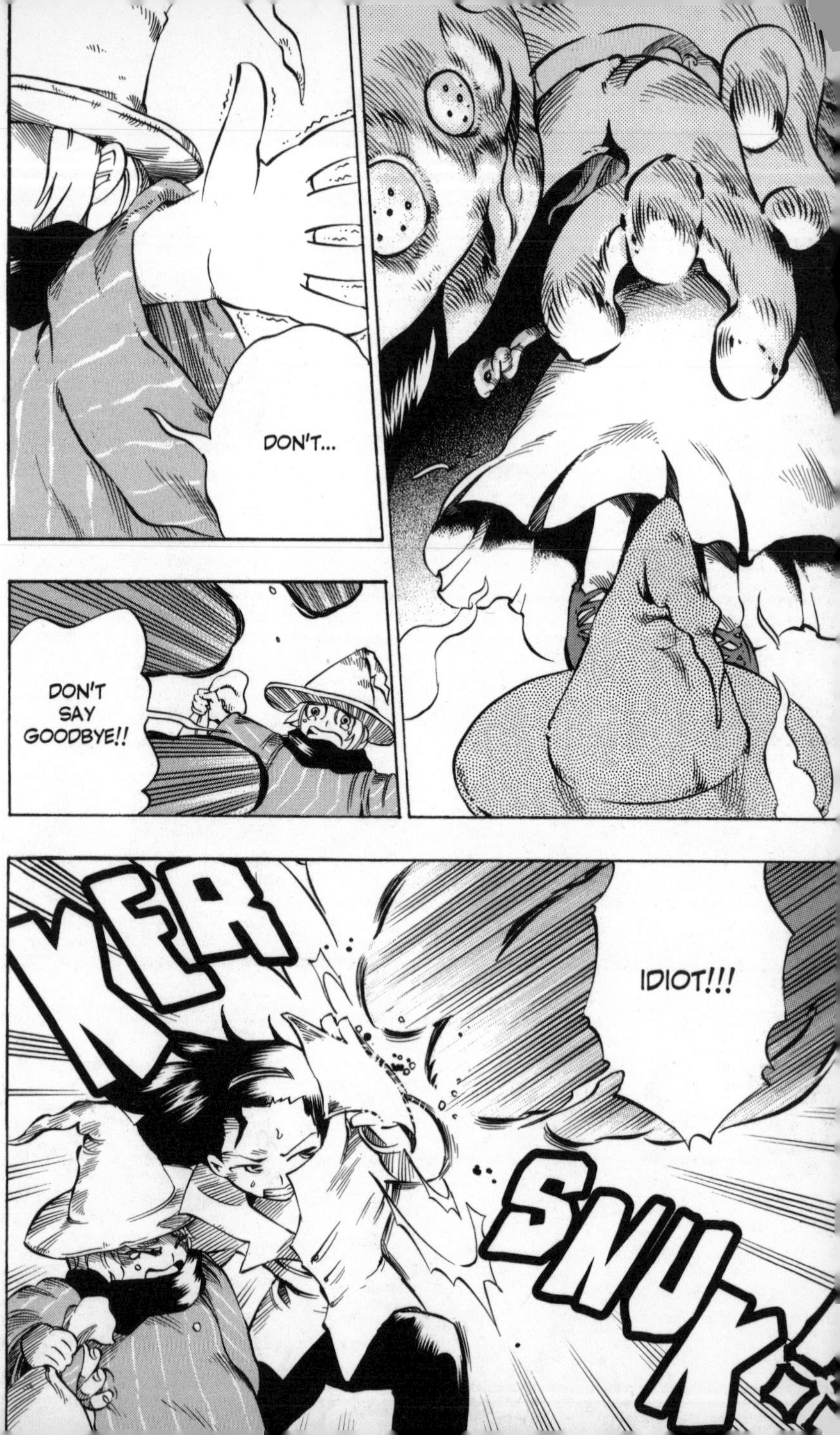

DON'T...
DON'T SAY GOODBYE!!
IDIOT!!!
KFR
SNUK

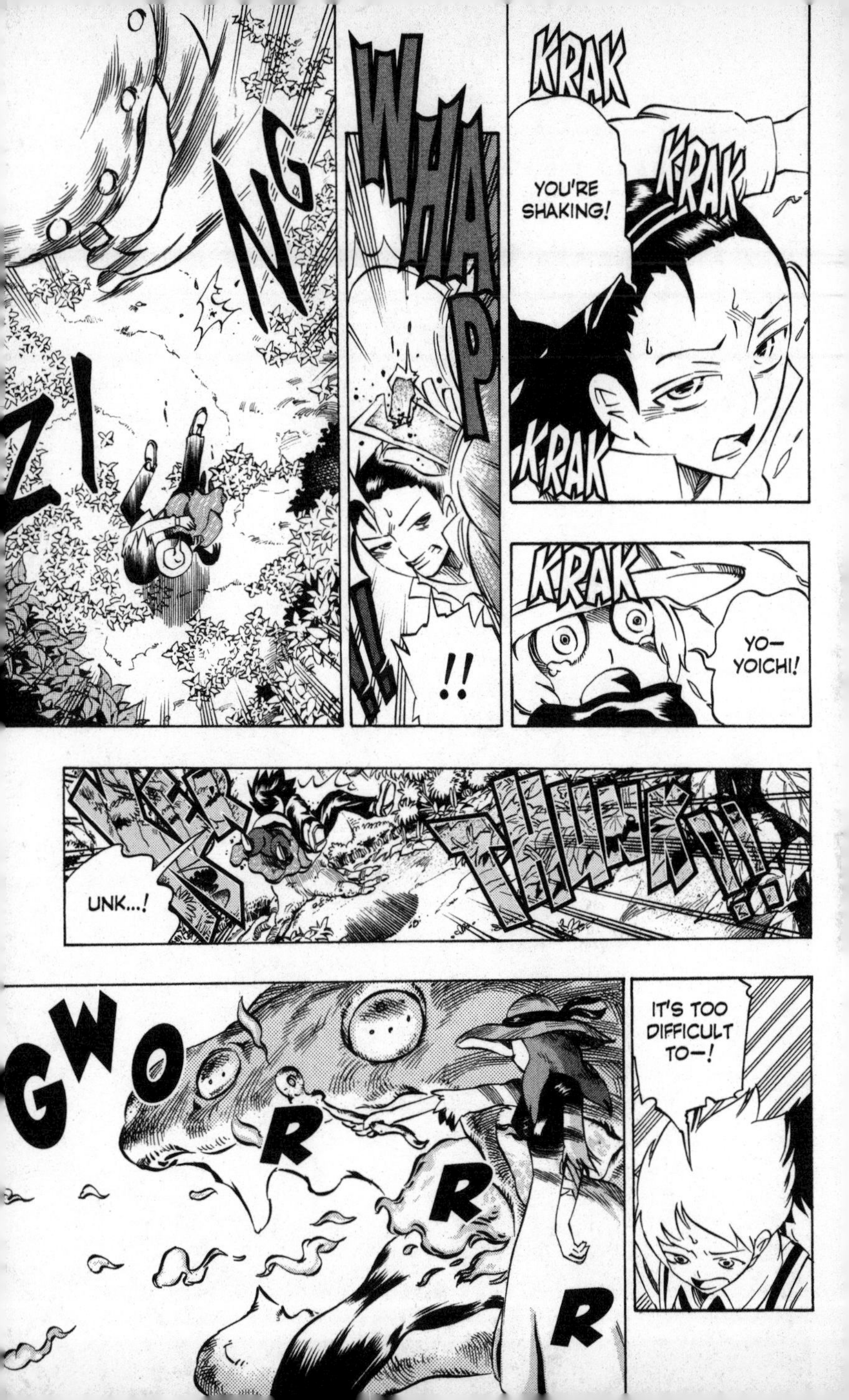
KRAK
KRAK
YOU'RE SHAKING!
KRAK
KRAK
YO— YOICHI!
WHAP
!!
ZING
THUNK!!
UNK...!
IT'S TOO DIFFICULT TO—!
GWORRR

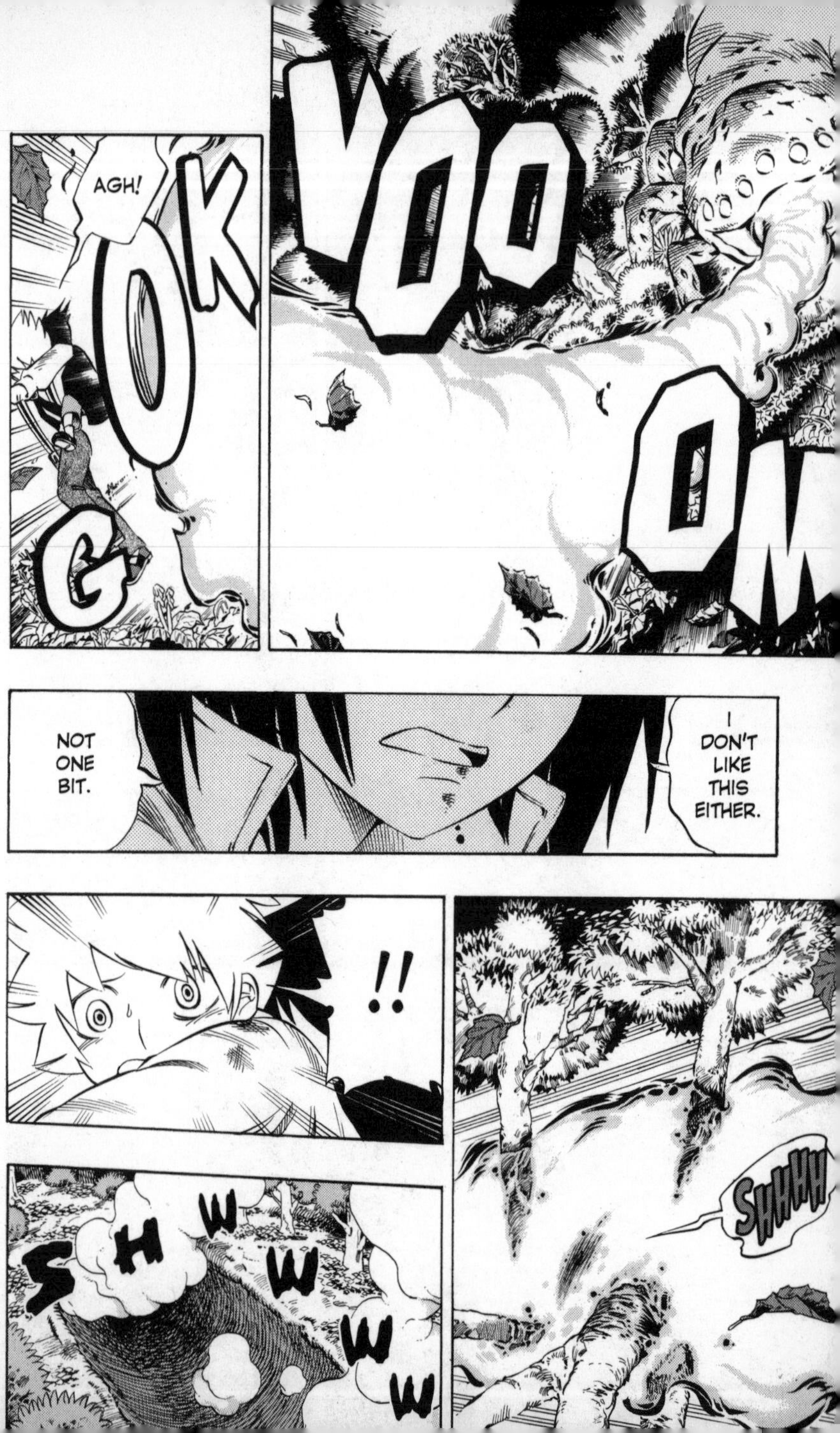
VOOOM
AGH!
GOK
I DON'T LIKE THIS EITHER.
NOT ONE BIT.
SHHHH
!!
SHWWWWW

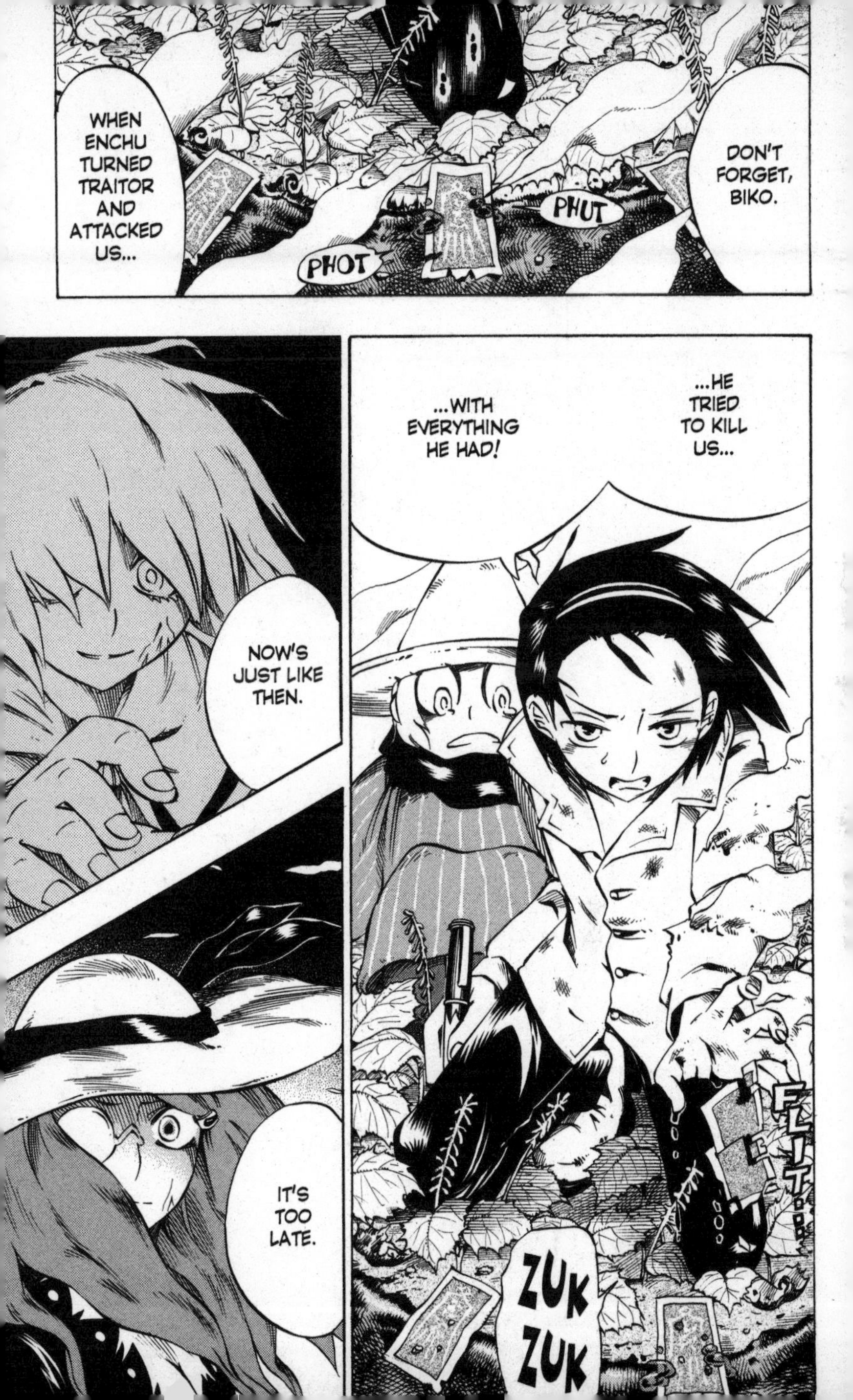
DON'T FORGET, BIKO.
PHUT
WHEN ENCHU TURNED TRAITOR AND ATTACKED US...
PHOT
...HE TRIED TO KILL US...
...WITH EVERYTHING HE HAD!
FLIT
ZUK ZUK
NOW'S JUST LIKE THEN.
IT'S TOO LATE.

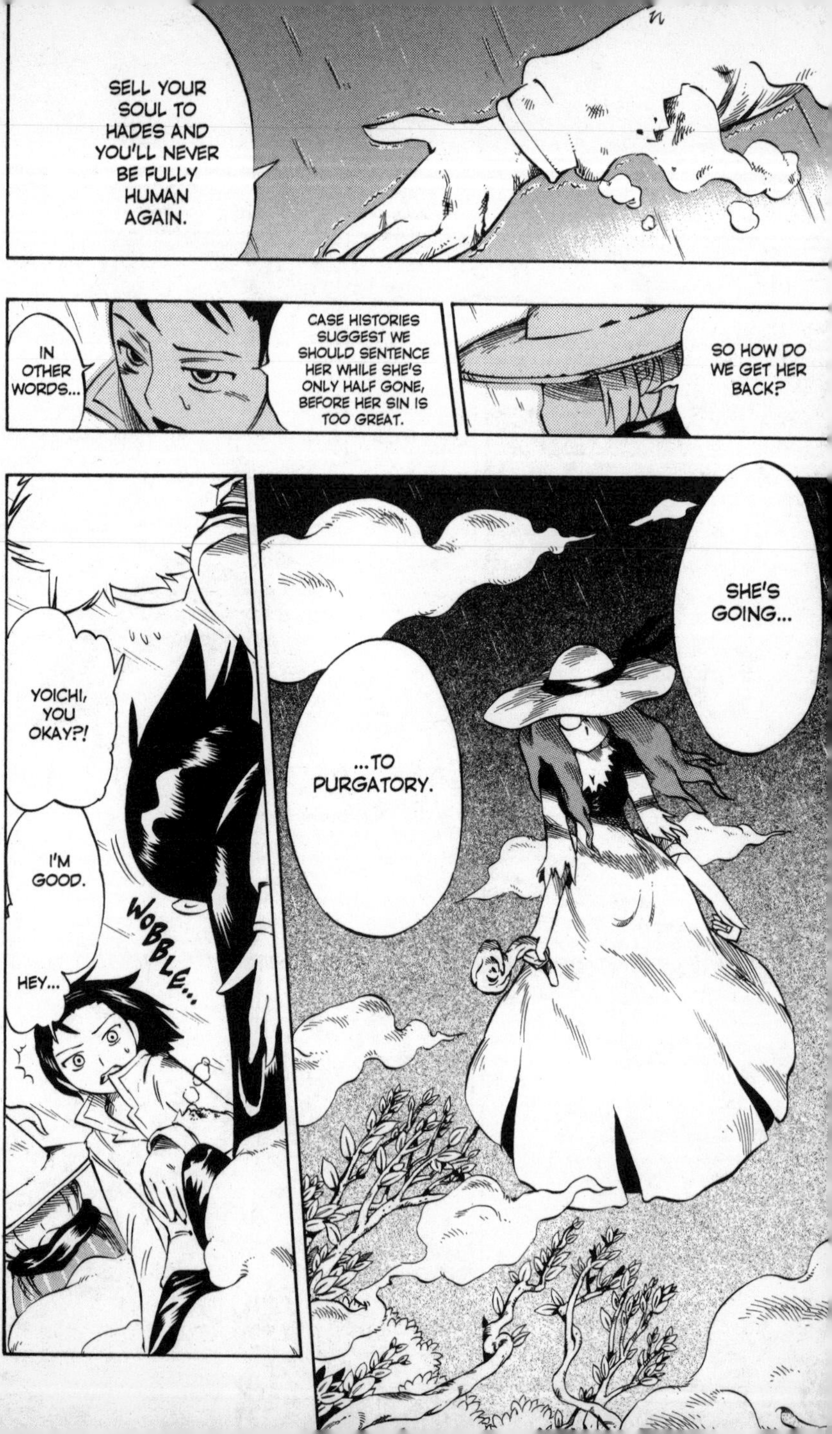
SELL YOUR SOUL TO HADES AND YOU'LL NEVER BE FULLY HUMAN AGAIN.
SO HOW DO WE GET HER BACK?
CASE HISTORIES SUGGEST WE SHOULD SENTENCE HER WHILE SHE'S ONLY HALF GONE, BEFORE HER SIN IS TOO GREAT.
IN OTHER WORDS...
SHE'S GOING...
...TO PURGATORY.
YOICHI, YOU OKAY?!
I'M GOOD.
WOBBLE...
HEY...

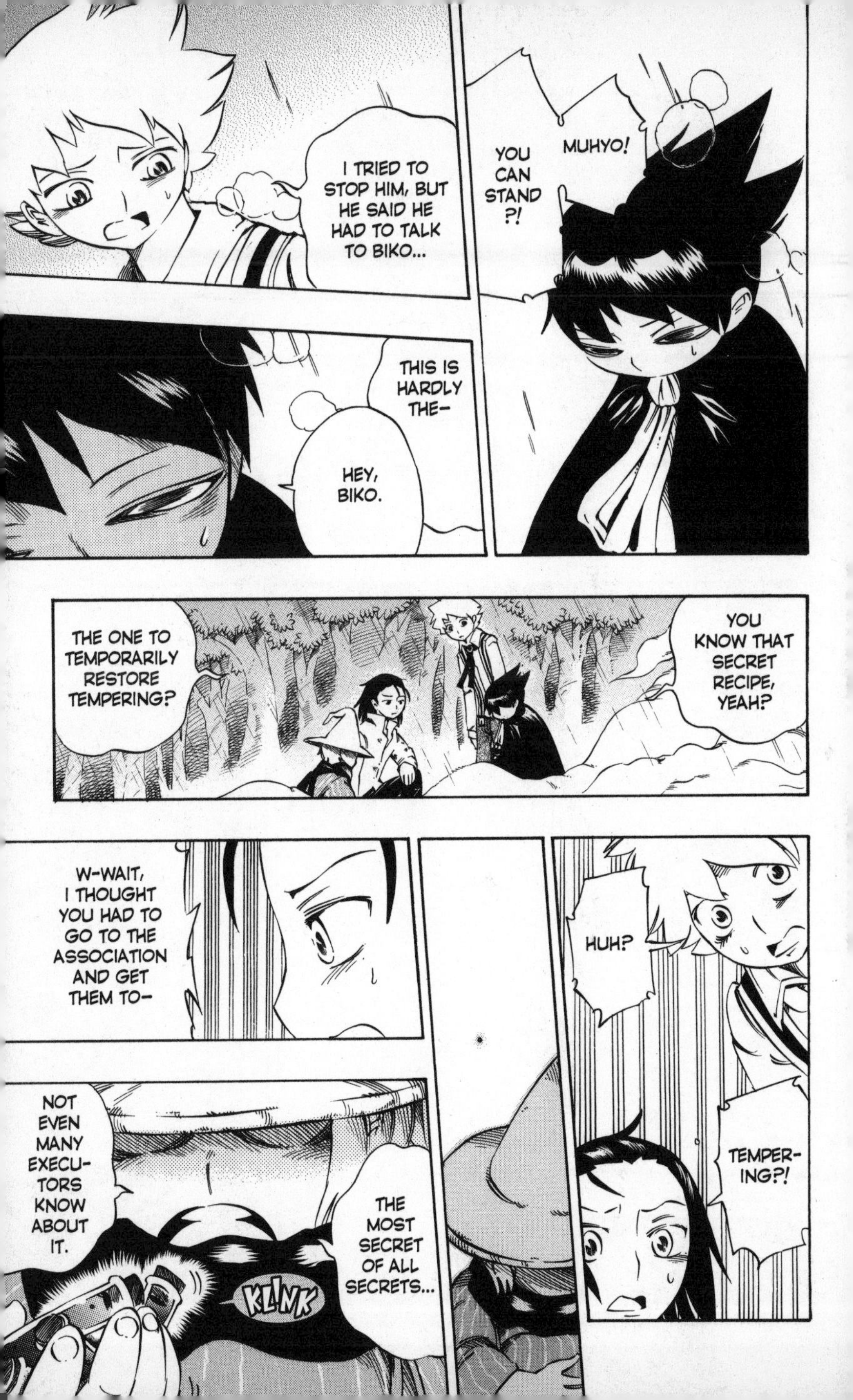
MUHYO!
YOU CAN STAND?!
I TRIED TO STOP HIM, BUT HE SAID HE HAD TO TALK TO BIKO...
THIS IS HARDLY THE-
HEY, BIKO.
YOU KNOW THAT SECRET RECIPE, YEAH?
THE ONE TO TEMPORARILY RESTORE TEMPERING?
HUH?
W-WAIT, I THOUGHT YOU HAD TO GO TO THE ASSOCIATION AND GET THEM TO-
TEMPER-ING?!
THE MOST SECRET OF ALL SECRETS...
KLINK
NOT EVEN MANY EXECU-TORS KNOW ABOUT IT.

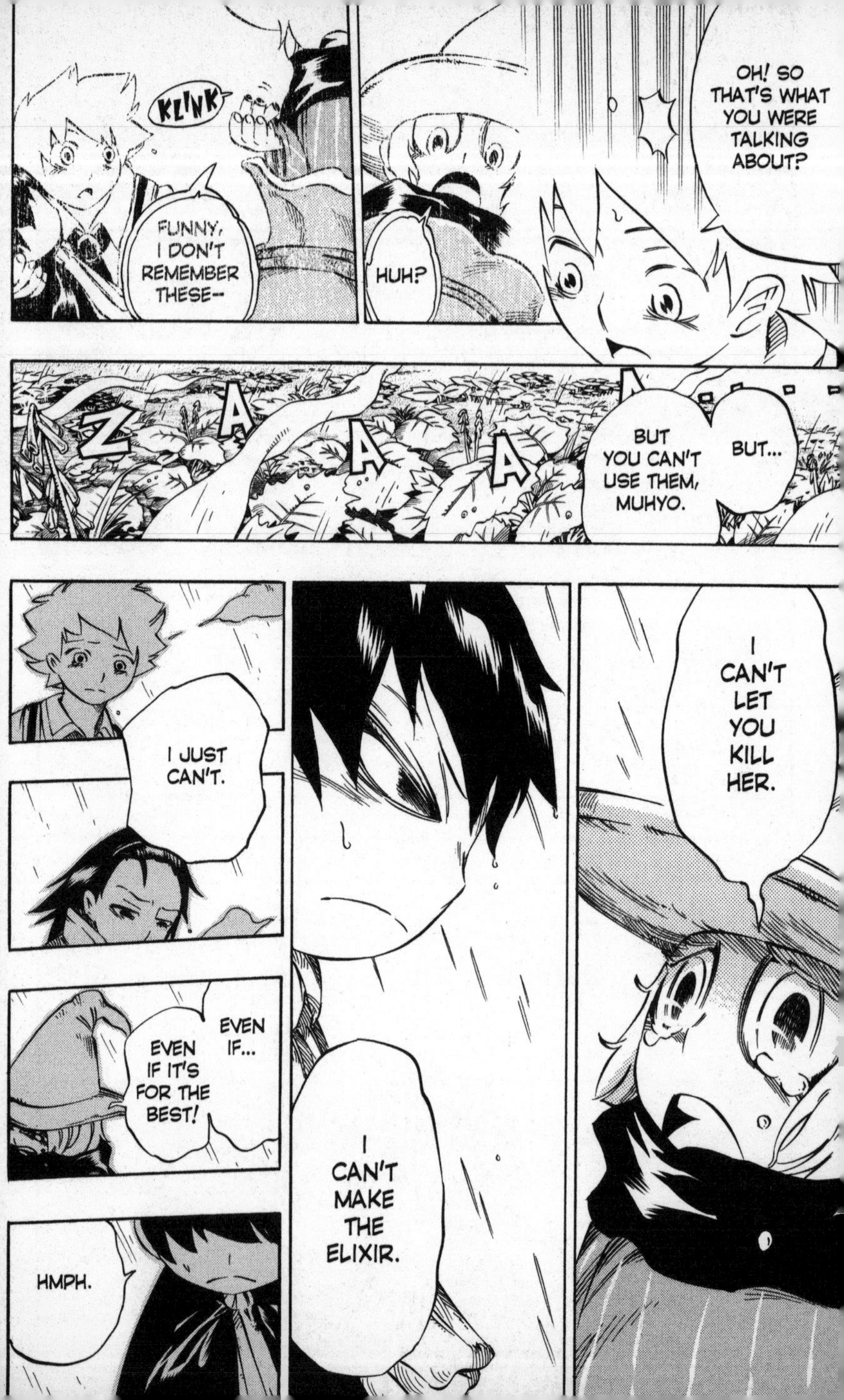
OH! SO THAT'S WHAT YOU WERE TALKING ABOUT?
HUH?
KLINK
FUNNY, I DON'T REMEMBER THESE--
BUT...
BUT YOU CAN'T USE THEM, MUHYO.
ZAAAA
I CAN'T LET YOU KILL HER.
I CAN'T MAKE THE ELIXIR.
I JUST CAN'T.
EVEN IF...
EVEN IF IT'S FOR THE BEST!
HMPH.

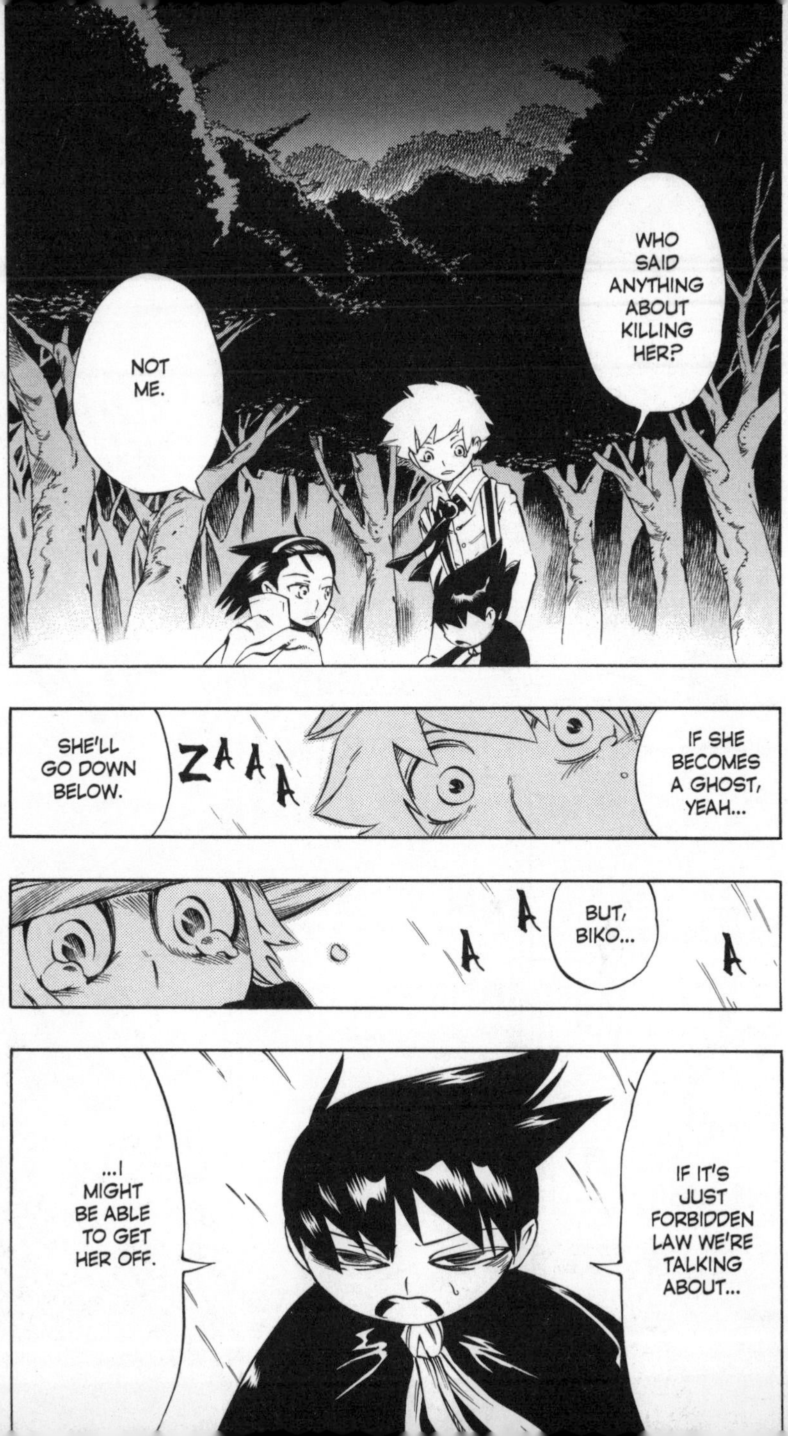
WHO SAID ANYTHING ABOUT KILLING HER?
NOT ME.
IF SHE BECOMES A GHOST, YEAH...
ZAAAA
SHE'LL GO DOWN BELOW.
A
BUT, BIKO...
A
A
IF IT'S JUST FORBIDDEN LAW WE'RE TALKING ABOUT...
...I MIGHT BE ABLE TO GET HER OFF.

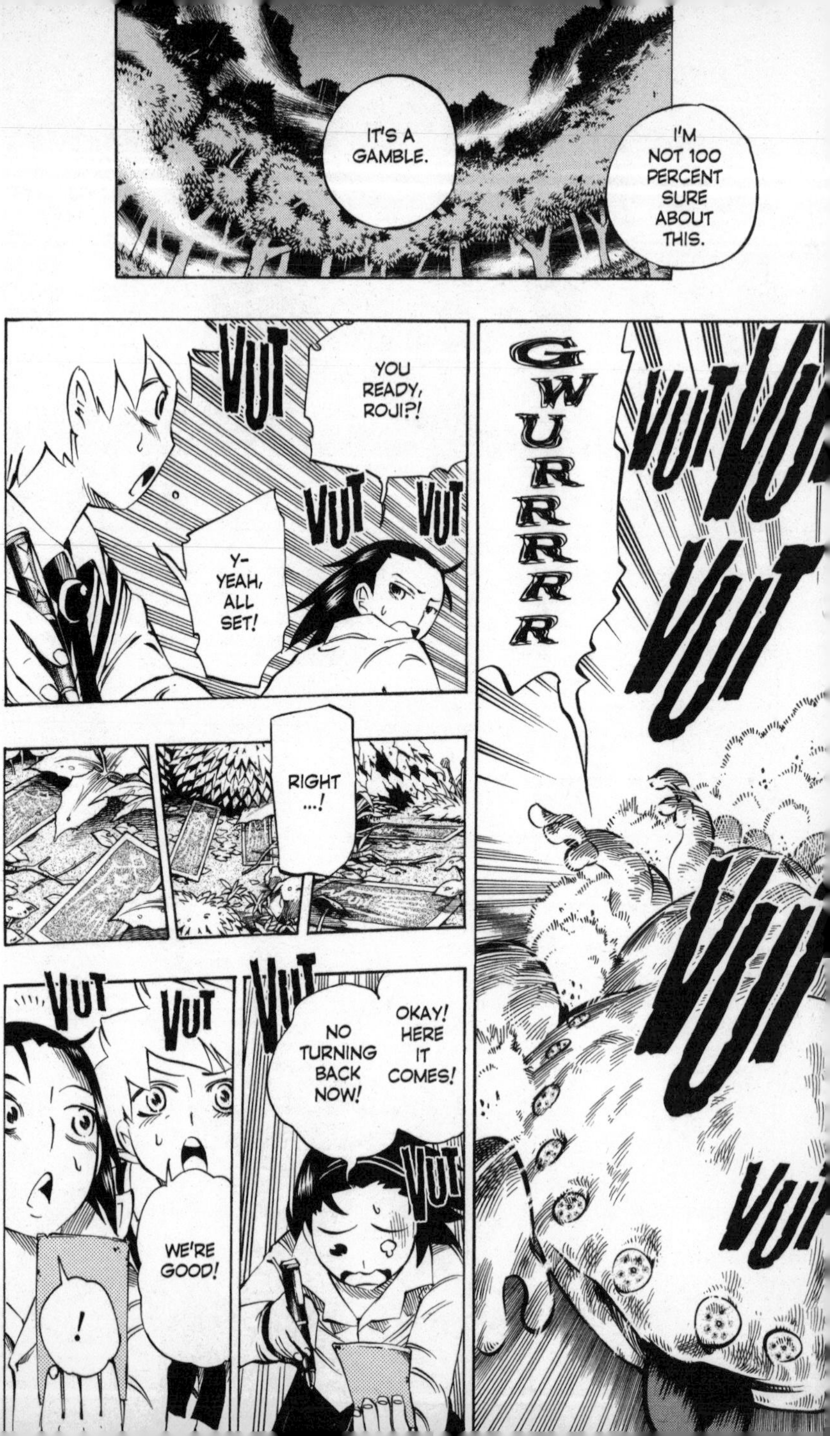
I'M NOT 100 PERCENT SURE ABOUT THIS.
IT'S A GAMBLE.
GWURRRRR
VUT
VU
VUT
VUT
VUT
VUT
YOU READY, ROJI?!
VUT
VUT
Y-YEAH, ALL SET!
RIGHT ...!
VUT
OKAY! HERE IT COMES!
NO TURNING BACK NOW!
VUT
VUT
VUT
WE'RE GOOD!
!

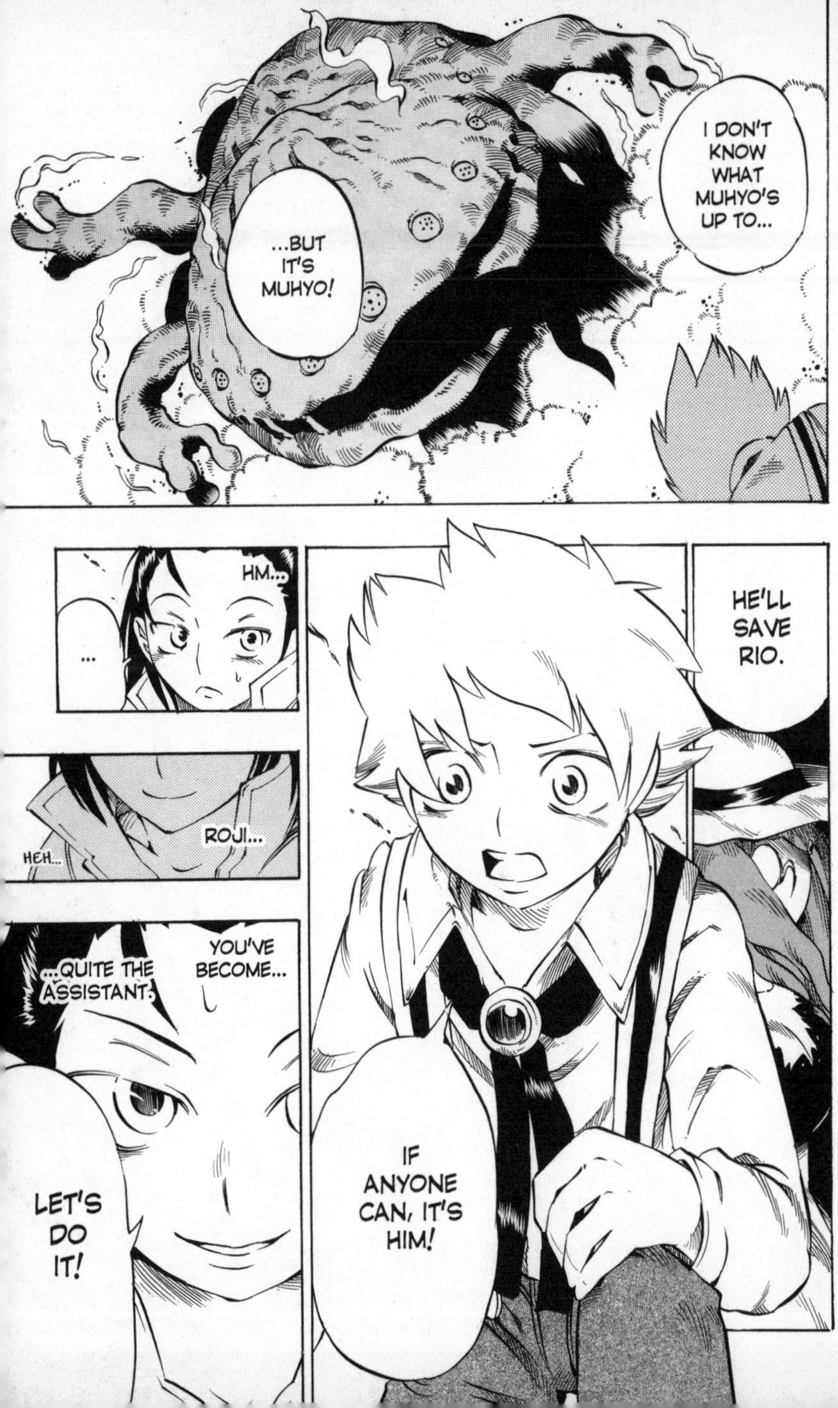
I DON'T KNOW WHAT MUHYO'S UP TO...
...BUT IT'S MUHYO!
HE'LL SAVE RIO.
IF ANYONE CAN, IT'S HIM!
HM...
...
ROJI...
HEH...
YOU'VE BECOME...
...QUITE THE ASSISTANT.
LET'S DO IT!

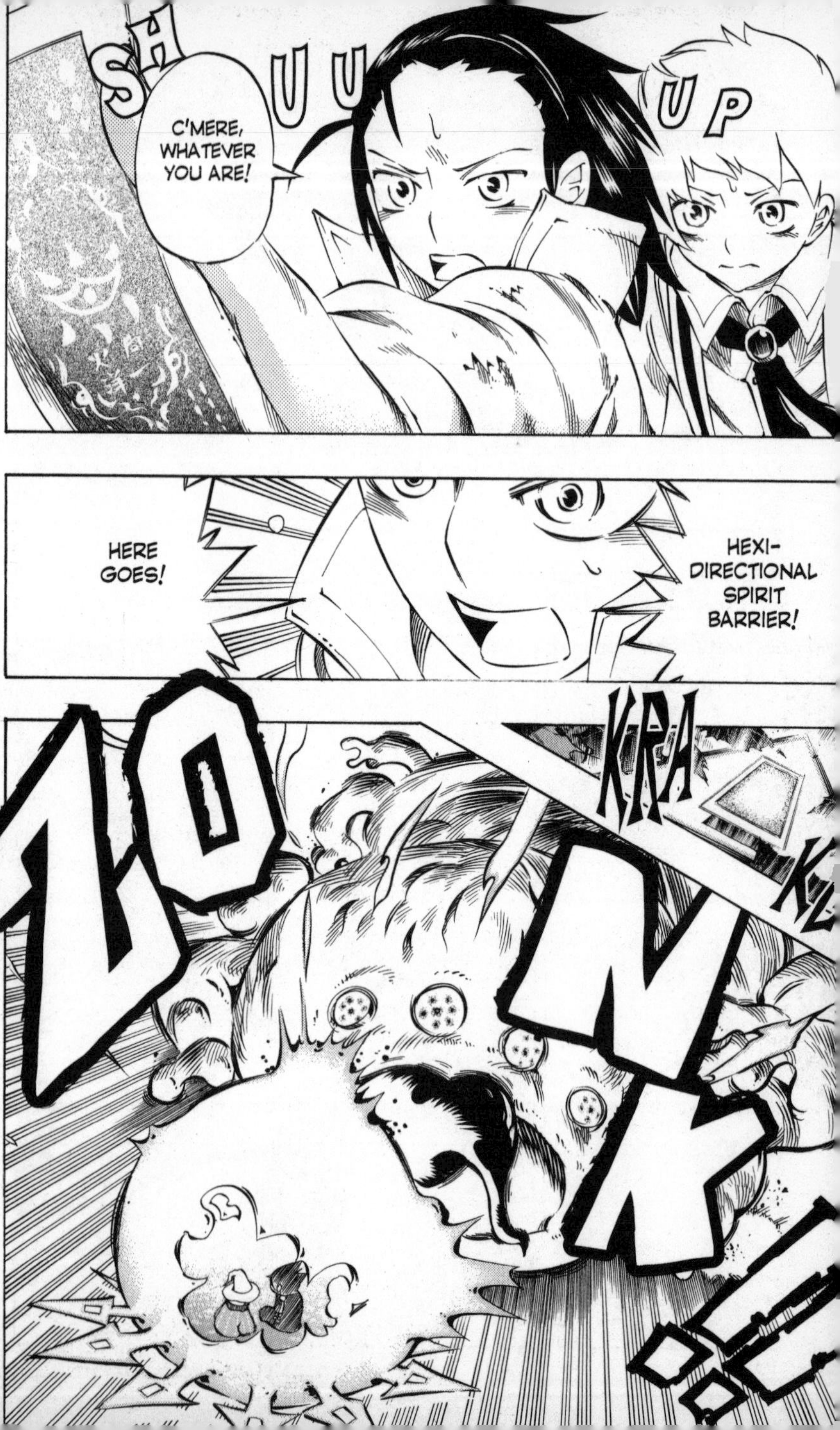

SHUUUP
C'MERE, WHATEVER YOU ARE!
HEXI-DIRECTIONAL SPIRIT BARRIER!
HERE GOES!
ZOOM

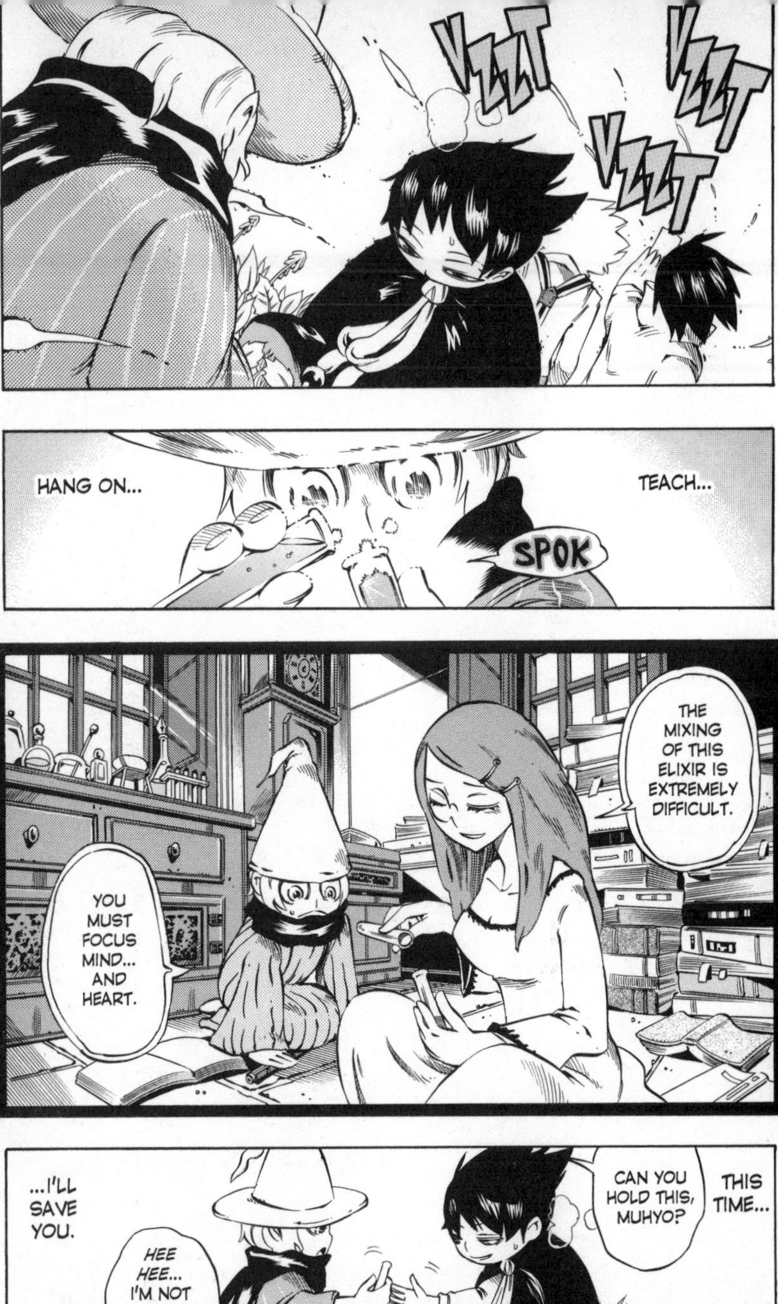
VZZT
VZZT
VZZT
TEACH...
SPOK
HANG ON...
THE MIXING OF THIS ELIXIR IS EXTREMELY DIFFICULT.
YOU MUST FOCUS MIND... AND HEART.
THIS TIME...
CAN YOU HOLD THIS, MUHYO?
...I'LL SAVE YOU.
HEE HEE... I'M NOT *THAT* WEAK.

VOLUME 4: SAD TIMES AHEAD (THE END)

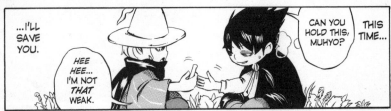

In The Next Volume...

Biko attempts to concoct an elixir that will
rejuvenate Muhyo, but will Muhyo's powers
be restored in time for him to face the
treacherous Enchu?

Available June 2008!

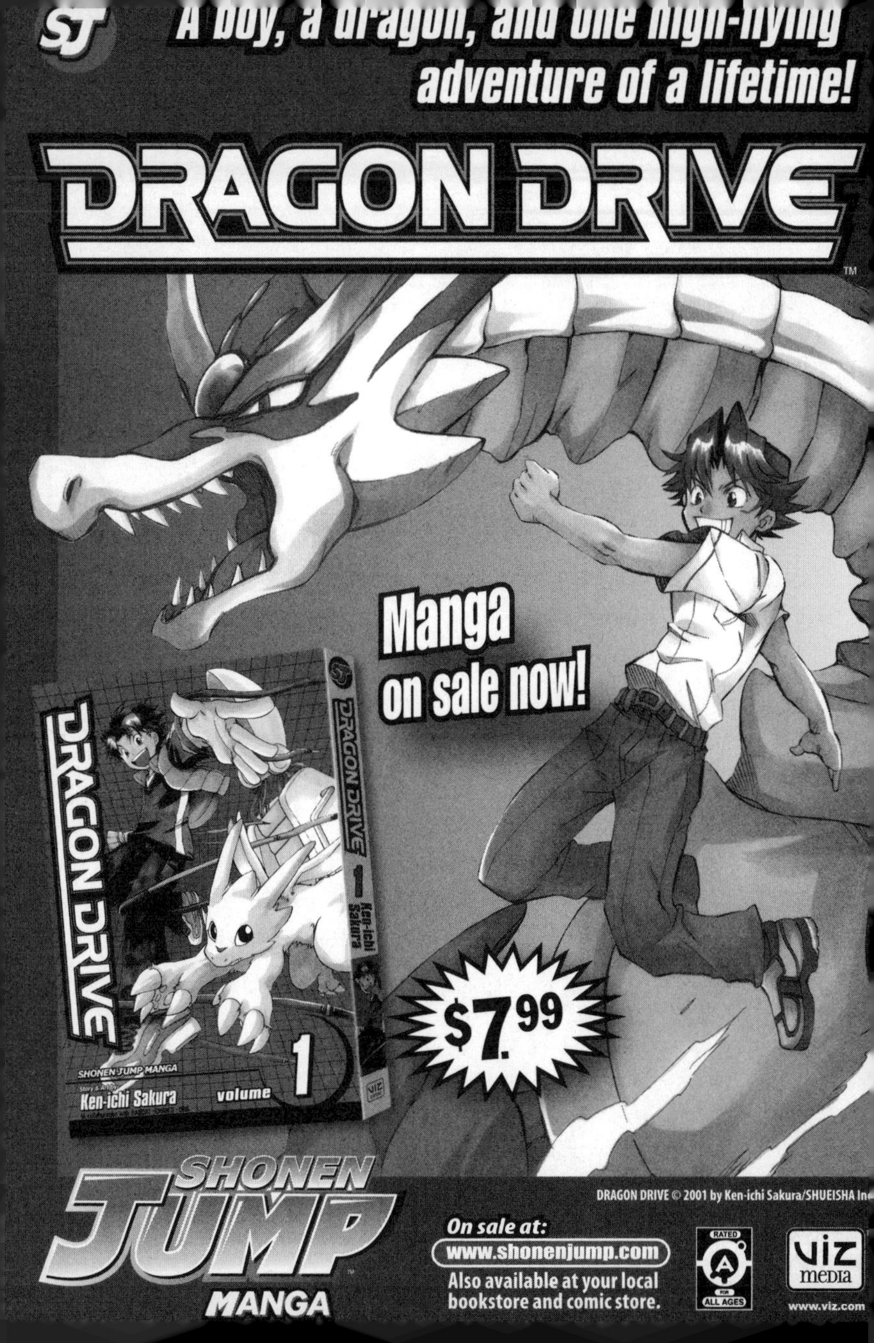

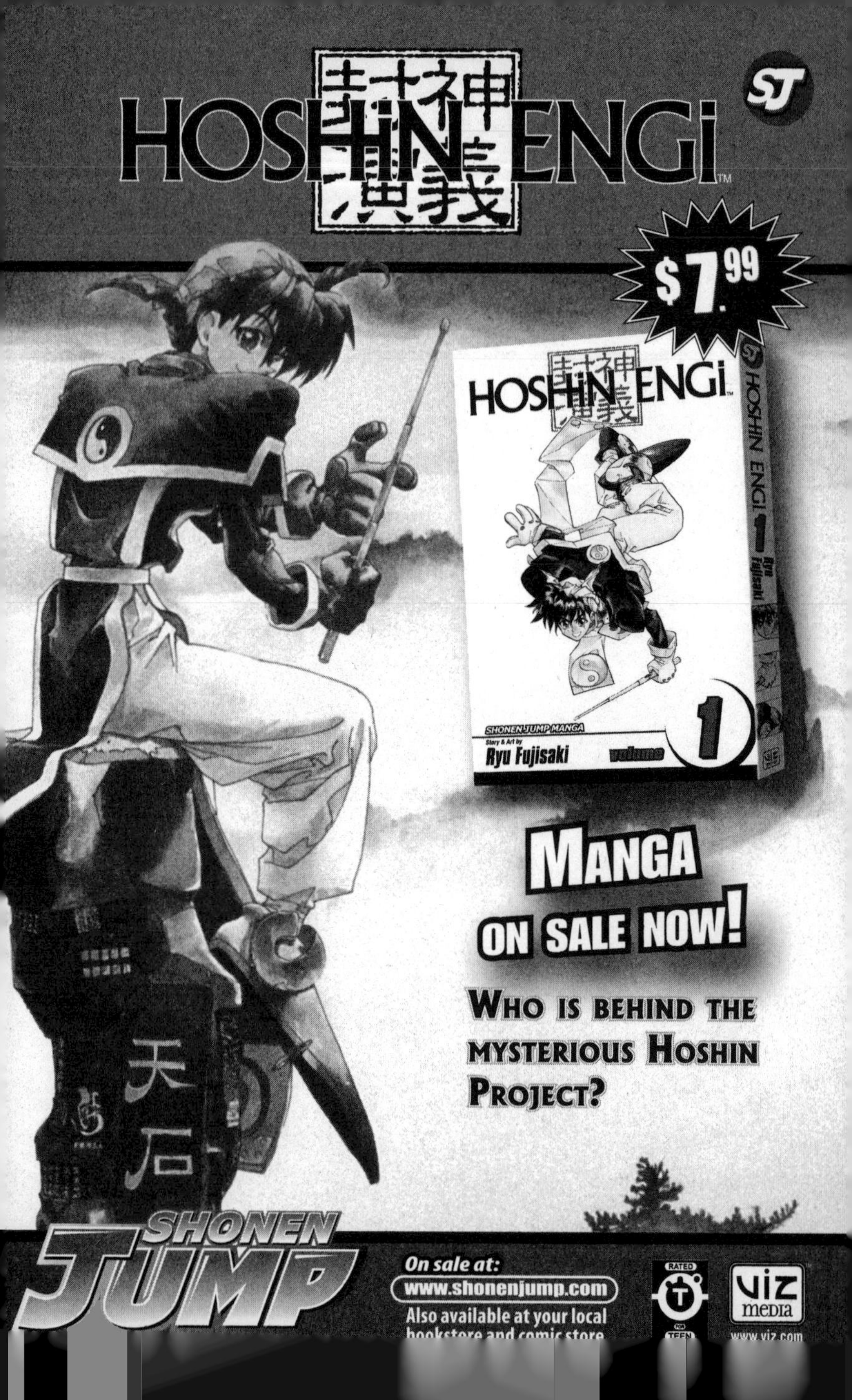

封神演義
HOSHIN ENGI™
SJ
$7.99
HOSHIN ENGI
SHONEN JUMP MANGA
Story & Art by
Ryu Fujisaki
volume 1
MANGA
ON SALE NOW!
WHO IS BEHIND THE MYSTERIOUS HOSHIN PROJECT?
SHONEN JUMP
On sale at:
www.shonenjump.com
Also available at your local bookstore and comic store.
RATED T TEEN
VIZ media
www.viz.com

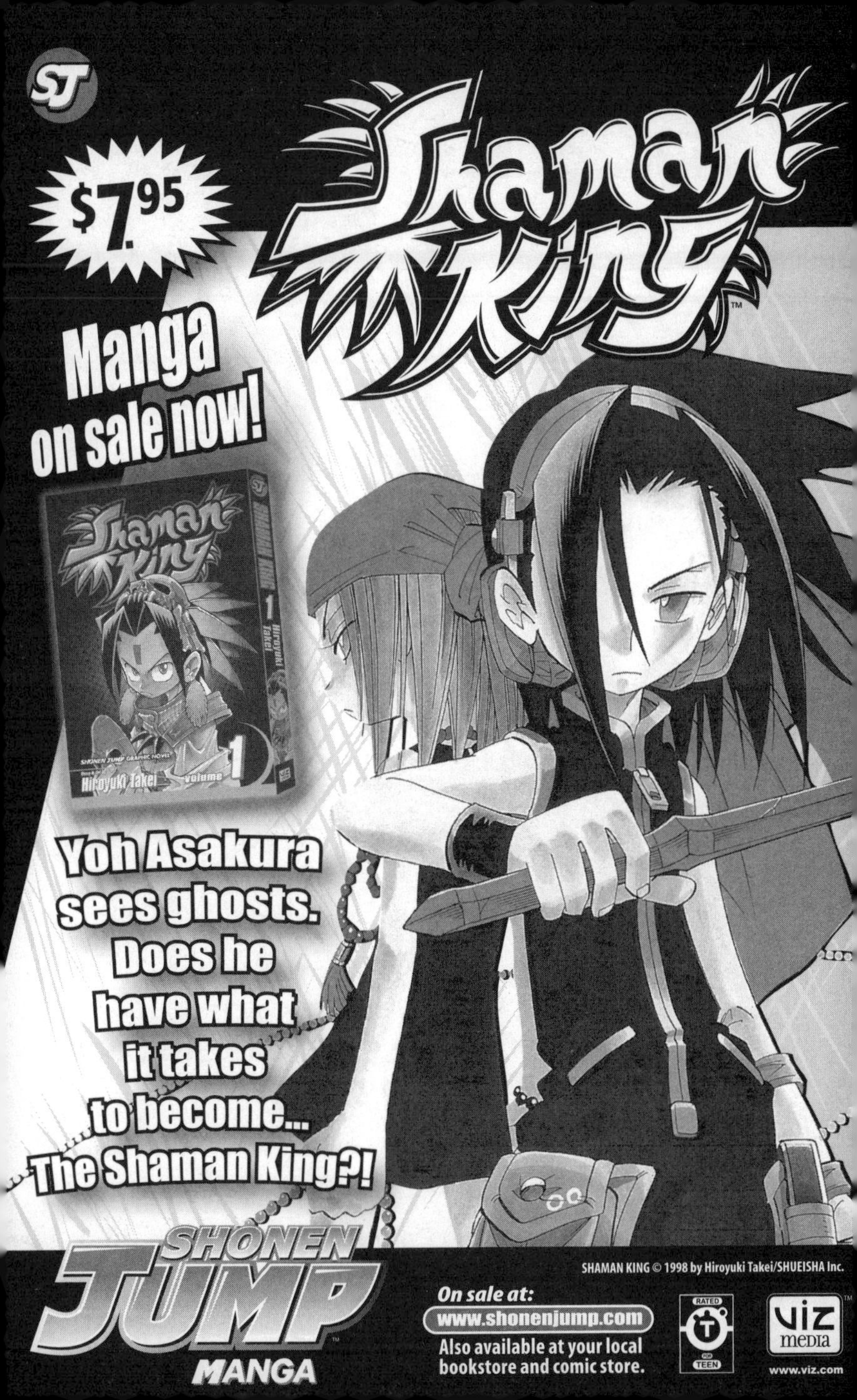
SJ
$7.95
Shaman King™
Manga on sale now!
Shaman King
SHONEN JUMP GRAPHIC NOVEL
Hiroyuki Takei volume 1
Yoh Asakura sees ghosts. Does he have what it takes to become... The Shaman King?!
SHONEN JUMP™ MANGA
SHAMAN KING © 1998 by Hiroyuki Takei/SHUEISHA Inc.
On sale at:
www.shonenjump.com
Also available at your local bookstore and comic store.
RATED T FOR TEEN
VIZ media
www.viz.com

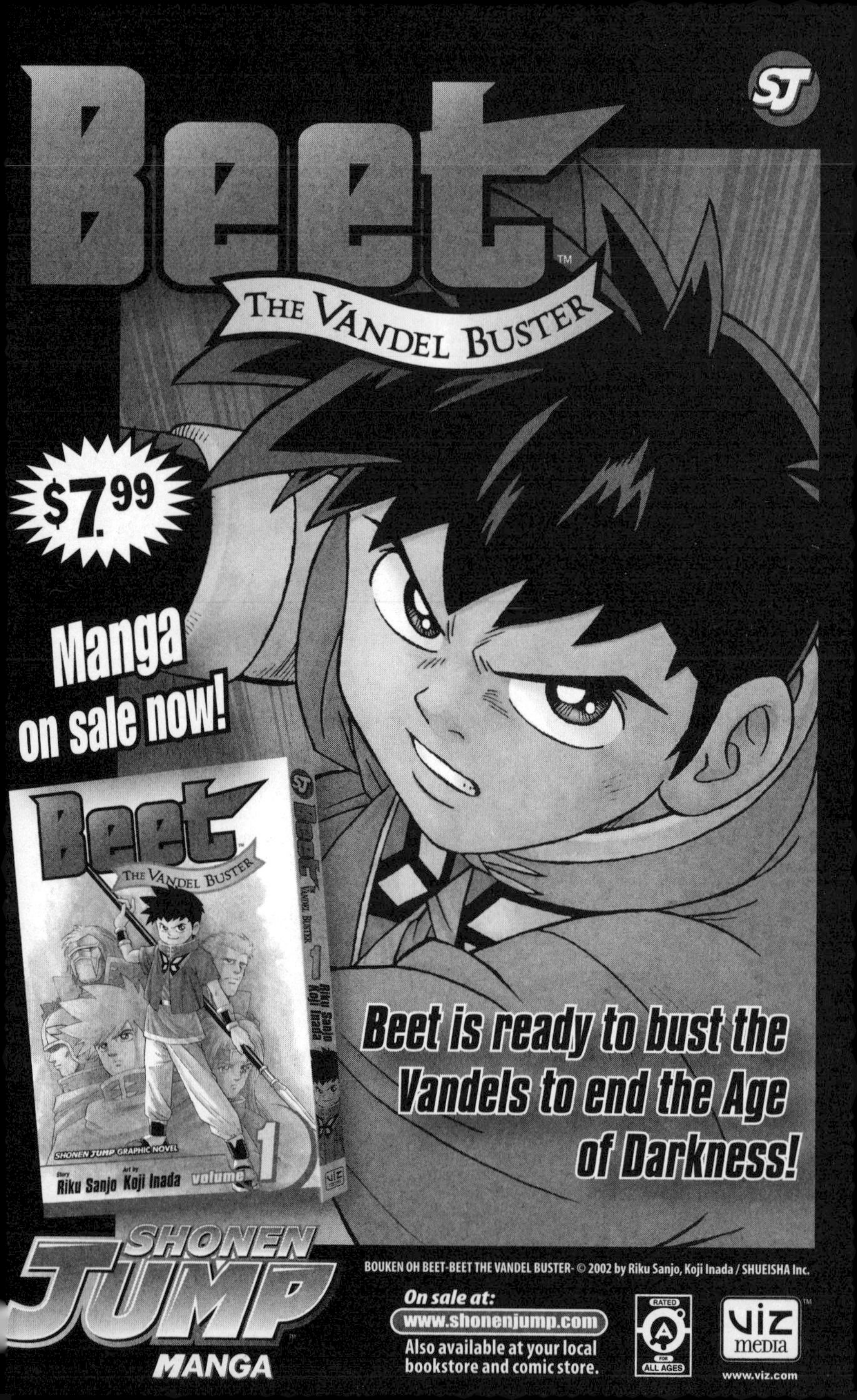
SJ
Beet™
THE VANDEL BUSTER
$7.99
Manga on sale now!
Beet™ THE VANDEL BUSTER
SHONEN JUMP GRAPHIC NOVEL
Story Riku Sanjo Art by Koji Inada volume 1
Beet is ready to bust the Vandels to end the Age of Darkness!
SHONEN JUMP MANGA
BOUKEN OH BEET-BEET THE VANDEL BUSTER- © 2002 by Riku Sanjo, Koji Inada / SHUEISHA Inc.
On sale at:
www.shonenjump.com
Also available at your local bookstore and comic store.
RATED A FOR ALL AGES
VIZ media
www.viz.com

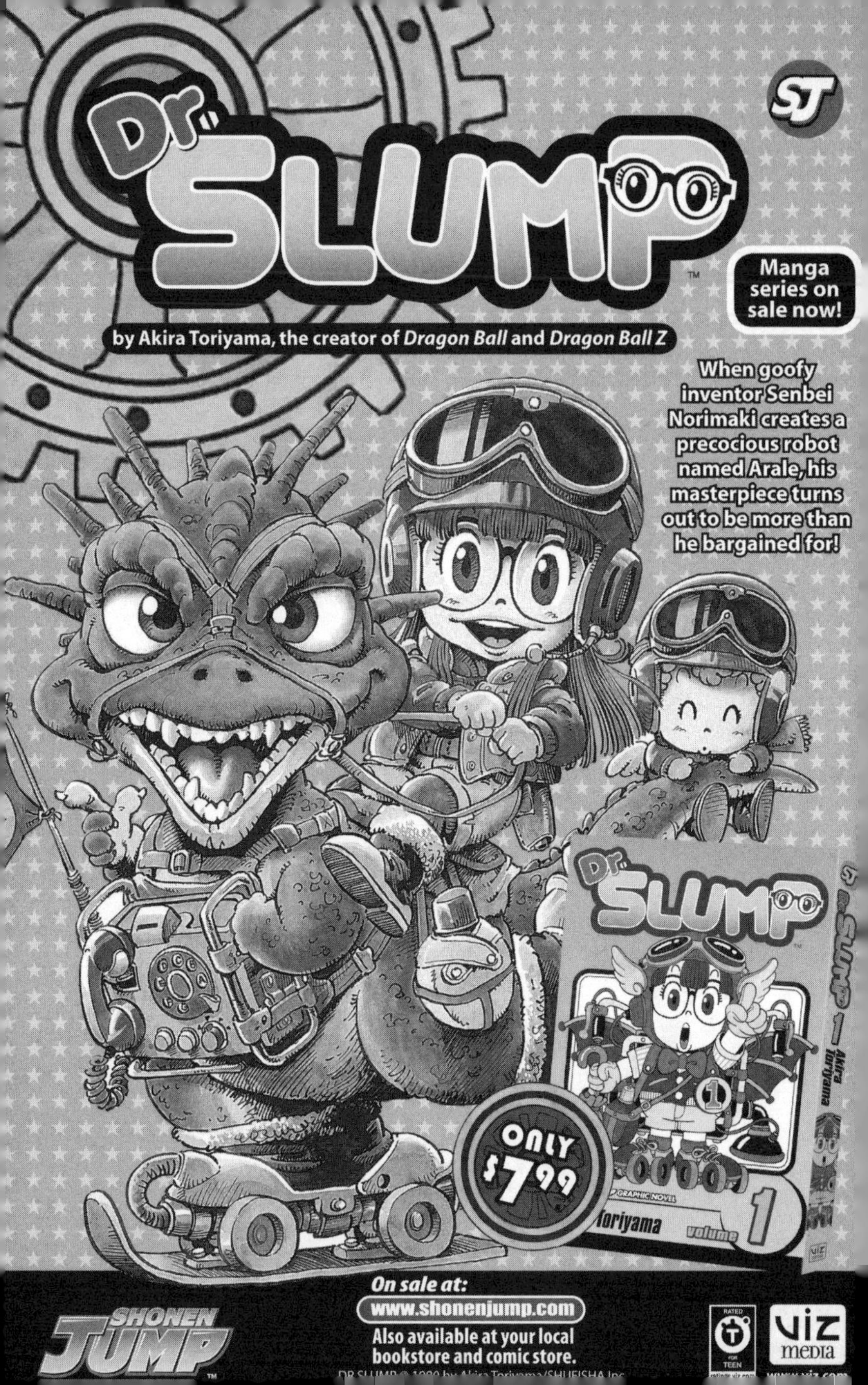

Dr. SLUMP™
SJ
Manga series on sale now!
by Akira Toriyama, the creator of *Dragon Ball* and *Dragon Ball Z*
When goofy inventor Senbei Norimaki creates a precocious robot named Arale, his masterpiece turns out to be more than he bargained for!
ONLY $7.99
On sale at:
www.shonenjump.com
Also available at your local bookstore and comic store.
SHONEN JUMP
RATED T FOR TEEN
VIZ media

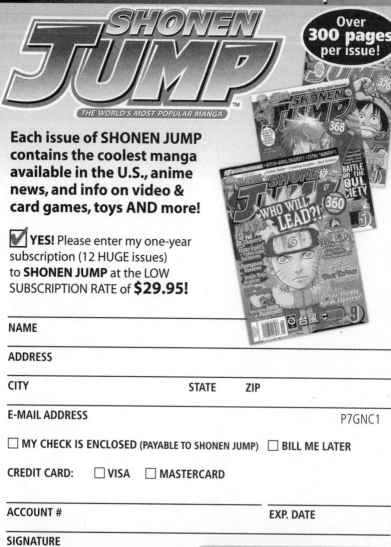